GUIDE TO SOUTHERN AFRICAN
GAME & NATURE RESERVES

CHRIS AND TILDE STUART'S
GUIDE TO SOUTHERN AFRICAN
GAME & NATURE RESERVES

NEW
HOLLAND

First published in the UK in 1992 by
New Holland (Publishers) Ltd
37 Connaught Street, London W2 2AZ

ISBN 1 85368 190 3

Editors: Tessa Kennedy, Sue Matthews
Designer: Jenny Camons
Cover designer: Neville Poulter
Phototypeset by Struik DTP
Originated by Unifoto (Pty) Ltd
Printed and bound by National Book Printers

Cover photographs: *Top left:* Fly fishing at St Lucia (R. de la Harpe); *Top right:* Giraffe and kudu at
the Chudob waterhole, Etosha National Park (G. Cubitt); *Left centre:* Royal Natal National Park
(R. de la Harpe); *Right centre:* Mbiso bush camp, Itala Game Reserve (R. de la Harpe); *Below left:*
Ivory Lodge, a private safari lodge near Hwange National Park (G. Cubitt); *Below right:* Lion at a
buffalo kill, Timbavati Game Reserve (G. Cubitt).

PUBLISHER'S NOTE
Every effort has been made to ensure the accuracy of the information published in the *Guide to
Southern African Game and Nature Reserves*. However, changes are taking place all the time,
particularly with regard to the accommodation and facilities provided by the reserves, and we can
accept no liability for inaccuracies or omissions. Tariffs, especially, are constantly changing, and
we would like to emphasise that the prices given are intended as no more than a comparative
indication of the price that visitors can expect to pay.

CONTENTS

ACKNOWLEDGEMENTS

Many individuals and organisations contributed, directly or indirectly, to the compilation of this guide and it is not possible to acknowledge them all individually. No doubt many more names should be listed below, and we ask pardon of those who assisted us but whose names have unintentionally escaped mention.

The directors and staff (particularly those at the reserves) of conservation and game departments throughout southern Africa, as well as town clerks and other members of local authority staff, are sincerely thanked for supplying information relevant to their particular areas of control. However, as is usually the case when compiling a book of this nature, there are always some individuals who deserve special mention: Debbie Abrahamson; D. J. Ackerman (National Parks Board); J. L. Anderson and his colleagues (KaNgwane Parks Corporation); D. R. Aniku (Department of Wildlife, National Parks and Tourism, Botswana); W. A. Astle; P. S. M. Berry; Ms E. Coetzee (Ministry of Wildlife, Conservation and Tourism, Namibia); Keith Cooper (Wildlife Society of Southern Africa); Ms B. Crook (Physical Planning Directorate, Natal Provincial Administration); J. E. W. Dixon (Nature Conservation Division, Ciskei); Niels Ferreira (Directorate of Nature Conservation, Orange Free State); S. P. Fourie (Directorate of Nature Conservation, Transvaal); Ian Gaigher (University of Venda); Hans Grobler (Natal Parks Board); E. D. M. Lloyd; Margaret M. Makungo (Zambia National Tourist Board); Ian Manning (World Wildlife Fund Rhino Project, Zambia); Josephine Mehl (National Hotels Development Corporation, Zambia); A. Moore (National Parks and Wildlife Management, Zimbabwe); Messrs Mphande and H. E. Nzima (Department of National Parks and Wildlife, Malawi); Lindy Nauta (Robin Binckes Public Relations); Peet Peens (National Parks Board); E. D. Scarr (Parks, Recreation and Beaches Department, Durban); Swaziland National Trust Commission; A. van Wyk (Department of the Chief Minister, Division of Land Affairs and Tourism, Lebowa).

We should also like to express our appreciation to the staff of Struik Publishers, particularly to Peter Borchert for his support, to Leni Martin and Jenny Ramsay, and latterly Tessa Kennedy and Sue Matthews for editing the manuscript, and to Jenny Camons for putting together a bewildering array of maps and text into a pleasing form.

CHRIS AND TILDE STUART
NIEUWOUDTVILLE, 1992

KEY TO MAP SYMBOLS

	Game or nature reserve		Urban area	■	Building
	Other conservation area	— ·· — ···	International boundary	*	Place of interest
	River	— · — ··	Self-governing homeland boundary	Ⓟ	Picnic site
	Waterfall	– – – – –	Provincial boundary	Ⓗ	Hide
	Water expanse	+—+—■—+—+	Railway line and station	Ⓥ	View-point
o	Waterhole	🏠	Self-catering accommodation	╂	Airstrip
⟋	Small dam	⌂	Trail hut	★	Lighthouse
↧	Marsh	⚠	Camping and caravan site	⌣	Hiking trail
⋯	Pan	∧	Bush camp	▲	Mountain peak

INTRODUCTION

For centuries the plains of southern Africa were the domain of great herds of game, which were attended by lion, leopard, cheetah and other predators. Within three hundred years of the arrival of Europeans at the south-western tip of the continent and their subsequent penetration northwards and eastwards into the land's interior, the great migratory herds – of blue and black wildebeest, red hartebeest, eland, quagga and springbok – had all but disappeared. Many fell to the gun, and those that survived were pushed into the wilder areas further to the north and east, to be replaced by domestic herds of cattle and flocks of sheep and goats. The migratory herds were a phenomenon of the past, but most of the species – the quagga and bluebuck being notable exceptions – may still be seen, albeit in greatly reduced numbers, in many of the game reserves of southern Africa.

Not only were the animals themselves killed, but large areas of the vegetation on which they fed have been destroyed or drastically changed. A prime example is the Karoo, in the interior of South Africa, which has been overgrazed by livestock to such an extent that the expanses of grassland that once sustained the antelope herds have become tracts of scrub that barely support goats.

In the nineteenth century it was the hunter who made the major impact on southern Africa's wildlife. In this century more subtle, but no less destructive, forces have been at work. Vast areas of grassland have been replaced by vast areas of maize, wheat, groundnuts, sugar cane and forest plantations; the permanent destruction of the natural vegetation has left environments that can support little wildlife. Agricultural practices have often resulted in erosion of the soil and this in turn leads to increasing desertification. Industry and agriculture have played a major role in polluting land, water and sky, and even large reserves such as the Kruger National Park have felt the effects of toxic chemicals. Exotic vegetation, introduced intentionally or accidentally, has taken hold in many areas, and even in some of the wildest regions alien species have become permanent features of the flora.

It is against such threats as these that conservationists endeavour to protect southern Africa's natural wildlife and vegetation in game and nature reserves. The concept is not new. At the end of the nineteenth century Paul Kruger, president of the Zuid-Afrikaansche Republiek, realised that the great concentrations of game he had known in his youth were fast disappearing, and proclaimed Africa's first formal conservation area, the Pongola Game Reserve. Unfortunately, it was deproclaimed in 1921, but efforts are once again being made to provide protection for this unique area. Kruger is perhaps better known in conservation terms for initiating the effort that resulted in the proclamation of the Sabie Game Reserve in 1898, the forerunner of the national park that now bears his name. In Natal, a province with a proud record of conservation, three reserves – the Umfolozi, Hluhluwe and St Lucia game reserves – were proclaimed in 1897, and they remain Africa's oldest surviving conservation areas. The number of reserves increased very slowly for the first five decades of this century, but in the past thirty years growing conservation awareness has resulted in many new areas being set aside to protect wildlife. It seems likely, however, that this increase will taper off rapidly as prices of land soar and burgeoning human populations exert more urgent demands on available land.

The conservation areas of southern Africa fall into several categories: national parks, game reserves controlled at national, provincial or municipal level, and those that are privately owned. In some countries, mainly Zambia and Zimbabwe, there are also game management and safari areas. The legal status of each category differs from one country to another, but in general national parks enjoy the highest level of legal protection; human activities are strictly controlled and exploitation, except for management purposes, is forbidden. Game reserves are governed by specific rules and regulations laid down by the authority under whose jurisdiction they fall. Municipal and privately owned reserves have the disadvantage that they are relatively easy to deproclaim or, in the latter case, to change hands and be used for non-conservation purposes. However, these reserves are numerous and often play a valuable role in protecting threatened habitats and occasionally even specific organisms; a good example are the many 'pocket handkerchief' reserves in South Africa's floristically rich south-western Cape Province. At the other end of the scale, game management and safari areas allow a certain level of exploitation, such as subsistence fishing or trophy hunting.

Around the coast of South Africa there are also a number of reserves that have been set aside to protect marine organisms. Exploitation of resources in these areas is strictly limited, and enquiries about regulations governing such aspects as protected species and bag limits should be made on an individual basis.

As well as protecting the natural environment and wildlife, game and nature reserves have a secondary, but also very important, function: at a number of different levels they serve to promote in visitors an understanding of their environment and an awareness of the need for conservation. A few are exclusively education-orientated, catering for groups, usually of school children, who attend intensive courses. Many others offer wilderness trails on which, often over a period of several days, a trained and knowledgeable ranger guides small parties of hikers around the locality, explaining the significance of what they see. At a more modest level, many of the smaller nature reserves provide visitors with a brochure from which they can follow self-guided trails.

Game reserves are usually associated with large areas such as Kruger, Hwange, Etosha, Chobe and South Luangwa. It is not only these great reserves, however, that have much to offer. We hope that, with the aid of this guide, readers will discover some of the smaller, also fascinating reserves of the region, and get to know environments new to them. To watch elephants at a waterhole or lions on a kill in Chobe, Etosha, Kruger or Hwange is a thrilling experience, but it can be just as exciting to watch Cape sugarbirds displaying amongst the proteas of the Helderberg Nature Reserve, or to observe the antics of fiddler crabs in the mangrove swamp of the Umlalazi Nature Reserve.

Guidelines for visitors to game and nature reserves

Most people have an instinctive dislike for rules and regulations, but there are certain points which are worth bearing in mind, for your own well-being as well as that of the wildlife, when visiting a game park or nature reserve.

❏ First and foremost is that all animals and plants are protected in the designated conservation areas of southern Africa.

❏ Don't feed the animals. If you do, you are almost certainly signing the animal's death warrant; not only does it come to rely on hand-outs rather than forage for itself but, more seriously, it becomes a potential nuisance or even a threat to other visitors and in many cases has to be shot.

❏ In parks where visitors are requested to stay in the car, do so – not only for your own safety, but also to avoid disturbing the animals. Several game parks, particularly in Botswana, Zimbabwe, Zambia and Malawi, have unfenced camps, and where lion and spotted hyena are present it is not wise to sleep in the open, or even with open tent flaps.

❏ Only drive on public roads or designated tracks; taking shortcuts across the veld damages the vegetation and soil, and driving too close to animals disturbs them and creates potentially very dangerous situations.

❏ Build fires only in designated areas, and take great care to extinguish the coals properly after use. In most reserves the collection of firewood is forbidden, so take your own or use a gas stove.

❏ In the more remote areas it is very important to check roadconditions before setting out, as they change rapidly depending on the weather; a road that may be suitable for a 4x4 vehicle in the dry season is quite likely to be impassable in the wet. Maps for such areas are generally sketchy and travellers will also have to rely on the local inhabitants and police for directions. It is important that visitors to isolated areas be well equipped and self-sufficient; always carry spare water and extra fuel (fuel consumption increases in soft sand), a good set of tools, basic spares and a repair manual, as well as all basic camping requirements and extra food. People who wish to visit remote game parks but are unfamiliar with 'bush living' are advised to make their first trip with a safari company.

❏ A good first-aid kit and knowledge of first aid are prerequisite for travelling in the bush. Many reserves are far from medical facilities, and quick and correct first-aid treatment could be critical in an emergency. 'Travellers' diarrhoea' is a curse that descends at the most awkward times; if you are affected, replace lost fluids regularly with a solution comprising 1 cup boiled water, 2 teaspoons sugar, a pinch of salt and a pinch of bicarbonate of soda. If the quality of the local water seems dubious, boil it.

❏ Malaria, bilharzia and sleeping sickness are prevalent in many parts of southern Africa and visitors to those areas should take certain precautions. Malaria-carrying mosquitoes occur in the Transvaal Lowveld, in Natal north of Richard's Bay, along the Limpopo and Orange rivers, in northern Namibia and Botswana, and in Zimbabwe, Zambia and Malawi. Travellers in these regions should take a course of anti-malarial tablets and use insect repellents and mosquito nets. Organisms causing bilharzia live in shallow pans and slow-flowing rivers in subtropical areas; the best way to prevent the disease is to avoid contact with water that is likely to be infected. Sleeping sickness is carried by tsetse flies which occur mainly near waterholes and rivers north of the Zambezi River and in the extreme north of Botswana. They are attracted by dark colours and follow moving objects. Consult a doctor if you think you may have contracted any of these diseases.

How to use this book

This guide has been designed to give visitors to any of the several hundred game and nature reserves of the southern African subcontinent as much practical information as possible. The region covered is

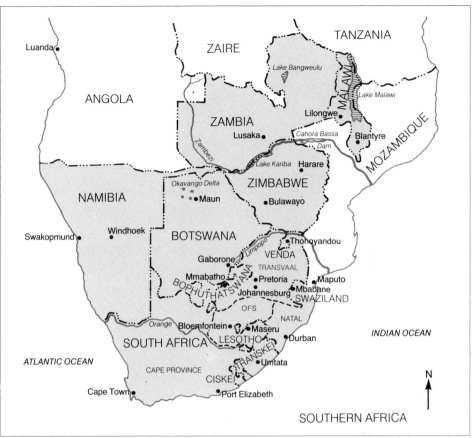

SOUTHERN AFRICA

indicated by the lightly shaded area in the map shown here (above), and has been divided into 19 areas: Transvaal; Boputhatswana; KaNgwane, Lebowa and Gazankulu; Venda; Swaziland; Natal and Kwazulu; Lesotho; Orange Free State and Qwaqwa; Transkei; Ciskei; Eastern Cape Province; Southern Cape Province; South-western Cape Province; Northern Cape Province and Karoo; Namibia; Botswana; Zambia; Malawi; and Zimbabwe. The chapter for each of these areas is prefaced by a regional map on which the reserves are identified by their numbers, and the reserves are then ordered alphabetically within the chapter.

In compiling the guide we have concentrated on reserves which do allow the general public access. In some cases, usually if an area would be damaged by an uncontrolled influx of visitors, permits must be obtained beforehand; they are generally available from the authority given under 'For further information'. Permits for other activities in the reserve, such as fishing or boating, can also be obtained from this source.

Accommodation is provided in a great many of the reserves covered, and its standard varies from basic to five-star luxury. As both the standard and the size of the self-catering complex or camping site affect many people's decision to stay in a particular reserve, we have, as far as possible, indicated both in the paragraph on accommodation. Visitors intending to stay at popular or well-known reserves, particularly during school holidays, are advised to book well in advance.

Although the information given in this book is aimed principally at independent travellers, many wildlife enthusiasts prefer to make use of the services of safari companies, particularly those which operate in the more remote areas of the subcontinent. A list of established operators is included at the back of the book.

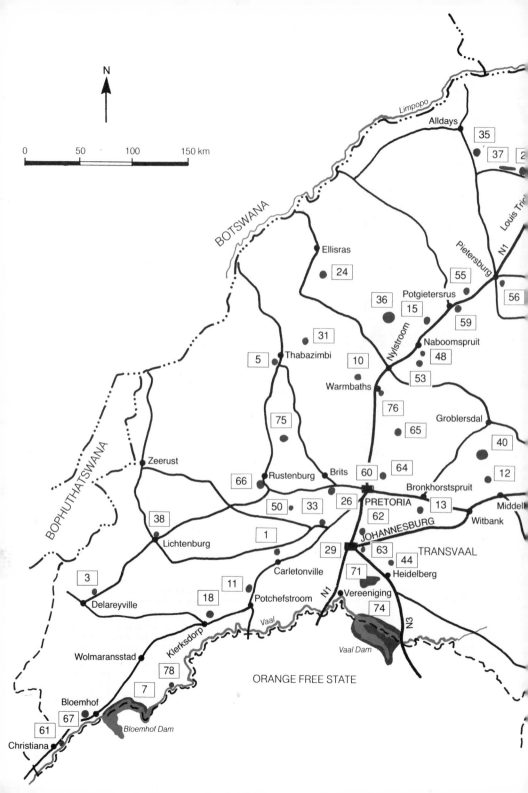

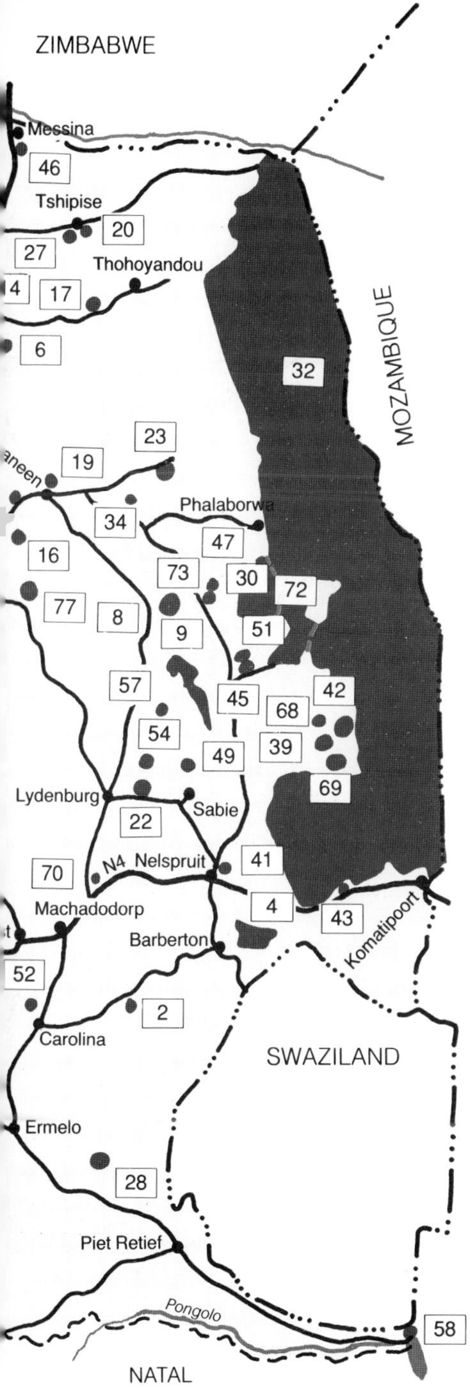

ZIMBABWE
Messina
46
Tshipise
20
27
Thohoyandou
17
6
32
MOZAMBIQUE
23
19
Phalaborwa
34
47
16
73
30
72
77
8
9
51
57
45
42
68
54
39
49
69
Lydenburg
22
Sabie
70
N4
Nelspruit
41
4
43
Komatipoort
Machadodorp
Barberton
52
2
Carolina
SWAZILAND
Ermelo
28
Piet Retief
Pongolo
58
NATAL

TRANSVAAL

1 Abe Bailey Nature Reserve
2 Badplaas Nature Reserve
3 Barberspan Nature Reserve
4 Barberton Nature Reserve
5 Ben Alberts Nature Reserve
6 Ben Lavin Nature Reserve
7 Bloemhof Dam Nature Reserve
8 Blydeberg Nature Reserve
9 Blyde River Canyon Nature Reserve
10 Bonwa Phala Game Farm
11 Boskop Dam Nature Reserve
12 Botshabelo Nature Reserve
13 Bronkhorstspruit Dam Nature Reserve
14 Buzzard Mountain Retreat
15 Doorndraai Dam Nature Reserve
16 Ebenezer Dam Nature Reserve
17 Entabeni State Forest
18 Faan Meintjes Nature Reserve
19 Fanie Botha Dam Nature Reserve
20 Greater Kuduland Safaris
21 Grootbosch Nature Reserve
22 Gustav Klingbiel Nature Reserve
23 Hans Merensky Nature Reserve
24 Hans Strijdom Dam Nature Reserve
25 Happy Rest Nature Reserve
26 Hartbeespoort Dam Nature Reserve
27 Honnet Nature Reserve
28 Jericho Dam Nature Reserve
29 Johannesburg
30 Klaserie Private Nature Reserve
31 Kransberg National Park
32 Kruger National Park
33 Krugersdorp Game Reserve
34 Lalapanzi Game Reserve
35 Langjan Nature Reserve
36 Lapalala Wilderness
37 Lesheba Wilderness
38 Lichtenburg Game Breeding Centre
39 Londolozi Game Reserve
40 Loskop Dam Nature Reserve
41 Lowveld National Botanic Garden
42 Mala Mala Game Reserve
43 Malelane Lodge
44 Marievale Bird Sanctuary
45 Matumi Game Lodge
46 Messina Nature Reserve
47 Mohlabetsi Game Reserve
48 Mosdene Private Nature Reserve
49 Mount Sheba Nature Reserve
50 Mountain Sanctuary Park
51 Ngangeni Game Farm
52 Nooitgedacht Dam Nature Reserve
53 Nylsvley Nature Reserve
54 Ohrigstad Dam Nature Reserve
55 Percy Fyfe Nature Reserve

The Transvaal, South Africa's second largest province, lies in the north-eastern part of the country, separated from Zimbabwe by the Limpopo River and with Mozambique extending down its eastern border. A large part of the province is taken up by the densely populated sprawl of the Witwatersrand region, and many of the resorts set aside for recreational purposes in the surrounding areas are heavily utilised. Very often the requirements for recreation and for conservation have been linked, and where a resort has been based on a dam, adjacent areas of land have been set aside in which existing game populations are protected and other species have been re-introduced.

A large proportion of the reserves are controlled by the Transvaal Provincial Administration's Directorate of Nature Conservation, but there are also approximately 750 registered game farms and 400 private nature reserves in the province. Although most of the latter are not open to the public, the sheer number of them does give an indication of how seriously nature conservation is taken.

Further evidence of the importance of conservation in the Transvaal lies in the fact that the Kruger National Park, a pioneer in conservation terms, was established here and now extends along almost the entire length of the province's eastern border. Moreover, the National Parks Board, which administers this and 15 other national parks throughout South Africa, has its headquarters in Pretoria.

Overvaal Resorts operates a number of large resorts adjacent to game reserves in the Transvaal, offering comfortable accommodation and many additional facilities. During off-season periods reduced rates for pensioners apply. The National Parks Board and the Directorate of Nature Conservation also offer pensioners certain discounts (see page 365).

Overvaal resorts and a number of Transvaal Provincial Administration reserves are in the process of privatizing and prospective visitors should ascertain their status in advance.

The Transvaal can be broadly divided into the Lowveld, Highveld and Kalahari regions. The Lowveld forms a broad band down the eastern part of the province and extends from the Soutpansberg north to the Limpopo River. It has typical bushveld vegetation, consisting of grassland with expanses of acacia or mopane woodland and scattered baobab trees. This area experiences hot, wet summers (between October and March) and mild, dry winters. The Highveld is that area of flat, open country that extends to the Orange Free State boundary in the south and the Cape Province in the south-west. Before the advent of mining and industrialisation it was covered by a vast 'sea' of grassland that was home to great herds of game. Today, most of the grassland has been put under the plough or has disappeared below urban sprawl, but small patches still survive in reserves. Summers here are warm, with rain falling during this season, and winter days are mild to cool, with cold, clear nights. The relatively small Kalahari region lies in the west, on the border with Botswana, and is generally drier than the rest of the Transvaal. Its vegetation comprises mainly scrub and thorny woodland.

The Transvaal's two major urban areas, Johannesburg and Pretoria, lie within 60 km of each other on the Highveld. Both have reserves and natural areas where visitors may find tranquillity in the midst of city bustle, and these are discussed under the heading of each city. Pretoria has the added advantage of being situated close to the Magaliesberg Natural Area, which encompasses most of the Magaliesberg range.

A number of reserves in the Transvaal are exclusively conservation areas and are therefore closed to the general public. These include: the Alice Glöckner Nature Reserve, near Suikerbosrand, which protects areas of fynbos (heath) and sour grassland on rocky ridges; Botha's Vlei, near Warmbaths, where one of the few remaining examples of turf thornveld typical of the Springbok Flats is conserved; De Bad Nature Reserve, north of Lydenburg, which is only 17,4 ha in extent but protects elements of mixed bushveld, sour bushveld and gallery forest along the

Spekboom River; Komatipoort Nature Reserve where typical Lowveld bush and riverine woodland are protected at the confluence of the Crocodile and Komati rivers; the Lillie Nature Reserve where the rare cycad *Encephalartos eugene-maraisii* grows; the Patatabos and Helpmekaar nature reserves within the Woodbush State Forest; the Sterkspruit Nature Reserve which protects water supplies for the farming of trout and other freshwater fish; the Tienie Louw, Thorncroft and Cythna Letty reserves near Barberton, where rare aloes are protected; the Verloren Vlei Nature Reserve north of Dullstroom which protects one of the highest grassland plateaux in South Africa, as well as rare bird species;

Vertroosting Nature Reserve, near Nelspruit, where a rare red-hot poker species is protected; and Witbad Nature Reserve, near Piet Retief, which conserves 550 ha of species-rich sourveld. Special permits are sometimes issued for these reserves; anyone wishing to visit one of them should apply to the Transvaal Directorate of Nature Conservation (see page 365).

Within the boundaries of Transvaal, and previously part of that province, are the independent states of Venda and Bophuthatswana, and the self-governing homelands Gazankulu, Lebowa, KwaNdebele and KaNgwane. The national parks and nature reserves in these areas are dealt with in their respective chapters.

1   ABE BAILEY NATURE RESERVE

Location: Southern Transvaal; north-west of Carletonville.
Access: From Carletonville follow the R500 in the direction of Randfontein for about 5 km, then turn left towards Welverdiend. After a similar distance take the signposted right turn to the reserve. By prior arrangement only; apply to the officer-in-charge.
Accommodation: None. Dormitories for school groups are being developed by the Wildlife Society of Southern Africa.
Other facilities: Guided tours; viewing hide; educational programmes.
Open: Throughout the year.
Opening time: 07h00 to 17h00.
For further information: The Officer-in-charge, Abe Bailey Nature Reserve, P.O. Box 13, Carletonville 2908. Tel: (01491) 2908. For information on educational programmes in the reserve, contact the Education Officer of the Wildlife Society (see page 365).

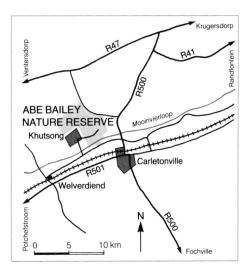

Until recently the Abe Bailey Nature Reserve was controlled by the Wildlife Society of Southern Africa. Most of it is now managed by the provincial conservation authorities, but the Wildlife Society retains control over a small area where qualified teaching staff run an environmental education centre   The main feature of this approximately 6 000-ha reserve is the extensive wetland area in which large numbers of waterbirds congregate. Among the 250 or more bird species which have been recorded in the area, Cape vultures from the Magaliesberg are regular visitors, attracted by a vulture 'restaurant'. The open grassland and acacia savannah in the reserve provide grazing for a number of introduced game species, including red hartebeest, black wildebeest, blesbok and springbok.

2   BADPLAAS NATURE RESERVE

Location: South-eastern Transvaal; east of Carolina.
Access: From Carolina follow the R38 eastwards towards Barberton for 52 km. The en-

trance to the reserve lies on the left just beyond the town of Badplaas, and is signposted. From Barberton travel westward on the R38 for 74 km.

Accommodation: Overvaal Badplaas resort has a hotel with 49 rooms, all with air conditioning. Self-catering accommodation comprises 43 rondavels, 10 chalets and 69 small flats, each of which has air conditioning, a toilet and an equipped kitchen; most have their own bathroom; bedding supplied (R30 to R84 per unit per night). The camping site has 270 stands (some with a power point) and full ablution facilities (R16 to R20 for 2 persons, R4 for each additional person).

Other facilities: Shop selling fresh produce, alcohol; restaurants and snack bars; hot mineral baths; swimming pools; wide range of sporting activities, including tennis, bowls and horse-riding; game-viewing in the well-stocked nature reserve.

Open: Throughout the year.

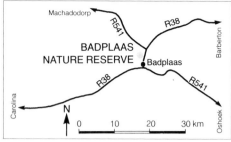

Opening time: Reserve – 14h00 to 17h00; 07h00 to 17h00 during school holidays. Resort – 24 hours.

For further information: The Resort Manager, Overvaal Badplaas Mineral Baths, P.O. Box 15, Badplaas 1190. Tel: (01344) 4-1020.

Primarily a popular holiday resort centering on hot mineral baths, Badplaas also boasts an attractive 1 000-ha nature reserve. A network of good roads, as well as paths for walking or horse-riding, criss-cross the grass-covered hillsides, on which it is relatively easy to observe the game. A number of game species, such as red hartebeest, black wildebeest, blesbok, eland and springbok, have been introduced.

3 BARBERSPAN NATURE RESERVE

Location: South-western Transvaal; northeast of Delareyville.

Access: From Delareyville take the R47 northeastwards towards Sannieshof and travel about 19 km before turning left onto the gravel road to Deelpan. Follow signposts from here to the entrance to the reserve. From Sannieshof follow the R47 south-westwards for 20 km, then take the right turn to Deelpan.

Accommodation: Camping only, with pit toilets, running water and outdoor fireplaces. There are hotels, self-catering accommodation and fully equipped camping sites in the area.

Other facilities: Picnic site; walks; birdwatching; fishing in a limited area; various watersports in a demarcated sector of the pan.

Open: Throughout the year.

Opening time: 07h00 to 16h00.

Speed limit: 40 km/h.

For further information: The Officer-in-charge, Barberspan Nature Reserve, P.O. Barberspan, 2765. Tel: (0144322) 1202.

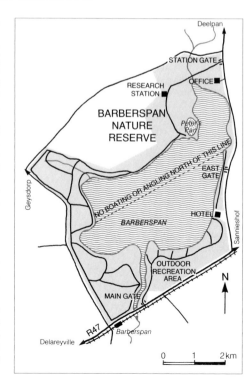

More than 350 bird species, of which the majority are water-related, have been recorded at the Barberspan Nature Reserve, making this one of the most important waterfowl sanctuaries in southern Africa. As such it is used as a base by researchers for ringing species whose migration patterns they wish to determine. Large numbers of flamingoes visit from time to time, presenting a memorablesight as they feed at the pan, and other visitors include red-knobbed coots, and night herons, as well as various egret and duck species. The reserve extends over 3 086 ha (including the 1 800-ha pan), its flat terrain covered mainly by grassland which supports black wildebeest, springbok, blesbok, red harte-beest, Burchell's zebra and ostrich.

4   BARBERTON NATURE RESERVE

Location: South-eastern Transvaal; north-east of Barberton.
Access: From Barberton the R38 to Kaap-muiden traverses the reserve.
Accommodation: None. There are hotels, self-catering accommodation and a camping site in Barberton.
Other facilities: To be developed.
Open: Throughout the year.
Opening time: Traversed by public roads.
For further information: Barberton Publicity Association. Tel: (01314) 2-2121.

1. DR HAMILTON NATURE RESERVE*
2. NELSHOOGTE NATURE RESERVE*
3. CYTHNA LETTY NATURE RESERVE*
4. THORNCROFT NATURE RESERVE*
5. TIENIE LOUW NATURE RESERVE*
* No access to the general public

Barberton Nature Reserve lies in an area steeped in gold-mining history, and with its neighbour, KaNgwane's 56 000-ha Songimvelo Nature Reserve, forms a considerable conservation area. Having only recently been proclaimed, the Barberton reserve is in the early stages of development, but promises to take a leading part in the conservation of the Lowveld environment.

This is rugged, hilly country, covered mainly by grassland, but also by areas of open bushveld and riverine forest. A number of human activities, mining in particular, are still practised in the area, and these have had an adverse effect on local mammal populations. However, a variety of smaller species, such as baboon, vervet monkey, rock dassie and common duiker survive. Birdlife is prolific, more than 300 species having been recorded. Summers are warm to hot, and winter days are mild to cool, although the nights can be cold, particularly in the mountains.

5   BEN ALBERTS NATURE RESERVE

Location: North-western Transvaal; south-west of Thabazimbi.
Access: From Thabazimbi follow the R510 southward for 5 km before taking the clearly signposted right turn to the reserve.
Accommodation: A small camping site.
Other facilities: Game-viewing roads; and a picnic site.
Open: Throughout the year.
Opening time: Winter – 08h00 to 18h00; summer – 07h00 to 19h00.
For further information: The Warden, Ben Alberts Nature Reserve, P.O. Box 50, Thabazimbi 0380. Tel: (01537) 2-1509.

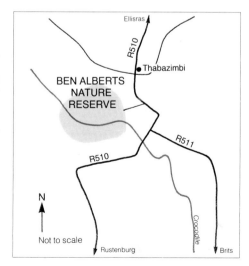

The Ben Alberts Nature Reserve, owned by ISCOR but open to the public, covers more than 2 000 ha

. A river valley runs through the hilly terrain, and a network of roads allows for good viewing of a wide variety of species, including white rhinoceros, eland, kudu and giraffe.

6 BEN LAVIN NATURE RESERVE

Location: Far northern Transvaal; south-east of Louis Trichardt.

Access: From Louis Trichardt travel southward on the N1 for 3 km, then turn left towards Elim; 1 km further on turn right to Fort Edward and follow this good gravel road for 5 km to the clearly marked reserve entrance on the left. If travelling from Pietersburg, do not take the gravel road to Elim at Bandelierskop, well to the south of Louis Trichardt. An entrance fee is charged.

Accommodation: 2 4-bed lodges with bathroom, fully equipped (R25 per person per night); 2 5-bed huts with toilet and cold water basin (communal ablution facilities available), fully equipped (R20 per person per night); large tents with stretchers can be hired (R8 per person per night). Camping site with full ablution facilities (R5 per person per night).

Other facilities: 40-km network of good to fair roads for game-viewing; 4 walking trails; hides at waterholes; night drives by arrangement with the warden; curio shop; an educational programme, aimed principally at school groups, is being developed. The nearest shop selling food and drink is at Louis Trichardt.

Open: Throughout the year.

Opening time: 06h00 to 19h00 (arrangements can be made for later arrival).

For further information: The Warden, Ben Lavin Nature Reserve, P.O. Box 782, Louis Trichardt 0920. Tel: (01551) 3834.

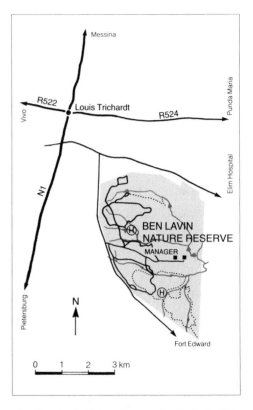

A property of the Wildlife Society of Southern Africa, the Ben Lavin Nature Reserve is situated within sight of the Soutpansberg, the most northerly mountain range in South Africa. It lies on farmland originally owned by Ben Lavin, a keen conservationist whose widow donated the land to the Wildlife Society, with the purpose of allowing people to 'get close to nature'. In accordance with this idea, visitors are allowed to walk freely through the beautiful flat to undulating country characteristic of the 2 500-ha reserve, as they can follow one of the four marked trails that pass through sweet and mixed bushveld and riverine vegetation. The trails are circular and vary from 3 to 8 km in length.

Whether they are on foot or travelling along the good road network, visitors can expect to see a wide variety of mammal species, including kudu, nyala, eland, waterbuck, bushbuck, impala, sable, blue wildebeest, tsessebe, giraffe, warthog and Burchell's zebra. Rock dassies occur on Tabajwane Hill, banded and dwarf mongooses are often seen along the 8-km Tabajwane trail, and bushbuck, reedbuck and leguaans are likely to be spotted on the Fountain Trail, which follows the Doring River. Troops of vervet monkeys frequent the camps, and at night the calls of thick-tailed bushbabies and black-backed jackals are frequently heard.

The birdlife is also very varied – 238 species have been recorded – and the most productive areas for birdwatchers are along the rivers in the south; being able to wander at will in the reserve makes birdwatching particularly rewarding.

One of a number of reptiles which visitors may be lucky enough to see is the African rock python, the only python species in this part of Africa.

1. Bourke's Luck Potholes are one of the most visited sites in the Blyde River Canyon area.

2. Young ostriches in mixed savannah in the Doorndraai Dam Nature Reserve.

3. The Three Rondavels are a prominent feature in the Blyde River Canyon Nature Reserve.

4. One of the well-equipped log cabins at Buzzard Mountain Retreat.

5. The forest habitat of Buzzard Mountain Retreat harbours samango monkeys and red duiker.

6. The Ebenezer Dam Nature Reserve, south of Magoebaskloof.

7. The roan, one of the rarest antelopes in South Africa, occurs naturally in the Hans Strijdom Dam Nature Reserve.

8. Purple gallinules are common waterbirds which may be seen at many dams in Transvaal nature reserves.

9. Happy Rest Nature Reserve lies on the southern slopes of the Soutpansberg.

10. The backdrop of the Soutpansberg and large baobab trees dominate the Honnet Nature Reserve.

11. The crowned crane, a rare crane species in Jericho Dam Nature Reserve.

12. Witpoortjie Falls in the Witwatersrand National Botanic Garden, Johannesburg.

A welcome development at the Ben Lavin reserve is the establishment of an environmental awareness programme. Summers in this region are hot, and rain falls at this time of the year; winters are generally mild, but temperatures drop sharply at night.

7   BLOEMHOF DAM NATURE RESERVE

Location: Extreme south-western Transvaal; north-east of Christiana.
Access: From Christiana follow the R29 towards Klerksdorp; 6 km beyond Bloemhof take the signposted turn-off to the reserve.
Accommodation: Camping site.
Other facilities: Picnic sites; watersports allowed (fee charged for boats); swimming; fishing (fee charged); game-viewing drives

(it is necessary to obtain permission from the officer-in-charge to enter the game area; access is from the R29).
Open: Throughout the year.
Opening time: 08h00 to 18h00.
For further information: The Officer-in-charge, Bloemhof Dam Nature Reserve, Private Bag X7, Bloemhof 2660. Tel: (018022) 1122.

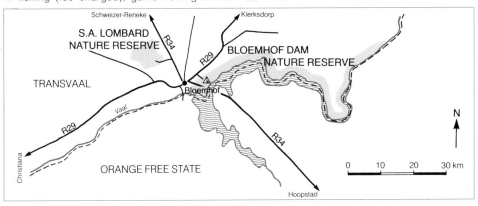

Situated on the northern bank of the Bloemhof Dam, this reserve comprises 22 211 ha of flat, open grassland with a scattering of small trees. Game species that have been released here include white rhinoceros, blesbok, black wildebeest and Burchell's zebra. Waterbirds are attracted to the dam, and the open plains are ideal for watching larks and other grassland species.

8   BLYDEBERG NATURE RESERVE

Location: Eastern Transvaal; west of Hoedspruit.
Access: From the N4 (Middelburg/Nelspruit) two route possibilities: taking the R36, 8 km west of Waterval Boven, travel through Lydenburg, and continue to within 25 km of Hoedspruit, turning south onto the Driehoek road. From Nelspruit take the R40 to just beyond Acornhoek and turn left onto the R531. Blydeberg is 3 km down the Driehoek road.
Accommodation: 4 6-bed (including 4 bunk beds) wooden chalets, fully equipped. Semi-open kitchen with all requirements, including stoves, fridges and lamps; open-air showers (hot and cold water) and flush toilets. Two-man tents with camping equipment can be hired;

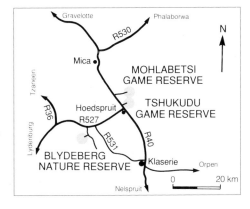

camping sites available (own equipment). Self-catering or full-catering. Rates range from R25 (camping site) to R95 per person per night (chalet with full catering). Slightly lower tariffs for chalets in low season.

Other facilities: Walking trails (self-guided, or in the company of reserve staff, for which there is a charge); game-viewing hide; night drives; fishing. Fuel and provisions are available 5 km from the reserve.

Open: Throughout the year.

Opening time: Arrivals should be planned to take place between 14h00 and sunset.

For further information: Blydeberg Nature Reserve, P.O. Box 612, Hoedspruit 1380 or Bushveld Breakaways, P.O. Box 926, White River 1240. Tel. (01311) 5-1998. Fax: (01311) 5-0383.

Blydeberg is located between the Blyde River and the Transvaal Drakensberg and covers 3 000 ha, with typical Lowveld vegetation. A variety of game species is present and more than 250 species of bird are said to be resident.

9 BLYDE RIVER CANYON NATURE RESERVE

Location: The Eastern Transvaal; north of Nelspruit.

Access: To reach Blydepoort Holiday Resort, from Nelspruit take the R37 to Sabie, then the R532 to Graskop; continue on the R532 (passing the turn-off to God's Window viewpoint and later to the Bourke's Luck Potholes) to the signposted right turn into the resort (also known as the F. H. Odendaal Camp). To reach the Sybrand van Niekerk Camp, from Nelspruit take the R40 to Klaserie, then turn left onto the R531, and after 19 km turn left again at the signpost to the resort. From Tzaneen, take the R36 southward, turning left onto the R531 for the Sybrand van Niekerk Camp, or onto the R532 for the Blydepoort Holiday Resort. The routes to both camps are clearly signposted.

Accommodation: *Overvaal Blydepoort* has 98 2- to 5-bed chalets, each with air conditioning, a fully equipped kitchen, a bathroom, carport and outdoor fireplace; bedding supplied (R22 to R40 per person per night; off-season rates and reduction for pensioners available). The camping site has 48 stands (some with a power point), ablution facilities and outdoor fireplaces (R16 to R20 for 2 persons, R4 per additional person).

Overvaal Sybrand van Niekerk has 78 6-bed chalets, each with air conditioning, a fully

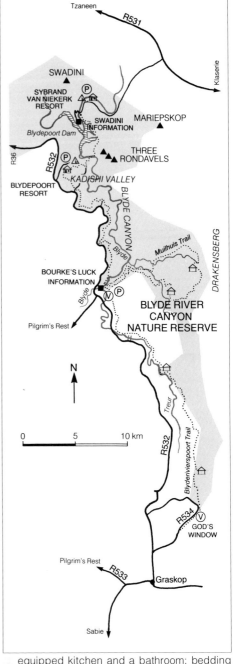

equipped kitchen and a bathroom; bedding is supplied (R36 to R38 per person per night; off-season rates and reduction for pensioners available). The camping site has 198 stands (some with a power point), ablution facilities and outdoor fireplaces (R20 to R25 for 2 persons, R4 per additional person). Hiking trail huts have bunks, mattresses, basic ablution facilities, cooking utensils, fireplaces and firewood.

Other facilities: Nature trails (varying in length) at Bourke's Luck Potholes, Kadishi Valley and Swadini, and hiking trails which pass through the reserve; viewpoints; picnic sites with fireplaces at Bourke's Luck Potholes and the 2 resorts; game-viewing in the Swadini area; very limited road system; information centres at Bourke's Luck and Swadini. The 2 camps offer most of the facilities associated with pleasure resorts.

Open: Throughout the year.

Opening time: Reserve – sunrise to sunset; resorts – 24 hours.

Beware: Malaria.

For further information: (including overnight trails) The Officer-in-charge, Blyde River Canyon Nature Reserve, P.O. Box 281, Hoedspruit 1380. Tel: 0020, ask for 15.

(Blyde River Canyon Hiking Trail) The Regional Director, Eastern Transvaal Forest Region, Private Bag X503, Sabie 1260. Tel: 0131512, ask for 196.

(Blydepoort Holiday Resort) Overvaal Blydepoort, Private Bag X368, Ohrigstad 1122. Tel: (013231) 901 or 881.

(Sybrand van Niekerk Resort) Overvaal Sybrand van Niekerk, P.O. Box 281, Hoedspruit 1380. Tel: 0020, ask for Blydedam 1, 2 or 3.

Archaeological evidence indicates that this part of the Eastern Transvaal has known human habitation since the Middle Stone Age. Rock paintings show that Bushmen once roamed the Blyde River Canyon and its surroundings, and in the Kadishi Valley there are ruins of stone walls that were built between the seventh and the nineteenth centuries. Towards the end of the last century the area attracted the attentions of gold prospectors.

Despite such a long history of human activity, the canyon is still an area of outstanding natural beauty; its nature reserve covers 22 664 ha of rugged and deeply incised landscape, with extensive sheer quartzite cliffs, river torrents and dramatic waterfalls.

This is an amazingly rich floristic region which encompasses five of South Africa's 71 recognised veld types, including open grassland, subtropical rain forest and protea forest. The variety of vegetation is influenced by extremes in altitude, soil conditions and climate, resulting in a mixture of naturally growing plants that are also found in the Cape Province, Natal, the Transvaal Lowveld and central Transvaal.

The diversity of vegetation types provides habitats for a wide range of mammals, including grey rhebok, oribi, Sharpe's grysbok, klipspringer, bushbuck, steenbok and hippopotamus, as well as all the primate species (baboon, vervet and samango monkeys, and thick-tailed and lesser bushbabies) that occur in southern Africa. The birdlife, too, is very rich.

Summers on the plateau are pleasant, and winters cold. At Swadini, however, summer days are often unpleasantly hot, whereas winters are milder than on the plateau. Mist and low cloud often occur during the summer rainy season.

10   BONWA PHALA GAME FARM

Location: Northern Transvaal; north-west of Warmbaths.

Access: From Warmbaths (on N1 – Pretoria/Nylstroom) take the R516 towards Mabula; watch out for signpost on the left. Private airstrip.

Accommodation: Main camp - 4 2-bed thatched huts with *en-suite* showers (hot and cold water) and electricity; rustic bush camps available. Main camp rates: R195 per person per day; R220 per person per day sharing for conferences. Rates include all meals, game-viewing drives and trails.

Other facilities: Accompanied game drives and walking trails; swimming pool; bar.

Open: Throughout the year.

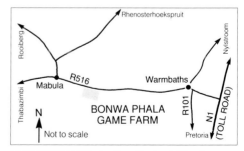

For further information: Bushveld Breakaways, P.O. Box 926, White River 1240. Tel: (01311) 5-1998. Fax: (01311) 5-0383. (Bonwa Phala), Tel: (015331) 4101 or 4767.

Bonwa Phala lies in typical bushveld below the Waterberg mountain range. Game species include giraffe, Burchell's zebra, white rhinoceros, kudu and impala. Summers are warm to hot but winters (particularly at night) can be cold.

11 BOSKOP DAM NATURE RESERVE

Location: South-western Transvaal; north of Potchefstroom.
Access: From Potchefstroom follow the tarred R501 towards Carletonville for about 20 km before turning left at the signpost to Boskop.
Accommodation: Camping site with ablution facilities (R7 per stand per night).
Other facilities: Game-viewing; picnic sites; fishing (a permit is required); boating and swimming in the dam.
Open: Throughout the year.
Opening time: 08h00 to 18h00.
For further information: The Officer-in-charge, Boskop Dam Nature Reserve, P.O. Box 24, Boskop 2528. Tel: (0148) 2-2430.

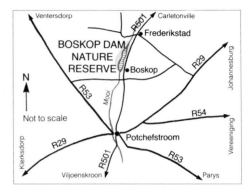

Although the Boskop Dam is primarily a haunt for fishing and watersport enthusiasts (no power boats are permitted), the surrounding nature reserve does stock a number of game species.

Blesbok, black wildebeest, red hartebeest and eland occur, and the dam attracts a wide variety of bird species.

12 BOTSHABELO NATURE RESERVE

Location: South-eastern Transvaal; north of Middelburg.
Access: From Middelburg take the R35 towards Groblersdal and Loskop Dam; after 6km a signpost indicates the turn-off to the reserve.
Accommodation: Overnight accommodation for 147 people, in rooms containing between 2 to 20 beds; a caravan park with 30 stands for caravans/tents.
Other facilities: Restored mission village; 3 walking trails; a living South Ndebele village picnic sites; refreshment kiosk; curio shop.
Open: Throughout the year.
Opening time: 07h00 to 18h00.
For further information: Middelburg Town Council, P.O. Box 14, Middelburg 1050. Tel: (0132) 2-3897 or 2-5331. Fax: (0132) 2-1041.

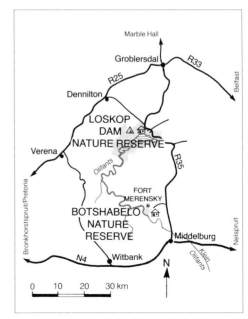

Situated in the valley of the Klein Olifants River, the Botshabelo Nature Reserve hosts 24 game species, including eland, oribi, springbok, black wildebeest and Burchell's zebra, as well as the rare Olifants River cycad. Additional attractions are a restored mission village with accommodation, and an occupied South Ndebele village.

13 BRONKHORSTSPRUIT DAM NATURE RESERVE

Location: South-central Transvaal; east of Pretoria/Johannesburg.

Access: From Pretoria travel eastward along the N4 for about 60 km, then turn right onto the R25; continue southward for a short distance, turn left onto the R42 to Delmas and watch out for the signpost to the reserve on the right. From Johannesburg take the R22, turn left onto the R42 to Bronkhorstspruit north of Delmas, and continue for about 20 km to the reserve turn-off.

Accommodation: Camping site with ablution facilities.

Other facilities: Watersports; fishing. The nearest shops or petrol supplies are at Bronkhorstspruit or Delmas.

Open: Throughout the year.

Opening time: 06h00 to 20h00.

For further information: The Officer-in-

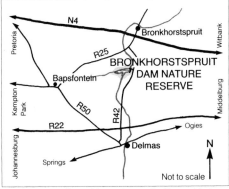

charge, Bronkhorstspruit Dam Nature Reserve, P.O. Box 583, Bronkhorstspruit 1020. Tel: (01212) 2-1621.

Its proximity to the densely populated Witwatersrand and Pretoria region makes the 1 285-ha Bronkhorstspruit Dam Nature Reserve a heavily utilised recreational area. A number of game species, including black wildebeest and blesbok, have been released into the reserve, and a variety of waterbirds frequent the dam.

14 BUZZARD MOUNTAIN RETREAT

Location: Far northern Transvaal; west of Louis Trichardt.

Access: From Louis Trichardt take the tarred R522 towards Vivo; after about 15 km watch out for the small sign indicating the reserve on the right, and low stone walls marking the entrance; turn into the entrance gate and continue to the second house. The camp lies 3 km further on and can only be reached on foot or by transport arranged with the owner. Advance booking is essential.

Accommodation: 2 7- and 9-bed cottages; 3 cabins, each with a fully equipped kitchen and ablution facilities nearby (R20 to R30 per person per night, reduced rate for children). A small camping site.

Other facilities: Network of trails.

Open: Throughout the year.

Opening time: Check with the owner.

For further information: John Greaves, Buzzard Mountain Retreat, P.O. Box 441, Louis Trichardt 0920. Tel: (01551) 4196.

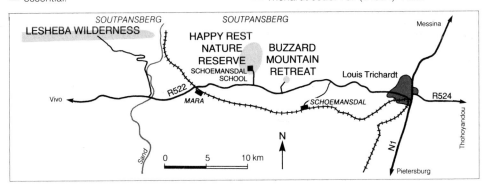

The Buzzard Mountain Retreat is a small, privately owned area situated high on the southern slopes of the Soutpansberg range in northern Transvaal. It has several short trails from which there are superb views of the surrounding countryside, and its indigenous forest, open heathland and steep cliffs offer sanctuary to a wide array of plant species. These include the cycad *Encephalartos transvenosus*, or Modjadji cycad which forms forests in the Modjadji Nature Reserve in Lebowa; the Soutpansberg is the only other known natural location of these ancient plants.

Forest-dwelling animals, such as bushbuck, red duiker, bushpig and samango monkey, may be seen, and the very rich birdlife includes crowned and black eagles, gymnogene, crested guineafowl and narina trogon.

15 DOORNDRAAI DAM NATURE RESERVE

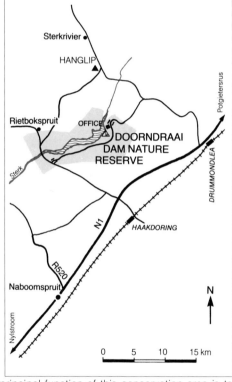

Location: North-central Transvaal; south-west of Potgietersrus.

Access: From Potgietersrus travel 17 km southward on the N1, turn right onto the tarred Sterkrivier road, and follow this road to the signposted turn-off to the reserve. From Naboomspruit travel northward on the N1 for 36 km, then turn left onto the above-mentioned tarred Sterkrivier road. A single internal gravel road running the length of the reserve is open to the public.

Accommodation: Camping site with ablution facilities and outdoor fireplaces (R7 per stand per night).

Other facilities: Picnic sites; watersports (boat permits can be obtained at the office); swimming; fishing; game-viewing.

Open: Throughout the year.

Opening time: 06h00 to 20h00.

Beware: Bilharzia.

For further information: The Officer-in-charge, Doorndraai Dam Nature Reserve, P.O. Box 983, Potgietersrus 0600. Tel: (015423) 629.

While the Doorndraai Dam is popular with anglers and watersport enthusiasts, nature-lovers are drawn more to the surrounding reserve. Lying among the foothills of the Waterberg, the 7 229-ha Doorndraai Dam Nature Reserve consists mainly of hilly country, with numerous kloofs and waterfalls. The dominant vegetation is sour bushveld, with a considerable variety of tree species. The principal function of this conservation area is to protect rare game species such as sable antelope and tsessebe, but a variety of other species may also be seen. The area around the dam can be rewarding for birdwatchers.

16 EBENEZER DAM NATURE RESERVE

Location: North-eastern Transvaal; south-west of Tzaneen.

Access: From Tzaneen take the R36 in the direction of Duiwelskloof and a short distance from the town turn left onto the R528 towards Haenertsburg; after about 35 km turn right towards the Ebenezer Dam. An entrance fee is charged.

Accommodation: A camping site with ablution facilities.

Other facilities: The reserve is still being developed.
Open: Throughout the year.
Opening time: Check with the officer-in-charge.
For further information: The Officer-in-charge, Ebenezer Dam Nature Reserve, P.O. Box 1397, Tzaneen 0850. Tel: (01523) 5-3109.

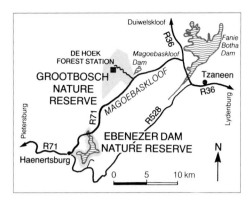

This recently proclaimed reserve in the popular Magoebaskloof holiday area is still being developed. It covers 95 ha of land around the dam, which is fed by the Broederstroom and Helpmekaar rivers, and attracts a wide variety of ducks and other waterbirds.

17 | ENTABENI STATE FOREST

Location: Far northern Transvaal; east of Louis Trichardt.
Access: From Louis Trichardt take the R524 eastwards towards Thohoyandou and after about 37 km watch out for the turn-off to Entabeni State Forest on the left (the turn-off is on a rise and easily missed). Tall trees line the gravel road into the forest. Permit essential (apply to address below); no vehicles are allowed within the reserves.
Accommodation: There are hotels and a camping site in Louis Trichardt.
Other facilities: The Entabeni section of the Soutpansberg Hiking Trail passes through the area.
Open: Throughout the year, although the better season for visiting the forest is winter.

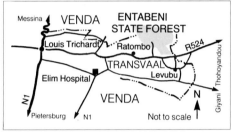

Opening time: Sunrise to sunset.
For further information: (including details about the Soutpansberg Hiking Trail) The Regional Director, Northern Transvaal Forest Region, Private Bag 2413, Louis Trichardt 0920. Tel: (01551) 2201 or 5-1152.

The three reserves within the Entabeni State Forest – the Entabeni Nature Reserve (880,8 ha), the Ratombo Nature Reserve (172 ha) and the Matiwa Nature Reserve (181,6 ha) – were all proclaimed to protect blocks of indigenous forest on the slopes of the Soutpansberg. A feature of this section of the Soutpansberg Hiking Trail are the excellent views over the plains to the south.

As well as bushbuck, which are common, the forest harbours red duiker, samango monkey, white-tailed mongoose, caracal and leopard. Birds too, although elusive, are abundant, and a variety of raptors may be sighted, including the crowned eagle which breeds here.

In this summer-rainfall area mist and low cloud also occur between November and March; winter days are usually mild.

18 | FAAN MEINTJES NATURE RESERVE

Location: South-western Transvaal; north of Klerksdorp.
Access: From Klerksdorp take the R30 towards Ventersdorp and follow signposts to the reserve. An entrance fee is charged.
Accommodation: 1 6-bed chalet; 2 4-bed chalets; all self-contained. There are also hotels and a camping site in Klerksdorp.
Other facilities: Picnic site; 40-km road network for game-viewing.
Open: Throughout the year.
Opening time: 10h00 to 18h00 (17h00 in winter).
Speed limit: 20 km/h.

For further information: The Department of Parks, Recreation and Farming, Klerksdorp Town Council, P.O. Box 99, Klerksdorp 2570. Tel: (018) 2-3635 or 2-5700. Fax: (018) 64-1780.

The open plains and sand ridges of the Faan Meintjes Nature Reserve are covered with both sweet and sour grassland, interspersed with occasional patches of bush. The reserve has been well stocked with a number of different game species, and visitors can expect to see white rhinoceros, giraffe, sable, eland, gemsbok, black wildebeest, blesbok, waterbuck, impala and springbok.

19 FANIE BOTHA DAM NATURE RESERVE

Location: North-eastern Transvaal; north of Tzaneen.
Access: From Tzaneen take the R36 northwards, then follow signposts to the reserve, which is a short distance out of town.
Accommodation: A camping and caravan site with 150 stands, ablution facilities (with electrical points) and outdoor fireplaces (R12 per stand per night).

Other facilities: Picnic sites; boating; fishing (permits obtainable at the office).
Open: Throughout the year.
Opening time: 05h00 to 20h00.
Beware: Bilharzia.
For further information: The Officer-in-charge, Fanie Botha Dam Nature Reserve, P.O. Box 1397, Tzaneen 0850. Tel: (01523) 5-3109.

Primarily a water-related recreational area, the Fanie Botha Dam lies in a picturesque setting, with extensive forest plantations on the hill slopes overlooking the water. Game in the surrounding reserve is restricted to common duiker and bushbuck, but many bird species are attracted to the dam. The reserve covers 2 850 ha, including the dam.

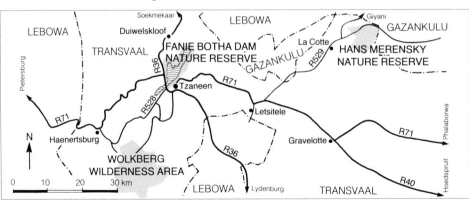

20 GREATER KUDULAND SAFARIS

Location: Far northern Transvaal; north of Louis Trichardt.
Access: From Louis Trichardt travel northward on the N1 for about 60 km before turning right onto the R525 to Tshipise. Continue to the Tshipise resort and about 1,5 km beyond

it take the right turn to Greater Kuduland Safaris.
Accommodation: A luxury hutted camp accommodates a maximum of 14 people for at least 2 nights; each hut has a bathroom and air conditioning; the rustic main building

houses a lounge/dining room, and there is an outdoor informal eating area (R150 per adult per day, all-inclusive; special rates for children and group bookings). There are also 2 bush camps.

Other facilities: Guided game-viewing trails; 3- to 5-day hiking trails; game-viewing drives; hunting safaris; swimming; canoeing.
Open: Throughout the year.
Opening time: 24 hours.
Beware: Malaria.
For further information: Greater Kuduland

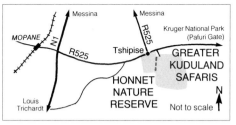

Safaris, P.O. Box 1385, Louis Trichardt 0920. Tel: (01551) 9663 or (015539) 664/5.

Mopane and mixed bush, with occasional baobab trees, cover the flat to hilly terrain of this 10 000-ha private reserve in the northern Transvaal bushveld. A great number of game species – including buffalo, Burchell's zebra, eland, kudu, impala, blue wildebeest, gemsbok, nyala, red hartebeest, waterbuck and klipspringer – occur naturally or have been introduced and, although rarely seen, leopard and cheetah are also present. Several dams attract waterfowl, and in total more than 200 bird species have been observed in the reserve.

Summer days tend to be very hot in this area, but winter days are mild, with cold nights.

21 GROOTBOSCH NATURE RESERVE See map Ebenezer Dam Nature Reserve

Location: North-eastern Transvaal; west of Tzaneen.
Access: From Tzaneen take the R71/R36 northwards towards Duiwelskloof and after about 7 km turn left onto the R71 towards Pietersburg; continue for about 9 km and just after passing the Magoebaskloof Dam on the right, turn right to the De Hoek State Forest. A permit is essential (can be obtained from the Regional Director). Access is limited to hikers on the Magoebaskloof Hiking Trail.

Accommodation: A hut at De Hoek Forest Station provides hikers with bunks, toilets, fireplaces and wood; otherwise they may camp at specified areas on the trail.
Other facilities: None.
Open: Throughout the year but may be closed in the rainy season (summer).
Opening time: Sunrise to sunset.
For further information: The Regional Director, Northern Transvaal Forest Region, Pvt. Bag X2413, Louis Trichardt 0920. Tel: (01551) 2202.

Situated within the De Hoek and Woodbush State Forest, this 4 625-ha reserve was proclaimed recently to protect the largest indigenous evergreen forest in the Transvaal. Among the many species which thrive here are tree ferns, yellowwoods, white and red stinkwood, forest mahogany and red beech.

Part of the strenuous Magoebaskloof Hiking Trail passes through the reserve, and observant hikers may spot forest birds such as long-crested eagle, gymnogene, rameron pigeon and Knysna and purple-crested louries. Mammals in the area include bushbuck and red duiker.

22 GUSTAV KLINGBIEL NATURE RESERVE

Location: Eastern Transvaal; east of Lydenburg.
Access: From Lydenburg take the R37 towards Sabie; the Gustav Klingbiel Nature Reserve lies to the left of the road a short distance out of town.
Accommodation: A hiking trail hut. There is accommodation in Lydenburg.
Other facilities: An overnight hiking trail and 3 nature trails; picnic sites with fireplaces;

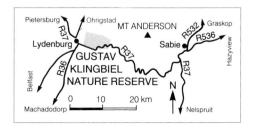

game-viewing; a museum complex including an auditorium and a curio/craft shop.
Open: Throughout the year.
Opening time: Winter – 08h00 to 16h00; summer – 07h30 to 16h00 (08h00 to 17h00 at weekends).
For further information: The Town Clerk, Lydenburg Town Council, P.O. Box 61, Lydenburg 1120. Tel: (01323) 2121 or 2130. Fax: (01323) 5-1108.

The 2 200-ha Gustav Klingbiel Nature Reserve on the slopes of Mount Anderson supports a number of antelope species, from the majestic eland to the diminutive steenbok, and more than 100 bird species. Also of interest are archaeological ruins from the Later Iron Age, and the remains of Anglo-Boer War forts.

23 | HANS MERENSKY NATURE RESERVE See also map Fanie Botha Dam Nature Reserve

Location: North-eastern Transvaal; north-east of Tzaneen.
Access: From Tzaneen take the R71 towards Gravelotte, turning left onto the R529 (signposted Eiland) after 25 km. Continue on the R529 for about 40 km to the reserve entrance.
Accommodation: The Overvaal Eiland Resort has 103 4- to 5-bed rondavels, each with a fully equipped kitchen and bathroom, and some with a lounge/dining room; bedding provided (R26 to R34 per person per night).The camping site has 450 stands (some with power points), ablution facilities and outdoor fireplaces (R16 to R20 for 2 persons, R4 per additional person). The hiking trail hut has beds and a cooking shelter.
Other facilities: Trails ranging in length from 1 to 34 km; game-viewing bus tours (private cars are not allowed on the road network); a reconstructed Tsonga kraal open-air museum. The resort offers hot springs and swimming pools; a wide variety of sporting activities, including fishing and horse-riding; restaurants and a cafeteria; shops selling fresh produce and alcohol; fuel supplies; an unregistered airstrip.
Open: Throughout the year.
Opening time: Sunrise to sunset.
Beware: Malaria; bilharzia; crocodiles.
For further information: (including hiking trails) The Officer-in-charge, Hans Merensky Nature Reserve, Private Bag X502, Letsitele 0885. Tel: (015238) 633. (Eiland Resort) Resort Manager, Eiland Resort, Private Bag 527, Letsitele 0885. Tel: (015238) 759. Bookings for bus tours and Tsonga Kraal Open-air Museum to be done in advance at the Visitor Centre, Tel: (015238) 727.

The vegetation of the 5 182-ha Hans Merensky Nature Reserve is typical of the Lowveld, comprising a mixture of mopane, combretum woodland and grassland. Riverine woodland fringes the Letaba River – which forms the northern boundary of the reserve – providing suitable habitat for hippopotamus and crocodile.

The reserve, originally set aside to conserve and breed sable antelope and giraffe, is now home to many other game species, including kudu, impala, waterbuck, blue wildebeest, common duiker and bushbuck. Leopard also occur, but these nocturnal predators are rarely seen.

As in most summer-rainfall areas, the best time for game-spotting is during the dry winter months, when the less dense vegetation allows a clearer view. Moreover, summer days in this area can be uncomfortably hot.

24 HANS STRIJDOM DAM NATURE RESERVE

Location: North-western Transvaal; north-west of Nylstroom.

Access: From Nylstroom take the R517 towards Ellisras; after approximately 120 km turn right onto a gravel road signposted to the Hans Strijdom Dam.

Accommodation: Camping site with ablution facilities.

Other facilities: Picnic sites with fireplaces; watersports allowed on the dam; fishing; walking trails; game-viewing and birdwatching.

Open: Throughout the year.

Opening time: 06h00 to 20h00.

Speed limit: 30 km/h.

Beware: Bilharzia; malaria during summer rains; crocodiles.

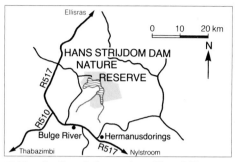

For further information: The Officer-in-charge, Hans Strijdom Dam Nature Reserve, P.O. Box 473, Ellisras 0555. Tel: (01536) 3-3384.

The rugged, hilly terrain around the Hans Strijdom Dam on the north-western fringes of the Waterberg is the natural habitat of the rare roan antelope and Sharpe's grysbok, and these and other game species are protected in this 3 686-ha reserve. The two walking trails through the reserve's savannah woodland offer visitors rewarding game-viewing and birdwatching opportunities; longer trails are being developed.

Summer days can be unpleasantly hot in this area.

25 HAPPY REST NATURE RESERVE See map Buzzard Mountain Retreat

Location: Far northern Transvaal; west of Louis Trichardt.

Access: From Louis Trichardt take the tarred R522 towards Vivo; after about 20 km turn right to the Schoemansdal Veld School which is in the reserve. Entrance by prior arrangement with the school principal.

Accommodation: Only for school or youth groups.

Other facilities: Paths through the reserve.

Open: Throughout the year.

For further information: The Principal, Schoemansdal Veld School, P.O. Box 737, Louis Trichardt 0920. Tel: (01551) 4181.

Situated on the southern slopes of the Soutpansberg range, the 1 585-ha Happy Rest Nature Reserve extends from the base of the mountains to their peaks and includes steep cliffs, pockets of indigenous forest (including some cycads) and elements of montane fynbos (heath). The birdlife in this varied scenery is rich.

26 HARTBEESPOORT DAM NATURE RESERVE

Location: South-central Transvaal; west of Pretoria.

Access: From Pretoria the most direct route to the Hartbeespoort Dam is to take the R27 towards Rustenburg; to reach the Kommandonek sector, travel about 30 km along the R27, turn left onto the R512, left again towards Kosmos, then follow signposts to Kommandonek; to reach the Oberon Re-

creational Area, follow the R27 for 18 km, turn left to link up with the R512, then turn right and continue to Oberon, following the signposts. A number of other roads lead to different parts of the dam.

Accommodation: Camping sites at Kommandonek and Oberon, each with ablution facilities and outdoor fireplaces. There are various types of accommodation nearby.

Other facilities: A wide range of watersports; fishing (permit required); game-viewing at Kommandonek; there are picnic sites for day visitors.
Open: Throughout the year.
Opening time: Officially controlled areas –

06h00 to 18h00; elsewhere – 24 hours.
Beware: Bilharzia.
For further information: The Officer-in-charge, Hartbeespoort Dam Nature Reserve, P.O. Box 903-034, Broederstroom 0240. Tel: (01205) 5-1353.

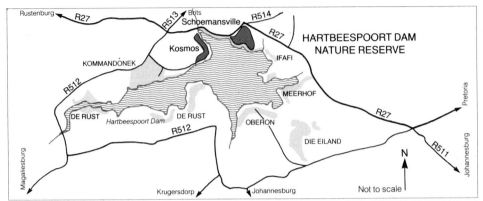

The Hartbeespoort Dam Nature Reserve, which falls within the much larger Magaliesberg Natural Area, comprises the dam itself plus a number of conservation areas scattered along its shore. As a unit, the reserve is under the control of the Transvaal Directorate of Nature Conservation. It serves as a major 'playground' to city-dwellers of Pretoria and the Witwatersrand region, and consequently its vegetation, animals and birdlife are subjected to considerable pressure.

The vegetation of the reserve is predominantly mixed bushveld, and tree species such as sweet thorn, white stinkwood, karee, wild olive and buffalo-thorn are common. Oberon is best known as a bird sanctuary, and Kommandonek has a fenced-off game camp, where kudu, bushbuck, common duiker, red hartebeest, Burchell's zebra and steenbok may be seen.

This is also a good birding area, and Cape vultures can be observed at their roosting cliffs just west of Kommandonek.

27 HONNET NATURE RESERVE See map Greater Kuduland Safaris

Location: Far northern Transvaal; north-east of Louis Trichardt.
Access: From Louis Trichardt travel northward on the N1 for 57 km before turning right onto the R525 to Tshipise; 30 km further on take the clearly signposted right turn to the reserve and Overvaal Tshipise resort.
Accommodation: Overvaal Tshipise resort has a hotel with 37 double rooms (R72 to R85 per room per night). Self-catering accommodation comprises 102 rondavels, each with a fully equipped kitchen, bathroom and air conditioning (R40 to R50 for 2 persons per night). A camping site has 300 stands (some with a

power point) and ablution facilities (R14 to R17 for 2 persons, R3 per additional person). A trail hut accommodates 12 hikers.
Other facilities: Hiking and nature trails; guided horse trails; fishing. Overvaal Tshipise offers most facilities associated with a pleasure resort, including fuel supplies.
Open: Throughout the year.
Opening time: Resort – 24 hours.
Beware: Malaria; bilharzia.
For further information: The General Manager, Overvaal Tshipise Resort, P.O. Box 4, Tshipise 0901. Tel: (015539) 624 or 661 (resort), 724 (hotel).

The Honnet Nature Reserve provides those staying at the Overvaal Tshipise resort with the opportunity to take short forays into the bush to spot such game species as giraffe, sable, blue wildebeest, tsessebe and Burchell's zebra. The terrain of this 2 200-ha reserve on the northern slopes of the Soutpansberg is flat to rugged, and its vegetation, like that of the adjacent Greater Kuduland Safaris, comprises mainly mopane woodland. The area becomes very hot in summer.

28 | JERICHO DAM NATURE RESERVE See regional map

Location: South-eastern Transvaal; south-east of Ermelo.
Access: From Ermelo take the R65 eastwards towards Amsterdam and Swaziland, and after approximately 45 km turn right onto a graded gravel road signposted to the reserve and Sheepmoor; follow signposts to the reserve. Alternatively, from Ermelo follow the R29 towards Piet Retief for 42 km, turn left onto a graded gravel road to Sheepmoor, and follow signposts to the reserve.

Accommodation: Camping site with outdoor fireplaces (small fee).
Other facilities: Picnic sites; watersports; fishing (permit required); birdwatching.
Open: Throughout the year.
Opening time: 06h00 to 18h00.
For further information: The Officer-in-charge, Jericho Dam Nature Reserve, P.O. Box 74, Amsterdam 2375. Tel: (013421) 307.

Although it also supports a few small game species, the 2 186-ha Jericho Dam Nature Reserve is known primarily as a haunt for birdwatchers.

Among the many species that have been recorded here, two rare crane species, wattled and crowned cranes, may be seen.

29 | JOHANNESBURG

Chudleigh View
Lucky St, Northcliff. This small reserve on the highest ridge in Johannesburg offers superb views of the city and the Magaliesberg to the north.

Florence Bloom Bird Sanctuary
Road No. 3, Victory Park. Situated in Delta Park between Blairgowrie and Victory Park, this 10-ha sanctuary provides refuge for almost 200 bird species. Many of these congregate around two small dams and can be observed from hides nearby. The bird sanctuary is open at all times.

Harvey Nature Reserve
Vera Rd, Cyrildene. The varied vegetation of this small, undeveloped reserve on the Linksfield Ridge supports a large number of birds. Visitors are free to wander along the network of paths that criss-cross the area, and the reserve is open at all times.

Klipriviersberg Nature Reserve
Fairway Ave, Mondeor. This 550-ha reserve in south Johannesburg conserves indigenous vegetation among rocky ridges, providing habitat for some 150 bird and several small mammal species.

Part of the guided Bloubos Spruit Hiking Trail passes through the reserve, although it is accessible to trailists only on the second Sunday of each month. The reserve is open at all times throughout the year.

Kloofendal Nature Reserve
Galena Ave, Roodepoort. The Kloofendal Nature Reserve, about 150 ha in extent, is an attractive haven situated around a dam within the city of Roodepoort. A number of easy walks and two self-guided trails allow the visitor to explore the kloofs, koppies and low cliffs that are the main features of the landscape.

The indigenous vegetation supports more than 120 bird species. The reserve's facilities include picnic sites and an amphitheatre for open-air events.

Of historical interest – and now a national monument – is the first mine shaft that produced a viable supply of gold on the Witwatersrand. The Kloofendal Nature Reserve is open daily in summer from 08h00 to 18h00.

Korsman Bird Sanctuary
The Drive, Westdene (Benoni). Situated on the Westdene Pan just to the south of the Benoni Lake Golf Course, the 50-ha Korsman Bird Sanctuary attracts large numbers of waterfowl, including flamingoes. Access to the bird hide within the perimeter fence is restricted to members of the Witwatersrand Bird Club, but the birds can also be seen from the pathway just outside the fence.[*]

Langermann Kop Reserve
Juno St, Kensington. Langermann Kop is a small, rocky ridge covered with dense indigenous bush, including proteas. The reserve is open at all times.

Melrose Bird Sanctuary
James and Ethel Gray Park, Melrose. More than 120 bird species have been recorded in this 10-ha sanctuary owned by the Johannesburg Municipality.

A small vlei in the reserve attracts many waterbirds, which find ideal roosting and breeding sites in the fringing reedbeds. The sanctuary is open from sunrise to sunset.

Melville Koppies Nature Reserve
Judith Rd, Emmarentia. Intended mainly to protect indigenous plantlife on outcrops of the Witwatersrand ridge, the 66-ha Melville Koppies Nature Reserve also provides a refuge for birds and other wildlife. A booklet is available, and guided tours are arranged by the Johannesburg Council for Natural History (Tel: 011 – 646-3612).

Archaeological research has shown that this area has been occupied by man for about 100 000 years, and the Archaeological Society (P.O. Box 42050, Craighall 2024) can supply information about interesting sites in the reserve. Melville Koppies is open from September to April on the third Sunday of the month, from 15h00 to 18h00.

Olifantsvlei Nature Reserve
South-western Johannesburg. The N1 and the R553 cut through this, Johannesburg's largest and probably most valuable, nature reserve. Plans to develop its potential are being drawn up, but at present it is a relatively wild wetland area with extensive reedbeds and a rich birdlife.

The Wilds
Houghton Dr., Houghton. The Wilds is a 20-ha area of rocky ridges, streams and established gardens.

Short nature trails take the visitor into a variety of plant habitats, including elements of fynbos (heath), as well as past several cycad species. The reserve is open at all times.

Witwatersrand National Botanic Garden
Malcolm Rd, Roodepoort. In its 225 ha this botanic garden conserves one of the few remnants of the Witwatersrand's original vegetation. Most of it has been left in its natural state, but in the small area developed as a formal garden a large collection of southern African cycads and an impressive array of Transvaal succulents are displayed. There is also a comprehensive collection of ferns. Several trails and paths wind through the natural area.

From Mondays to Fridays the garden opens at 08h00 and closes at 16h00; on Sundays and public holidays it remains open until 17h00.

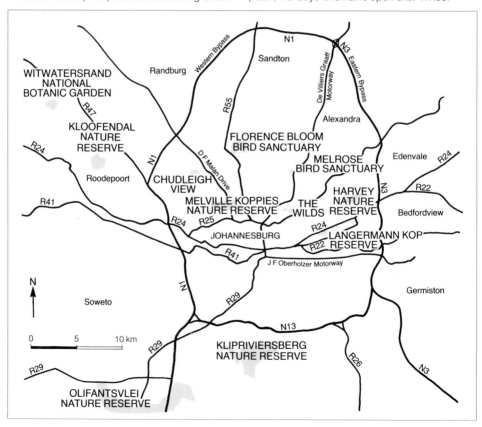

30 KLASERIE PRIVATE NATURE RESERVE

Location: Eastern Transvaal; south of Phalaborwa.
Access: Only through Clive Walker Trails; transport for visitors is provided from Johannesburg.
Accommodation: A tented camp with ablution facilities; meals provided.
Other facilities: 5-day walking trails guided by an armed and experienced field officer (maximum 8 persons); nocturnal game- viewing drives.
Open: Throughout the year.
Beware: Malaria.
For further information: Clive Walker Trails, P.O. Box 645, Bedfordview 2008. Tel: (011) 453-7645/6/7. Fax: (011) 453-7649.

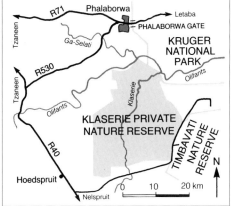

The Klaserie Private Nature Reserve, owned by more than 100 private individuals, covers approximately 60 000 ha on both sides of the Klaserie River. Its vegetation is typical of the Transvaal Lowveld, with woodland fringing the riverbanks, and it supports a wide variety of game animals, including elephant, giraffe, kudu, buffalo and a large population of impala. Predators are represented by lion, leopard, spotted hyena and many smaller species. The reserve's birdlife is similar to that of the neighbouring Kruger National Park.

31 KRANSBERG NATIONAL PARK

This recently proclaimed national park is situated in the Kransberg north-east of Thabazimbi and covers approximately 15 000 ha, although it is hoped that another 12 000 ha will be added soon. At this stage the park is closed to visitors, but facilities are to be developed.

For information on the latest progress contact the National Parks Board (see page 365).

32 KRUGER NATIONAL PARK

Location: Eastern Transvaal; on the Mozambique border, extending from Zimbabwe to within a few kilometres of Swaziland
Access: The Kruger National Park has 8 public entrance gates: Pafuri, Punda Maria, Phalaborwa, Orpen, Paul Kruger (to Skukuza), Numbi, Malelane and Crocodile Bridge.
To reach *Pafuri:* From Louis Trichardt take the N1 northward and after about 60 km turn right onto the R525 towards Tshipise; continue past the Overvaal Tshipise Resort to the Pafuri gate, which is approximately 130 km from the N1. The nearest camp, Punda Maria, is about 60 km further on. There is no petrol station between Tshipise and Punda Maria (about 160 km).
Punda Maria: From Louis Trichardt take the R524 eastward, passing through Thohoyan-

dou, to reach the gate after about 140 km. Punda Maria camp is 8 km further on.
Phalaborwa: From Pietersburg follow the R71 eastward for 214 km, passing through Tzaneen and the town of Phalaborwa before reaching the gate. The nearest camp (Letaba) is 50 km further on.
Orpen: From Tzaneen (north) or Nelspruit (south) follow the R40 to Klaserie, then take the clearly signposted turn-off to Orpen and continue for 45 km to the gate. The small Orpen camp is near the gate, but the larger Satara is 45 km further on.
Paul Kruger: From the R40 turn onto the R536 near Hazyview and continue for about 45 km to the gate. Skukuza is 13 km further on.
Numbi: From Nelspruit take the R40 to White River, then follow the R538 for approximately

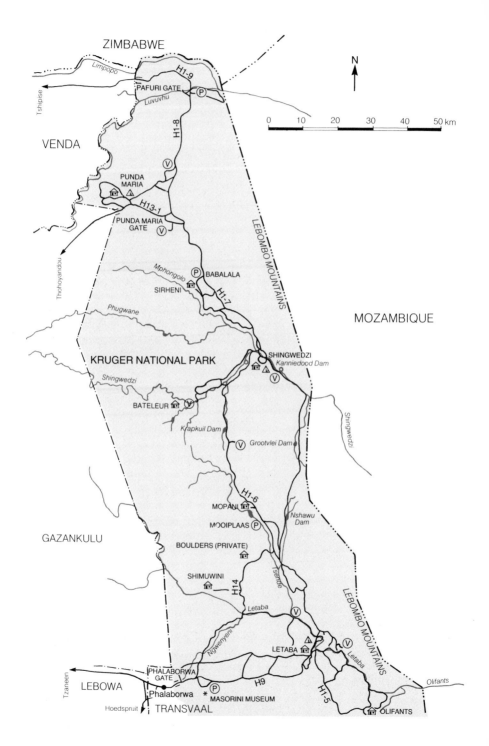

ZIMBABWE

Limpopo

H1-9

PAFURI GATE (P)

Luvuvhu

Tshipise

N

0 10 20 30 40 50 km

VENDA

H1-8

(V)

PUNDA
MARIA

H13-1

PUNDA MARIA
GATE (V)

Thohoyandou

Mphongolo (P) BABALALA

SIRHENI

H1-7

Phugwane

LEBOMBO MOUNTAINS

MOZAMBIQUE

KRUGER NATIONAL PARK

Shingwedzi

SHINGWEDZI
Kanniedood Dam

(V)

BATELEUR (V)

Shingwedzi

Krapkuil Dam

(V) *Grootvlei Dam*

H1-6

MOPANI

MOOIPLAAS (P)

*Nshawu
Dam*

GAZANKULU

BOULDERS (PRIVATE)

SHIMUWINI

H14

Tsende

Letaba

(V)

LEBOMBO MOUNTAINS

LETABA

(V)

Letaba

Ngwenyeni

PHALABORWA
GATE

LEBOWA

Tzaneen

Phalaborwa

* MASORINI MUSEUM

H9

Hoedspruit

TRANSVAAL

H1-5

Olifants

OLIFANTS

13. Impala lilies have been planted in many of the rest camps in the Kruger National Park.

14. Despite the Kruger Park's large size, the authorities have to cull buffalo to prevent overgrazing.

15. Jock of the Bushveld is one of the Kruger Park's private camps.

17. The Kruger National Park has a large lion population.

16. A group of waterbuck cows and well-grown calves in the Kruger National Park.

18. The evening settles on Letaba camp in the Kruger National Park.

19. White-fronted bee-eaters can sometimes be seen in woodland fringing the Kruger National Park's rivers.

20. A fine example of a fever tree, a species which grows only in the eastern half of the park.

21. Elephant bulls moving through mopane woodland near Shingwedzi.

23. The Kruger Park is one of the few areas in South Africa where marabou stork can be seen.

22. The impala is the most abundant antelope species in the Kruger National Park.

24. Instead of being fenced Boulders camp, in the northern half of the park, is built on stilts.

25 km before turning right onto the R569; continue for 7 km along this road to Numbi. Pretoriuskop lies 8 km beyond the gate.

Malelane: From Nelspruit follow the N4 towards Komatipoort and after about 70 km take the clearly signposted left turn to the gate, which is 3 km further on. The nearest major camp is Berg-en-dal, 12 km away.

Crocodile Bridge: From Nelspruit follow the N4 towards Komatipoort for about 110 km before turning left to the Crocodile Bridge gate, which is about 10 km further on. The camp of the same name is a short distance from the gate.

Skukuza has an airfield which is served by regular commercial flights to and from Johannesburg and Durban.

Accommodation/Facilities: The Kruger Park's 24 rest camps (including one for campers only) offer visitors a wide variety of accommodation, ranging from private camps, which accommodate 12 to 19 people and must be booked as a unit, to town-like Skukuza, the park's headquarters. Rates range from R25 to R70 per person per night; the private camps cost between R720 and R960 per night. Some camps have guest cottages which are occupied for certain periods by private organisations or individuals who have donated them, but are available to the public at other times (rates on application). Berg-en-dal, Letaba, Lower Sabie, Olifants, Satara, Shingwedzi and Skukuza have accommodation for paraplegic visitors. All the camping sites have ablution blocks and communal cooking facilities excepting Balule where a lapa with wash-up facilities is provided. No power points are installed at camping sites. (Rates are between R8 and R15 per stand per night plus R7 per adult and R5,50 per child under 16 per night; children under 2 stay free.)

Balule, a small camp on the Olifants River, has 3-bed huts with no refrigerator or electricity. There is an ablution block and a caravan and camping site. The nearest shop and petrol station are at Olifants.

Berg-en-dal, a medium-sized camp in the south-west, has 6-bed family cottages and 2- and 3-bed huts, each with a bathroom, kitchen and air conditioning; self-contained guest cottages; and a caravan and camping site. It also has a laundry, restaurant, shop selling fresh produce, petrol station, conference facilities and swimming pool.

Crocodile Bridge, a small camp in the south-east, has 2- and 3-bed huts, each with a bathroom, refrigerator, hotplate and air conditioning; and a camping site with space for 12 caravans or tents. There is a shop (no fresh produce) and petrol station.

Letaba, one of the larger camps and centrally situated, has 6-bed family cottages, each with a bathroom, kitchen and air conditioning; 2- and 3-bed huts, each with a bathroom, refrigerator, hotplate and air conditioning; 2- and 3-bed huts, each with a bathroom, refrigerator and air conditioning; 2 self-contained guest cottages; and a caravan and camping site. The camp provides laundry facilities, a restaurant, a shop selling fresh produce, a petrol station and a garage with workshop facilities. A 2-roomed unit is available for maids or chauffeurs.

Lower Sabie, a medium-sized camp in the south, has 5-bed family cottages, each with a bathroom, kitchen and air conditioning; 2- and 3-bed huts, each with a bathroom, hotplate, refrigerator and air conditioning; 2- and 3-bed huts, each with a bathroom, refrigerator and air conditioning; 1-, 2-, 3-, 5- and 6-bed huts, each with a refrigerator and air conditioning; self-contained guest cottages; and a caravan and camping site. There is a restaurant, a shop selling fresh produce, and a petrol station.

Mopani, situated roughly halfway between Letaba and Shingwedzi, offers accommodation in family cottages, 4-bed huts and a guest house. The thatched buildings are spaciously arranged and there is a swimming pool.

Olifants, a large camp on the Olifants River, has 6-bed family cottages and 2- and 3-bed huts, each with a bathroom, kitchen and air conditioning; 2- and 3-bed huts, each with a bathroom, refrigerator and air conditioning; and a self-contained guest cottage. The camp has a restaurant, shop selling fresh produce, petrol, and conference facilities.

Orpen, a small camp close to the Orpen gate, has 2- and 3-bed huts, a communal ablution block and a kitchen unit. There is a small shop (no fresh produce) and a petrol station.

Pretoriuskop, in the south-west, has 6-bed family cottages, each with a bathroom, kitchen and air conditioning; 6-bed huts, each with a bathroom, refrigerator and air conditioning; 2-, 3- and 4-bed huts, each with a bathroom, refrigerator and air conditioning; 2-, 3-, 5- and 6-bed huts, each with a refrigerator and air conditioning; 2- and 3-bed huts, each with a bathroom, refrigerator, hotplate and air conditioning; 2-bed huts, each with air conditioning; 2 self-contained guest cottages; and a caravan and camping site. The camp has a restaurant, shop selling fresh produce, petrol, and a swimming pool.

Punda Maria, a small camp in the far north,

has 4-bed family cottages and 2- and 3-bed huts, each with a bathroom, kitchen and air conditioning; 2- and 3-bed huts, each with a bathroom, refrigerator and air conditioning; and a caravan and camping site. There is also a restaurant, shop selling fresh produce, and petrol station.

Satara, the second largest camp, lies in the central sector of the park between the Olifants and Sabie rivers. It has 6-bed family cottages, each with a bathroom, kitchen and air conditioning; 2- and 3-bed huts, each with a bathroom, refrigerator and air conditioning; self-contained guest cottages; and a caravan and camping site. The camp has a laundry, restaurant, shop selling fresh produce, petrol station and garage with workshop facilities.

Shingwedzi, a medium-sized camp in the northern sector, has 4-bed family cottages, each with a bathroom and kitchen; 2- and 3-bed huts, each with a bathroom and kitchen; 3- and 5-bed huts, each with a bathroom, refrigerator, and air conditioning in the 5-bed huts; 3-bed huts, each with a refrigerator; a self-contained guest cottage; and a caravan and camping site. There is a restaurant, shop selling fresh produce, petrol station and swimming pool.

Skukuza, the largest camp and the park's headquarters, has 4- and 6-bed family cottages, each with a bathroom, kitchen and air conditioning; 2- and 3-bed huts, each with a bathroom, refrigerator, hotplate and air conditioning; 2- and 3-bed huts, each with a bathroom, refrigerator and air conditioning; 7 self-contained guest cottages; dormitory accommodation for school groups; and a caravan and camping site. The camp also has restaurants, a shop selling fresh produce, banking, post office and conference facilities, a library and information centre, a petrol station and a garage with workshop facilities.

The following fully equipped camps are private and must be booked as a unit by one group: *Boulders*, a secluded camp north of Letaba, accommodates 12 people in 4 2-bed huts and a 4-bed cottage. Provisions and fuel can be obtained either in Phalaborwa or at Letaba, where visitors should book in.

Jock of the Bushveld, between Skukuza and Berg-en-dal, accommodates 12 people in 3 cottages. Provisions and fuel can be obtained at Berg-en-dal, Pretoriuskop, Skukuza or Lower Sabie; visitors should book in at Berg-en-dal.

Malelane, just inside the park in the south, accommodates 18 people in luxury huts in spacious grounds. The nearest major camp is Berg-en-dal, where provisions and fuel can

be obtained and visitors should book in.

Nwanetsi, east of Satara, accommodates 16 people in 6 bungalows, each with 2 or 3 beds. Satara is the nearest major camp where fuel and provisions can be obtained, and visitors should book in there.

Roodewal, between Olifants and Satara, accommodates 19 people in a 4-bed cottage and 3 5-bed huts. The nearest camps for fuel and provisions are Olifants, Satara and Orpen, but visitors should book in at Olifants.

Maroela camping site, overlooking the Timbavati River near Orpen, accommodates 20 caravans and is administered by the Orpen camp.

Bushveld camps are slightly larger than private camps and offer accommodation in fully equipped, serviced huts; these huts may be reserved individually. Supplies and fuel must be purchased in the nearest large camp. The following camps all fall into this category: *Bateleur*, about 40 km north-west of Shingwedzi, offers accommodation in 7 family cottages.

Mbyamiti, situated in the extreme south of the park near Crocodile Bridge, has 10 5-bed huts and 5 4-bed huts.

Shimuwini is located between Phalaborwa and Mopani and has 5 4-bed huts, 9 5-bed huts and one 6-bed hut. The closest shop or fuel station is at either Mopani, Phalaborwa or Letaba.

Sirheni adjoins the Sirheni Dam, midway between Shingwedzi and Punda Maria, and has 5 4-bed huts and 10 6-bed huts.

Talamati is positioned somewhat south of a line between Orpen and Satara on the southern bank of the normally dry Nwaswitsontso River. There are 9 6-bed huts and 6 4-bed huts. Nearest shop and fuel station is at Orpen or Satara.

Wilderness trails: To allow visitors to appreciate the Bushveld at close quarters, 6 wilderness trails – the Wolhuter, Bushman, Olifants, Nyalaland, Metsi-Metsi and Sweni – have been established. On a Monday or Friday a maximum of 8 people meet their ranger guide and set out for the 2-day, 3-night trail. Each is based at a bush camp where bedding, cooking and eating utensils, and food are provided, and from which daily walks are undertaken.

The Wolhuter and Bushman trails are based in the south-western corner of the park, near Berg-en-dal; the Olifants trail camp is near the confluence of the Olifants and Letaba rivers; the Nyalaland trail camp is in the far north, just south of the Luvuvhu River; and the recently established Metsi-Metsi trail is based in the

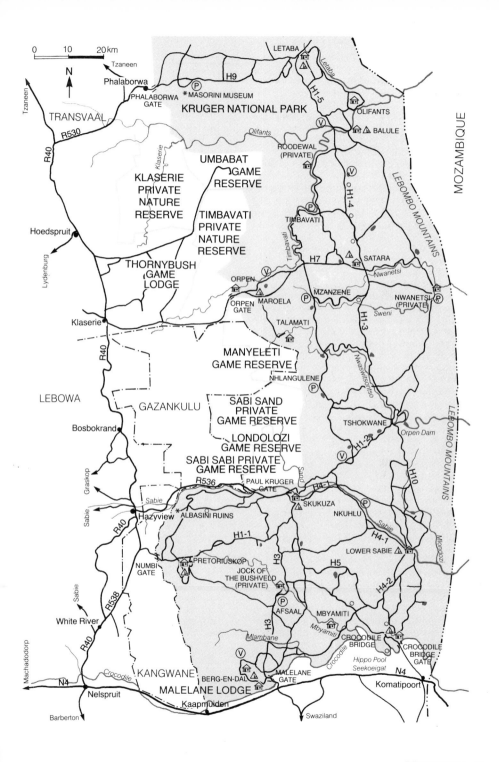

central area between Tshokwane and Satara camp.

The Sweni trail is also based in the central area and traillists meet at Orpen camp. These trails must be booked in advance.

Other facilities: Game-viewing on tarred and graded gravel roads (some of the low-lying gravel roads may be flooded in summer); waterholes and dams which make game-viewing particularly rewarding during the dry winter months; picnic sites with hot water for tea or coffee.

Speed limit: 40 to 50 km/h.

Beware: Malaria.

Open: Throughout the year.

Opening times:

	Camps open	Gates open	Camps/ Gates close
January	05h00	05h30	18h30
February	05h30	05h30	18h30
March	05h30	05h30	18h00
April	06h00	06h00	17h30
May - August	06h30	06h30	17h30
September	06h00	06h00	18h00
October	05h30	05h30	18h00
Nov/December	04h30	05h30	18h30

For further information: (and bookings) National Parks Board (see page 365).

One of the best-known game reserves in the world, the Kruger National Park is named after Paul Kruger, president of the Zuid-Afrikaansche Republiek, who had the foresight to establish the Sabie Game Reserve in the Transvaal Lowveld in 1898. In 1903 the Shingwedzi Game Reserve was proclaimed, and 23 years later the two reserves were combined and renamed the Kruger National Park. Major James Stevenson-Hamilton was appointed the Sabie Reserve's first warden in 1902 and he continued his work in the amalgamated reserves. When he took up his position he found that game was scarce in the area, much of it having fallen to the guns of hunters and poachers who killed for meat, hides and ivory. In the face of considerable opposition, he gradually built up a force of rangers to control the poaching, succeeded in increasing the numbers of animals in the park as well as its extent, and won over public opinion. By the time he retired in 1946, the Kruger National Park was firmly established not only as the pioneering conservation area of South Africa, but also as a major tourist attraction. Since then it has gained a reputation as a centre for wildlife management and research. Considerable progress has been made, too, in providing accommodation and facilities – including a network of tarred roads – for tourists. The authorities are trying, however, to maintain a balance between the demands of tourism and those of conservation.

Covering 19 455 km^2, some 350 km in length and with an average width of 60 km, this sanctuary has a variety of plants, mammals, birds, reptiles and invertebrates to match its size. Most of the park consists of flat grass- and bush-covered plains, broken by the low Lebombo Mountains extending along much of the border with Mozambique and by rocky outcrops scattered throughout, most noticeably in the north and the south-west. Several major rivers – the Limpopo at the northern border, the Luvuvhu, Shingwedzi, Letaba, Olifants, Timbavati, Sabie and, at the southern border, the Crocodile – flow across the park from west to east. Many of the smaller ones carry water only during the summer rainy season. The park's vegetation can be broadly divided into a number of zones. North of the Olifants River it is dominated by mopane scrub and woodland, with elements of red bushwillow, particularly to the west of the main north/south road. Towards Punda Maria the vegetation becomes more varied, with other species, notably baobabs in the north-east, evident among the mopane. South of the Olifants, in the Satara plains area and the eastern half of the park down to the Crocodile River, large expanses of grassland interspersed with knobthorn, leadwood and marula trees provide extensive grazing areas for large herds. Towards the south-west grassland gives way to mixed woodland which is dominated by a variety of acacia and bushwillow species, but also includes tamboti, marula, silver clusterleaf and sicklebush. The major watercourses are lined by riverine woodland which includes many large wild fig trees; one of the finest of these forests borders the Luvuvhu River. In all, more than 200 tree species grow in the Kruger National Park.

Although most of the mammals are distributed throughout the park, some show a preference for certain vegetation types. Elephants, roan antelope, tsessebe and eland are seen mainly in the mopane woodland of the northern sector, whereas Burchell's zebra, blue wildebeest, impala, giraffe and black rhinoceros prefer the central and southern areas. Lion, whose favoured prey is zebra and wildebeest, also prevail in these sectors. White rhinoceros occur mainly in the south-west. Hippopotamus and crocodiles can be seen along rivers throughout the park, and certain antelopes, such as bushbuck and nyala, prefer riverine forest, particularly in the north. Cheetah and leopard roam the entire region, the latter usually by night. Wild dogs, spotted hyenas and black-backed jackals are other predators likely to be seen. Buffalo are common throughout the park, and other species frequently observed include kudu, sable antelope, waterbuck, warthog, baboon and vervet monkey

. The smaller antelope species, such as steenbok, common duiker, Sharpe's grysbok, klipspringer and reedbuck, are less easily seen. The varied vegetation supports many diverse bird species, making the park a birdwatcher's paradise. Waterbirds, raptors, owls, louries, cuckoos, bee-eaters, parrots and hornbills are just some of the groups represented. Although the entire area is good 'bird country', the rivers and their environs, the area around Punda Maria and to the north, and the southern and south-western parts are consistently productive.

This is a summer-rainfall area, with the highest rainfall occurring in the south and south-west and decreasing northwards. In summer, when it can be extremely hot, game-viewing is more comfortable in the cooler early morning and late afternoon hours. In this season many species produce their young, and birdwatching is most rewarding. However, the game tends to disperse and the animals are difficult to see in the lush vegetation. Many people prefer to visit the park in winter, when the days are generally mild and the nights cool. In the dry season the animals are inclined to concentrate around waterholes and can be watched at leisure.

33 | KRUGERSDORP GAME RESERVE

Location: Southern Transvaal; west of Krugersdorp.
Access: From Krugersdorp take the R24 towards Magaliesburg; the reserve lies out of town, on the right. An entrance fee is charged.
Accommodation: 12 2-bed rondavels (R50 per weeknight; R150 per weekend) and 6 6-bed chalets (R70 per weeknight; R200 per weekend). A camping and caravan site with 18 stands and ablution facilities (R20 per day).
Other facilities: Picnic sites; restaurant and take-away outlet (no shop); guided trails are sometimes arranged by the Wildlife Society; network of roads for game-viewing; separate enclosures in which lion, white rhinoceros and buffalo are kept.

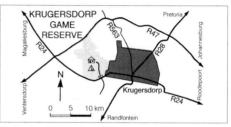

Open: Throughout the year.
Opening time: 08h00 to 17h00.
For further information: Krugersdorp Game Reserve, P.O. Box 5237, Krugersdorp West 1742. Tel: (011) 665-1735. Fax: (011) 665-1735.

Because of its proximity to Johannesburg, the Krugersdorp Game Reserve attracts large numbers of visitors over weekends and public holidays. It covers approximately 1 400 ha, comprising open grassland, bushveld and woodland which support a wide variety of introduced game species. Giraffe, eland, roan, sable, blesbok, springbok, impala, black wildebeest, red hartebeest, nyala and waterbuck roam the hillsides and riverbanks, while potentially dangerous lion, buffalo and white rhinoceros are confined in special enclosures. More than 140 bird species have been recorded here.

34 | LALAPANZI GAME RESERVE

Location: North-eastern Transvaal; between Tzaneen and Phalaborwa.
Access: From Tzaneen take the R71 towards Gravelotte for about 44 km; turn left onto the gravel road to Eiland. Continue for 1.5 km, turn right onto the Letaba Ranch road and continue for 27 km to the reserve entrance on the right. Booking is essential, no casual visitors. A private airstrip (1.2 km) can be used.
Accommodation: 4 4-bed thatched chalets, en suite. Thatched central dining area and fully equipped kitchen (full board or self-catering).Camping sites available.

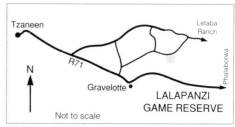

Other facilities: Guided game-viewing drives and walks; bar; swimming pool.
Open: Throughout the year.

Opening time: 07h00 to 22h00; by arrangement only.
For further information: The Manager, Lalapanzi Game Reserve, P.O. Box 218, Gravelotte 0895. Tel: (0152312), ask for 1511.

Lalapanzi covers 2 000 ha of typical Lowveld vegetation, dominated by combretum/mopane woodland. The reserve protects a wide range of animals, including eland, giraffe, gemsbok, waterbuck, tsessebe, kudu, impala, blue wildebeest, common duiker, nyala and Burchell's zebra. A number of carnivores are also present, such as leopard, caracal and serval. Over 180 bird species have been recorded.

35 LANGJAN NATURE RESERVE

Location: Far north-western Transvaal; north of Pietersburg.
Access: From Pietersburg follow the tarred R521 through Vivo and continue towards Alldays; about 22 km from Vivo watch out for the signpost to the reserve. Alternatively, from Louis Trichardt take the scenic R522 along the edge of the Soutpansberg to Vivo, then turn right onto the R521 and continue to the reserve. Access is strictly by arrangement/booking only.
Accommodation: 4 rondavels with primitive facilities, beds and mattresses provided; fireplaces; bring own bedding, crockery, cutlery, cooking utensils, camping chairs, etc.; maximum 16 people. No camping.
Other facilities: Guided game-viewing tours (to be arranged in advance); walking trails.
Open: Throughout the year.
Opening time: (Office) 07h45 to 12h30; 13h30 to 16h15.
For further information: The Officer-in-charge, Langjan Nature Reserve, P.O. Box 15, Vivo 0924. Tel: (015562) 1211.

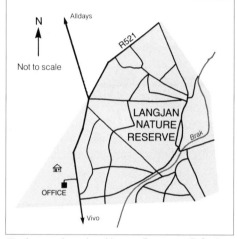

The flat landscape of this somewhat remote semi-desert reserve (average annual rainfall 350 to 400 mm) lies only 800 m above sea-level and offers clear views of the Soutpansberg to the south and the Blouberg to the south-west. Its vegetation is typical of the Kalahari thornveld and includes acacias, marula and tamboti.

The reserve was originally proclaimed to protect the last wild herd of gemsbok in the Transvaal, which had dwindled drastically before being brought up to its current strength. Other species that can be seen are red hartebeest, eland, giraffe and ostrich. Black-backed jackal, leopard and several small predators also occur. Like the vegetation, many of the 300 bird species recorded are typical of the Kalahari belt, and include crimson-breasted shrike, pied babbler, barred warbler and tawny eagle.

In this northern area of South Africa summer temperatures are very high, but winters are mild to cold and long, dry and dusty.

36 LAPALALA WILDERNESS

Location: North-western Transvaal; north-west of Nylstroom.
Access: From Nylstroom follow the R517 for 60 km to Vaalwater, then turn right towards Melkrivier; after 40 km turn left onto a gravel road at the signpost to Melkrivierskool, and continue for 5,5 km before bearing left and driving another 17 km to Doornleegte; turn left onto the Visgat road and follow this to the Lapalala Wilderness office. Each camp is

about half an hour's drive from the entrance; no driving is allowed within the reserve, except to gain access to the camps. A gravel, 1 200-m airstrip can be used by arrangement.

Accommodation: 6 camps (8-bed Tambuti, 6-bed Marula, 6-bed Lepotedi, 4-bed Munadu, 4-bed Umdoni, 2-bed Mukwa) comprising rustic huts (R32 to R43 per person per night). All camps have ablution facilities and fully equipped kitchens; take your own food, drink and charcoal. Bookings must be made for a minimum of 2 nights. *Kolobe Lodge:* 4 separate, thatched and fully equipped rondavels, *en suite* (16 people); full-catering, game-viewing drives, swimming pool, all-weather tennis court, conference facilities.

Other facilities: Walking trails, out of 8-bed, tented Mogonono Bush Camp, are organised by the Wilderness Trust of Southern Africa; 3-, 4- and 5-day courses for children aged 11-16 are conducted from the Lapalala Wilderness School; the Black Rhino Trail, with tented camp. There is no shop, and the nearest fuel supply is at Vaalwater.

Open: Throughout the year.

Opening time: Summer – sunrise to 18h30; winter – sunrise to 17h30.

Beware: Crocodiles in the river system.

For further information: Lapalala Wilderness (Pty) Ltd, P.O. Box 645, Bedfordview 2008. Tel: (011) 453-7645/6/7. Fax: (011) 453-7649. Wilderness Trust of Southern Africa, P.O. Box 577, Bedfordview 2008. Tel: also (011) 453-7645/6/7.

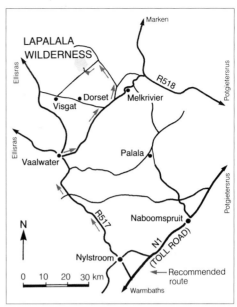

Lapalala is a privately owned conservation area established in the Waterberg with the purpose of making the visitor more aware of his environment. Unless on an organised trail, hikers are free to walk where they please in this 24 400-ha wilderness of mountain landscapes and extensive tracts of woodland. A number of game species, such as white rhinoceros, Burchell's zebra, blue wildebeest, kudu, impala, waterbuck, bushbuck, baboon and vervet monkeys, occur here. Other species, such as sable, roan, tsessebe, black rhinoceros, giraffe and so on, are kept in an area where the newly-opened Kolobe Lodge is situated. More than 270 bird species have been observed in the reserve.

37 LESHEBA WILDERNESS See map Buzzard Mountain Retreat

Location: Far northern Transvaal; west of Louis Trichardt.

Access: From Louis Trichardt follow the R522 towards Vivo for 35 km; shortly after crossing the Sand River turn right onto a gravel road (the signpost is set back from the main road) and follow this for 10 km – passing a farmhouse on the left – until you reach the main entrance gate at the top of the mountain. Although it is a steep climb, the road can be negotiated by most vehicles. Alternatively, from Pietersburg take the R521 to Vivo, turn right onto the R522 towards Louis Trichardt, and travel 36 km along this road before turning left onto the gravel road into the mountains. Except to gain access to the camps, no driving is permitted within the wilderness area. There is a landing strip for guests who prefer to fly in.

Accommodation: There are 2 camps, Duluni and Hamasha, each accommodating 12 people in cottages; each cottage has a bathroom, fully equipped kitchen, dining area and outdoor fireplaces (R45 per person per night, depending on the number of guests). Booking is essential, and must be for a minimum of 2 nights.

Other facilities: Self-guided walking trails; game-viewing; game-viewing drives by night in open 4x4 vehicles (R50 per vehicle);

guided day trips to Bushman paintings or the vulture drinking hole (R100 per vehicle). Nearest fuel supply at Louis Trichardt.
Open: Throughout the year.
Opening time: April to August – sunrise to 18h00; September to March – sunrise to 19h00.
Speed limit: 30 km/h.
Beware: Malaria.
For further information: Lesheba Wilderness, P.O. Box 795, Louis Trichardt 0920. Tel: 015562, ask for 3004.

Lesheba Wilderness extends for 18 km along the top of the western part of the Soutpansberg range. High, sheer cliffs and rugged hillsides are interspersed with valleys of open savannah grassland which support white rhinoceros, Burchell's zebra, eland, kudu, red hartebeest, blue wildebeest, waterbuck, impala and reedbuck. Areas of high canopy forest are inhabited by red duiker, samango monkey, bushbuck and bushpig. Other species that may be seen are leopard, mountain reedbuck, klipspringer, common duiker, Sharpe's grysbok, and warthog, as well as vervet monkey, baboon and thick-tailed and lesser bushbabies. The varied birdlife includes a breeding colony of Cape vultures.

38 LICHTENBURG GAME BREEDING CENTRE

Location: South-western Transvaal; north of Lichtenburg.
Access: From Lichtenburg take the R52 towards Koster and turn left at the 4-way stop; continue for 2 km to the entrance gate.
Accommodation: Municipal camping site.
Other facilities: Picnic sites with fireplaces; network of good roads for game-viewing.
Open: Throughout the year.
Opening time: Summer – 08h00 to 18h00; winter – 08h30 to 17h30.
For further information: The Officer-in-charge, Lichtenburg Game Breeding Centre, P.O. Box 716, Lichtenburg 2740. Tel: (01441) 2-2818.

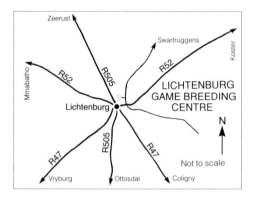

As well as being a nature reserve, this 6 000-ha area serves as a game breeding centre for the National Zoological Gardens in Pretoria, to which it belongs. Its terrain is flat and covered mainly with grassland and pockets of mixed bush. Thirty-five mammal species occur, including white rhinoceros and red hartebeest, plus exotic species such as Père David and axis deer, and pygmy hippopotamus. A wetland area attracts a wide range of waterbirds, which may be watched from a hide.

39 LONDOLOZI GAME RESERVE

Location: Eastern Transvaal; north-east of Hazyview, on the western border of the Kruger National Park.
Access: From Hazyview take the R536 towards Skukuza and follow it for 36 km before turning left onto a gravel road (1 km past Lisbon Store); continue for 28 km to the camp, following signposts to Londolozi. Daily Comair flights to Skukuza from Johannesburg and Durban can be met, or air charters can be arranged; private aircraft may land at Londolozi's 980-m airstrip.
Accommodation: *Main camp* has luxury thatched chalets, each with a bathroom, for a

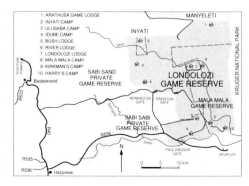

25. Accommodation at Londolozi's bush camp is extremely comfortable.

26. The cheetah is one of several predators in the Londolozi Game Reserve.

27. The Mala Mala Game Reserve offers luxurious accommodation.

29. Messina Nature Reserve was originally proclaimed to protect the baobab.

28. Clivia thrives in the Lowveld National Botanic Garden in Nelspruit.

30. Mountain Sanctuary Park, like many parts of the Magaliesberg, offers excellent hiking opportunities.

31. The restored Royal Hotel provides accommodation for visitors to the Pilgrim's Rest Nature Reserve.

32. The Steenbok Hiking Trail hut in the Suikerbosrand Nature Reserve.

33. Burchell's zebra have been introduced into the Van Riebeeck Nature Reserve in Pretoria.

34. The Timbavati Private Nature Reserve is the home of a number of 'white' lions.

35. Game-viewing in an open-topped vehicle at the Sabi Sand Private Game Reserve.

36. Thabina Falls in the unspoilt Wolkberg Wilderness Area.

37. The Sabie River flows past Sabi Sand's River Lodge.

maximum of 12 couples, plus rustic rondavels, also with a bathroom each; *Tree camp* has luxury bedrooms, each with a bathroom, for a maximum of 4 couples; *Bush camp* has cabins, each with a bathroom, for a maximum of 8 couples. Tariffs include all meals, daily guided walking safaris and game-viewing drives; there are reduced rates for children.

All bookings must be made in advance.
Other facilities: Guided trails; game-viewing drives; swimming pool.
Open: Throughout the year.
Beware: Malaria.
For further information: Londolozi Game Reserve, P.O. Box 1211, Sunninghill Park 2157. Tel: (011) 803-8421. Fax: (011) 803-1810.

The 18 000-ha Londolozi Game Reserve lies within the area known as Sabi Sand, a large, privately owned and managed conservation area comprising also Mala Mala, Inyati and Sabi Sabi. This area falls within the typical Lowveld bush country and a great variety of game species occur, including elephant, white rhinoceros, buffalo, hippopotamus, a wide range of antelope, and lion, leopard, cheetah and spotted hyena. The birdlife is rich.

40 LOSKOP DAM NATURE RESERVE See map Botshabelo Nature Reserve

Location: South-central Transvaal; north of Middelburg.
Access: From Middelburg take the R35 northwards towards Groblersdal, reaching the entrance to the reserve, to the left of the road, after about 45 km.
Accommodation: Overvaal Loskop has 25 4- to 5-bed A-frame log cabins (R112,50 per night); 9 6-bed family cabins (R164 per night); 18 3-bed cabins (R74,75 per night); 15 2-bed log cabins (R81 per night). The camping site has 250 stands (70 with power points), ablution facilities and braai sites (R23 for 2 people per night, R4,50 per additional person; sites with electricity: R29 for 2 people per night,

R4,50 per additional person).
Other facilities: Walking trail; game-viewing; boating and fishing (permits for both can be obtained from the office). The resort offers a variety of recreational facilities.
Open: Throughout the year.
Opening time: Resort – 24 hours; reserve – 07h00 to 17h00.
Beware: Bilharzia; crocodiles.
For further information: The Officer-in-charge, Loskop Dam Nature Reserve, Private Bag X606, Groblersdal 0470. Tel: (01202) 4184. (Resort) The Manager, Overvaal Loskop, Private Bag X1525, Middelburg 1050. Tel: (01202) 3075/6. Fax: (01202) 3916.

The Loskop Dam Nature Reserve was established in 1942 around the dam of the same name and for many visitors its main attraction is the excellent fishing in the dam. Others come to view the numerous game species – white rhinoceros, buffalo, Burchell's zebra, impala, kudu, blue wildebeest, mountain reedbuck, waterbuck, sable, eland and nyala – that inhabit the mixed bush and grassland of the predominantly hilly terrain. Carnivores are represented by leopard, brown hyena, black-backed jackal and a number of smaller species. Approximately 250 bird species have been recorded.

41 LOWVELD NATIONAL BOTANIC GARDEN

Location: South-eastern Transvaal; Nelspruit.
Access: Clearly signposted from Nelspruit town centre.
Accommodation: None. There are hotels and a camping site in Nelspruit.
Other facilities: Picnic site; 2-km nature trail; pathways; information centre.
Open: Throughout the year.
Opening time: 07h00 to 16h30.
Beware: Bilharzia.
For further information: The Lowveld National Botanic Garden, P.O. Box 1024, Nelspruit 1200. Tel: (01311) 2-5531.

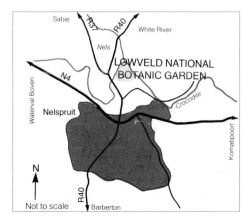

The Lowveld National Botanic Garden covers 150 ha, about a quarter of which has been cultivated and consists of formal planted areas, whereas the remaining area of the garden is maintained in its natural state. Lying along the banks of the Crocodile River, the garden boasts a variety of vegetation types, including typical Lowveld bush, marsh, gallery forest and plants associated with rocky slopes. Some 500 plant species grow here, including many trees. To date 245 bird species have been recorded, and a number of reptile and small mammal species occur.

42 MALA MALA GAME RESERVE See map Londolozi Game Reserve

Location: Eastern Transvaal; north-east of Hazyview, adjoining the Kruger National Park.
Access: From Hazyview follow the R536 towards Skukuza for 36 km, then turn left onto a gravel road; follow signposts to Kirkman's Camp, Harry's or Mala Mala camp. Daily commercial flights to Skukuza from Johannesburg or Durban can be met; private or chartered aircraft can land at the Mala Mala airstrip.
Accommodation: *Mala Mala* camp has luxurious rondavels, each with a bathroom and air conditioning; the Sable Suite for up to 16 guests in 1 party; a central dining area; 24-hour electricity. The accommodation is up-market, catering mainly for overseas visitors. *Kirkman's Camp* has semi-detached, 1-bedroomed cottages, each with a bathroom and air conditioning; central lounge and dining areas; 24-hour electricity.'Kirkman's Cottage' consists of 2 cottages, each with 2 double bedrooms, sharing a private swimming pool and boma. *Harry's* has 7 double rooms, each with a bathroom and air conditioning; a central lounge and dining area. No casual visitors are admitted.
Other facilities: Game-viewing drives accompanied by rangers; accompanied walks can be arranged; swimming pools; bars; curio shops.
Open: Throughout the year.
Beware: Malaria.
For further information: Mala Mala Rattray Reserves, P.O. Box 2575, Randburg 2125. Tel: (011) 789-2677. Fax: (011) 886-4382.

The Mala Mala Game Reserve has a worldwide reputation for its luxurious accommodation and excellent game-viewing, and it does indeed offer the opportunity to combine the wildness of the bush with the comforts of a 5-star hotel. Bordered to the east by the Kruger National Park and to the west by the Londolozi and Sabi Sand game reserves, Mala Mala covers 30 000 ha of typical Lowveld bush country and supports the 'Big Five' – lion, elephant, leopard, buffalo and rhinoceros – as well as a great number of other species. Like other bushveld areas, it is rich in bird species too.

43 MALELANE LODGE See map Kruger National Park (south)

Location: South-eastern Transvaal; west of Komatipoort.
Access: From the N4 (Nelspruit/Komatipoort) turn onto the Malelane Gate (Kruger National Park) road just beyond Malelane village. The turn-off to the Lodge is on the right and clearly signposted.
Accommodation: There are 102 rooms in air-conditioned chalets, all are *en-suite*; typical hotel amenities.
Other facilities: Guided walks and drives in private reserve; restaurant; bars; swimming pools; conference facilities.
Open: Throughout the year.
Beware: Malaria.
For further information: Malelane Lodge, P.O. Box 392, Malelane 1320. Tel: (013133) 2294. Fax: (013133) 2522.

A 350-ha private game reserve, which lies on the banks of the Crocodile River and adjoining the southern border of the Kruger National Park, is attached to the Lodge. Game includes giraffe, kudu, impala, blue wildebeest and Burchell's zebra. Birdlife is abundant.

44 MARIEVALE BIRD SANCTUARY

Location: Southern Transvaal; north-east of Nigel.
Access: From Nigel take the R42 towards Delmas and follow signposts to Marievale.

Accommodation: None.
Other facilities: 3 birdwatching hides, each with a pit toilet close by; picnic area; a system of hiking trails, starting at the main gate where a large board provides the necessary information.
Open: Throughout the year.
Opening time: Sunrise to sunset.
For further information: The Officer-in-charge, Marievale Bird Sanctuary, P.O. Box 12137, Daggafontein 1573. Tel: (011) 734-9642.

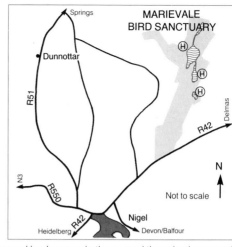

Marievale, one of the premier bird sanctuaries in the Transvaal, is surrounded by the mining activity of the East Rand. A little more than 1 000 ha of it is owned by the Transvaal conservation authorities, and an additional 400 ha is leased from the Anglo-American Corporation. Mining operations have modified the landscape, with embankments, for example, having created large wetland areas. Large reed beds occur in these, and there is also a small area of open grassland. Approximately 280 bird species have been recorded at the sanctuary, including large flocks of spurwing geese which gather here in winter.

---

45 MATUMI GAME LODGE

Location: Eastern Transvaal; south-east of Hoedspruit.
Access: From Tzaneen take the route to Hoedspruit and then follow the R40 southwards, turning left onto the Orpen Gate (Kruger National Park) road; after 2,8 km turn left and after 6 km turn right into Matumi. From Nelspruit drive north on the R40 and then follow the above instructions. Book in advance.
Accommodation: 12 4-bed and 2 6-bed thatched, air-conditioned chalets, full-catering (R95 per person per night). Bush lapa for overnight trail (take own sleeping bag).
Other facilities: Walking trails; game-viewing hides; game-viewing drives; swimming pool; various activities in camp; fishing (barbel, bream, yellowfish).
Open: Throughout the year.

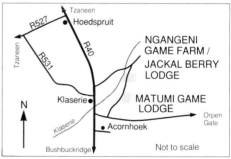

Beware: Malaria.
For further information: Matumi Game Lodge, P.O. Box 57, Klaserie 1381. Tel: 0131732, ask for 4313. Fax: 0131732, ask for Dataline 4313.

Matumi is located on the banks of the Klaserie River, amid typical Transvaal Lowveld vegetation. A variety of game species is present, including giraffe, and birdlife is rich, particularly along the densely wooded river banks.

---

46 MESSINA NATURE RESERVE

Location: Far northern Transvaal; south of Messina.
Access: From Messina take the N1 southwards; the nature reserve lies next to the motorway, on the left.
Accommodation: None. There are hotels and a camping site in Messina.
Other facilities: Picnic site; network of roads

for game-viewing (rough in parts, but suitable for most vehicles); nature trails (with permission from the authority).
Open: Throughout the year.
Opening time: 07h45 to 16h15.
For further information: The Officer-in-charge, Messina Nature Reserve, P.O. Box 78, Messina 0090. Tel: (01553) 3235.

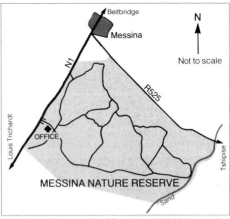

The Messina Nature Reserve was originally proclaimed to protect the great number of baobab trees which grow in this area and have been declared a national monument. Another notable feature in the 4 700-ha reserve are the ancient rock formations in the bed of the Sand River, estimated to be 3 800 million years old. In addition to the baobabs, the reserve's mopane-dominated bushveld supports nyala, kudu, impala, sable, blue wildebeest, Sharpe's grysbok, giraffe, leopard and a host of smaller species. More than 200 bird species have been recorded, and 53 different reptiles are known to occur.

---

47 | MOHLABETSI GAME RESERVE See map Blydeberg Nature Reserve

Location: Eastern Transvaal; east of Hoedspruit.
Access: Hoedspruit lies on the R40 (Nelspruit/Gravelotte); continue north on the R40 beyond Hoedspruit for 10 km, turn right and follow the signposts.
Accommodation: Thatched bungalows with *en-suite* bathrooms in two separate camps, for small groups (R185 per person per day); full-catering. Book in advance.
Other facilities: Game drives and walks (included in tariff); bar; swimming pools (heated in winter).
Open: Throughout the year.
Beware: Malaria.
For further information: Bushveld Breakaways, P.O. Box 926, White River 1240. Tel: (01311) 5-1998. Fax: (01311) 5-0383.

Vegetation is typical of the Lowveld, with a variety of game species, including buffalo.

---

48 | MOSDENE PRIVATE NATURE RESERVE

Location: North-central Transvaal; east of Naboomspruit.
Access: From Naboomspruit take the R519 towards Roedtan and after about 10 km turn right into Boekenhout Road; the farm entrance is on the left after 2 km. All visitors should report to one of the homesteads on arrival.
Accommodation: Camping only at sites indicated by the owner; R5 per night. Visitors are requested to take all their rubbish away with them, and to obey the reserve regulations.
Other facilities: None.
Open: Throughout the year.
Opening time: Sunrise to sunset but visitors are permitted to arrive after dark by prior arrangement with the owners of the reserve.
For further information: R.G. Galpin, P.O.

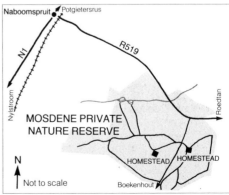

Box 28, Naboomspruit 0560. Tel: (01534) 3-1933 or 3-1938 or 3-1685.

Although Mosdene Private Nature Reserve is a commercial, 5 421-ha cattle ranch, the owners allow birdwatchers and other natural history enthusiasts access to it on a limited and controlled basis. The property includes four main vegetation types: open vlei and flood plain, tamboti veld, dense seringa woodland and extensive areas of thornveld.

Several game species occur, but the main appeal of Mosdene lies in its amazing bird population; more than 400 species have been recorded here.

49 MOUNT SHEBA NATURE RESERVE

Location: Eastern Transvaal; south of Pilgrim's Rest.
Access: From Pilgrim's Rest take the R533 westward towards Lydenburg, turning left at the Mount Sheba signpost after about 12 km; follow this dirt road to the resort.
Accommodation: The Mount Sheba Hotel has luxury suites, time-share cottages (R140 to R165 per person per night).
Other facilities: Nature trails; squash; tennis; trout dam; walks; snooker; mountain bicycles; solarium.
Open: Throughout the year.

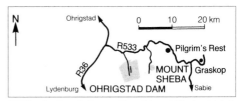

For further information: Mount Sheba Hotel, P.O. Box 100, Pilgrim's Rest 1290. Tel: 0131532, ask for 17. Fax: 0131532, ask for 17 and ask to be put through to fax. Johannesburg sales: Tel: (011) 788-1258.

The 500-ha Mount Sheba Nature Reserve is best known for the indigenous forest it conserves, one of the few pockets of such forest left in the Transvaal. More than 100 tree species have been identified, including yellowwood, white stinkwood, Cape chestnut, ironwood and mountain cedar, and many ferns, mosses and creepers thrive in the damp forest environment. Typical forest mammals, such as red duiker, bushbuck and samango monkey, are occasionally seen, whereas the varied, and noisier, birdlife is more conspicuous.

This area receives high rainfall (up to 1 500 mm a year), most of which occurs in summer, and it lies within the escarpment mist belt.

50 MOUNTAIN SANCTUARY PARK

Location: Southern Transvaal; west of Pretoria.
Access: From Pretoria take the R27 towards the Hartbeespoort Dam, then skirt the southern edge of the Magaliesberg along the R512, R560 and R24, passing Pelindaba, Skeerpoort and Hekpoort; just beyond Maanhaarrand turn right towards Breedt's Nek and follow this road to the Mountain Sanctuary Park turn-off. An entrance fee is charged to the park.
Accommodation: Chalets; camping site.
Other facilities: Picnic sites with fireplaces; swimming; walking.
Open: Throughout the year.
Opening time: Sunrise to sunset.
For further information: Mountain Sanctuary

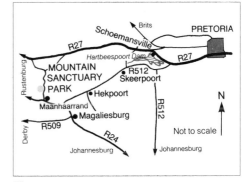

Park, P.O. Box 187, Kroondal 0350. Tel: (0142) 75-0114.

A 960-ha private reserve in the Magaliesberg Natural Area, the Mountain Sanctuary Park is a haven for those who enjoy exploring this mountain range and its vegetation and wildlife.

The scenic views are one of the most appealing aspects of the park.

51 NGANGENI GAME FARM See map Matumi Game Lodge

Location: Eastern Transvaal; south-east of Hoedspruit.

Access: From the R40 take the Orpen Gate (Kruger National Park) road for 3.5 km; turn left. The Jackal Berry Lodge entrance is 8 km along this road.

Accommodation: *Jackal Berry Lodge* has 3 double-bedded thatched huts with *en-suite* bathrooms; bunkhouse with 4 double-bedded rooms and bush shower. Book in advance. Full-catering (R135 per person per day); self-cater-ing (R65 per person per day). Meals served in a thatched lapa. Fridge and deepfreeze available for those bringing their own food.

Other facilities: Accompanied walks and drives (included in tariff); swimming pool.

Open: Throughout the year.

Beware: Malaria.

For further information: Bushveld Break-aways, P.O. Box 926, White River 1240. Tel: (01311) 5-1998. Fax: (01311) 5-0383. (Ngangeni) Tel: (0131732) 2811.

Located in the subtropical Transvaal Lowveld, Ngangeni fronts on the Klaserie River and has a variety of game species, including giraffe, Burchell's zebra, nyala, waterbuck and blue wildebeest.

52 NOOITGEDACHT DAM NATURE RESERVE

Location: South-eastern Transvaal; north of Carolina.

Access: From Carolina take the R36 towards Machadodorp and after 1 km turn onto the tarred road signposted to the Nooitgedacht Dam.

Accommodation: Camping allowed, but only basic facilities are provided; no drinking water. There is a hotel and a camping site in Carolina.

Other facilities: Fishing; watersports; game-viewing and birdwatching. Game-viewing and birdwatching take place mainly from motorboats and the camping sites. Guests are not permitted to wander freely in the reserve but group walks can be organised.

Open: Throughout the year.

Opening time: 06h00 to 18h00.

For further information: The Officer-in-charge, Nooitgedacht Dam Nature Reserve,

P.O. Box 327, Carolina 1185. Tel: (01344) 3-2603.

The Nooitgedacht Dam, covering an area of 750 ha and lying in the centre of the 3 420-ha reserve, is fed by the Vaalwater, Boesmanspruit and Witkloof rivers, and contains bass, carp, yellowfish and barbel. The vegetation surrounding it consists of species typical of the Highveld grassland, with extensive beds of thatch-grass which provide roosting and nesting sites for a wide variety of bird species. Large flocks of spurwing and Egyptian geese are seasonal visitors, and blue cranes also occur. The reserve contains Burchell's zebra, springbok, blesbok, red hartebeest, vaalribbok, duiker and steenbok.

53 NYLSVLEY NATURE RESERVE

Location: Central Transvaal; south of Naboomspruit.

Access: From Naboomspruit follow the N1 towards Nylstroom and after 13 km turn off to Boekenhout; after crossing the railway line watch out for the Nylsvley signpost on the left.

Accommodation: A camping site with basic ablution facilities. Booking is essential.

Other facilities: Escorted trips; picnic sites.

Open: Throughout the year.

Opening time: 06h00 to 18h00.

For further information: The Officer-in-charge, Nylsvley Nature Reserve, P.O. Box 508, Naboomspruit 0560. Tel: (01534) 3-1074.

At Nylsvley the Nyl River forms a 16 000-ha grass flood plain, one of the largest in South Africa. Of this, 3 100 ha is protected in the Nylsvley Nature Reserve, and more in the neighbouring Mosdene Nature Reserve. Apart from the grass- and reed-covered flood plain, the vegetation comprises mainly mixed bushveld, with trees such as silver clusterleaf, wild seringa, umbrella thorn and red bushwillow.

A wide variety of mammal species inhabit this bushveld, and roan, tsessebe, reedbuck, kudu, waterbuck and vervet monkey may be seen. However, Nylsvley is best known for its birdlife, of which more than 400 species have been recorded. When the Nyl River overflows its banks during the summer rains, an outstanding habitat for waterbirds is created. Up to 12 000 herons of 17 species, 19 000 ducks of 17 species and an estimated 43 000 crakes flock to the vlei, and 85 of the 94 waterbird species known to have bred in southern Africa have been recorded here on the Nyl. Spring and summer are the most productive birdwatching seasons.

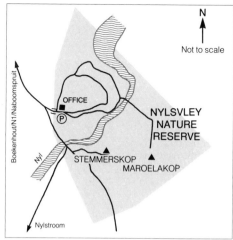

54 | OHRIGSTAD DAM NATURE RESERVE See Mount Sheba Nature Reserve

Location: Eastern Transvaal; north-east of Lydenburg.
Access: From Lydenburg take the R36 towards Ohrigstad and after about 30 km turn right onto the R533 to Pilgrim's Rest; the reserve turn-off is about 7 km further on, on the right.
Accommodation: A camping site with basic ablution facilities (R5 per stand).

Other facilities: Picnic sites; boating in small craft; boardsailing; fishing.
Open: Throughout the year.
Opening time: 06h00 to 18h00.
For further information: The Officer-in-charge, Ohrigstad Dam Nature Reserve, Private Bag X1018, Lydenburg 1120. Tel: (01323) 851.

This 2 563-ha reserve lies in rugged, hilly country, with the Ohrigstad Dam as its focal point. The vegetation comprises mainly grassland on the open slopes and indigenous forest in the kloofs and gorges. A variety of game species, such as klipspringer, common duiker and mountain reedbuck, occur naturally in the area, and several other species have been introduced. The birdlife is varied.

55 | PERCY FYFE NATURE RESERVE

Location: North-central Transvaal; north-east of Potgietersrus.
Access: From Potgietersrus take the N1 towards Pietersburg; after a short distance turn left and follow the signposts to the Percy Fyfe Nature Reserve, which is about 35 km from Potgietersrus.
Accommodation: There is a camping site with an ablution block, field kitchen and hall, for organised groups only (groups must supply own tents).
Other facilities: Picnic area; walks through game camps; game-viewing drives.
Open: Throughout the year.

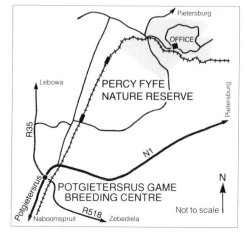

Opening time: 08h00 to 17h00.
For further information: The Officer-in-charge, Percy Fyfe Nature Reserve, P.O. Box 217, Pietersburg 0700. Tel: (01541) 5678.

Named after the farmer who donated the property to the provincial conservation authorities, the Percy Fyfe Nature Reserve consists mainly of open grassland and granite outcrops. It is primarily a breeding centre for roan and tsessebe, and these rare antelope species are enclosed in separate camps in the 3 032-ha reserve. Other game species also occur throughout the area.

56 PIETERSBURG NATURE RESERVE

Location: Northern Transvaal; Pietersburg.
Access: From the centre of Pietersburg follow signposts to the Union Park camping site and the nature reserve. An entrance fee is charged.
Accommodation: Union Park, adjacent to the reserve, has 6-bed, fully equipped chalets, and a camping site with a large ablution block.
Other facilities: Walking trail; gravel roads in good condition for game-viewing; picnic site at Union Park.
Open: Throughout the year.
Opening time: September to March – 07h00 to 18h00; April to August – 08h00 to 17h00.
For further information: The Town Clerk, Pietersburg Municipality, P.O. Box 111, Pietersburg 0700. Tel: (01521) 2011.

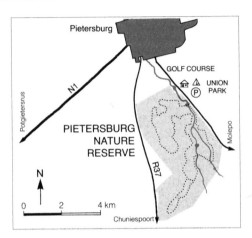

At 2 800 ha, Pietersburg's municipal nature reserve is one of the largest in the Transvaal. Its open, grass-covered plains are dotted with clumps of bush, allowing easy viewing of the game, which includes white rhinoceros, eland, red hartebeest, blesbok, gemsbok, impala and Burchell's zebra. An extensive 'aloe forest' on a low rocky ridge in the reserve makes an attractive sight when the plants are in flower.

57 PILGRIM'S REST NATURE RESERVE

Location: Eastern Transvaal; surrounding Pilgrim's Rest.
Access: Public roads (the R533 and the minor road northward to Bourke's Luck) traverse the reserve.
Accommodation: None in the reserve itself. In Pilgrim's Rest, Overvaal Resorts has 2 hotels, 11 historic cottages and a camping site with 250 stands.
Other facilities: Hiking and rambling trails; trout fishing (a permit can be obtained from the information centre); horse-riding trails; picnic sites with fireplaces; information centre. Overvaal Pilgrim's Rest offers many of the facilities normally associated with a holiday resort.
Open: Throughout the year.
Opening time: Sunrise to sunset.
For further information: The Officer-in-

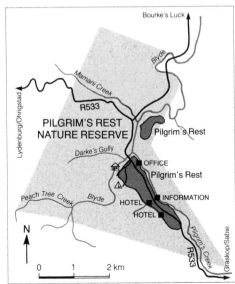

charge, Chief Directorate Works, Private Bag X519, Pilgrim's Rest 1290. Tel: 0131532, ask for Pilgrim's Rest 28. (Resort) The General Manager, Overvaal Pilgrim's Rest, P.O. Box 59, Pilgrim's Rest 1290. Tel: 0131532, ask for Pilgrim's Rest 4.

This reserve, covering 1 899 ha, surrounds the historic village of Pilgrim's Rest, and evidence of the mining activity of a century ago can still be seen. Set among hills and falling within the mountain sourveld vegetation zone, the reserve is covered mainly by grassland, with remnant riverine forest flanking the Blyde River and its tributaries. Alien vegetation is abundant, but attempts are being made to eradicate the invasive plants.

No game animals have been introduced, but visitors may see mountain reedbuck and common duiker. To date 180 bird species have been recorded here, including such rarities as the blue swallow, broad-tailed warbler, Cape eagle owl and narina trogon. Keen birdwatchers are advised to visit the reserve when it is quiet, avoiding the school holidays. A comprehensive birdlist is available. Summer days in this region are warm and humid, and nights are cool; winters are cold, and heavy frosts sometimes occur.

58 PONGOLA NATURE RESERVE

Location: Extreme south-eastern Transvaal; south-east of Piet Retief.
Access: From Piet Retief follow the R29 towards Golela for approximately 140 km, then watch out for the signpost to the reserve. Also accessible from Natal via the N2.
Accommodation: None.
Open: By prior arrangement.
Opening time: Sunrise to sunset.
Beware: Malaria; bilharzia.
For further information: The Officer-in-charge, Pongola Nature Reserve, P.O. Box 29, Golela 3990. Tel: (03843) 5-1012.

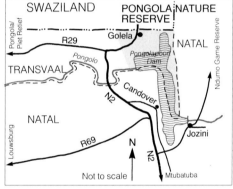

In 1894 a 20 000-ha game reserve was proclaimed in the Pongola corridor, a narrow wedge of Transvaal between Natal and Swaziland, by President Paul Kruger. It was deproclaimed in 1921 after several years of neglect, but when the Pongolapoort (originally named Jozini) Dam was constructed in the 1970s a reserve was once again established in the region. The 10 485-ha sanctuary lies in an area which rises onto a plateau and is characterised by impressive cliffs, wooded gorges and mixed grassland and bush. A large number of rare plant species occur. Some of the more common antelopes, such as impala, blue wildebeest, reedbuck, mountain reedbuck, bushbuck and red and common duiker, can be seen in the reserve, and it also shelters the rare suni. White rhinoceros, buffalo and giraffe have been introduced. Regrettably, poaching has increased from Natal on the eastern boundary and also from Swaziland. Other unusual inhabitants include several uncommon lizard species and a number of birds such as the bearded robin, brown-headed parrot and lemon-breasted canary. Tigerfish occur in the dam.

59 POTGIETERSRUS GAME BREEDING CENTRE See map Percy Fyfe Nature Reserve

Location: Northern Transvaal; Potgietersrus.
Access: From Potgietersrus take the N1 northwards, watching out for signposts to the reserve a short distance out of the town. An entrance fee is charged.
Accommodation: A camping site is opposite the entrance to the reserve. There is also a hotel nearby.

Other facilities: Picnic sites with fireplaces; circular game-viewing drive.
Open: Throughout the year.
Opening time: Summer – 08h00 to 18h00; winter – 08h30 to 17h30.
For further information: The Officer-in-charge, Potgietersrus Game Breeding Centre, P.O. Box 170, Potgietersrus 0600. Tel: (01541) 4314.

Like the Lichtenburg Game Breeding Centre, the 1 000-ha Potgietersrus reserve is owned by the National Zoological Gardens and maintained as a game breeding centre. As well as rare southern African game animals, several exotic species – llama and pygmy hippopotamus for example – may be seen here. Of the southern African species, black rhinoceros, waterbuck, tsessebe, giraffe and Burchell's zebra roam the flat, open grassland and the bush-covered hillsides, one of which features an extensive area of euphorbias. Many bird species are present.

60 PRETORIA

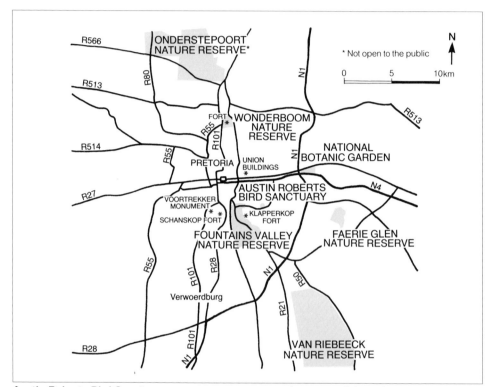

Austin Roberts Bird Sanctuary
Boshoff St, New Muckleneuk. Named after the naturalist whose book on South African birds has become a standard work, the 11-ha Austin Roberts Bird Sanctuary protects no less than 170 bird species in a limited area. Many are waterbirds, attracted to a small dam where visitors may watch them from a hide. A few game species have been introduced. Visitors have access to the hide only at weekends and on public holidays from 09h00 to 16h00, although passers-by can easily see into the sanctuary.

Faerie Glen Nature Reserve
Manitoba Dr., Faerie Glen. This 97-ha area in the eastern part of Pretoria protects a broad spectrum of natural vegetation, which in turn provides food and shelter for a variety of bird species. The reserve is open at all times throughout the year.

Fountains Valley Nature Reserve
Maria van Riebeeck Ave and Johann Rissik Dr. pass through the reserve. A recreational area within the city, Fountains Valley Nature Reserve offers a number of amenities, including a camping site, picnic sites with fireplaces, and a swimming pool. Some 60 ha have been set aside for recreation, while the remainder of the 500-ha area is inhabited by a number of game species and an interesting array of birds. The reserve is open throughout the year from 07h00 to 20h00.

Pretoria National Botanic Garden
Cussonia Ave, near CSIR. Despite its name, this garden does not form part of the network managed by the National Botanic Gardens of South Africa, but is administered by the Botanical Re-

search Institute whose plant collections it contains. More than 5 000 indigenous species are grouped according to major vegetation types, allowing visitors to appreciate to best advantage the diversity of southern Africa's flora. The 76-ha garden is open daily from 06h00 to 18h00.

Van Riebeeck Nature Reserve
Access from Delmas Rd (R50). Bankenveld, the vegetation type covering the Van Riebeeck Nature Reserve, is characterised by its wide variety of both woody and herbaceous plant species. This rich vegetation in turn supports many game animals, including eland, Burchell's zebra, springbok, red hartebeest, steenbok, common duiker and the rare oribi. Access to the reserve

is limited to visitors on specially arranged bus tours; applications should be made to the Director, Department of Parks and Recreation, Pretoria City Council, P.O. Box 1454, Pretoria 0001. Tel: (012) 313-7198.

Wonderboom Nature Reserve
Voortrekkers Rd (R101) passes through the reserve. This 90-ha reserve in north Pretoria was proclaimed to protect a huge fig, *Ficus salicifolia*. By the way it has propagated itself, this 'wonderboom' looks like a grove of trees but is in fact only one, estimated to be about a thousand years old. A nature trail meanders through the reserve, and there are picnic sites near the tree. The reserve is open from 06h00 to 17h00.

61 ROB FERREIRA NATURE RESERVE

Location: Extreme south-western Transvaal; north of Christiana.
Access: From Christiana follow the R29 towards Bloemhof and after 3 km take the clearly signposted right turn to the reserve.
Accommodation: Overvaal Rob Ferreira has 14 4-bed luxury rooms with air conditioning; 86 2- and 5-bed bungalows, each with a bathroom and fully equipped kitchen, some with a dining/lounge area (R29 to R38 per person per night; off-season rates available). The camping site has 500 stands (some with power points) and full ablution facilities (R16 to R20 for 2 persons, R4 per additional person).
Other facilities: Network of roads for game-viewing (in own vehicle or a bus); hiking trails; fishing. The resort has most of the facilities

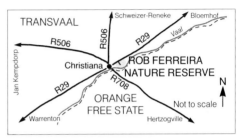

associated with a popular holiday centre.
Open: Throughout the year.
Opening time: Reserve – 07h00 to 17h00; resort – 24 hours.
For further information: The General Manager, Overvaal Rob Ferreira Resort, P.O. Box 19, Christiana 2680. Tel: (0534) 2244.

The Rob Ferreira Nature Reserve lies on the north bank of the Vaal River and covers approximately 2 500 ha of flat, open grassland which makes spotting game relatively easy. All species likely to be seen have been introduced, and include white rhinoceros, eland, red hartebeest, black wildebeest, blesbok, gemsbok, springbok, impala and Burchell's zebra. Birdwatching along the bank of the Vaal can be rewarding.

62 ROLFE'S PAN NATURE RESERVE See regional map

Location: Southern Transvaal; Boksburg.
Access: From the N12 in Boksburg take the R21 in the direction of Jan Smuts Airport/Kempton Park and then the first exit, to Jet Park/Bartlett; turn left, and then left again into Kelly Rd; cross the 4-way stop and the Rolfe's Pan Nature Reserve lies directly ahead. It is open only to members of the Witwatersrand Bird Club and

other organised groups.
Accommodation: None.
Other facilities: Picnic sites with fireplaces.
For further information: The Officer-in-charge, Rolfe's Pan Nature Reserve, P.O. Box 12137, Daggafontein 1573. Tel: (011) 734-9642 or The Hon. Officer, Tel: (011) 975-2054 (home).

Also known as Carlos Rolfe's Bird Sanctuary, this reserve is primarily a haven for birds. Some 130 species have been recorded, and the pan of the reserve's name supports one of the largest inland breeding colonies of the grey-headed gull. Sacred ibis also breed here in substantial numbers. The 100-ha reserve is fringed by grassland, exotic trees and land that is being allowed to return to its natural state.

63 RONDEBULT BIRD SANCTUARY

Location: Southern Transvaal; Germiston.
Access: From central Germiston follow the N3 southwards as far as the R103/R554 exit and take this in the direction of Heidelberg; where the R103 and R554 diverge, follow the R554 to the left, into Van Dyk Rd, and shortly after crossing the railway line watch out for signposts to the sanctuary on the right.
Accommodation: None.
Other facilities: Birdwatching hides; short walks. Guided visits can be arranged through the Witwatersrand Bird Club or the Wildlife Society (see page 365).
Open: Throughout the year.
Opening time: 08h00 to 17h00 (arrangements can be made for an extension of these hours).
For further information: The Director, Department of Parks, Sport and Recreation,

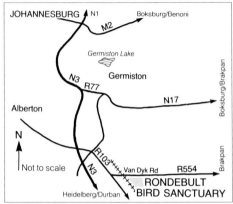

Germiston Municipality, P.O. Box 374, Germiston 1400. Tel: (011) 51-0355.

Rondebult, one of South Africa's premier urban bird sanctuaries, was officially opened to the public in 1978. Comprising open water, marsh, reed beds and open grassland, this wetland is particularly well known for the diversity of waterbird species it attracts. A list of all species observed would run to more than 150, many of which have bred in the 94-ha sanctuary. A visit to Rondebult is highly recommended.

64 ROODEPLAAT DAM NATURE RESERVE

Location: Southern Transvaal; east of Pretoria.
Access: From Pretoria take the N1 northwards towards Pietersburg and at the Wonderboom/Cullinan interchange turn right to travel eastwards along the R513; at the 4-way stop turn left towards Moloto and Roodeplaat Dam, and continue for 10 km to the reserve entrance on the right.
Accommodation: 5 camping sites with ablution facilities; each stand has a fireplace and wooden tables and benches; stands at 2 sites have light sockets (R7 per stand per night).
Other facilities: Walking trails; a network of roads for game-viewing; visitor centre; picnic sites with fireplaces and drinking water ; fishing; watersports (except water- and jet-skiing) are allowed.
Open: Throughout the year.
Opening time: 08h00 to 18h00.

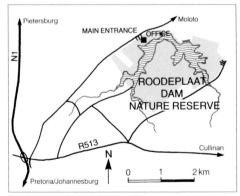

For further information: The Officer-in-charge, Roodeplaat Dam Nature Reserve, P.O. Box 15163, Lynn East 0039. Tel: (012) 808-1164.

Roodeplaat Dam Nature Reserve was proclaimed in 1977 and covers a total of 1 667 ha, with the dam as its centre. The vegetation in this area, known as sourish mixed bushveld, comprises open savannah with scattered common hookthorn trees, and sweet thornveld on the dam's western shore. A number of rare plant species, including *Aloe pretoriensis*, occur. The bushveld supports such game species as impala, kudu, sable, blue wildebeest, waterbuck, red hartebeest, common duiker, steenbok and Burchell's zebra. A total of 224 bird species have been recorded, with waterbirds being particularly well represented.

65 RUST DER WINTER DAM NATURE RESERVE

Location: South-central Transvaal; north of Pretoria.

Access: From Pretoria follow the N1 northwards in the direction of Warmbaths and after about 40 km turn right at the Pienaarsrivier/Rust de Winter off-ramp. The entrance is about 30 km further on, on the right-hand side.

Accommodation: None.

Other facilities: Picnic sites; watersports; fishing. There is no shop or fuel at the reserve.

Open: Throughout the year.

Opening time: 06h00 to 18h00.

Beware: Crocodiles; bilharzia.

For further information: The Officer-in-charge, Rust der Winter Dam Nature Reserve, Poste Restante, Rust de Winter 0406. Tel: 0121712, ask for 2422.

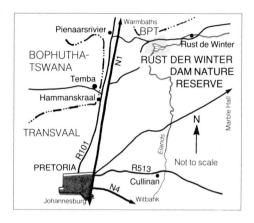

With the dam as its focal point, the Rust der Winter Dam Nature Reserve is predominantly a recreational resort frequented by anglers and watersport enthusiasts. It covers 1 654 ha in total, and its vegetation comprises thornveld in the north and a variety of bushveld species on the rocky slopes to the south of the dam. This is a popular venue with birdwatchers, as the dam and surrounding bush attract a wide variety of bird species, including European migrants.

66 RUSTENBURG NATURE RESERVE

Location: Southern Transvaal; south-west of Rustenburg.

Access: From the centre of Rustenburg the reserve is clearly signposted. The north gate gives access to the group camp and hiking trail; other visitors should use the east gate, where the reserve office and visitor centre are located. An entrance fee is charged.

Accommodation: Camping site with ablution facilities, fireplaces and wood, water; to be booked in advance (R7 per stand per night). 2 hiking trail huts, each with 10 beds, cooking pots and grid, paraffin lamps and firewood, a pit toilet and water (R4 per person per night). A small camp accommodating 60 is available for organised groups (R2 per person).

Other facilities: Visitor information centre; picnic sites; self-guided nature trail (about 2 hours); 2-day hiking trail.

Open: Throughout the year.

Opening time: 08h00 to 16h00.

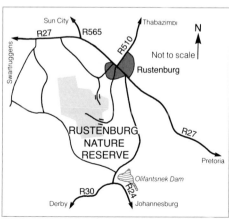

For further information: The Officer-in-charge, Rustenburg Nature Reserve, P.O. Box 511, Rustenburg 0300. Tel: (0142) 3-1050.

The Rustenburg Nature Reserve lies at the western end of the Magaliesberg Protected Natural Environment, about 100 km from Pretoria and Johannesburg. Originally established on the farm Rietvallei, which once belonged to President Kruger, it has been gradually expanded over the years and now covers some 4 257 ha. The reserve is dominated by the rocky ridges of the Magaliesberg, with well-wooded ravines on the rugged slopes. A large valley basin and an extensive plateau together form an important water catchment area, from which the main watercourse flows into a large, reed-filled marsh.

Although broadly defined as sour bushveld, the vegetation is varied, comprising grassland, scrub, mixed woodland, and even scattered pockets of fynbos (heath). More than 115 tree and bush species are known to grow in this mountain reserve, as well as a number of rare plants such as *Aloe peglerae* and the succulent *Frithia pulchra*.

Oribi, common duiker, klipspringer, reedbuck, mountain reedbuck, kudu, red hartebeest and sable are among the 13 antelope species that roam the reserve. The smallest of these and other small mammals are preyed upon by leopard, caracal, brown hyena and black-backed jackal, but these are seldom seen.

Some 230 bird species have been observed here, and a Cape vulture breeding colony is situated just to the east of the reserve. Both martial and black eagles occur.

67 S.A. LOMBARD NATURE RESERVE See map Bloemhof Dam Nature Reserve

Location: Extreme south-western Transvaal; north-west of Bloemhof.
Access: From Bloemhof take the R34 towards Schweizer-Reneke and after 5 km turn left onto a gravel road signposted to the reserve. Entry only by arrangement with the authority.
Accommodation: None.
For further information: The Officer-in-charge, S.A. Lombard Nature Reserve, P.O. Box 174, Bloemhof 2660. Tel: (01802) 3-1953.

This 3 663-ha reserve is predominantly flat, open grassland, with some scattered scrub. It was originally developed as a station for problem animal control and hound training, but is now a conservation area for plains antelope, which include gemsbok, eland, springbok, red hartebeest, blesbok and black wildebeest.

68 SABI SABI PRIVATE GAME RESERVE See map Londolozi Game Reserve

Location: Eastern Transvaal; north-west of Hazyview.
Access: From Hazyview take the R536 towards Skukuza and after about 35 km turn left onto a good gravel road towards Sabi Sabi; after about 3 km turn right and drive 5 km further to the entrance gate. Arrangements can be made for visitors to be met from commercial flights to Skukuza at no extra charge.
Accommodation: *Bush Lodge* has 25 2-bed thatched chalets, each of which has a bathroom, air conditioning and overhead fan (R875 per person per night, fully inclusive of all meals, guided game-viewing in open Landrovers, walking safaris and night sa- faris). *River Lodge* has 20 2-bed thatched chalets, each of which has a bathroom and air conditioning (rates same as Bush Lodge). Substantially reduced tariffs are made available to South Africans from May to September.
Other facilities: Both lodges are fully licensed and have a swimming pool, a curio shop and fully equipped conference facilities; Shangaan tribal dancing during open-air boma dinners.
Open: Throughout the year.
Beware: Malaria.
For further information: P.O. Box 52665, Saxonwold 2132. Tel: (011) 880-4840. Fax: (011) 447-2019.

Sabi Sabi Private Game Reserve borders the Kruger National Park and lies within Sabi Sand Private Game Reserve.

Habitat varies from acacia bushveld and open grass plains to combretum and riverine forest. Elephant, lion, leopard, rhinoceros and buffalo are all present, as well as giraffe, Burchell's zebra, cheetah, hyena, wild dog, hippopotamus, crocodile and all antelope species. Over 350 species of birds have been recorded.

SABI SAND
PRIVATE GAME RESERVE See map Londolozi Game Reserve

Location: Eastern Transvaal; north-west of Hazyview.

Access: Arrangements can be made for visitors to be met from commercial flights to Skukuza. *Inyati:* From Hazyview take the R536 towards Skukuza and after about 35 km turn left onto a good gravel road, following signposts to Inyati; continue for about 12 km to the Newington gate; the camp is 12 km further on. Visitors may use the 900-m airstrip if arrangements are made in advance. *Arathusa:* From the R40 (Bosbokrand/Hoedspruit) turn off to Acornhoek and travel for 34,4 km (the first 12 km are tarred); turn right, passing the Manyeleti road and continue for 6 km. Keep bearing left and after 12,1 km you will arrive at the entrance gate to Sabi Sand. Arathusa Game Lodge lies a further 3,9 km ahead, on the right. *Ulusaba:* From Nelspruit take the R538, turning off after Hazyview onto the R536 in the direction of Skukuza (Paul Kruger Gate, Kruger National Park) for 37,5 km. At the Ulusaba signpost, turn left along the dirt road to Sabi Sand's Kingston Gate; the lodge lies 24 km along this road. The route is clearly marked. *Idube:* Follow the same route as for Ulusaba but turn off 34,6 km along the R536. Shortly after this left turn, cross the motorgate, bearing right after 8 km, and left after a further 7 km; a further 4 km will bring you to Sabi Sand's Newington Gate. The signpost to Idube is a further 7 km ahead.

Accommodation: *Inyati Game Lodge* has 9 2-bed luxury chalets, each with a bathroom, lounge and air conditioning; a communal dining room and bar (R520 per person per night sharing, including meals, 2 game-viewing drives and accompanied walks). *Arathusa Game Lodge* has 5-bed, thatched, *en-suite* rondavels; minimum of 8 and a maximum of 15 guests; fully catered (R165 per person per night). *Ulusaba: Rock Lodge* has 4 *en-suite* bedrooms (maximum 8 guests), lounge and dining room, self-catering, take your own food and drink (R1 400 per night per group of 8); *Ntomo Bush Camp* caters for 6 guests, 3 bedrooms with showers, central dining area and kitchen, self-catering (R1 000 per night per group of 6). *Idube: Idube Lodge* provides luxury accommodation with air conditioning for a maximum of 10 people; the bush camp provides accommodation in well-equipped tents (maximum 10 guests). Full-catering is provided (lodge: R320 per person per night sharing; bush camp: R175 per person per night sharing). No children under 13 are accommodated. Advance booking is essential for all camps in Sabi Sand Private Game Reserve.

Other facilities: *Inyati:* Game-viewing drives in open vehicles; accompanied walks; swimming pool. *Arathusa:* Game-viewing drives in open vehicles; accompanied walks; plunge pool; conference facilities; private airstrip. *Ulusaba:* Game-viewing drives in open vehicles, including night drives; accompanied walks; swimming pool at Rock Lodge; private airstrip (gravel, 1 000 m). *Idube:* Game-viewing drives from the lodge only; accompanied walking trails; swimming pool; conference facilities.

Open: Throughout the year.

Beware: Malaria.

For further information: (Inyati) Inyati Game Lodge (Pty) Ltd, P.O. Box 38838, Booysens 2016. Tel: (011) 493-0755. Fax: (011) 493-0837. (Arathusa, Ulusaba and Idube) Bushveld Breakaways, P.O. Box 926, White River 1240. Tel: (01311) 5-1998. Fax: (01311) 5-0383.

The Sabi Sand Private Game Reserve is owned by a number of private individuals, and each camp or lodge is managed as a separate entity. In terms of conservation and game and veld management, however, the whole reserve is run as a single unit.

Inyati is situated in the north-western corner of the 58 000-ha reserve, straddling the Sand River where crocodiles and hippopotamus abound. Arathusa lies in the north-east, close to the boundary with Manyeleti Game Reserve; Ulusaba and Idube are located in the north-west. The vegetation of the reserve resembles that of the neighbouring Kruger National Park, and the bird and animal life, too, are similar. All the major game species are present, including elephant, buffalo, lion and leopard. Game-viewing is best during the dry winter months.

70

SAMANGO FOREST PRIVATE NATURE RESERVE

Location: S.E. Transvaal; west of Nelspruit.

Access: Lies on the N4 between Waterval Boven and Nelspruit; from Cross Roads Garage (Lydenburg turn-off, R36) continue east-

wards on the N4 to Hemlock turn-off; follow signposts to Samango Forest Lodge (13 km).
Accommodation: 4-bedroomed lodge (maximum 8 persons), with two bathrooms, kitchen, dining and sitting room, solar lighting; take your own food, drink, linen and towels (1-8 persons R300 per night).
Other facilities: Trails and pathways; camp attendant to do basic chores; firewood.
Open: Throughout the year.
For further information: Tel: (01311) 4-4586.

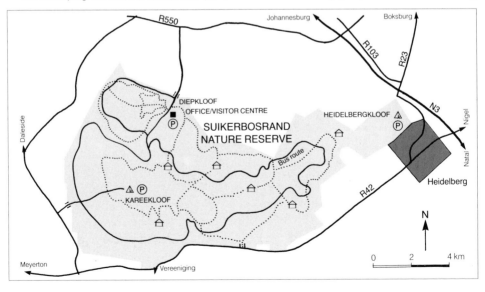

The Samango Forest Lodge is located in mountainous terrain, with areas of indigenous forest and plantations. The reserve takes its name from the samango monkey troops which inhabit the area. Baboons, vervet monkeys, klipspringer, bushbuck, mountain reedbuck and both the red and common duikers occur. Birdlife is abundant. Terraces built by the Bakoni people more than 150 years ago can still be seen.

71 SUIKERBOSRAND NATURE RESERVE

Location: Southern Transvaal; south of Johannesburg.

Access: From Johannesburg follow the N3 towards Heidelberg. To reach *Diepkloof* (reserve headquarters), take the R550 exit westwards and follow signposts to the reserve; *Overvaal Kareekloof*, from Heidelberg take the R42 towards Meyerton and follow signposts, or drive through the reserve from Diepkloof; *Overvaal Heidelbergkloof*, follow signposts from Heidelberg. All access points are signposted.

Accommodation: *Overvaal Heidelbergkloof* has a camping site with 145 stands (with power

points), ablution facilities and communal kitchens (R20 to R29 for 2 persons, R4,50 per additional person). *Overvaal Kareekloof* has a camping site with 120 stands (most with power points), ablution blocks and kitchen facilities (R17,50 to R30 for 2 persons, R4 per additional person). Camps for youth groups, with ablution and kitchen facilities (R2 per person per night). 6 hiking trail huts, each accommodating 10 hikers, with outdoor fireplaces, gas lamps, water and firewood. Meditation hut.

Other facilities: Hiking trail varying in length from 1 to 6 days; day walks 10 or 17 km long

and a 4,5 km trail; information centre, with a variety of interpretive literature; a 60-km game-viewing route; picnic sites. Overvaal Heidel-bergkloof and Overvaal Kareekloof offer most facilities associated with pleasure resorts.
Open: Throughout the year.
Opening time: Reserve – 07h00 to 18h00; resorts – 24 hours.

For further information: (Reserve) The Officer-in-charge, Suikerbosrand Nature Reserve, Private Bag H616, Heidelberg (T) 2400. Tel: (0151) 2181/2/3. (Resort bookings) Overvaal Heidel-bergkloof: P.O. Box 721, Heidelberg 2400. Tel: (0151) 2413. Fax: (0151) 6758. Overvaal Kareekloof: P.O. Box 372, Meyerton 1960. Tel: (0166) 5334 or 5485. Fax: (0166) 5628.

The Suikerbosrand Nature Reserve, covering 13 337 ha, is intensively utilised for environmental education, outdoor recreation and resource management. Lying so close to the most densely populated area in southern Africa, it plays an extremely important role in conservation.

A large variety of vegetation types can be seen here, ranging from open grassland on hillsides and plains to wooded gorges and acacia woodland, marshland and fynbos (heath). The sugarbush (*suikerbos*) from which the reserve takes its name, is a common sight.

Mountain reedbuck, common duiker and steenbok were here when the Suikerbosrand Nature Reserve was proclaimed, but since then species such as blesbok, springbok, red hartebeest, black wildebeest, oribi, eland, kudu and Burchell's zebra have been re-introduced and have thrived. Cheetah and brown hyena have been released here, and a number of smaller predator species also occur.

More than 200 bird species have been recorded.

72 TIMBAVATI PRIVATE NATURE RESERVE

Location: Eastern Transvaal; north-east of Lydenburg.
Access: From Lydenburg take the R36 north-ward through Ohrigstad and over the Abel Erasmus Pass, before bearing right onto the R531 and continuing on the R527 to Hoed-spruit; turn right onto the R40 and after 6 km turn left onto Argyle Rd; follow this road for 35 km, then turn right to the Timbavati gate and drive on to Tanda Tula camp; to reach the adjoining Motswari and M'Bali game lodges, continue on Argyle Rd for 24 km, then follow signposts to Motswari, which is 3 km further on. M'Bali is 9 km from Motswari. The last 41 km of this route is on gravel. Arrangements can be made to meet visitors on commercial flights to Phalaborwa; Motswari has a 1 385-m airstrip.
Accommodation: *Tanda Tula* has 7 2-bed rondavels, each with air conditioning and a bathroom; a communal bar/lounge and dining area (R475 per person per night). *Motswari* has 11 2-bed and 4 single bungalows, each with a bathroom and overhead fan; communal dining area and bar (R540 per person per night, all meals and 2 game-viewing drives included). *M'Bali* has 8 2-bed habitents; communal dining area and bar (R275 per person per night, all meals, 2 game-viewing walks and a boat ride included).
Other facilities: Morning and evening game-viewing drives in an open 4x4 with armed rangers; 3-day hiking trails; walking trails under the guidance of armed rangers; hides

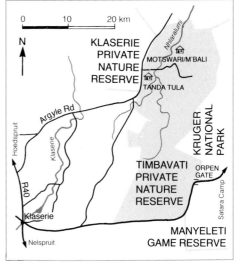

at waterholes; swimming pool and curio shop; Motswari and Tanda Tula have conference facilities.
Open: Throughout the year.
Opening time: 24 hours.
Beware: Malaria.
For further information: (Tanda Tula camp) Safariplan (Pty) Ltd, P.O. Box 4245, Randburg 2125. Tel: (011) 886-1810/1/2/3/4. (Motswari and M'Bali camps) Motswari Game Lodges, P.O. Box 67865, Bryanston 2021. Tel: (011) 463-1990/1/2. Fax: (011) 864-5353.

Similar in most respects to the adjacent Kruger National Park, the 22 000-ha Timbavati Private Nature Reserve has a wide spectrum of game species, including large populations of giraffe, impala, blue wildebeest and Burchell's zebra. The 'Big Five' (elephant, lion, leopard, buffalo and rhinoceros) are all present. The area is particularly well known for its white lions, individual animals which lack melanin pigment in the hair. A major attraction of the reserve is its birdlife, which encompasses some 240 species. Timbavati, like many of the other commercial game lodges in the Eastern Transvaal, appeals particularly to overseas travellers and businessmen who enjoy the luxury and personal attention offered, and who wish to see as much wildlife as possible in a limited time.

73 TSHUKUDU GAME RESERVE See map Blydeberg Nature Reserve

Location: Eastern Transvaal; north of Hoedspruit.
Access: The Tshukudu Game Reserve lies on the R40, 4.3 km north of Hoedspruit and to the east of the road; entrance is clearly signposted.
Accommodation: Thatched bungalows with private facilities (R200 per person per day including all meals, game-viewing drives and walks); bush camp with rustic, thatched, timber chalets, with separate ablution facilities (R100

per person per day including meals; R55 if self-catering).
Other facilities: Accompanied game-viewing drives (also night drives) and walks; swimming pool; bar.
Open: Throughout the year.
For further information: Lolly and Ala Sussens, P.O. Box 289, Hoedspruit 1380. Tel: (0131732) 6313. Fax: (0131732) 6313.

Tshukudu covers 5 000 ha of Lowveld woodland and is home to a wide range of game species, including buffalo, giraffe, white rhinoceros, kudu, blue wildebeest, Burchell's zebra, warthog and impala. Large predators are also present.

74 VAAL DAM NATURE RESERVE

Location: Extreme southern Transvaal; south of Johannesburg.
Access: From Johannesburg take the N3 towards Durban; to reach the north bank of the Vaal Dam, 63 km south of Heidelberg turn right onto the R54; to reach the south bank, continue on the N3 to Villiers, then turn right onto the R51; after 21 km turn right again onto the R716 and continue towards Oranjeville.
Accommodation: A camping site with ablution facilities is being developed.
Other facilities: Picnic sites; watersports; fishing.
Open: Throughout the year.
Opening time: 07h00 to 18h00.
For further information: The Officer-in-charge,

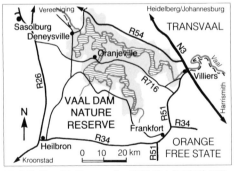

P.O. Box 12, Deneysville 1932. Tel: (01618) 777.

The Vaal Dam is one of the prime recreational centres for inhabitants of the Witwatersrand and surrounding urban areas, its attractions being a variety of watersports and fishing. Some 500 ha of land around the dam has been proclaimed a reserve but, because of the dam's popularity, only a few corners can be considered quiet. Most of the reserve is typical of the Highveld, with extensive grassland and scattered scrub. The birdlife is varied and particularly abundant near the dam shore.

75 VAALKOP DAM NATURE RESERVE

Location: South-western Transvaal; north-west of Brits.

Access: From Brits take the R511 towards Thabazimbi and after about 38 km, at Beestekraalstasie, turn left towards the Vaalkop Dam and Rustenburg; at the next junction turn right onto the Vaalkop Dam road, follow this for 12 km and then turn left; the entrance to the reserve is 2 km further on.

Accommodation: Camping is permitted but only basic facilities (toilets and drinking water) are provided.

Other facilities: Fishing (permit can be obtained from the officer-in-charge).

Open: Throughout the year.

Opening time: 06h00 to 20h00.

For further information: The Officer-in-charge, Vaalkop Dam Nature Reserve, P.O. Box 1846, Rustenburg 0300. Tel: (012117) 676.

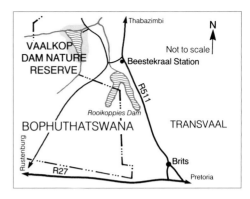

This reserve has a total area of 3 996 ha, of which the dam occupies 1 045 ha. The vegetation is typical of the Bushveld zone, comprising mixed broad-leafed and acacia species which attract a wide variety of bird species. The dam is a popular venue for anglers.

WARMBATHS NATURE RESERVE

Location: Central Transvaal; Warmbaths.

Access: From Overvaal Warmbaths.

Accommodation: Overvaal Warmbaths has over 100 2- and 4-bed fully equipped chalets; 48 2-bed rooms, each with a bathroom (R30 to R133 per night). A camping site has 294 stands, with ablution facilities (R14 to R24 for 2 persons per night).

Other facilities: Game-viewing tours in the reserve. The resort has many of the facilities associated with a popular holiday centre.

Open: Throughout the year.

Opening time: Reserve – by arrangement; resort – 24 hours.

For further information: The General Manager, Overvaal Warmbaths, P.O. Box 75, Warmbaths 0480. Tel: (015331) 2200.

This small reserve is accessible only by means of tours from the adjacent resort, to which it belongs. Its vegetation is typical of the Bushveld, and a few animals, such as kudu, red hartebeest, impala and Burchell's zebra, may be seen.

WOLKBERG WILDERNESS AREA See also map Fanie Botha Dam Nature Reserve

Location: North-eastern Transvaal; south-east of Pietersburg.

Access: From Pietersburg take the R71 eastwards, reaching Haenertsburg after about 60 km; follow signposts to Serala Forest Station. From Tzaneen follow signposts to the New Agatha Forest Station. Private vehicles not allowed into the area. A hiking permit is essential.

Accommodation: A camping site at the Serala entrance has ablution facilities; maximum 60 campers, with no more than 10 in a group; no fires permitted.

Other facilities: Network of hiking trails.

Open: Throughout the year.

Opening time: Sunrise to sunset.

For further information: The Officer-in-charge, Private Bag X102, Haenertsburg 0730. Tel: (0152222) 1303.

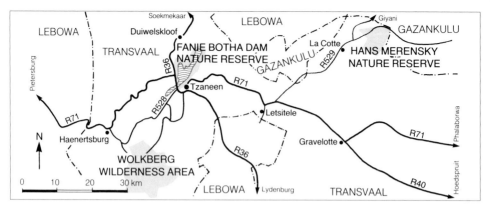

The Wolkberg Wilderness Area, covering some 22 009 ha in the northern part of the Transvaal Drakensberg, is an important water catchment zone, yielding some 20 000 000 m³ of water each year. Several streams rise in the area, and their clear, cool waters are appreciated by hikers on the rugged mountain slopes. The highest point within the conservation area is Serala Peak (2 050 m), and the Iron Crown (2 126 m) lies just outside it.

Mountain sourveld and bushveld savannah are the dominant vegetation types, with pockets of dense forest growing in the deep ravines and on south- and east-facing upper slopes. A great many plant species thrive here, including many rarities. Mammals that may be encountered are bushbuck, common duiker, grey rhebok, reedbuck, klipspringer, baboon, samango and vervet monkey, and dassie; other species such as leopard and brown hyena are more secretive and rarely seen. A number of reptiles occur, and hikers should be on the lookout for berg and puff adders, black mambas and pythons. More than 150 bird species have been recorded. Thunderstorms are common in this part of the summer-rainfall area, and mists occur all year round. Winter nights can be cold

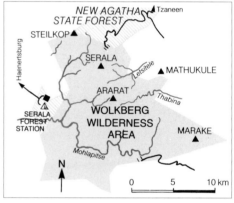

78 WOLWESPRUIT NATURE RESERVE

Location: South-western Transvaal; south-east of Wolmaransstad.

Access: From Wolmaransstad take the R504 to Leeudoringstad and there follow signposts to Kommandodrif; at the junction south of Leeudoringstad take the road to Klipspruit, and then the road to Rustfontein, continuing to the reserve entrance.

Accommodation: Primitive camping sites along the river bank without ablution facilities but with a field toilet, fireplace and rubbish bin.

Other facilities: Picnic area; game-viewing; fishing.

Open: Throughout the year.

Opening time: Sunrise to sunset.

For further information: The Officer-in-charge, Wolwespruit Nature Reserve, P.O. Box 237, Leeudoringstad 2640. Tel: (01813) 705.

The Wolwespruit Nature Reserve, covering 1 521 ha, has as its border a stretch of the Vaal River and is frequented mainly by fishermen. Games species that can be seen include black wildebeest, blesbok, red hartebeest, common duiker, springbok, Burchell's zebra and ostrich.

N

0   50   100   150 km

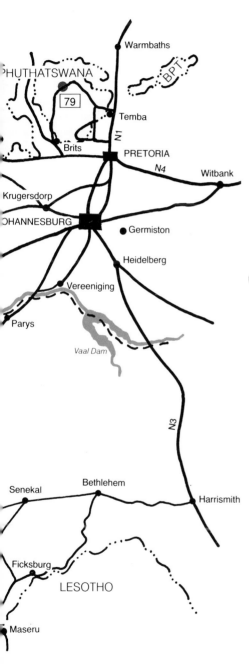

BOPHUTHA-TSWANA

79 **Borakalalo National Park**
80 **Botsalano Game Reserve**
81 **Lotlamoreng Dam – Cultural Village and Nature Reserve**
82 **Maria Moroka National Park**
✓83 **Pilanesberg National Park** Rino

The Republic of Bophuthatswana, declared independent in 1977, consists of seven geographically separate parcels of land scattered through the south-western Transvaal, north-eastern Cape Province and the Orange Free State. Together they make up the domain of the Batswana people.

The landscape is predominantly flat to undulating and supports a variety of vegetation types, such as Kalahari thornveld, which consists of sparse grassland dominated by various thorn tree species; bushveld savannah, which is grassland mixed with varying densities of woodland; and open grassland. Most of the region's rain (300 to 750 mm a year) falls during the summer months, and during this time the days are warm to hot; winter days are usually mild, but nights are cold and frost is common.

Bophuthatswana's five national parks, all recently established, are controlled by the National Parks and Wildlife Management Board. They offer the following types of accommodation: private camps for a maximum of 12 people (R300 per camp per night, excluding food); dormitories (R25 per person per night); tented camps (R60 per tent per night); caravan sites (R8 per person per night); cottages (R70 per cottage per night). All rates are substantially reduced for mid-week bookings. There is an entrance fee of R4,50 per adult and R3 per child.

It is wise to carry a passport or identity document when travelling in Bophuthatswana, although an entry visa is not required.

BORAKALALO NATIONAL PARK

Location: Within south-western Transvaal; north of Brits.

Access: From Brits take the R511 to Thabazimbi. After approximately 60 km, turn right at Leeupoort; 6 km further on, turn right again at the Klipvoor Dam sign and continue for 26 km, turning left at the Borakalalo signpost.

Accommodation: *Phudufudu Camp* has 4 2-bed tents, a communal lounge/dining room, fully equipped kitchen (guests must bring and prepare their own food) and ablution facilities; *Moretele Camp* has 2- and 3-bed tents with communal cooking and ablution facilities; private tents are also permitted at this site. *Pitjane camping site* has 20 stands with ablution facilities. Moretele and Phudufudu camps must be booked in advance.

Other facilities: Self-guided day walks; guided hiking and horseback trails for organ-ised groups; 60-km network of game-viewing roads; fishing (permits are available at the office); shop selling food and drink.

Open: Throughout the year.

Opening time: October to March – 05h00 to 20h00; April to September – 06h00 to 19h00.

Beware: Bilharzia.

For further information: The Reservations Officer, Borakalalo National Park, P.O. Box 240, Jericho 0264, Bophuthatswana. Tel: (0140) 2-1107 or tel. 0020, ask for Jericho 1441. Fax: (0140) 2-1107.

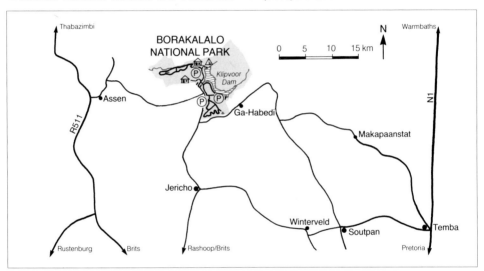

The topography of this 14 000-ha reserve – Bophuthatswana's second largest – varies widely from rolling sandveld to rocky outcrops, gorges and valleys. The vegetation consists of mixed bushveld, marsh and grassland, with riverine woodland and scrub fringing the Moretele River.

More than 30 large mammal species can be seen within the park, including white rhinoceros, giraffe, Burchell's zebra, sable, tsessebe, gemsbok and waterbuck. Some 300 bird species have been recorded. The 1 000-ha Klipvoor Dam in the park is a popular angling spot, famous for its large fish.

BOTSALANO GAME RESERVE

Location: Within south-western Transvaal; north of Mmabatho.

Access: From Mmabatho follow the R52 in the direction of Lobatse for about 20 km. At the Botswana border post at Ramatlhabama turn right towards Jagersfontein, and after 8 km turn left onto the Klippan/Botsalano road. The reserve's entrance is 10 km from this turn-off.

Accommodation: *Mogobe Tented Camp* has 4 2-bed tents with a fully equipped communal

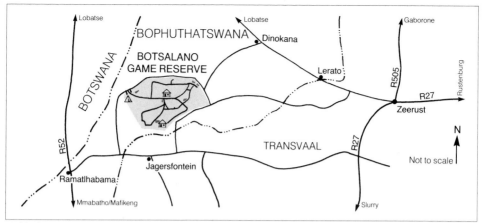

kitchen and an ablution block. Near the entrance gate there is a camping site with 10 stands and full ablution facilities.

Other facilities: A network of game-viewing roads; conducted game-viewing drives; accompanied walks (by prior arrangement); picnic sites with fireplaces; trophy hunting.

Open: Throughout the year.

Opening time: Monday to Friday – 07h30 to 17h00; Saturday and Sunday – 06h30 to 18h30. Overnight visitors must check in before 16h30.

For further information: The Reservations Officer, Pilanesberg National Park, P.O. Box 1201, Mogwase 0302, Bophuthatswana. Tel: (0140) 2-2405 or 2-2377/8, or PR Officer (0140) 89-5156/9. Fax: (0140) 2-1468.

The landscape of this reserve is dominated by outcrops of quartzite, ironstone and lava, which form low, gently sloping hills covered with grassland, woodland and woodland savannah. A wide range of game species, including white rhinoceros, giraffe, springbok, impala, eland, gemsbok, sable, waterbuck and blue wildebeest, have been re-introduced into this recently established, 5 800-ha reserve.

81 LOTLAMORENG DAM – CULTURAL VILLAGE AND NATURE RESERVE

Location: Within south-western Transvaal; south of Mafikeng.

Access: From Mafikeng follow the R27 in the direction of Vryburg for 4 km; the turn-off to the reserve is on the left and is clearly sign-posted.

Accommodation: None. There are hotels and a caravan and camping site in Mafikeng.

Other facilities: Bird sanctuary; access to Lotlamoreng Dam; information centre; African cultural centre and 'living' museum.

Open: Throughout the year.

Opening time: Sunrise to sunset.

For further information: The Tourist Officer, Lotlamoreng Dam, Private Bag X2078, Mmabatho 8670. Tel: (0140) 89-5156/9. Fax: (0140) 2-1468.

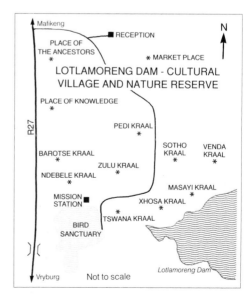

The main attraction of Lotlamoreng is the 'living village concept', in which the traditional ways of life of nine different tribes of southern Africa are represented.

Birdwatchers will find a visit to the reserve rewarding. A waterbird sanctuary is attracting an increasing number of birds; the recently completed walk-in aviary will eventually house more than 70 different species of birds indigenous to the Lotlamoreng Dam area.

82 MARIA MOROKA NATIONAL PARK

Location: Within central Orange Free State; east of Bloemfontein.
Access: From Bloemfontein take the R64 to Thaba Nchu, then follow signposts to the Thaba Nchu Sun Hotel.
Accommodation: None. The Thaba Nchu Sun Hotel lies on the park's southern border.
Other facilities: Guided and self-guided walking trails, ranging in length from 1,5 to 10 hours; guided game-viewing drives; fishing in the Groothoek Dam.
Open: Throughout the year.
Opening time: Sunrise to sunset.
For further information: The PR Officer, Bophuthatswana National Parks Board, Private Bag X2078, Mmabatho 8670. Tel: (0140) 89-5156/9. Fax: (0140) 2-1468.

With the Groothoek Dam taking up much of the southern area and the Thaba Nchu Mountain on its northern border, the Maria Moroka National Park is a scenically attractive reserve. Open plains of sweet grassland and low shrub savannah support re-introduced populations of springbok, blesbok, red hartebeest, eland and Burchell's zebra, totalling some 1 500 head of game.

More than 150 bird species have been recorded, including raptors and the rare, endemic blue korhaan.

83 PILANESBERG NATIONAL PARK

Location: Within south-western Transvaal; north of Rustenburg.
Access: From Rustenburg follow the R510 in the direction of Thabazimbi for 56 km before turning left at the signpost to the reserve; Manyane Gate, which must be used by overnight visitors, lies 6 km from the turn-off. Day visitors can also enter at Bakgatla, Bakubung or Kwa Maritane; these entrances are clearly signposted, and all access roads to the park are tarred.
Accommodation: *Manyane, Mankwe, Kololo* and *Metswedi camps* provide tented accommodation with varying levels of luxury and service. *Bosele Camp* provides dormitory-type accommodation in wooden huts for groups of up to 180; all meals are supplied. *Manyane*

caravan and camping site has 100 stands and ablution facilities.
Other facilities: A 100-km network of roads; conducted walks; self-guided wilderness trails; organised game-viewing drives; hides; walk-in aviary; picnic sites with fireplaces; restaurants; education centre; swimming pool; shop selling food and drink.
Open: Throughout the year.
Opening time: April to August – 05h30 to 19h00; September to March – 05h00 to 20h00.
For further information: The Reservations Officer, Pilanesberg National Park, P.O. Box 1201, Mogwase 0302, Bophuthatswana. Tel: (0140) 2-2405 or 2-2377/8. Fax: (0140) 2-2405 or 2-2377/8.

A huge volcanic crater rising 600 m above the surrounding plain provides a dramatic setting for this 50 000-ha park. Founded in 1979, Pilanesberg National Park has rapidly become one of southern Africa's premier tourist attractions. An ambitious game-stocking programme, started in the 1970s, has proved highly successful and a wide range of game species have now been re-introduced to their former haunts. They include elephant, black and white rhinoceros, buffalo, Burchell's zebra, hippopotamus, giraffe, kudu, eland, red hartebeest, sable, waterbuck, tsessebe and impala. Cheetah, leopard and brown hyena also occur.

Two distinct vegetation zones, namely Kalahari thornveld and sour bushveld, meet in this area, resulting in a diversity of habitats which has contributed to the success of the restocking venture. The most productive game-viewing areas lie in the valleys, with the main concentrations of game occurring during the dry winter season.

With its great diversity of habitats and the fact that the Pilanesberg National Park lies in the transition zone of the arid Kalahari and the moist Lowveld vegetation, it is no wonder that this reserve has become a haven for birdwatchers. More than 300 bird species have been recorded, including thirty different raptors. These range from the Martial, Black and Fish eagles to the smaller Rock Kestrel and African Hobby. The vultures are represented by the frequently seen Cape Vulture, as well as the White-backed and Lappet-faced vultures. A 'vulture restaurant' is located in the vicinity of Manyane Gate. Other groups of birds that are well represented are the cuckoos, francolins, larks, babblers and warblers.

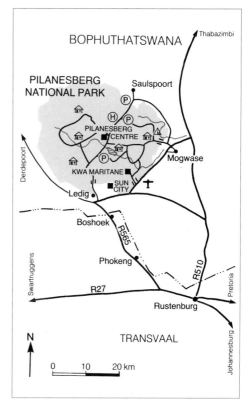

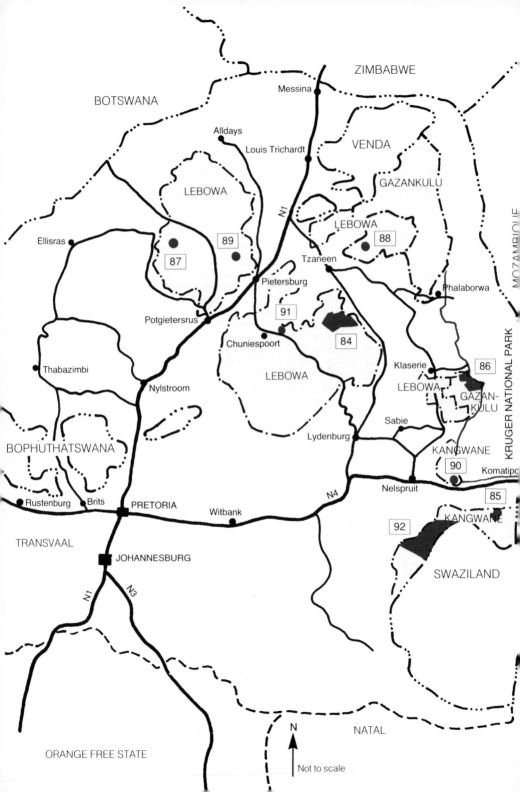

KANGWANE, LEBOWA AND GAZANKULU

KaNgwane, Lebowa and Gazankulu are all self-governing homelands that form part of the mosaic of tribal states within the province of Transvaal.

KaNgwane consists of two blocks of land, the larger bordering on Swaziland and Mozambique, and the smaller adjoining the south-western boundary of the Kruger National Park. The area receives a relatively high rainfall (up to 1 600 mm in the southern mountains), most of which falls during the summer months. Summer temperatures are generally high, particularly in the lower-lying areas, but winter nights are often cold.

Lebowa is made up of several separate parcels of land containing a variety of landscapes and vegetation which range from mountain massifs to rolling hills, and from great expanses of savannah to pockets of indigenous forest. This diversity of habitats supports a varied wildlife, although in most areas large game animals disappeared long ago or their numbers have been greatly reduced. Lebowa's climate is similar to Transvaal's, with hot, wet summers and dry, warm winters.

The third self-governing state, Gazankulu, consists of two main blocks of land, both of which lie in the Lowveld. Although there is some hilly country in the north, most of the terrain is flat.

There are no formal entry requirements to these areas, but it is advisable to carry proof of identity.

All reserves are open from sunrise to sunset throughout the year.

84 — LEKGALAMEETSE NATURE RESERVE

Location: Eastern-central Lebowa, within the Eastern Transvaal; south of Tzaneen.
Access: From Tzaneen take the R36 southwards for 43 km. Turn right at Ofcolaco and continue for 3,5 km. Turn right at 'The Downs' signpost onto a gravel road and travel for 10,5 km to the reserve's entrance. Permits are required.

Accommodation: 8 furnished 2- or 5-bed log cabins; hiking huts on overnight hiking trail.
Other facilities: Short walks; 2- and 3-day hiking trails; picnic sites with fireplaces.
Information: Tourism Official, Lekgalameetse Nature Reserve, P.O. Box 186, Trichardtsdal 0890. Tel: 0152302, ask for 1514.

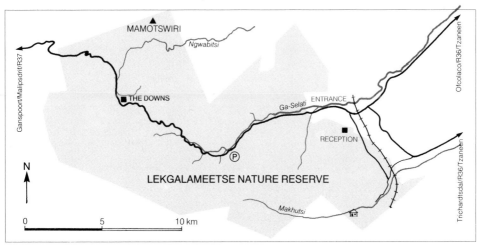

This is a rugged, mountainous reserve, covered by indigenous forests and mixed bush and grassland. Extending over a total area of 19 500 ha, the Lekgalameetse Nature Reserve is intersected by numerous rivers and streams, and fine views of the surrounding country can be obtained from Mamotswiri Mountain (1 838 m). Its varied animal life includes bushbuck, common duiker, mountain reedbuck, klipspringer, samango monkey, baboon, thick-tailed bushbaby and leopard. A number of interesting and rare forest birds occur in the reserve. Between 800 and 1 100 mm of rain falls in the area during the summer months and mist occurs fairly frequently.

85 MAHUSHE SHONGWE GAME RESERVE

Location: KaNgwane, within the Eastern Transvaal; south-east of Nelspruit.
Access: From Nelspruit take the N4 eastwards towards Komatipoort. Outside Malelane take the Jeppes Reef turn; continue for 12 km to the Tonga road. Turn left and continue for 15 km. Turn right to Mzinti; the reserve entrance is within 3 km on the right.
Accommodation: An exclusive tented camp with 4 2-bed tents, each with its own bathroom; central kitchen/lapa; self-catering.
Other facilities: Nyala trail; birdwatching; swimming pool.
Open: Throughout the year.
Opening time: Sunrise to sunset.
Beware: Malaria; bilharzia.

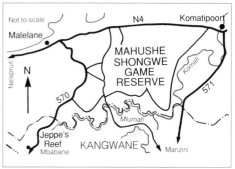

For further information: KaNgwane Parks Corporation (see page 365).

Mahushe Shongwe covers 700 ha and is situated on the Lebombo Flats. The Mzinti River, a tributary of the Komati, flows through the reserve.

There are a number of game species present. The birdlife is abundant and as many as 164 species have been recorded on weekend visits.

86 MANYELETI GAME RESERVE

Location: Gazankulu, within the Eastern Transvaal; north of Nelspruit.
Access: From Nelspruit take the R40 northwards; after approximately 140 km turn off onto the R531 towards Orpen Gate (Kruger National Park) and after another 36 km turn right at the signpost to the reserve. From Acornhoek travel approximately 43 km along a fairly rough gravel road to the Acornhoek entrance gate which is well signposted.
Accommodation: The main camp has self-contained and standard rondavels, and dormitories for schoolchildren. Limited camping facilities are available on special request. An Educational Bush Camp (Ndzhaka) accommodates groups of up to 45. Khoka Moya Trails operate 2 camps in the reserve. Lowveld Environmental Awareness Trails (LEAT) operate a rustic camp.
Other facilities: The main camp – game-viewing drives; short walks with game scouts on

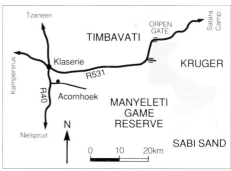

request; reptile park; swimming pool; curio shop; educational film shows available; restaurant; bar; shop selling food and drink; post office and fuel. Khoka Moya Trails – game-viewing walks and drives. LEAT – walking trails; 'primitive' trails for the more adventurous.
Open: Throughout the year.

Opening time: From 06h00 to 18h00.
Beware: Malaria.
For further information: (Main camp and Ndzhaka) The Manager, Manyeleti Game Reserve, P.O. Manyeleti 1362. Tel: 0020, ask for Manyeleti 3. (Khoka Moya Trails) Safariplan, P.O. Box 4245, Randburg 2125. Tel: (011) 886-1810/14. (LEAT) Lowveld Environmental Awareness Trails, P.O. Box 3756, Nelspruit 1200. Tel: (011) 442-9592 or (01311) 5-1307.

The vegetation and wildlife of the Manyeleti Game Reserve are similar to those of the adjacent areas of the Kruger National Park. Elephant, white rhinoceros, buffalo, hippopotamus, a broad spectrum of antelope species, giraffe, lion, leopard, cheetah and spotted hyena can be seen. The birdlife is rich and varied.

87 MASEBE NATURE RESERVE

Location: North-western Lebowa, within northern Transvaal; north-west of Potgietersrus.
Access: From Potgietersrus take the R518 towards Marken for 90 km; turn right at the Skrikfontein turn-off immediately before the left turn to Overyssel, continue to the T-junction and then turn left. Entrances to the reserve are about 5 km from this junction. Alternatively, continue along the R518 to Marken; turn right at the T-junction and follow the Mogalakwenastroom road to the gates. This is a developing reserve and prospective visitors should contact the authority beforehand.
Accommodation: None at present. Bungalows, a camping site and other facilities are being developed.
Other facilities: Walking trails.
Open: Throughout the year.

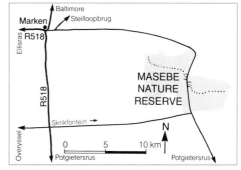

Opening time: Sunrise to sunset.
For further information: Department of the Chief Minister, Division Land Affairs and Tourism, Lebowa (see page 365).

The Masebe Nature Reserve, previously known as Haakdoorndraai, has a number of caves and shelters with evidence of Bushman habitation, including paintings. These, together with the rugged scenic setting, make the reserve well worth a visit. The vegetation is predominantly woodland with many large tree species such as marula, tamboti and paperbark albizia. Eland, kudu, impala, waterbuck, red hartebeest, sable and zebra are present. The birdlife is diverse and includes many raptor species.

88 MODJADJI NATURE RESERVE

Location: North-eastern Lebowa, within the Eastern Transvaal; north-east of Duiwelskloof.
Access: From Duiwelskloof take the R36 towards Soekmekaar and travel for about 10 km; where the R36 bears left, carry straight on towards Ga-Kgapane, following this road as it bears right towards the reserve.
Accommodation: None at present; cottages and a camping site are being developed.
Other facilities: Short trails; picnic sites with fireplaces; information centre.
Open: Throughout the year.
Opening time: Sunrise to sunset.
For further information: Department of the Chief Minister, Division Land Affairs and Tourism, Lebowa (see page 365).

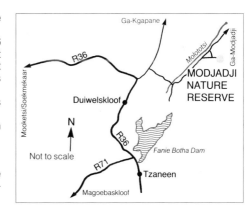

The Modjadji area has a long and fascinating tribal history dominated by a succession of Modjadji, or rain queens, the latest of which lives on land adjoining this 305-ha reserve. The main purpose of the Modjadji Nature Reserve is to protect the largest known concentration of a single cycad species in the world, namely the Modjadji cycad, *Encephalartos transvenosus*. This prehistoric plant can exceed 10 m in height, but most grow to between 5 and 8 m. Game species have been introduced and inhabit the lower-lying savannah woodland. These include blue wildebeest, nyala, impala, waterbuck and bushbuck. More than 170 bird species have been recorded.

89 MOLETSI NATURE RESERVE

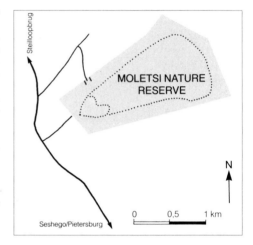

Location: Northern Lebowa; north-west of Pietersburg.
Access: From Pietersburg take the R521 northwards for about 3 km, turn left and continue to Seshego. Immediately after Seshego take the right turn towards Steilloopbrug and, 40 km from Pietersburg, turn right into the reserve. Two prominent rock outcrops are useful landmarks at the entrance. Permission to visit the reserve must be obtained in advance.
Accommodation: None.
Other facilities: Self-guided trails; picnic sites with fireplaces; ablution facilities; information centre; vulture 'restaurant'.
Open: Throughout the year.
Opening time: Sunrise to sunset.
For further information: Department of the Chief Minister, Division Land Affairs and Tourism, Lebowa (see page 365).

This 204-ha reserve is dominated by rock outcrops and a mixture of trees, bush and grassland savannah. It is of particular interest to birdwatchers as the rare bald ibis and Cape vulture breed here, as well as several other raptors. Mammals that may be seen include impala, common duiker, steenbok, klipspringer, baboon and rock dassie.

90 MTHETHOMUSHA GAME RESERVE

Location: KaNgwane, within the Eastern Transvaal; east of Nelspruit.
Access: From Nelspruit take the N4 eastwards towards Komatipoort for approximately 36 km and turn left into the Matsulu road. Within 1 km turn left at the Bongani signpost and follow this road to the reserve.
Accommodation: *Bongani Mountain Lodge* is an exclusive luxury bush camp with full-catering. Chalets range from luxurious double rooms with twin bathrooms to the Nkosi suite.
Other facilities: Full conference facilities for 60; swimming pool; picnic site for day visitors.
Beware: Malaria.
For further information: KaNgwane Parks Corporation (see page 365) or Game Lodge Reservations, Tel: (011) 883-4345. Fax: (011) 83-2556.

38. The blue korhaan is protected in the Maria Moroka National Park.

39. Safari tents at Manyane in the Pilanesberg National Park offer comfortable accommodation.

40. Giraffe thrive once more in the Pilanesberg National Park, which has undergone major restocking.

41. The Modjadji cycad, which can grow higher than 10 metres, in the Modjadji Nature Reserve.

42. Buffalo, a highly dangerous species, being released in the Mthethomusha Game Reserve.

43. The attractive entrance to the Manyeleti Game Reserve.

44. Warthogs are often seen at waterholes in Nwanedi National Park.

45. The rest camp at Nwanedi.

46. The rugged terrain of the Songimvelo Nature Reserve is softened in parts by grassland.

47. A collection of equipment used by poachers is displayed at Mlilwane Wildlife Sanctuary.

48. Giraffe, once widespread throughout Swaziland, have been re-introduced at Mlilwane.

49. The upper Mahulungwane Falls, one of many beautiful features in the Malolotja Nature Reserve.

50. The main camping site at Malolotja.

This 9 000-ha reserve is bounded by the Kruger National Park to the east and by the Crocodile River Gorge to the south. The landscape is dominated by granite hills and outcrops, while the vegetation consists of mixed sourish woodland and grassland savannah. Game includes elephant, rhinoceros, buffalo, leopard and giraffe. The birdlife is rich and varied; more than 200 species have been recorded to date.

91 POTLAKE NATURE RESERVE

Location: Central Lebowa, within the Eastern Transvaal; south-east of Pietersburg.
Access: From Pietersburg follow the R37 towards Burgersfort for 85 km. Shortly after crossing the Olifants River turn left into the reserve. This is a developing reserve and anyone wishing to visit it should contact the Chief Nature Conservator beforehand.
Accommodation: None.
Other facilities: Walking trails; hiking trail with tented camping site; picnic sites; interpretive centre; kiosk and curio shop.
For further information: Department of Land Affairs and Tourism, Lebowa (see page 365).

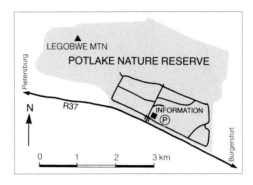

Potlake Nature Reserve covers 2 786 ha of rugged hills and open flats dominated by acacia woodland. Species seen include giraffe, zebra, wildebeest, eland, gemsbok, kudu and waterbuck.

92 SONGIMVELO GAME RESERVE

Location: South-western KaNgwane, within the Eastern Transvaal; south-east of Barberton, running along the Swaziland border.
Access: From Badplaas take the R38 towards Barberton; 1 km from Badplaas take the Lochiel turn-off. After about 22 km the road becomes gravel; continue straight on for approximately 10 km; turn left at the Songimvelo signpost.
Accommodation: None. A fully serviced luxury tented camp is under construction.
Other facilities: Hiking trails for organised groups; horseback safaris.
Open: Throughout the year.
Beware: Malaria; bilharzia.
For further information: KaNgwane Parks Corporation (see page 365). (Horseback safaris) Bushveld Breakaways, P.O. Box 926,

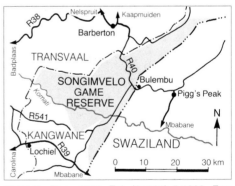

White River 1240. Tel: (01311) 5-1998. Fax: (01311) 5-0383.

One of this reserve's many attractions is the archaeological remains of early man to be found in the area, dating back to between 200 and 400 BC, as well as numerous remnants of the Barberton goldrush that occurred here in the latter half of the last century. Covering 56 000 ha, the Songimvelo Game Reserve promises to become one of the conservation showpieces of southern Africa. It lies in mainly rugged, mountainous terrain, the highest point in the area being Mlembe Peak at 1 851 m. The reserve is to be developed as a multiple-use conservation area and certain human activities will continue.

In addition to the two major vegetation structures, namely grassland and savannah woodland, and shrub forest, elements of the Cape Floral Kingdom grow in higher areas and three cycad species can also be found here. There are currently 20 species of ungulates in the reserve, including hippo, giraffe and rhino. Predators include leopard and caracal. Birdlife is rich with 309 species recorded to date.

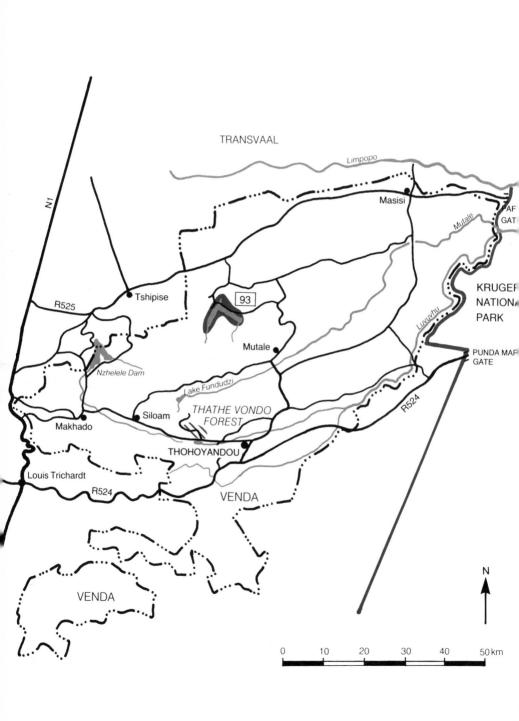

TRANSVAAL

Limpopo

N1

Masisi

AF
GAT

R525

Tshipise

Mutale

93

KRUGER
NATIONA
PARK

Mutale

Luvuvhu

PUNDA MAR
GATE

Nzhelele Dam

Lake Fundudzi

*THATHE VONDO
FOREST*

Siloam

R524

Makhado

THOHOYANDOU

Louis Trichardt

R524

VENDA

VENDA

N

0   10   20   30   40   50 km

VENDA

93 Nwanedi National Park

The Republic of Venda adjoins the far northern sector of the Kruger National Park and covers approximately 6 500 km² This is a land steeped in tribal legend and tradition, with many sites of great historical significance. Strict tribal laws govern entry to a number of sacred areas and must be respected at all times.

Much of Venda is taken up by the Soutpansberg Mountains, some of whose peaks rise to 1 900 m above sea-level. Between the mountains and the Limpopo River to the north the dry Malonga Flats are covered by mopane woodland, whereas to the south mixed bushveld dominates. On the south-facing mountain slopes indigenous forests flourish, the largest of which falls within the extensive Thathe Vondo plantation. This is a summer-rainfall area, with up to 1 500 mm falling annually at the highest altitudes. Summer days are usually hot and humid, but winters are mild.

Although Venda has no official border posts, all visitors or people in transit must carry a passport or South African identity document. Visitors intending to stay longer than 14 days must obtain permission to do so from the Department of Internal Affairs, Private Bag X2249, Thohoyandou 0907, Republic of Venda.

93 NWANEDI NATIONAL PARK

Location: North-western Venda, within northern Transvaal; north-east of Louis Trichardt and north of Thohoyandou.

Access: From Louis Trichardt head north on the N1 in the direction of Messina for 57 km, then turn right onto the R525 and drive 34 km to Tshipise; continue on this road for another 20 km before turning right and following the signpost to the reserve. The entrance is approximately 7 km from this turn-off. From Thohoyandou a route passes through the mountains, but part of this road is gravel (a long section is in the process of being macadamized). This route is approximately 70 km long and well signposted.

Accommodation: Self-catering accommodation consists of fully equipped, 4-bed rondavels each with a bathroom and kitchenette, and a block of luxury family rooms (R55 per rondavel per night without food; luxury accommodation R78 per person per night sharing, dinner, bed and breakfast). There are also caravan and camping sites with ablution facilities (R8 per tent per night; R10 per caravan per night).

Other facilities: Walking trails; game-viewing roads; fishing; à la carte restaurant; shop; the

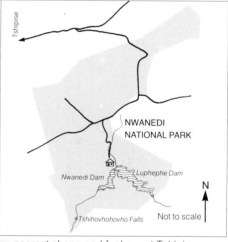

nearest shops and fuel are at Tshipise.

Open: Throughout the year.

Opening time: 06h00 to 18h00.

Beware: Malaria.

For further information: Venda Tourism, P.O. Box 9, Sibasa, Venda. Tel: (015581) 4-1577. Fax: (015581) 2-1298.

The northern slopes of the Soutpansberg provide a wonderfully scenic backdrop to this rugged reserve. Most visitors come here for the fishing offered in the Nwanedi and Luphephe dams, or to walk to the scenic Tshihovhohovho Falls. Game-viewing in the mopane and mixed woodland can be rewarding, and such species as white rhinoceros, Burchell's zebra, warthog, kudu, blue wildebeest, impala, eland, nyala, common duiker and klipspringer may be seen. Cheetah and lion are penned in separate enclosures.

Daytime temperatures in summer are often high in this area; the average annual rainfall is relatively low, at 250 mm.

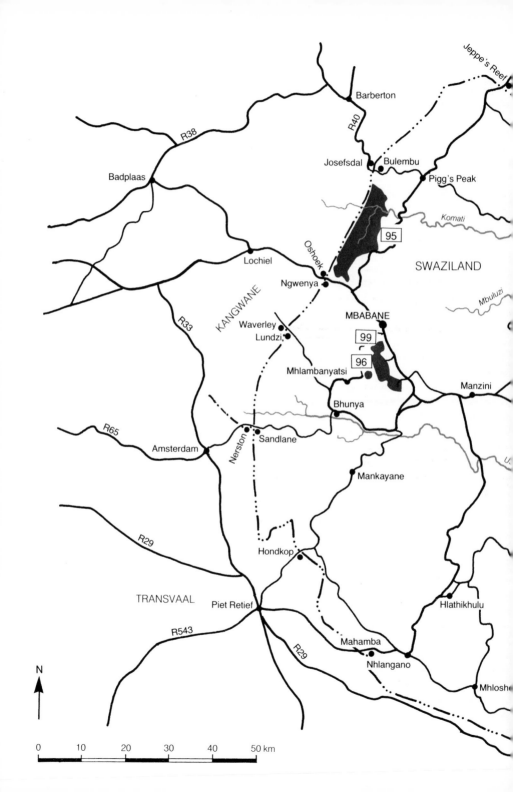

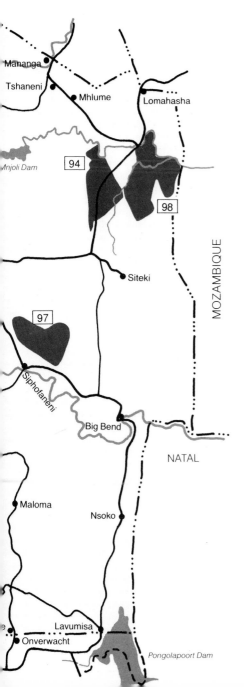

SWAZILAND

94 Hlane National Park
95 Malolotja Nature Reserve
96 Meikles Mount
97 Mkhaya Nature Reserve
98 Mlawula Nature Reserve
99 Mlilwane Wildlife Sanctuary

One of Africa's smallest countries, the tiny kingdom of Swaziland covers 17 363 km² of highly diverse landscapes and habitats, ranging from dramatic mountain scenery to open woodland savannah. It is surrounded by Mozambique, Ka-Ngwane, Transvaal and Natal.

The control and management of Swaziland reserves fall mainly within the hands of the Swaziland National Trust, although private individuals, notably Ted and Liz Reilly, have played a major role. Most of Swaziland's larger mammal species were hunted to extinction, but in recent years many animals have been re-introduced, in particular elephant, black and white rhinoceros and several antelope species.

Visitors to Swaziland must be in possession of valid passports, and nationals other than South Africans may require visas. Border posts close and open at different times, with most closing at 16h00, a few at 22h00. The unit of currency is the lilangeni (plural emalangeni) which is divided into 100 units.

Climatically, Swaziland varies from temperate in the higher altitudes to subtropical in the Lowveld. Rain falls in the summer months (November to March) and average annual amounts recorded range from over 2 000 mm in the mountainous north-west to approximately 500 mm in parts of the thornveld savannah. Malaria and bilharzia are widespread, particularly in the lower-lying areas.

HLANE NATIONAL PARK

Location: North-eastern Swaziland; east of Mbabane.

Access: From Mbabane take the main tar road to Manzini and drive straight through the town; continue for approximately 65 km in the direction of Mhlume and Tshaneni. This road enters Hlane once the second road-over-rail bridge has been crossed; the entrance signpost is on the left.

Accommodation: Thatched huts with bedding and towels provided (E35 per person per night without bath; E45 per person per night with bath); Bhubesi camp, fully equipped, self-catering (E60 per person per night); all accommodation is half price for children under 16. There is a camping site with ablution facilities (E10 per person per night).

Other facilities: Walking is permitted; game-viewing. There are no shops or fuel supplies.

Open: Throughout the year.

Opening time: Sunrise to sunset.

Beware: Malaria; all barbed wire fences are electrified.

For further information: The Officer-in-charge, Hlane National Park, P.O. Box 216, Simunye, Swaziland. Tel: (09268) 6-1037 or 6-1591/2/3. Fax: (0194) 6-1594.

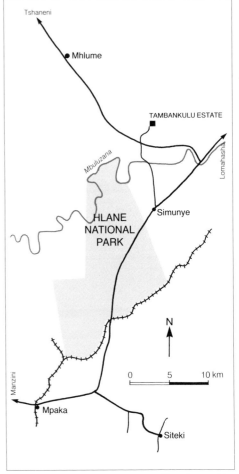

The Hlane National Park is situated in the Swaziland Lowveld and covers approximately 30 000 ha. Part of this area was set aside by King Sobhuza as a royal hunting ground and was proclaimed a reserve in 1967. This is one of the few conservation areas in southern Africa where natural mortality is allowed to take its course, and this policy results in a high incidence of scavenger species such as vultures and jackals.

The vegetation is predominantly mixed bushveld and savannah. Game-viewing in the northern part of the park is at its best during the dry season when the animals concentrate at the rivers to drink. Species that can be seen are Burchell's zebra, white rhinoceros, warthog, kudu, impala, waterbuck, bushbuck, nyala, common duiker, steenbok and giraffe. The authorities are planning to re-introduce other species in the future.

The area has a subtropical climate with hot, wet summers and generally mild winters. Winter nights can be very cold.

MALOLOTJA NATURE RESERVE

Location: North-western Swaziland; north-west of Mbabane.

Access: From the Oshoek border post follow the road towards Mbabane for 7 km; at Motshane take the left turn towards Pigg's Peak and after 18 km watch out for the signpost to Malolotja reserve on the left.

Accommodation: Self-catering accommodation comprises 5 6-bed luxury log cabins, bedding supplied (E120 per cabin per night at weekends, E80 during the week). There is a camping site with 15 stands (E9 per person per night). A number of small camping sites for hikers on overnight trails are scattered throughout the reserve; they accommodate a maximum of 10 hikers but have no facilities (E6 per person per night).

Other facilities: More than 200 km of hiking trails ranging in duration from 1 to 7 days; a 15-km network of game-viewing drives (the dirt roads are rough in places and closed during summer rains); picnic sites with fireplaces; trout fishing; horse-riding; swimming in bilharzia-free rivers. There are no shops or fuel in the reserve.

Open: Throughout the year.

Opening time: Winter – 07h00 to 18h00; summer – 06h30 to 18h30.

Speed limit: 25 km/h.

Beware: Be prepared for sudden weather changes, particularly on longer hikes.

For further information: The Senior Warden, Malolotja Nature Reserve, P.O. Box 1797, Mbabane, Swaziland. Tel: (09268) 4-3060. (Bookings for log cabins) Malolotja Bookings, P.O. Box 100, Lobamba, Swaziland. Tel: (09268) 6-1178/9.

Opened to the public in 1984, the 18 000-ha Malolotja Nature Reserve is the last true wilderness area in Swaziland and as such is a paradise for hikers. The conservation area is dominated by the rugged mountains of the Silotwane, Mgwayisa and Ngwenya ranges, and includes two of Swaziland's highest mountains, Ngwenya (1 837 m) and Silotwane (1 680 m), as well as its highest waterfall, Malolotja Falls (100 m). In addition to the mountainous terrain there are beautiful valleys, deep river gorges, and grass-covered plains. It also boasts some of the world's oldest and best-preserved sedimentary rocks, and the Lion Cavern which, dated at 41 000 BC, is the oldest known site of mining activity.

The great variety of habitats and vegetation types, ranging from open grassland to forest, makes this one of the most interesting botanical areas in Swaziland. A number of rare plant species are protected in the reserve, including the woolly, Barberton and Kaapsehoop cycads. Protea and erica species are among the elements of the Cape Floral Kingdom which can be seen here, and the profusion of small flowering plants justifies a visit to the reserve's herbarium so that their identities may be determined. The reserve boasts a rich array of aloes, orchids and amaryllids. Trees are well represented in the valleys and the forest fever tree *Anthocleista grandiflora* reaches its southernmost limits in the riverine forests of Malolotja.

Mountain reedbuck, grey rhebok, oribi, klipspringer, common and red duiker and many smaller mammals occurred in the reserve before its proclamation, and other species – such as Burchell's zebra, warthog, blue and black wildebeest, red hartebeest, blesbok and common reedbuck – have been re-introduced. Predators are represented by leopard, caracal, black-backed jackal and aardwolf, amongst others. The herpetofauna of the reserve is diverse with 18 species of amphibians and 54 species of reptiles currently recorded. Venomous snakes are few and the Nile crocodile does not occur in any of the rivers.

More than 280 bird species have been recorded, and those that breed at Malolotja include the endangered blue swallow, the rare bald ibis, which nests on the cliffs alongside the Malolotja Falls during the winter months, and the blue crane, which nests in the upland marshes during the wet summer months. The proteas attract several sunbird species, as well as Gurney's sugarbird. Other species that are worth looking out for are Stanley's bustard, the black-rumped buttonquail and the broad-tailed warbler.

Most of the area's rain falls between September and February, when days are mild to hot and nights are mild. Mists often occur during summer. Winter days are generally mild to warm, although temperatures frequently fall to below freezing at night.

96 MEIKLES MOUNT

Location: Western Swaziland; south of Mbabane, bordering Mlilwane Wildlife Sanctuary.
Access: From Mbabane take the Mhlambanyati road. The Meikles Mount turn-off is 18 km from Mbabane on the left-hand side.
Accommodation: 7 2- to 6-bed equipped and self-contained thatched cottages (rates on application).
Other facilities: Walking trails; horse-riding; fishing; excellent birdwatching; swimming pool; a variety of other sporting facilities; a small shop.
Open: Throughout the year.
Opening time: Sunrise to sunset.
For further information: Meikles Mount, P.O. Box 13, Mhlambanyati, Swaziland. Tel: (09268) 7-4110.

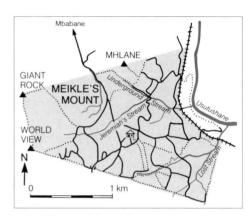

Covering more than 300 ha, Meikles Mount is run as a commercial timber farm, although there are considerable areas of natural vegetation which are dominated by grassland interspersed with pockets of indigenous forest. Water provided by springs, streams and the Usutushane River – which forms the estate's western boundary with Mlilwane – is abundant. To date more than 120 bird species have been recorded, and various game species such as common duiker, reedbuck, kudu, monkeys and warthog may be seen on the farm.

97 MKHAYA NATURE RESERVE

Location: South-central Swaziland; south-east of Manzini.
Access: From Mbabane travel along the main tarred road to Manzini; 6 km beyond the town take the right fork and continue on the tarred road to Phuzumoya via Siphofaneni; immediately after crossing the bridge over the railway at Phuzumoya turn left and follow the farm road, crossing the bed of the Mzimpofu River (do not stop, as the bed is sandy; if the river is flowing do not attempt to cross it – arrangements will be made to fetch you); drive through a gate and follow the railway line, then turn through the first gate on the left and continue to Mkhaya, which is some 3 km from the railway bridge at Phuzumoya. Entry to the reserve is by prior arrangement only.
Accommodation: Spacious luxury canvas tents, each with a pit toilet and running water; 'honeymoon tent', isolated from others; central summer house and kitchen (E190 per person per day, all-inclusive of meals and game-

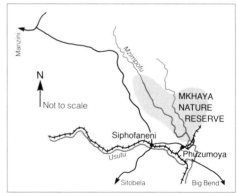

viewing drives in open Landrovers; half price for children under 14).
Other facilities: Tours, including a main meal, 2 jeep drives and refreshments, for day visitors by prior arrangement (E80 per person); guided vehicle tours; walking trails; rafting (halfday to

3 days) on the Great Usutu River (E80 in addition to the daily rate for visitors staying at Mkhaya; E96 for day visitors, including lunch and refreshments on the river).
Open: Throughout the year.
Opening time: By arrangement.

Beware: Most barbed wire fences are electrified; malaria.
For further information: Mkhaya Nature Reserve, P.O. Box 33, Mbabane, Swaziland. Tel: (09268) 6-1037 or 3-4371 or 6-1591/2/3. Fax: (09268) 6-1594.

One of Swaziland's newest reserves and officially recognized as its refuge for endangered species, Mkhaya offers a real 'into Africa' experience. It covers 6 200 ha and can be divided into two principal vegetation types: broadleaf sandveld savanna in the north, and acacia savannah in the south. Riverine woodland is encountered along the main drainage lines.

A major effort has been made to re-introduce game animals that once occurred naturally in Swaziland, such as elephant, hippopotamus, black and white rhinoceros, Burchell's zebra, waterbuck, kudu, nyala, reedbuck and blue wildebeest plus tsessebe, roan antelope, eland, giraffe, red duiker, crocodile and ostrich, as well as many smaller species. Most of the carnivores in the reserve are the smaller ones, such as black-backed and side-striped jackal, although spotted hyena are also present.

The birdlife is abundant, and as many as 100 species have been recorded on a weekend visit. Raptors are well represented and include bateleur, martial, tawny, Wahlberg's, booted and crowned eagles, and four vulture species.

Summer days are hot (up to 40°C), with most of the annual average rainfall of 500 mm falling during this season; winter days are warm, but nights can be cold.

98   MLAWULA NATURE RESERVE

Location: North-eastern Swaziland; east of Hlane Nature Reserve, bordering Mozambique.
Access: From Mbabane take the tar road to Manzini and travel approximately 6 km further before taking the left fork towards Mhlume and Tshaneni; beyond Hlane watch out for signposts to the reserve. From Komatipoort take the R571, crossing into Swaziland at the Mananga border post; 5 km beyond the border turn left to Mhlume and continue past the town for approximately 30 km, then turn right and watch out for signposts. Soon after crossing the Mbuluzi River, turn left and follow the road for approximately 5 km to the reserve entrance.
Accommodation: 2 camping sites with ablution facilities and thatched shelters (E9 per person per night, plus a small entrance fee). A tented camp offers 3 2-bed tents (bedding supplied).
Other facilities: Accompanied or self-guided walks (guide book available); Landrover tours on request; game-viewing drives on tracks (the condition of these varies); canoeing on river; fishing (a permit is necessary); vulture 'restaurant' and viewing hide. There are no shops or fuel.
Open: Throughout the year, but movement is limited during the rainy season.
Opening time: Sunrise to sunset.
Beware: Malaria; bilharzia; crocodiles and hippopotamus in the river.
For further information: The Senior Warden,

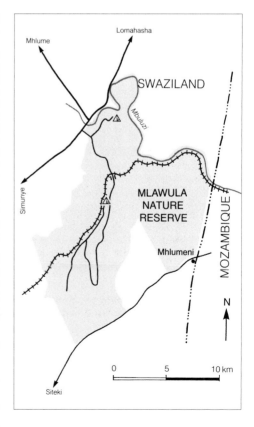

Mlawula Nature Reserve, P.O. Box 312, Simunye, Swaziland. Tel: (09268) 3-8885. Alternatively, the Swaziland National Trust Commission, P.O. Box 100, Lobamba, Swaziland.

The Mlawula Nature Reserve comprises four conservation areas (Mlawula, Ndindza, Mbuluzi and the geographically separate Simunye) that are managed as a unit and together cover approximately 18 400 ha. Archaeologists have made several interesting finds in the area over the years, including the oldest known record of modern man (dating back 110 000 years), as well as many Early and Middle Stone Age remains.

The reserve ranges in altitude from the Lebombo Mountains (highest point 573 m) to the Lowveld and incorporates a wide variety of vegetation types, including dry thorn savannah, open grassland with characteristic 'islands' of bushes, and moist woodland. The reserve protects a large number of endemic plant species, including such rarities as the Umbuluzi cycad.

The mammal fauna of the area is rich and varied, and the visitor may see hippopotamus, Burchell's zebra, blue wildebeest, eland, waterbuck, mountain reedbuck, Sharpe's grysbok, red duiker, leopard and spotted hyena. Samango monkeys live in the more densely wooded areas. The varied vegetation, and the dry and moist woodland in particular, have encouraged a diversity of birdlife and more than 300 species, including many rarities, have been recorded to date.

Summers are hot and humid, and winters mild to warm, although winter nights are often cold.

99 MLILWANE WILDLIFE SANCTUARY

Location: West-central Swaziland; south of Mbabane.

Access: From Mbabane take the main road south towards Manzini, turning right after about 10 km at the signpost to Mlilwane. The internal gravel roads are generally in good condition. The rest camp lies 24 km from Mbabane and 27 km from Manzini. An entrance fee is charged.

Accommodation: Mlilwane offers thatched huts (with or without bath; bedding and towels supplied), grass beehive huts and a log cabin (with or without bedding). Rates per person per night range from E20 to E45. There is also a rustic camping site with ablution facilities (E10 per adult per night). A discount is given on bookings for mid-week visits.

Other facilities: A network of game-viewing roads; self-guided and guided walking trails; organised open Landrover drives, including night drives; guided horse-trails; educational courses for groups; a licensed restaurant; campfire catering can be arranged; picnic sites with fireplaces; a swimming pool; a shop well stocked with provisions which include fresh meat and alcohol.

Open: Throughout the year.

Opening time: Sunrise to sunset. Visitors staying at the camp may leave and enter the reserve after sunset.

Speed limit: 25 km/h.

Beware: Malaria; crocodiles.

For further information: Mlilwane Wildlife Sanctuary, P.O. Box 33, Mbabane, Swaziland. Tel: (09268) 6-1037 or 6-1591/2/3. Fax: (09268) 6-1594.

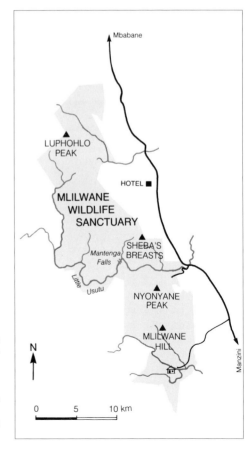

Mlilwane Wildlife Sanctuary, the first area of land in Swaziland to be set aside for conservation purposes, was officially opened to the public in 1964. Before being proclaimed, the land was farmed on a commercial basis and was mined for tin, as several abandoned pits bear witness. Extensive areas of erosion resulting from these activities can still be seen, but efforts are being made to reclaim the land. Today Mlilwane plays an important role in environmental education.

Riverine and montane forest, broadleaf savannah, sour grassland and bushveld predominate in the 4 545-ha reserve. It has been restocked with a great variety of game species that once roamed freely throughout Swaziland, including white rhinoceros, giraffe, Burchell's zebra, buffalo, sable, blue wildebeest, eland, kudu, waterbuck, reedbuck and common duiker. Hippopotamus and crocodile frequent the rivers near the camp, and the presence of these and several of the larger mammals close to camp offers excellent opportunities for photography. The wide variety of vegetation types guarantees a productive visit for the birdwatcher, as bird species typical of both highveld and lowveld areas are represented.

In this summer-rainfall area the average annual rainfall exceeds 1 000 mm, most of which occurs between October and April. Summers are hot to mild, and winter days are generally mild, but temperatures can fall sharply at night.

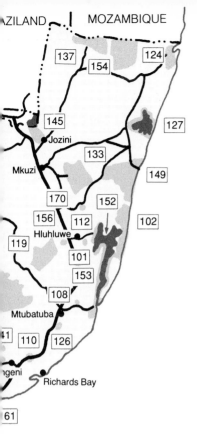

NATAL AND KWAZULU

100 Albert Falls Public Resort Nature Reserve
101 Bona Manzi Game Park
102 Cape Vidal State Forest
103 Chelmsford Public Resort Nature Reserve
104 Coleford Nature Reserve
105 Craigie Burn Public Resort Nature Reserve
106 Dlinza Forest Nature Reserve
107 Doreen Clark Nature Reserve
108 Dukuduku Indigenous Forest Area
109 Durban
110 Enseleni Nature Reserve
111 Entumeni Nature Reserve
112 False Bay Park
113 Ferncliffe Forest
114 Giant's Castle Game Reserve
115 Goedetrouw Public Resort Nature Reserve
116 Harold Johnson Nature Reserve
117 Hazelmere Public Resort Nature Reserve
118 Himeville Nature Reserve
119 Hluhluwe Game Reserve
120 Ilanda Wilds Nature Reserve
121 Itala Game Reserve
122 Kamberg Nature Reserve
123 Klipfontein Public Resort Nature Reserve
124 Kosi Bay Nature Reserve
125 Krantzkloof Nature Reserve
126 Lake Eteza Nature Reserve
127 Lake Sibaya
128 Loteni Nature Reserve
129 Mfuli Game Ranch
130 Mhlopeni Nature Reserve
131 Midmar Public Resort Nature Reserve
132 Mkhomazi and Mzimkulu Wilderness
    Areas; Mzimkulwana Nature Reserve
133 Mkuzi Game Reserve
134 Mlambonja and Mdedelelo Wilderness Areas
135 Moor Park Nature Reserve
136 Mount Currie Nature Reserve
137 Ndumo Game Reserve
138 New Germany Nature Reserve
139 North Park Nature Reserve
140 Ntendeka Wilderness Area
141 Nyala Game Ranch
142 Ocean View Game Park
143 Oribi Gorge Nature Reserve
144 Paradise Valley Nature Reserve
145 Pongolapoort Public Resort Nature
    Reserve
146 Queen Elizabeth Park Nature Reserve
147 Royal Natal National Park
148 Rugged Glen Nature Reserve
149 Sodwana Bay National Park
150 Spioenkop Public Resort Nature Reserve

N

50   100   150 km

151 Springside Nature Reserve
152 St Lucia Game Reserve
153 St Lucia Park
154 Tembe Elephant Reserve
155 The Swamp Nature Reserve
156 Ubizane Game Ranch
157 Umdoni Bird Sanctuary
158 Umfolozi Game Reserve
159 Umgeni Valley Nature Reserve
160 Umhlanga Lagoon Nature Reserve

161 Umlalazi Nature Reserve
162 Umtamvuna Nature Reserve
163 Uvongo Nature Reserve
164 Vergelegen Nature Reserve
165 Vernon Crookes Nature Reserve
166 Vryheid Nature Reserve
167 Wagendrift Public Resort Nature Reserve
168 Weenen Nature Reserve
169 Windy Ridge Game Park
170 Phinda Resource Reserve

Natal, the smallest of South Africa's provinces, makes up for its size by the diversity of its habitats, which range from subtropical forest to mountains some 3 000 m above sea-level. From Transkei in the south to Mozambique in the north, the warm waters of the Indian Ocean lap the highly popular eastern coastline. The province has an admirable conservation record and the principal controlling body, the Natal Parks Board (see page 365), manages 75 areas. Incorporated within Natal are a number of scattered segments of land which together form KwaZulu. The KwaZulu authorities are making an important contribution to the protection of the environment, and the Bureau of Natural Resources (see page 365) controls an increasing number of conservation areas.

The two major recreation and conservation regions in Natal are the Drakensberg and the St Lucia complex, both of which are becoming increasingly popular with tourists. The Drakensberg, in the west of Natal, is the highest and most spectacular range of mountains in South Africa and forms the border between Natal and Lesotho. The highest point is Thaba Ntlenyana, which rises to 3 482 m, but a number of other peaks exceed 3 000 m. The great sandstone base of the mountains has been eroded into numerous caves and overhangs, once home to Bushmen but now used by hikers. This is a very popular holiday area, especially with mountaineers, hikers and trout fishermen. Recreational demands must be balanced against the fragility of the environment, and this is by and large achieved in the Mkhomazi, Mzimkulu, Mlambonja and Mdedelelo wilderness areas, the Rugged Glen, Giant's Castle, Mzimkulwana, Kamberg, Loteni and Vergelegen nature reserves, and the Royal Natal National Park. A considerable part of the Drakensberg region is occupied by state forest land, control of most of which has recently been transferred to the Natal Parks Board. These areas are open to the general public, but permits are required. The main entry points are at Cathedral Peak, Monk's Cowl, Highmoor, Mkhomazi, Cobham and Garden Castle, and there are public camping sites at Cathedral Peak and Monk's Cowl, which can be reached by car. The Drakensberg is a summer-rainfall area and has a pleasant summer climate, although thunderstorms are common.

Winters are cold, and snow and rapidly blanketing cloud often make conditions hazardous for hikers, who should always carry proper equipment and be prepared for any eventuality. Thefts from hikers on the upper altitudes of Drakensberg reserves on the Lesotho border appear to be on the increase, therefore be alert and hike in groups.

The St Lucia complex is made up of a number of reserves linked to Lake St Lucia. This body of water is, in fact, not a lake but a 60-km long estuary, one of the most important coastal wetlands in southern Africa. The channel where the estuary opens into the sea is extremely narrow and it is this, together with the freshwater inflow from the Mkuzi, Mzinene, Hluhluwe, Mfolozi and Nyalazi rivers, that holds this rich environment in its precarious balance. The conservation areas linked to the St Lucia complex are St Lucia Game Reserve, St Lucia Park, False Bay Park, Cape Vidal State Forest (including Eastern Shores State Forest), Mapelane Nature Reserve (incorporating Mhlatuze State Forest), Sodwana Bay National Park and State Forest, and St Lucia and Maputaland marine reserves. Summers in this area are generally hot and humid; winters are mild, with cool nights.

Durban, the principal city in Natal, has an amazing number of small reserves and other conservation areas, despite its large population and ongoing development. Many of these areas have the MOSS (Metropolitan Open System) to thank for their existence. Within the Greater Durban area there are currently 13 reserves that have been proposed for development (see the map of Durban on page 110).

Although not proclaimed national parks or nature reserves, there are several areas in Natal which contain indigenous forest and its associated wildlife. These areas fall under the control of the Regional Director of the Natal Forest Region and the KwaZulu Bureau of Natural Resources, and although some are closed to the public, a few – such as Dukuduku, Weza and Cedara – allow limited access for walking and hiking; contact the Regional Director, Water Affairs and Forestry, Natal, for further details (see page 365).

At present there are a number of established nature reserves and natural areas in Natal and KwaZulu that are closed to the public, although some may become accessible in a year or two. Amatikulu Nature Reserve, on the coast between Tugela and Mtunzini, contains coastal forest and estuarine habitats which support a small number of game species; for further information contact the KwaZulu Bureau of Natural Resources. Assagay Nature Reserve, a small wetland area at the source of the Mhlatuzana River between Durban and Pietermaritzburg, should be open to the public within the next two years; for further information contact Assagay Health Committee, P.O. Box 196, Hillcrest 3650. The following reserves fall under the control of the Natal Parks Board: Blinkwater Nature Reserve, near Seven Oaks, protects one of the four most important breeding localities for South Africa's most endangered bird, the blue swallow; Karkloof Nature Reserve, 20 km north of Howick, covers 936 ha of indigenous forest and open grassland; Richards Bay Nature Reserve protects 1 200 ha of land adjacent to the large port and town of Richards Bay; Tugela Drift Nature Reserve, 6 km north of Colenso, covers 41 ha and offers excellent views of the Tugela River and the Anglo-Boer War battlefields at Colenso; Umgeni Vlei Nature Reserve, in the lower Drakensberg foothills southwest of Mooi River, is an important area encompassing the headwaters of the Mgeni River and providing breeding habitat for several pairs of wattled cranes; Umvoti Vlei Nature Reserve, 11 km from Greytown, covers 267 ha of open water, mixed swamp and reed beds, all of which provide ideal conditions for waterfowl.

Accommodation in Natal's reserves is of a high standard, particularly in those controlled by the Natal Parks Board. Bungalows have a lounge/dining room and bathroom; crockery, cutlery, a refrigerator and linen are provided and food is prepared by a cook. Bush camps are equipped with linen, cutlery, crockery, cooking utensils, a small refrigerator and stove. Cabins have a lounge/dining room, bathroom and fully equipped kitchenette; linen is provided. Chalets have a lounge/dining room, bathroom and fully equipped kitchenette; linen is provided. Cottages have a lounge/dining room, bathroom and fully equipped kitchen; linen is provided and a cook is in attendance. Dormitory cabins have a bedroom with four double bunks and a bathroom and fully equipped kitchenette. Leisure homes have a lounge, bathroom and fully equipped kitchen. Lodges are equipped on a more luxurious scale, and have a lounge/dining room, bathroom and fully equipped kitchen; linen is provided and a cook is in attendance. Log cabins have a bathroom and fully equipped kitchen; linen is provided. Rondavels have a bathroom and fully equipped kitchenette. Rest huts are provided with cutlery, crockery, a refrigerator and linen; communal bathrooms are used, and food is prepared by cooks in a central kitchen. Rustic cabins are equipped with cutlery, crockery, a hot plate and a refrigerator; communal bathrooms are used; linen is provided. Rustic cottages have fully equipped kitchens, and rustic huts share basic ablution facilities and are provided with crockery, cutlery, cooking utensils, but meals are prepared over open fires. Trail/mountain huts are supplied with a gas cooker, cold water and toilet. Caves have basic toilet facilities only. Rates for the different types of accommodation range from R4 to R120 per person per night.

All bookings and enquiries should be directed to the Reservations Officer, Natal Parks Board (see page 365). Bookings for camping sites should be made with the officer-in-charge of each reserve; fees for camping normally range from R3 to R25 per person per night. A small entrance fee is charged for most reserves, usually R2,50 per adult and between R5 and R10 per vehicle.

Natal's climate is generally warm to hot and humid in summer, when the rain falls; winters are usually mild, although it becomes cool at night. Temperatures are more extreme in the inland areas. Humidity is higher near the coast and, particularly in the north-eastern parts of the province, it can become uncomfortably hot and humid in summer.

100 ALBERT FALLS PUBLIC RESORT NATURE RESERVE

Location: Natal Midlands; north of Pietermaritzburg.

Access: From Pietermaritzburg take the R33 northwards towards Greytown for 20 km and turn left to Albert Falls. The reserve is 2 km from the turn-off and is clearly signposted.

Accommodation: 15 2-bed rondavels; 3 6-bed and 10 5-bed chalets. There is a camping site with 50 stands and a caravan site with 23 stands; both have ablution facilities.

Other facilities: Picnic sites; sailing and water-skiing permitted; fishing; tennis; squash; a swimming pool; game-viewing; walking. No pets are allowed.

Open: Throughout the year.

Opening time: October to March – 05h00 to 19h00; April to September – 06h00 to 18h00.

Beware: Bilharzia.

For further information: The Natal Parks Board (see page 365). (Camping site) The Officer-in-charge, Albert Falls Public Resort, P.O. Box 31, Cramond 3420. Tel: (03393) 202/3.

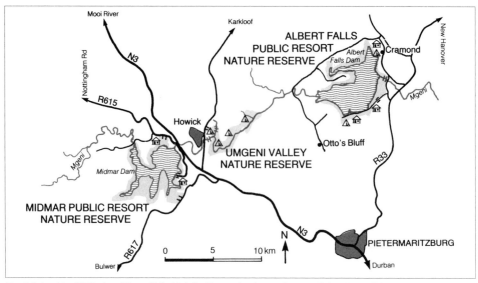

Established in 1975, the Albert Falls Public Resort is situated around the dam of the same name – the dam covers 2 274 ha and the land 816 ha. The adjoining nature reserve protects such species as Burchell's zebra, blesbok, impala, hartebeest, oribi and reedbuck. The area has a generally mild climate, but winters can be cold, particularly at night.

101 | BONA MANZI GAME PARK

Location: North-eastern Zululand; between Hluhluwe Game Reserve and Lake St Lucia, south of Hluhluwe village.

Access: Follow the N2 (main road from Durban) northwards from Mtubatuba to the Hluhluwe village turn-off. Turn right here to the village and at the 'T'-junction turn right and drive for 8 km to the signposted left turn-off to Bona Manzi. Book in advance.

Accommodation: Treehouses, equipped with bedding, kitchen requirements, gas cooker and coolbox. All treehouses have their own ablution facilities (hot and cold water). Self-catering only (take your own food and drink). There is also a game lodge and bush camp (contact the authority).

Other facilities: Game-viewing roads and tracks (walking is encouraged); day and night drives in a Landrover offered; swimming pool; deep freeze at office; firewood.

Open: Throughout the year.

Beware: Malaria.

Opening time: 24 hours (office hours – 09h00 to 17h00).

For further information: Bona Manzi Game Park, P.O. Box 48, Hluhluwe 3960. Tel: 03562, ask for 3530.

Bona Manzi is situated just to the west of Lake St Lucia, with vegetation typical of the area. Game species present include blue wildebeest, Burchell's zebra, nyala, impala, kudu, waterbuck and bushbuck. This is an interesting area for the birdwatcher and a checklist is available (also for mammals and trees). Summers are hot and humid.

CAPE VIDAL STATE FOREST See map St Lucia Park

Location: Coastal Zululand; north-east of Mtubatuba.
Access: From Mtubatuba follow the R620 for 25 km to St Lucia Estuary, then continue northwards on the gravel road past the Crocodile Centre. Once through the gate into the Eastern Shores State Forest, continue for about 30 km to the Cape Vidal reserve.
Accommodation: 15 5-bed and 6 8-bed log cabins; 1 8-bed bush camp; 5 angler cabins (1 8-bed, 1 13-bed, 1 20-bed, 2 12-bed); Mount Mabor, the overnight stop for the Mkizi trail,
sleeps 8 people. There is a camping and caravan site with 50 stands, and ablution facilities.
Other facilities: Fishing; snorkelling; guided 5-day trails from Cape Vidal; the Mkizi trail passes through the Eastern Shores State Forest.
Open: Throughout the year.
Opening time: Sunrise to sunset.
Beware: Malaria.
For further information: The Natal Parks Board (see page 365). (Camping site) The Officer-in-charge, Cape Vidal, Private Bag, St Lucia Estuary 3936. Tel: (035) 590-1404.

Although the Cape Vidal resort has been controlled by the Natal Parks Board for several years, the board has only recently taken over the state forest to the north, which covers the north-eastern section of Lake St Lucia. This 11 313-ha area comprises a continuous belt of sand-dune forest, indigenous forest clumps and open grassland. This is not a major game-viewing area, but a wide variety of bird and game species can be seen, and black rhino, buffalo, kudu and waterbuck have been introduced.

The Eastern Shores State Forest is a narrow, 13 873-ha strip lying between the lake and the Indian Ocean. Apart from commercial softwood plantations, the reserve consists of a band of sand-dune forest and extensive open grassland. Populations of side-striped jackal inhabit the latter area, and brown hyena have been re-introduced into the Cape Vidal State Forest area. Other game species occur naturally or have been re-introduced, and this and adjoining areas have the highest density of reedbuck in Africa, comprising some 6 000 to 7 000 head. The Mkizi self-guided trail provides the more energetic visitor with an excellent opportunity for birdwatching, seeing the game animals and wonderful views of the lake, the oceans and the pans.

CATHEDRAL PEAK STATE FOREST
See MLAMBONJA AND MDEDELELO WILDERNESS AREAS

CHELMSFORD PUBLIC RESORT NATURE RESERVE

Location: North-western Natal; south-west of Newcastle.
Access: From Newcastle take the R23 southwards; after 23 km, turn right at the signpost to Chelmsford Dam and follow further signposts to the resort for about 7 km .
Accommodation: *Leokop:* 8 5-bed chalets; *Richgate Park:* 4 5-bed chalets. 3 camping sites (Leokop has electrical points); ablution facilities.
Other facilities: Boating is allowed; fishing; game-viewing; games room.
Open: Throughout the year.
Opening time: 24 hours.
For further information: The Natal Parks Board (see page 365). (Camping site) Officer-in-charge, Chelmsford Public Resort, P.O. Box 3, Ballengeich 2942. Tel: (03431) 7-7205.

Chelmsford Dam, primarily a recreational area, attracts a variety of waterfowl species. The reserve is stocked with various game species.

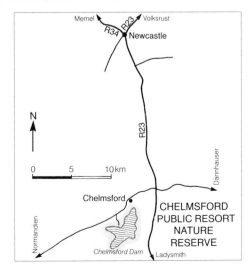

N

0   5   10 km

Memel   Volksrust
R34   Newcastle
R23
Chelmsford
Normandien
Chelmsford Dam   Ladysmith
Dannhauser

CHELMSFORD
PUBLIC RESORT
NATURE
RESERVE

104 COLEFORD NATURE RESERVE

Location: Foothills of the southern Drakensberg; south-west of Pietermaritzburg.

Access: From Pietermaritzburg take the R617 towards Underberg, take the Central Berg turn-off near Merrivale, passing through Bulwer; about 24 km beyond Bulwer turn left towards Coleford onto a graded gravel road; the reserve is 19 km from the turn-off. Alternatively, from Underberg turn off the R617 after 3 km onto the graded gravel road to the reserve.

Accommodation: 6 3-bed rest huts; 2 3-bed and 3 5-bed bungalows; 2 6-bed cottages, with communal lounge, kitchens and ablution facilities; 1 7-bed rustic cottage situated 5 km from the main camp. There are no facilities for camping or caravans.

Other facilities: Fishing for rainbow trout (a daily permit is available from the camp superintendent; fishing tackle can be hired); short walking trails; horses for hire; guided horse-trail through game area; tennis, croquet and deck quoits; game- and bird-viewing hide in the reserve; picnic sites for day visitors.

Open: Throughout the year.

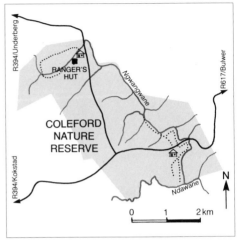

Opening time: April to September – 06h00 to 18h00; October to March – 05h00 to 19h00.

For further information: The Natal Parks Board (see page 365).

Covering 1 272 ha, Coleford Nature Reserve lies in the Underberg, South Africa's foremost trout fishing area, and is traversed by the Ngwangwana and Ndawana rivers which attract large numbers of anglers each year. Grassland predominates in the hilly game area, where black wildebeest, blesbok, oribi, reedbuck and other antelope can be seen.

105 CRAIGIE BURN PUBLIC RESORT NATURE RESERVE

Location: Natal Midlands; north of Pietermaritzburg.

Access: From Pietermaritzburg travel northwards on the N3 to Mooi River; turn eastwards onto the R622 to Greytown and continue for approximately 30 km. The reserve lies to the north of the road.

Accommodation: A small camping site (maximum 30 people).

Other facilities: Boating; fishing; picnic sites.

Open: Throughout the year.

Opening time: 24 hours.

For further information: The Camp Superintendent, Midmar Public Resort, Private Bag, Howick 3290. Tel: (0332) 30-2067/8/9.

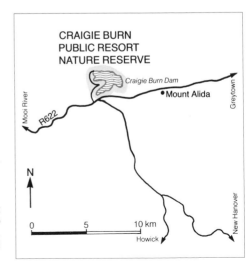

This is a small recreational resort covering about 330 ha on the banks of the Craigie Burn Dam. No specific area has been set aside for game animals, but birdwatchers will find a variety of waterbird species at the dam.

106 DLINZA FOREST NATURE RESERVE

Location: Zululand; in the town of Eshowe.
Access: In Eshowe take Kangella St and turn off onto either Natural Arch Dr. or Goatly Rd; both roads pass through the forest.
Accommodation: None. There are hotels and a caravan and camping site in Eshowe.
Other facilities: Footpaths; 6 picnic sites; 2 self-guided trails.
Open: Throughout the year.
Opening time: 07h00 to 17h00.
For further information: The Natal Parks Board (see page 365).

This 200-ha patch of indigenous forest is unusual in that it is situated in a large town. A number of tracks running through it are believed to have been cut by British soldiers who occupied the area shortly after the Anglo-Zulu War in 1879. Apart from a rich bird- and insect-life, several mammal species occur naturally, including bushbuck, red and blue duiker, vervet monkey and bushpig.

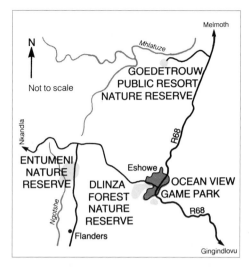

107 DOREEN CLARK NATURE RESERVE

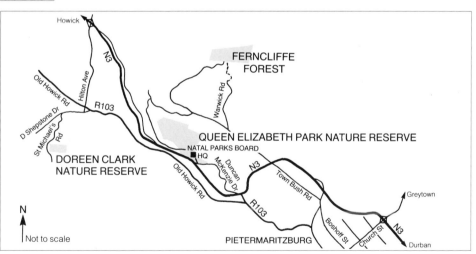

Location: Natal Midlands; just outside Pietermaritzburg.
Access: From Pietermaritzburg take the N3 towards Howick for about 10 km and turn left into Hilton Ave; at the T-junction turn right into David Shepstone Dr., then left into St Michael's Rd. The reserve lies to the left of this road.
Accommodation: None.
Other facilities: A picnic site; a short trail.
Open: Throughout the year.
For further information: The Natal Parks Board (see page 365).

The smallest of the Natal Parks Board nature reserves, this 5-ha patch of indigenous forest is of both botanical and ornithological interest.

DUKUDUKU INDIGENOUS FOREST AREA

Location: Zululand; north of Empangeni.
Access: From Empangeni follow the N2 north-wards for 56 km and turn right onto the R620 towards St Lucia, which goes through the forest.
Accommodation: None. Mtubatuba and St Lucia have a variety of accommodation.
Other facilities: A picnic site; 14 km of trails.
Open: Throughout the year.
Opening time: Sunrise to sunset.
For further information: Regional Director, Department of Water Affairs and Forestry: Zululand Forest Region, Private Bag X506, Eshowe 3815. Tel: (0354) 4-2087. Fax: (0354) 4-1892.

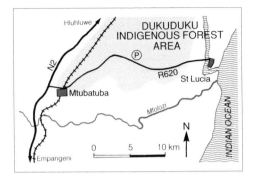

The Dukuduku Indigenous Forest Area forms part of the largest coastal lowland forest in Natal and is one of the few such forests that is ecologically self-sufficient. It borders Lake St Lucia to the east. Apart from the many plant species that are protected, there are a great number of insects, in particular butterflies, as well as a diversity of birds and smaller mammal species. Red duiker are regularly seen at the picnic site. The reserve is also one of only a handful of localities south of the Limpopo River where the Gaboon adder occurs.

This is a subtropical area, with relatively high humidity and summer rainfall.

DURBAN

Beachwood Mangroves Nature Reserve

Access from Leo Boyd Highway, north of Umgeni River mouth. This 76-ha reserve protects a mangrove swamp within the city's bounds. The swamp's evergreen trees provide a specialised habitat for a unique fauna which includes the amphibious fish called mudskippers, crabs and molluscs. The reserve is open at all times and houses a conservation educational centre. Guided tours can be arranged through the Natal branch of The Wildlife Society (see page 365).

Bluff Nature Reserve

Tara Rd, Jacobs. Best known for its birdlife, this 45-ha reserve also provides protection for 11 small mammal species in a habitat of coastal forest, shrub and grassland. A small vlei fringed with bullrushes is situated within the reserve. There are birdwatching hides, and a network of footpaths runs through the reserve, which is open from sunrise to sunset throughout the year.

Burman Bush Nature Reserve

Burman Dr., Morningside. The main attractions of this 45-ha patch of well-preserved indigenous woodland are the trees, rich birdlife and troops of vervet monkeys which inhabit the area. The reserve is open between 07h00 and 16h30 throughout the year and offers picnic sites, short walks and an information centre.

Kenneth Stainbank Nature Reserve

Coedmore Rd, Yellowwood Park. The Kenneth Stainbank Nature Reserve protects a substantial block of coastal forest and grassland along the Little Mhlatuzana River, as well as a number of game species, including blue and red duiker, bushbuck, nyala, impala, reedbuck and Burchell's zebra. A variety of smaller mammals, reptiles and bird species also occurs. The reserve, open between 06h00 and 18h00 throughout the year, offers nature trails and picnic sites. A special self-guided trail and picnic site for handicapped visitors has also been established. Guided trails for school groups can be arranged through The Senior Ranger, Kenneth Stainbank Nature Reserve, P.O. Box 53048, Yellowwood Park 4011. Tel: (031) 42-1125.

Palmiet Nature Reserve

David Maclean Dr., Morningside. This 60-ha reserve lies in the rugged Palmiet River valley. The vegetation of dense riverine forest and mixed scrub and grassland protects more than 150 tree species, as well as 145 different species of bird. There are picnic sites with fireplaces and several short trails through the reserve, which is open from sunrise to sunset throughout the year. The Natal branch of the Wildlife Society (see page 365) runs regular guided trails.

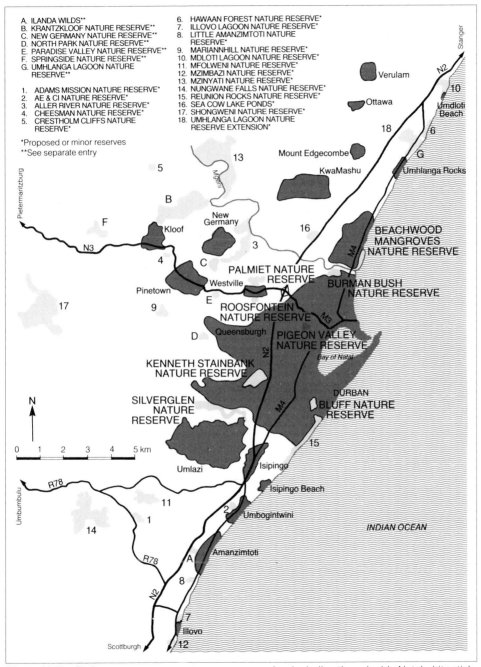

A. ILANDA WILDS**
B. KRANTZKLOOF NATURE RESERVE**
C. NEW GERMANY NATURE RESERVE**
D. NORTH PARK NATURE RESERVE**
E. PARADISE VALLEY NATURE RESERVE**
F. SPRINGSIDE NATURE RESERVE**
G. UMHLANGA LAGOON NATURE
   RESERVE**

1. ADAMS MISSION NATURE RESERVE*
2. AE & CI NATURE RESERVE*
3. ALLER RIVER NATURE RESERVE*
4. CHEESMAN NATURE RESERVE*
5. CRESTHOLM CLIFFS NATURE
   RESERVE**

6. HAWAAN FOREST NATURE RESERVE*
7. ILLOVO LAGOON NATURE RESERVE*
8. LITTLE AMANZIMTOTI NATURE
   RESERVE*
9. MARIANNHILL NATURE RESERVE*
10. MDLOTI LAGOON NATURE RESERVE*
11. MFOLWENI NATURE RESERVE*
12. MZIMBAZI NATURE RESERVE*
13. MZINYATI NATURE RESERVE*
14. NUNGWANE FALLS NATURE RESERVE*
15. REUNION ROCKS NATURE RESERVE*
16. SEA COW LAKE PONDS*
17. SHONGWENI NATURE RESERVE*
18. UMHLANGA LAGOON NATURE
   RESERVE EXTENSION*

*Proposed or minor reserves
**See separate entry

Pigeon Valley Park

King George V Avenue, Bulwer. Pigeon Valley Park is a nature reserve which was created to protect a remnant forest of indigenous tree species, including the valuable Natal white stinkwood. The rare spotted thrush is a notable winter visitor. The reserve is open from 07h00 to 16h30 throughout the year.

Roosfontein Nature Reserve

Spine Rd, Westville. This reserve extends along the Umbilo Valley and at present covers only 50 ha of mainly grassland vegetation which supports a diverse birdlife. There are, however, plans to extend it and to add trails and various other facilities. The reserve is open throughout the year: check with the Environmental Officer, Borough of Westville, P.O. Box 39, Westville 3630 for opening times.

Seaton Park

Lothian Rd, Park Hill. The 6-ha Seaton Park protects 3,5 ha of remnant coastal forest containing at least 89 tree species, which are labelled with their National Tree List numbers. To date 85 bird species have been spotted. The park is open throughout the year between 07h00 and 16h30.

Silverglen Nature Reserve

Clearwater Dam, Silverglen. Possibly the best pre-served piece of coastal bush and grassland in the Durban area, this 220-ha reserve protects several indigenous trees, including forest fever berry, velvet bushwillow and Natal camwood. A nursery has been established to combat an ongoing problem of illegal harvesting of plant parts by traditional healers. A total of 144 bird species has been recorded in the area. Facilities include picnic sites, trails and an information centre. The reserve is open from sunrise to sunset throughout the year.

Virginia Bush Nature Reserve

Kensington Dr., Virginia. This 38-ha area of re-generating coastal bush is fairly seriously infested by alien plants. Populations of bushbuck and blue duiker inhabit the reserve, as do a wide variety of bird species. There is a short trail and an information centre, and the reserve is open between 07h00 and 16h30 throughout the year.

EASTERN SHORES STATE FOREST

See CAPE VIDAL STATE FOREST

110 ENSELENI NATURE RESERVE

Location: Zululand; north-east of Empangeni.
Access: About 13 km from Empangeni the N2 enters the reserve.
Accommodation: None. Richard's Bay and Empangeni offer a variety of accommodation.
Other facilities: Picnic site; ablutions; a 5-km self-guided trail through the game area and a shorter trail through the nature reserve may be undertaken between 08h00 and 17h00; accompanied walks on request.
Open: Throughout the year.
Opening time: Sunrise to sunset.
Beware: Malaria.
For further information: The Natal Parks Board (see page 365).

Although only 293 ha in extent, this relatively small reserve conserves a variety of habitats. A 5-km Swamp Trail, part of which is on a boardwalk, passes among water myrtle trees, freshwater man-groves, papyrus beds and through a fig forest on the banks of the Nseleni River. The birdlife is extremely rich, and water-related species are particularly plentiful. A number of larger mammal species can be seen in the 143-ha game area, including nyala, impala, bushbuck, reedbuck, Burchell's zebra and blue wildebeest. Hippopotamus and crocodile occur in the Nseleni River. This is a subtropical region, and summers are hot and humid, while winters are mild.

111 ENTUMENI NATURE RESERVE See map Dlinza Forest Nature Reserve

Location: Zululand; north-west of Eshowe.
Access: From Eshowe take the tarred road towards Nkandla for 16 km. The reserve is signposted and lies 4 km to the west of the road.

Accommodation: None. There are hotels and a camping and caravan site in Eshowe.
Other facilities: Picnic site; pathways in the forest.

Open: Throughout the year.
Opening time: Sunrise to sunset.
For further information: The Natal Parks Board (see page 365).

Entumeni Nature Reserve is an island of mist-belt forest, surrounded by fields of sugar cane. It covers an area of 563 ha and provides a haven for birds such as starred robin, narina trogon and Knysna lourie. Mammals that live in this rich habitat are bushbuck, blue and red duiker and bushpig. Perhaps the most interesting aspect, however, is the abundance of plants and insect and other invertebrate species to be found in the forest.

112 FALSE BAY PARK See map St Lucia Park

Location: Coastal Zululand; north-east of Mtubatuba.
Access: From Mtubatuba follow the N2 northwards towards Mkuze for about 55 km; turn right to Hluhluwe village and continue eastwards through this settlement, following the signposts to the reserve.
Accommodation: 4 4-bed rustic huts on the Dugandlovu Trail. There is a camping and caravan site with 36 stands and ablution facilities.
Other facilities: Overnight Dugandlovu Trail; self-guided Mphophomeni Trail (7 or 10 km); shorter walks; fishing (bait available); boat hire; canoeing up to 50 m from shore; fuel, food and

alcohol are available at Hluhluwe village but curios, cool drinks and charcoal may be purchased in the park.
Open: Throughout the year. Military exercises are undertaken at certain times and restrictions are then placed on the use of trails and the lake; check with the officer-in-charge.
Opening time: Summer – 05h00 to 20h00; winter – 06h00 to 20h00.
Beware: Malaria; crocodiles.
For further information: The Natal Parks Board (see page 365). (Camping site) The Officer-in-charge, False Bay Park, P.O. Box 222, Hluhluwe 3960. Tel: 03562, ask for 2911.

Most of the 2 247-ha False Bay Park is covered by sand-dune forest, woodland and mixed thicket, while patches of open shoreline provide ideal camping and picnic sites. To date 160 bird species have been recorded here. This is also a good area for viewing red duiker, and the rare and shy suni may be seen in the sand-dune forest in the northern area of the park. Other mammal species which are likely to be spotted include bushpig, warthog, Burchell's zebra, waterbuck, bushbuck, reedbuck, nyala and common duiker.

113 FERNCLIFFE FOREST See map Doreen Clark Nature Reserve

Location: Natal Midlands; north-west of Pietermaritzburg.
Access: From Pietermaritzburg city centre take Town Bush Rd and continue past Grey's Hospital. At the D.V. Harris waterworks turn right and follow this road to the forest.
Accommodation: None. Pietermaritzburg has

a variety of accommodation.
Other facilities: Short trails.
Open: Throughout the year.
Opening time: Sunrise to sunset.
For further information: The Director of Parks, P.O. Box 31, Pietermaritzburg 3200. Tel: (0331) 42-3186.

Indigenous vegetation dominates this 250-ha mist-belt forest, which is inhabited by bushbuck, duiker and rock dassie. More than 100 bird species, including raptors, have been recorded, and other attractions include waterfalls and views over Pietermaritzburg.

114 GIANT'S CASTLE GAME RESERVE

Location: The central Drakensberg; west of Mooi River.

Access: 64 km from Mooi River take the road westwards to South Downs; continue past this

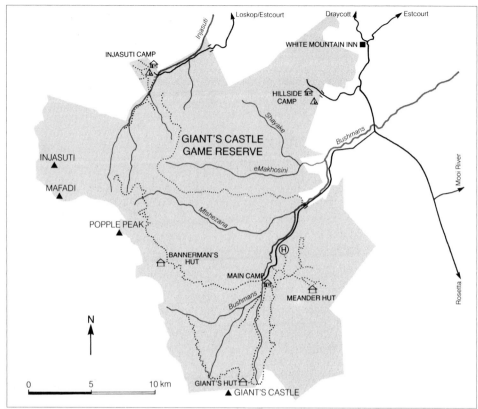

Loskop/Estcourt   Draycott   Estcourt

Injasuti

WHITE MOUNTAIN INN ■

INJASUTI CAMP

HILLSIDE CAMP

Shayake

GIANT'S CASTLE
GAME RESERVE

Bushmans

INJASUTI ▲

eMakhosini

Mooi River

MAFADI ▲

Mtshezana

POPPLE PEAK ▲

BANNERMAN'S HUT

MAIN CAMP

MEANDER HUT

Bushmans

Rosetta

N

0   5   10 km

GIANT'S HUT
▲ GIANT'S CASTLE

settlement and at the T-junction turn right towards Rockmount; at Rockmount turn left and follow this road to the reserve. Alternatively, 69 km from Estcourt follow the road westwards to Ntabamhlope and turn left to Rockmount; at Rockmount turn right and follow this road to the reserve. These access routes are clearly signposted. To reach Injasuti hutted camp, from Winterton follow the Cathkin Peak road for about 12 km, turn left at the Gorton Hall/Loskop Road crossroads, continue along this road for 10 km and, after crossing the Little Tugela River, turn right at the signpost to Injasuti. Alternatively, turn off the N3 at the Loskop interchange, follow the tarred Loskop road for 27 km, and turn left at the signpost to Injasuti; the camp lies 32 km from the turn-off on a gravel road. The condition of gravel access and internal roads may deteriorate during wet weather. Except to gain access to the camps, no driving is allowed within the reserve.

Accommodation: *Main camp:* 1 7-bed lodge, 4 6-bed cottages, 2 2-bed bungalows, 7 3-bed bungalows, 4 5-bed bungalows; communal lounge available. Situated well away from the main camp are mountain huts (1 4-bed and 2 8-bed) which can only be reached on foot. *Hillside camp:* 1 8-bed rustic hut and a camping site (60 people), with 2 ablution blocks. *Injasuti camp:* 17 6-bed cabins, 2 8-bed dormitory cabins and a camping site (80 people) with full ablution facilities; 2 8-bed caves.

Other facilities: Guided walking trails between September and May; fuel available at the Witteberg entrance (main camp); no shops within the reserve. *Main camp:* picnic sites; network of long and short trails (guided and self-guided); rock climbing (for the experienced only); stone birdwatching hide (booking is essential). *Hillside camp:* horse-riding; mounted trails (not for beginners); walking trails. *Injasuti camp:* walking trails; fishing allowed in Little Tugela River (angling permit and trout-fishing licence available from camp superintendent).

Open: Throughout the year.

Opening time: Sunrise to sunset.

Beware: Changeable weather conditions. Hikers going above the 2 300-m contour level must report to the warden before departure.

For further information: (Bookings for huts

52. The Dlinza Forest Nature Reserve provides sanctuary for the red duiker.

51. The rest camp of the Coleford Nature Reserve has comfortable bungalows and cottages.

53. Egyptian geese are attracted to the dam in the Chelmsford Nature Reserve.

54. The Albert Falls is the focal point of a popular resort and adjoining game area.

55. The Bluff Nature Reserve in Durban is popular with birdwatchers.

56. Fine examples of Bushman art in the caves of Giant's Castle.

57. A beautiful setting for a hiking hut in the Giant's Castle Game Reserve.

59. Nyala bulls at the Munywaneni waterhole in the Hluhluwe Game Reserve.

58. The Harold Johnson Nature Reserve lies on the south bank of the Tugela River.

60. Mhlangeni bush camp in Itala Game Reserve is set into the rocky hillside. The terrain here is mostly grassed hilltops and steep valleys, with some open savannah.

62. A leatherback turtle preparing to lay her eggs on the protected shore at Kosi Bay.

61 The recently expanded Kosi Bay Nature Reserve now incorporates areas once exploited by local fishermen.

63. Self-catering accommodation at the Kamberg Nature Reserve.

only at all 3 camps)The Natal Parks Board (see page 365). (Main Camp) The Camp Manager, Private Bag X7055, Estcourt 3310. Tel: (0363) 2-4718. (Hillside – camping site bookings only) The Officer-in-charge, Hillside, P.O. Box 288, Estcourt 3310. Tel: (0363) 2-4435. (Injasuti – camping site bookings only) The Camp Superintendent, Injasuti, Private Bag X7010, Estcourt 3310. Tel: 0020, ask for Loskop 1311. (Bird-watching hide) Tel: (0363) 2-4616.

Giant's Castle Game Reserve, named after the 3 314-m peak which towers above the reserve, was established in 1903, principally to protect the eland. Covering 34 638 ha, this mountainous reserve is a veritable paradise for those who enjoy walking and climbing in the mountains. A number of high peaks can be viewed from the reserve, among them the 3 409-m Injasuti Dome. Until the middle of the nineteenth century, when they were killed or driven from their stronghold, Bushmen occupied these mountains, sheltering in the numerous rock overhangs and caves. All that remains of their existence here are great numbers of rock paintings (in the main caves about an hour's walk from the main camp there are more than 500) and these alone make a visit to the area well worthwhile.

Most of the reserve consists of rolling grassed hills and ridges, high basaltic cliffs, wooded gorges, perennial streams and waterfalls, and a particularly fine patch of forest in the Injasuti area. Known mainly for its dramatic scenery, there are also many antelope species here, including eland, black wildebeest, blesbok, reedbuck, mountain reedbuck, grey rhebok, bushbuck, oribi, common duiker, red hartebeest and klipspringer. Black-backed jackal are fairly common, but are more frequently heard than seen. Rock dassies are frequently observed, and a small, hairy, short-tailed rodent called the ice rat lives among the boulders near the mountain summit. Approximately 140 bird species have been recorded.

115 GOEDETROUW PUBLIC RESORT NATURE RESERVE See map Dlinza Forest Nature Reserve

Location: Zululand; north of Eshowe.
Access: From Eshowe follow the R68 towards Melmoth for 13 km; turn right at the signpost to the reserve.
Accommodation: None.

Other facilities: Picnic sites; fishing.
Open: Throughout the year.
Opening time: Sunrise to sunset.
For further information: The Natal Parks Board (see page 365).

At present the Natal Parks Board controls a small section of Goedetrouw Dam and the surrounding area. The KwaZulu authorities are developing a much larger adjacent area. The vegetation consists mainly of acacia woodland and there is very little wildlife, although birds are attracted to the dam.

116 HAROLD JOHNSON NATURE RESERVE

Location: Zululand; north of Durban.
Access: From Durban follow the N2 northwards in the direction of Gingindlovu; 16 km north of Darnall take the signposted turn-off onto a good gravel road to the reserve (which is 100 km from Durban).
Accommodation: A camping site for about 50 people, with full ablution facilities.
Other facilities: Picnic sites overlooking the Tugela River; 2 self-guided trails of 1,8 and 7 km (these trails become muddy and slippery during the summer rainy season); historical sites.
Open: Throughout the year.
Opening time: Sunrise to sunset (day visitors may remain in the reserve after closing time by prior arrangement).
For further information: The Officer-in-charge, Harold Johnson Nature Reserve, P.O. Box 148, Darnall 4480. Tel: (0324) 6-1574.

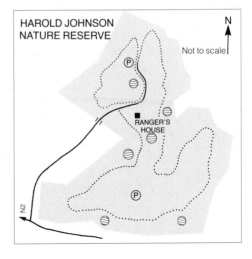

HAROLD JOHNSON NATURE RESERVE

N

Not to scale

RANGER'S HOUSE

N2

In the nineteenth century this area was the scene of conflicts between invading British soldiers and Zulu impis, and the Ultimatum Tree and Fort Pearson, both relics of this period, are incorporated in the reserve.

Most of the 104-ha reserve is situated on the steep southern bank of the Tugela River and it conserves a block of coastal forest, as well as a varied flora which includes a number of epiphytic orchids. The Remedies and Rituals Trail identifies a number of trees used by both white settlers and Zulus (a booklet is available at the office). Red, blue and common duiker, bushbuck, bushpig, Burchell's zebra and vervet monkey occur, and typical forest birds are present.

117 HAZELMERE PUBLIC RESORT NATURE RESERVE

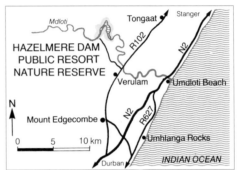

Location: North Coast; north of Durban.
Access: From Durban follow the N2 towards Tongaat; about 14 km north of Durban take the Mount Edgecombe/Umhlanga turn-off and bear left to Mount Edgecombe. Continue along this road in a north-westerly direction, ignoring turn-offs to Mount Edgecombe, Ottawa and Verulam; after passing under an arched bridge take the first left turn and follow signposts to Hazelmere Dam. The reserve is 10 km further on.
Accommodation: Camping site with ablution facilities and plug points.
Other facilities: Picnic sites; a variety of water-sports; swimming; walks; fishing (with licence).
Open: Throughout the year.
Opening time: Sunrise to sunset.
For further information: The Natal Parks Board (see page 365). (Camping site) Officer-in-charge, P.O. Box 1013, Verulam 4340. Tel: (0322) 33-2315.

This 304-ha reserve is open to the public, although it has not yet been proclaimed. The adjoining recreational resort is popular, and is zoned for a number of different activities.

118 HIMEVILLE NATURE RESERVE

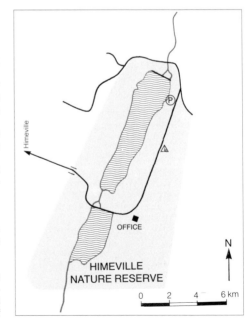

Location: Southern Drakensberg foothills; north-east of Underberg.
Access: From Underberg follow the R617 for 5 km northwards to Himeville. The reserve lies just to the north-east of Himeville village and is clearly signposted.
Accommodation: A camping and caravan site for 52 people; has ablution facilities. There is a hotel in Himeville.
Other facilities: Rowing boats for hire; trout fishing in the dams (permit and licences available at the reserve).
Open: Throughout the year.
Opening time: Sunrise to sunset.
For further information: The Officer-in-charge, Himeville Nature Reserve, P.O. Box 115, Himeville 4585. Tel: 033722, ask for 36.

The Himeville Nature Reserve, in the foothills of the Drakensberg, has a scenic setting and is a pleasant starting point for visiting other parts of this dramatic range. Two dams which take up much of the reserve's area make this a popular trout-fishing location. A variety of waterfowl is attracted to the dams, and a few antelope species, such as blesbok, may be seen.

119 HLUHLUWE GAME RESERVE

Location: Zululand; north-west of Mtubatuba.
Access: From Mtubatuba follow the N2 for about 50 km, turn left and continue to the Memorial Gate entrance of the reserve. Alternatively, follow the N2 for about 3 km, turn left onto the R618 towards Nongoma, and after 17 km turn right onto a graded gravel road; continue to the Gunjaneni Gate entrance of the reserve (during heavy rains this access may be closed). Roads in the reserve are graded gravel and usually in good condition. The reserve is 280 km from Durban.
Accommodation: 1 7-bed luxury lodge, 4 6-bed cottages and 20 2-bed rest huts.
Other facilities: Picnic sites at Hilltop camp, Maphumulo, Siwas ama Khosikazi and at the Gunjaneni Gate entrance; viewing sites; a game-viewing hide; an 84-km network of game-viewing drives, including 2 self-guided auto-trails with points of interest marked (pamphlet available from the office); Mbhombe self-guided walking trail (about 30 minutes) at Hilltop camp; guided walks from camp office; shop selling curios, books, film, cool drinks, charcoal and malaria tablets; fuel at Hilltop camp.

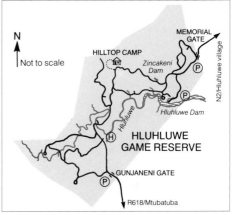

Open: Throughout the year.
Opening time: Summer – 05h00 to 19h00; winter – 06h00 to 18h00.
Speed limit: 40 km/h.
Beware: Malaria.
For further information: The Natal Parks Board (see page 365).

Proclaimed in 1897, the Hluhluwe Game Reserve is one of the oldest game reserves in Africa. It covers 23 067 ha and is linked to the nearby Umfolozi Game Reserve by a wide corridor of land which allows free movement of game between the two areas. Hluhluwe consists mainly of steep, wooded hills, grass-covered slopes and riverine woodland lining the Hluhluwe and the many other streams and rivers in the reserve.

An abundant water supply and dense bush make game-viewing difficult in summer, and the best time to visit is during the dry winter months (May to September). The roads in the north of the reserve and those between Seme and Gunjaneni Gate are usually productive, but the staff at Hillside camp can advise where visitors are most likely to see game. In summer the animals are more active in the early morning and late afternoon.

The reserve is a stronghold of the white rhinoceros, but a wide range of other mammal species also occur, including elephant, black rhinoceros, buffalo, giraffe, kudu, blue wildebeest, nyala, hippopotamus, impala, waterbuck, red duiker and Burchell's zebra. Samango monkeys are present in the forests and baboons range over most of the reserve. Lion, leopard, wild dog, cheetah and spotted hyena occur, but are difficult to spot. In all, 84 different mammals, as well as 425 bird species, have been recorded here.

Summers are hot, and it is at this time that most of the rain falls; mist and low cloud are fairly frequent. Winters are mild to cold, particularly at Hilltop camp.

120 ILANDA WILDS NATURE RESERVE

Location: South Coast; south of Durban.
Access: From Durban take the N2 southwards into Amanzimtoti; follow Umdoni Rd inland to its

T-junction with the Old South Coast Rd, turn left and follow this road to the Ilanda Wilds Nature Reserve.

Accommodation: None. There is a variety of accomodation in Amanzimtoti.

Other facilities: Picnic sites; short walking trails; trails guided by the Wildlife Society (see page 365).

Open: Throughout the year.

Opening time: Sunrise to sunset.

For further information: The Chief Health Inspector, Borough of Amanzimtoti, P.O. Box 26, Amanzimtoti 4126. Tel: (031) 903-2121. Fax: (031) 903-7382.

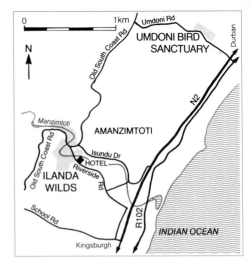

The Manzimtoti River flows through the 14-ha Ilanda Wilds Nature Reserve and provides a variety of rich habitats.

Coastal and riverine forest predominate, and more than 120 tree and shrub species have been recorded.

The area is well known for its excellent birdlife, with 161 resident species having been recorded in the reserve.

121 ITALA GAME RESERVE

Location: Northern Natal; north-east of Vryheid.

Access: From Vryheid take the R69 to Louwsburg, then follow the signposts to Itala.

Accommodation: 1 4-bed, 1 8-bed and 1 10-bed bush camp (fully equipped but take your own food, drink, torches and towels); camping site with cold water ablutions, flush toilets and a kitchen. *Ntshondwe Camp* (new, 200-bed camp): 2- to 5-bed thatched chalets (R55 per person per night), with lounge, kitchenette, bathroom and toilet (fully equipped; self-catering); 1 luxury lodge with 3 *en-suite* bedrooms,

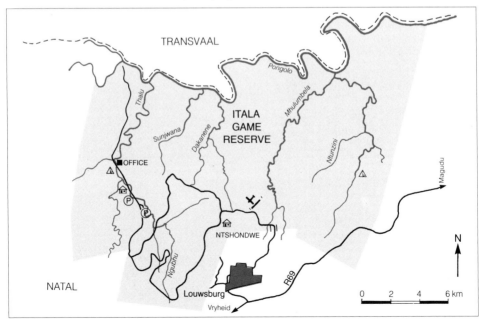

lounge, kitchen and private swimming pool (R120 per person per night).
Other facilities: 30-km gravel game-viewing road; 5-day wilderness trail, open from March to October; day walks with a game scout; picnic site. *Ntshondwe Camp:* restaurant; bar; take-away kiosk; curio shop; swimming pool; conference centre; mini supermarket.

Open: Throughout the year.
Opening time: Sunrise to sunset.
Beware: Malaria.
For further information: The Officer-in-charge, Itala Game Reserve, P.O. Box 42, Louwsburg 3150. Tel: (0388) 7-5239. (Bush camps) The Natal Parks Board (see page 365). (Ntshondwe Camp) Tel: (0388) 7-5190.

Proclaimed in 1972, this 30 000-ha game reserve lies in part of the old Pongola Game Reserve. The terrain consists mostly of grassed hilltops dotted with numerous aloes, steep valleys, and open woodland savannah, or bushveld. The northern boundary of the reserve lies on the south bank of the Pongolo River and several tributaries flow through the area.

There are 75 mammal species in Itala, and many of these, long extinct in the area, have been re-introduced. There are large populations of impala and reedbuck, and kudu, waterbuck, nyala, eland, tsessebe, blue wildebeest, giraffe, warthog, Burchell's zebra, black and white rhinoceros, and crocodile also inhabit the reserve. Rock dassies and klipspringer may be seen in the hilly parts. Cheetah and brown hyena have been re-introduced and leopard occur naturally. The great variety of habitats provide suitable environments for more than 400 bird species.

Summers are generally warm to hot. Winter days are generally mild, but nights can be very cold.

122 KAMBERG NATURE RESERVE

Location: Drakensberg foothills; north-west of Pietermaritzburg.
Access: From Pietermaritzburg follow the N3 towards Mooi River for 51 km and take the exit to Nottingham Road; from this village take the gravel road westwards, following the signposts to the reserve.
Accommodation: 1 6-bed cottage; 5 3-bed rest huts with a communal lounge; 10-bed farmhouse at 'Stillerust'.

Other facilities: 13 km of trout-fishing waters; fishing in dams throughout the year (permit available from the camp superintendent); short self-guided trails, including one designed to accommodate wheelchairs; visitors are allowed to tour the trout hatchery.
Open: Throughout the year.
Opening time: Sunrise to sunset.
For further information: The Natal Parks Board (see page 365).

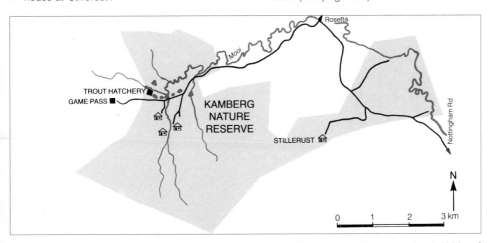

Kamberg Nature Reserve is set against the scenic backdrop of the Drakensberg, covering 2 232 ha of mostly grass-covered hill slopes, although yellowwoods and tree ferns may also be seen in the area. Common and mountain reedbuck, blesbok, black wildebeest, grey rhebok, eland, red hartebeest, common duiker and oribi occur in the reserve.

123 KLIPFONTEIN PUBLIC RESORT NATURE RESERVE

Location: Northern Natal; south of Vryheid.
Access: From Vryheid follow the R34 towards Melmoth for 6 km. The turn-off to the reserve is on the right and is clearly signposted.
Accommodation: There is a camping site with limited facilities.
Other facilities: Picnic sites; fishing; boating is allowed (boats should be registered with the Natal Parks Board before being launched).
Open: Throughout the year.
Opening time: Sunrise to sunset.
For further information: The Officer-in-charge, Klipfontein Public Resort Nature Reserve, P.O. Box 1774, Vryheid 3100. Tel: (0381) 4383.

This 4 562-ha reserve is situated around the Klipfontein Dam and is as yet undeveloped. For further information contact the officer-in-charge.

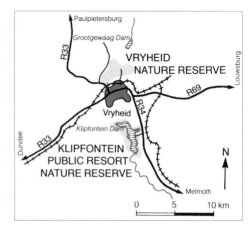

124 KOSI BAY NATURE RESERVE

Location: Extreme north-eastern Natal; north-east of Mkuze.
Access: From Mkuze take the R69 northwards in the direction of Candover; turn right to Jozini and continue past this village, following signposts towards Ndumo Game Reserve; keep bearing east, ignoring the turn-off to Ndumo, and continue to Kosi Bay. Much of this road is now tarred, although the last stretch is sandy and at present 4x4 vehicles are required (check with the authorities as the situation may have improved, and conditions vary according to the weather: access is often difficult during the summer rains). The distance from Mkuze is about 150 km.
Accommodation: At Nhlange Lake there are 1 2-bed, 1 5-bed and 1 6-bed fully equipped and staffed luxury lodges; a camping site with 15 stands and ablution facilities; 2 trail huts.
Other facilities: Trails accompanied by a game scout; guided 3-day hiking trail; turtle-viewing tours; fishing in certain areas. The nearest supplies are at KwaNgwanase. 'Bush' stores on the way to the reserve usually have fuel, but it is advisable to carry all you need.
Open: Throughout the year.
Opening time: Sunrise to sunset.
Beware: Malaria; Zambezi sharks and crocodiles; walk with caution on hippo paths.
For further information: The KwaZulu Bureau of Natural Resources (see page 365). (Camping site) The Officer-in-charge, Kosi Bay Nature

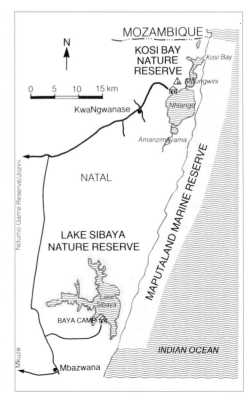

Reserve, P.O. Box 1, KwaNgwanase 3973. (Reservations) 367 Loop Street, Pietermaritz- burg 3201. Tel: (0331) 94-6698. Fax: (0331) 42-1948

Previously managed by the Natal Parks Board and now run by the KwaZulu authorities, this recently enlarged reserve encompasses 11 000 ha of the Kosi subtropical ecosystem. Kosi is not in fact a bay, but a series of four lakes (Nhlange, Mpungwini, Sifungwe and Amanzimnyama) separated from the Indian Ocean by a barrier of forested sand dunes and with only one outlet. Extensive mangrove swamps, fig forest and marshes provide suitable habitats for a fascinating array of creatures. A small population of hippopotamus inhabits the lake system, and although not common, crocodiles are present. Samango and vervet monkeys, red and blue duiker, bushbuck and bushpig occupy the forested areas. More than 250 bird species occur, including the endangered palmnut vulture. Kosi Bay is hot and humid in summer.

125 KRANTZKLOOF NATURE RESERVE

Location: Central Natal; north-west of Durban.
Access: From Durban take the N3 towards Pietermaritzburg and turn off at Kloof; follow the Kloof Falls road for 5 km to the reserve.
Accommodation: None.
Other facilities: 20 km of trails; guided walks on request; interpretive centre; picnic site.
Open: Throughout the year.
Opening time: Sunrise to sunset.
For further information: The Officer-in-charge, Krantzkloof Nature Reserve, P.O. Box 288, Kloof 3640. Tel: (031) 764-3515.

The Emolweni River and its steep forested banks are the main features of the 535-ha Krantzkloof Nature Reserve. A variety of rare plant and bird species are to be found in the area, including a number of cycads and the crowned eagle, which breeds here. Two species of duiker, blue and common, may be seen in the reserve, as well as bushbuck, bushpig and vervet monkey.

126 LAKE ETEZA NATURE RESERVE See regional map only

Location: Northern Natal; south of Mtubatuba.
Access: Lies on the eastern side of the N2 (from where it can be seen), between Kwa-Mbonambi and Mtubatuba; take the turn-off to Teza station.
Accommodation: None.
Other facilities: Short walking trails; floating birdwatching hide (maximum 10 people) reached by canoe.
Open: Throughout the year.
Opening time: Check with authority.
Beware: Malaria.
For further information: Natal Parks Board (see page 365).

The reserve covers 350 ha and contains a shallow pan with a papyrus swamp. Waterbirds are abundant and hippopotamus are present.

127 LAKE SIBAYA See map Kosi Bay Nature Reserve

Location: North-eastern Zululand; north-east of Mkuze.
Access: From Mkuze take the R69 towards Candover and after about 2 km turn right to Ubombo. Follow this road to Mbazwana, turn north and follow the signposts to Lake Sibaya.

Alternatively, a turn-off from the N2 north of Hluhluwe village leads to the reserve; this route is clearly signposted. Access roads are gravel and it is advisable to check their condition with the authorities.

Accommodation: *Baya Camp* has 3 4-bed and 4 2-bed rustic cabins. Bedding is provided, but visitors must bring all their own food, which is prepared in a central kitchen.

Other facilities: Walking trails; birdwatching hides; fishing is permitted; access to '9 Mile Beach'. There are no shops or fuel supplies in the reserve.

Open: Throughout the year.

Opening time: Sunrise to sunset.

Beware: Malaria; crocodiles; hippopotamus.

For further information: The KwaZulu Bureau of Natural Resources (see page 365). (Reservations) Central Reservations Office, Bureau of National Resources, 367 Loop Street, Pietermaritzburg 3201. Tel: (0331) 94-6698. Fax: (0331) 42-1948.

Lake Sibaya is South Africa's largest natural freshwater lake and covers between 60 and 70 km², depending on the level of water. Between the eastern shore and the sea is a range of sand dunes up to 165 m high, covered by a narrow belt of well-preserved forest.

Although Lake Sibaya has a rich mammal fauna, including such species as side-striped jackal, civet, reedbuck and hippopotamus, the area is best known for its varied birdlife, of which some 280 species have been recorded.

This summer-rainfall area is hot and humid during the summer months.

128 LOTENI NATURE RESERVE

Location: The Drakensberg; north-west of Pietermaritzburg.

Access: From Pietermaritzburg follow the N3 northwards to Howick; take the R103 to Nottingham Road and at this village follow the graded gravel R617 westwards for about 61 km to Lower Loteni; turn right and follow the signposts for 14 km to the entrance. The reserve can also be approached from the south via Underberg. Heavy rains occasionally make approach roads impassable.

Accommodation: 2 6-bed cottages, 12 3-bed bungalows and 1 10-bed rustic cottage. A camping site has 10 stands and ablution facilities.

Other facilities: Trout fishing (1 September to 30 April) in the Loteni River (a permit can be obtained from the camp superintendent); horse-riding; swimming; Settler's Homestead Museum; 12-km self-guided trail.

Open: Throughout the year.

Opening time: Sunrise to sunset.

For further information: The Natal Parks Board (see page 365). (Camping site) The Camp Superintendent, Loteni Nature Reserve,

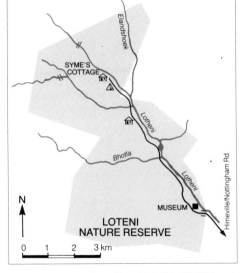

P.O. Box 14, Himeville 4585. Tel: 033722, ask for 1540 (during office hours).

Situated in the foothills of the Drakensberg, an area known as the Little Berg, the main attraction of this 3 984-ha conservation area is its dramatic scenic beauty. The grass-covered hill slopes and bush-covered valleys are home to common and mountain reedbuck, grey rhebok, eland, common duiker, bushbuck and oribi.

MAPELANE NATURE RESERVE See ST LUCIA COMPLEX

MAPUTALAND NATURE RESERVE See ST LUCIA COMPLEX

129 MFULI GAME RANCH

Location: Zululand; west of Empangeni.
Access: From Empangeni (just off the N2) take the R34 in the direction of Nkwalini and Melmoth for 29 km; the ranch is signposted. From Eshowe or Melmoth (R68), travel to Nkwalini and turn onto the R34 for 12,5 km.
Accommodation: 6-bed log cabins, air conditioned, serviced, self-catering, bedding supplied (rates vary between R45 and R90 per person per night depending on number of occupants; children: less R10 for each child under 12 years). Businessmen's and weekend specials available (out of season only); rates on application.
Other facilities: Self-guided and guided walks; day and night Landrover drives; swimming pool; restaurant.

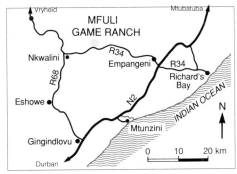

Open: Throughout the year.
For further information: Mfuli Game Ranch, P.O. Box 17, Nkwalini 3816. Tel: (03546) 620.

This is a small ranch (about 250 ha) set in very hilly terrain, with many indigenous trees, dominated by thornveld. Game species present are Burchell's zebra, blue wildebeest, nyala, impala and common duiker.

MHLATUZE STATE FOREST See ST LUCIA COMPLEX

130 MHLOPENI NATURE RESERVE

Location: Natal Midlands; north-west of Greytown.
Access: From Greytown take the R74 towards Muden; after 25 km turn left at the signpost to Mhlopeni, which is 6 km further on.
Accommodation: 4 bush camps (4 to 12 people), with cooking facilities, refrigerators, paraffin lamps and ablution facilities (R13 to R20 per person per night); camping site with ablution facilities (R5 per person per night).
Other facilities: Network of trails; guided walks; historical trails; game-viewing; information centre; swimming in natural pools.
Open: Throughout the year.
Opening time: Sunrise to sunset.

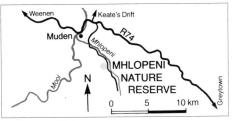

Beware: Ticks.
For further information: The Warden, Mhlopeni Nature Reserve, P.O. Box 386, Greytown 3500. Tel: (0334) 722.

Mhlopeni Nature Reserve lies in the Tugela River basin and takes its name 'peaceful valley of white rocks' from the white sandstone cliffs bordering the Mhlopeni River valley. Established in 1977 to rehabilitate land suffering from years of misuse, the vegetation consists mainly of acacia and grass savannah, with mixed scrub and aloes on the valley slopes. More than 230 bird species have been recorded, including black eagles which nest on the property. Rock dassies are particularly numerous and blesbok, impala, bushbuck, mountain reedbuck, common duiker and Burchell's zebra may be seen.

131 MIDMAR PUBLIC RESORT NATURE RESERVE See map Albert Falls Public Resort Nature Reserve

Location: Natal Midlands; north-west of Pietermaritzburg.

Access: From Pietermaritzburg take the N3 towards Howick for about 25 km; turn left onto the R617 and follow signposts to the Midmar Public Resort Nature Reserve.

Accommodation: 47 fully equipped 3-, 4-, 5- and 6-bed chalets and 16 4-bed rustic cabins. 4 camping and caravan sites with ablution blocks.

Other facilities: Game-viewing; launch tours; historical village museum; a restaurant; fishing; boating and watersports.

Open: Throughout the year.

Opening time: Daylight hours.

For further information: The Natal Parks Board (see page 365). (Camping sites) The Camp Superintendent, Midmar Public Resort, Private Bag, Howick 3290. Tel: (0332) 30-2067/8/9.

The Midmar Public Resort surrounds the 1 822-ha Midmar Dam, which is very popular with watersport enthusiasts. The adjacent nature reserve is stocked with black wildebeest, blesbok, springbok, red hartebeest, reedbuck, Burchell's zebra and oribi.

132 | MKHOMAZI & MZIMKULU WILDERNESS AREAS; MZIMKULWANA NATURE RESERVE

Location: The southern Drakensberg; north-west of Pietermaritzburg.

Access: From Pietermaritzburg follow the N3 northwards towards Howick for about 25 km; turn left onto the R617 at the Bulwer turn-off and continue to Himeville; about 3 km beyond Himeville turn left towards Sani Pass and continue to the bottom of the pass. Mzimkulu lies to the south of the road, Mzimkulwana to the north. For Mkhomazi continue on the R617 past the Sani Pass turn-off towards Lower Loteni, turning left to Vergelegen Nature Reserve; Mkhomazi Wilderness Area lies to the west of this reserve. During heavy rains approach roads are sometimes difficult to negotiate. No vehicles are allowed into any of the conserva-

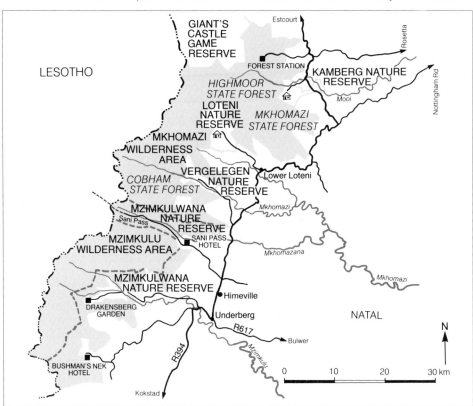

tion areas; permits are required (maximum 10 persons per party) and may be obtained from the entrance gates between 07h00 and 17h00 (22h00 on Fridays).

Accommodation: Designated caves for hikers; a hut at the top of Sani Pass has limited accommodation. There are many hotels and resorts in the Drakensberg foothills. Loteni and Vergelegen nature reserves have self-catering accommodation and facilities.

Other facilities: An extensive network of trails.

Open: Throughout the year.

Opening time: Sunrise to sunset.

For further information: (Mkhomazi) The Officer-in-charge Mkhomazi, P.O. Box 105, Nottingham Road 3280. Tel: (0333) 3-6444. (Mzimkulu and Mzimkulwana) The Officer-in-charge, Cobham, P.O. Box 116, Himeville 4585. Tel: 033722, ask for 1831. Fax: 033722, ask for fax 1831.

These three conservation areas form one continuous block covering approximately 105 000 ha and have been set aside to protect the water catchment area. Apart from the great cliffs and crags of the Drakensberg Escarpment, most of the slopes are covered by grassland and montane fynbos (heath), with pockets of indigenous forest and woodland in the gorges and along the many streams. Eland, mountain reedbuck, grey rhebok, oribi and klipspringer occur naturally throughout the area. The birdlife is not prolific, but there is a chance of seeing such rarities as the bearded vulture and bald ibis.

133 | MKUZI GAME RESERVE

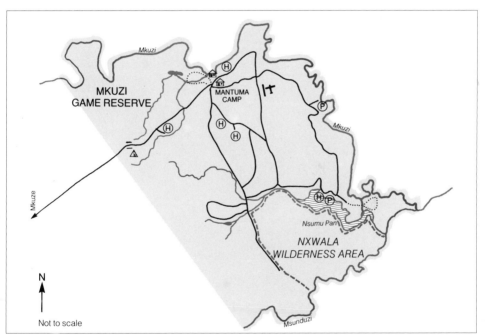

Location: North-eastern Natal; north-east of Mtubatuba.

Access: From Mtubatuba follow the N2 northwards, passing the turn-off to Hluhluwe village, and 35 km beyond this turn-off take the signposted exit; continue along this graded gravel road for 25 km, following signposts to the reserve. There are also signposts from Mkuze village.

Accommodation: An attractive camp 10 km from the entrance gate has 6 rest huts with separate ablution and kitchen blocks, 2 6/7-bed cottages, 5 4-bed bungalows, 2 duplex bungalows and 4 3-bed rustic huts (all self-catering). There is a camping and caravan site (maximum 60 persons) with ablution facilities at the entrance gate.

Other facilities: An 84-km network of game-viewing drives; a 57-km auto-trail; short accompanied walks; a 3-km self-guided or

accompanied walk through Mkuzi fig forest; picnic sites; game-viewing hides at waterholes; 2 bird observation platforms next to the Nsumu pan; shop selling curios, books and cool drinks; fuel at entrance gate. Game Lodge Reservations run private, guided walking trails in the Mkuzi Wilderness area (4 days; maximum 8 people).
Open: Throughout the year.
Opening time: Sunrise to sunset.

Speed limit: 40 km/h.
Beware: Malaria.
For further information: The Natal Parks Board (see page 365). (Camping site) The Camp Superintendent, Mkuzi Game Reserve, Private Bag X550, Mkuze 3965. Tel: 0020, ask for Mkuzi Game Reserve on the MRI line. (Wilderness walking trails) Game Lodge Reservations, P.O. Box 783968, Sandton 2146. Tel: (011) 883-4345/8. Fax: (011) 883-2556.

This 34 000-ha reserve was established in 1912 and, for its size, is one of the most rewarding conservation areas to visit in southern Africa. Vegetation consists of large tracts of open savannah woodland dotted with umbrella thorn and scented thorn trees, woodland thicket, riverine forest and an extensive forest of large sycamore fig trees. Nsumu Pan, with its fringing fever trees and expanses of water lilies, is home to hippopotamus and crocodile, and a fascinating array of waterbirds. Probably the greatest appeal of Mkuzi is the thatched game-viewing hides sited at waterholes and at Nsumu Pan. A few hours or a day spent at one of these hides can be very productive, and often more satisfying than continuously driving around. Game-viewing from the hides is best between June and October, and although animals may arrive to drink at any time, the most productive hours are usually from 09h00 to 12h00. For those who wish to drive, it is usually best to concentrate on the loop road, Nsumu Pan and the area between the entrance gate and the main camp. Both white and black rhinoceros occur, as do giraffe, hippopotamus, leopard, blue wildebeest, kudu, mountain reedbuck, bushbuck, waterbuck, eland, impala, nyala, reedbuck, red duiker, suni, Burchell's zebra and warthog. Baboons and vervet monkeys visit the waterholes and provide comic interludes. The birdlife is prolific, and 413 species have been recorded. Pelicans, fish eagles, purple gallinules, African jacanas, squacco herons and a variety of warblers are common, while the Nsumu Pan also attracts large numbers of ducks and geese. Recently a breeding colony of pink-backed pelicans moved here from False Bay on Lake St Lucia. Crested guineafowl are often encountered and a variety of other birds are attracted to the waterholes, including the woolly-necked stork and hamerkop.

Rain falls during summer and temperatures are warm to hot at this time. Winters are generally mild, but nights can be cold.

134 MLAMBONJA AND MDEDELELO WILDERNESS AREAS

Location: The Drakensberg; north-west of Pietermaritzburg.
Access: From Pietermaritzburg take the N3 towards Ladysmith; shortly after passing Frere turn left and follow the R615 to Winterton. To reach Mlambonja Wilderness Area from Winterton follow the gravel road westwards for 40 km to Cathedral Peak Hotel; to reach Mdedelelo Wilderness Area, take the tar road southwards to Cathkin Park and Champagne Castle Hotel. Permits are required. There are no internal roads.
Accommodation: Camping site with ablution

facilities; caves for hikers on the trail system; educational facility accommodating 50 people. There are numerous hotels, private accommodation and camping and caravan sites in the area.
Other facilities: Extensive trail system.
Open: Throughout the year.
Opening time: Sunrise to sunset.
Beware: Sudden changes in the weather.
For further information: The Natal Parks Board (see page 365). (Camping site) The Officer-in-charge, Cathedral Peak State Forest, Private Bag X1, Winterton 3340.

Mlambonja and Mdedelelo wilderness areas, formerly known as the Cathedral Peak Nature Reserve, together cover some 35 000 ha in the central part of the Drakensberg. This area is well known for its dramatic scenery, and is particularly favoured by mountaineers who respond to the challenge of such peaks as Cathedral and Cathkin, the Inner and Outer Horn, Champagne Castle and Monk's Cowl. Below the rock faces, the terrain consists mainly of steep, grass-covered slopes and deep kloofs with clumps of indigenous forest. Only trails traverse the wilderness areas, and hikers may see such naturally occurring species as grey rhebok, mountain reedbuck and klipspringer. The birdlife is not abundant but the rare bearded vulture does occur in the area.

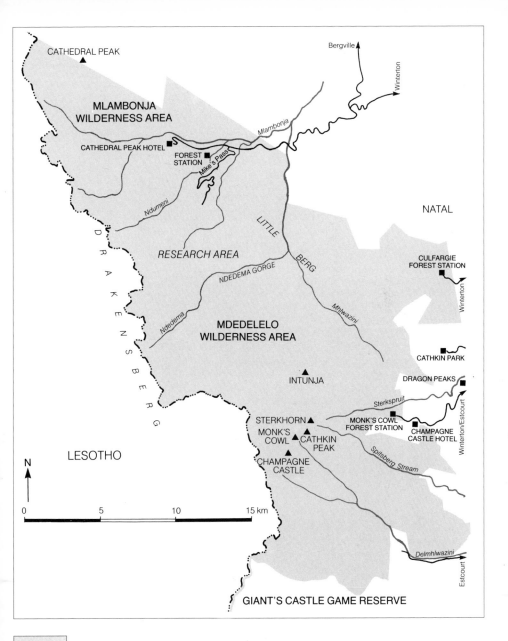

MOOR PARK NATURE RESERVE

Location: Natal Midlands; south-west of Est-court.
Access: From Estcourt take the Ntabamhlope road south-westwards towards Wagendrift

Dam for 12 km, following signposts.
Accommodation: None. The nearby Wagendrift Public Resort offers facilities for camping and caravans.

Other facilities: Picnic site; self-guided trail; an education centre for school groups; Wagendrift Dam.
Open: Throughout the year.
Opening time: Sunrise to sunset.
For further information: The Natal Parks Board (see page 365).

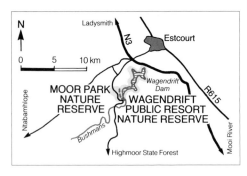

This reserve is situated at the head of the Wagendrift Dam and slopes down to the Bushmans River. Mixed acacia and grassland predominate and many game species have been introduced, including impala, black wildebeest and Burchell's zebra.

136 MOUNT CURRIE NATURE RESERVE

Location: Southern Drakensberg foothills; north of Kokstad.
Access: From Kokstad take the R394 towards Franklin; after about 500 m turn left onto the D623 graded gravel road to the reserve. The entrance gate lies about 5 km further on.
Accommodation: A camping and caravan site with ablution facilities. Kokstad has a hotel.
Other facilities: Boating; fishing (permit available at the gate); footpaths; game-viewing.
Open: Throughout the year.
Opening time: Sunrise to sunset.
For further information: The Officer-in-charge, Mount Currie Nature Reserve, P.O. Box 378, Kokstad 4700. Tel: (0372) 3844.

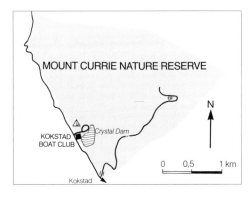

This reserve, established in 1981, covers 1 777 ha and consists mainly of grass-covered hillsides. The camping site is situated on the Crystal Dam and is a good starting point for those wishing to follow the many pathways. A short network of gravel roads south of the camping site runs through the lower-lying areas. Grey rhebok and mountain reedbuck are common, and several other mammal species may be seen, including springbok, blesbok, bushbuck, reedbuck, oribi and common duiker.

137 NDUMO GAME RESERVE

Location: North-eastern Natal; north-east of Mkuze.
Access: From Mkuze follow the N2 northwards towards Candover and after approximately 10 km take the exit to Jozini; drive through this settlement and continue northwards, following the signposts to Ndumo. The last 14-km stretch of this road is sandy and rough, but most vehicles should be able to negotiate it at low speed. From Jozini to Ndumo camp is just over 80 km.
Accommodation: 7 3-bed cottages with refrigerators, a cooking area with trained cooks and ablution facilities. There are no camping facilities. Advance booking is essential.

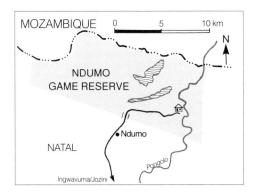

Other facilities: A network of game-viewing roads; open-vehicle tours can be booked; walks accompanied by game scouts (small fee levied; no children under 14 years); game-viewing hides. The nearest fuel and basic stores are 5 km away at Ndumo village.
Open: Throughout the year.
Opening time: Sunrise to sunset.

Speed limit: 40 km/h.
Beware: Malaria.
For further information: The KwaZulu Bureau of Natural Resources (see page 365). (Reservations) Central Reservations Office, Bureau of Natural Resources, 367 Loop Street, Pietermaritzburg 3201. Tel: (0331) 94-6698. Fax: (0331) 42-1948.

Despite its relatively small size (10 117 ha), the Ndumo Game Reserve is one of the most attractive reserves in southern Africa. Although there are no great herds of game to be seen, the fever tree and fig tree woodland, the many large pans and abundant birdlife (416 species have been recorded) more than make up for this. Several bird species are at the southernmost limit of their range here, making this a very rewarding area for birdwatchers. Look out for pink-throated twinspot, green-capped eremomela, yellow-spotted nicator, broad-billed roller, Pel's fishing owl, brown-headed parrot and southern banded snake eagle. The reserve is well watered and lies in the flood plain of the Pongolo River, attracting fish eagles and many other water-loving birds. Game species such as black and white rhinoceros, hippopotamus, impala, nyala, bushbuck, red duiker and suni occur, and crocodiles are common in the pans and river.

Summer months are usually hot, often with an uncomfortably high humidity level.

138 NEW GERMANY NATURE RESERVE

Location: Central Natal; west of Durban.
Access: From Durban take the N3 towards Pinetown; turn right into Old Main Rd and right again into Birdhurst Rd; at the T-junction turn left into Mountain Ridge Rd and right into Gilbert Dr. which will lead you to the reserve. Using the R613 from Durban, turn left into Stapleton Rd, right into the Old Main Rd, left into Birdhurst Rd; proceed as described above. Using the R628 from Durban, turn left into Blair Atholl and right into Methven Rd which leads into Mountain Ridge Rd; proceed as described above. From Pietermaritzburg take the N3 towards Durban; turn left into St John's Ave, right into Old Main Rd, left into Birdhurst Rd; proceed as described above. Using the R613 from Pietermaritzburg, turn left into St John's Ave and proceed as for the N3. The route to the reserve is clearly signposted.
Accommodation: A bush camp ideal for small conservation groups with 6 huts (maximum 12 persons) and ablution facilities.
Other facilities: Self-guided trails; information centre; game-viewing and birdwatching hide; picnic area with fireplaces; mini-conference facilities (booking is essential).
Open: Throughout the year.

Opening time: September to March – 06h00 to 18h00 (06h00 to 19h00 at weekends and public holidays); April to August – 07h00 to 17h00 (06h30 to 18h00 at weekends and public holidays). The reserve is closed on Mondays and Tuesdays.
For further information: The Superintendent Parks, Borough of New Germany, P.O. Box 2, New Germany 3620. Tel: (031) 705-4360. Fax: (031) 705-1499.

This 40-ha reserve, situated in the scenic hills of New Germany, has coastal grassland and indigenous forest vegetation, in which 122 tree species have been identified. Several indigenous plants have been planted in the gardens and picnic sites. A diversity of animals occurs in the reserve, including many small and nocturnal species. Regular sightings are made of Burchell's zebra, blue and common duiker, bushbuck, impala and vervet monkeys.

The birdlife is excellent: more than 150 species have been recorded.

139 NORTH PARK NATURE RESERVE See map Durban

Location: Central Natal; Queensburgh, west of Durban.
Access: From central Durban take the N2 southwards, turning right onto the M10 which joins the M5; turn off into Anderson Rd and continue to the reserve's entrance. The reserve lies 20 km from the city centre.

Accommodation: None.
Other facilities: Paths; picnic sites.
Open: Throughout the year.
Opening time: Sunrise to sunset.
For further information: The Officer-in-charge, North Park Nature Reserve, P.O. Box 288, Kloof 3640. Tel: (031) 764-3515.

North Park Nature Reserve protects a 53-ha block of coastal lowland forest along the Mhlatuzana River. Birdwatching is rewarding; bushbuck, blue and common duiker and banded mongoose may be seen.

140 NTENDEKA WILDERNESS AREA

Location: Zululand; east of Vryheid.
Access: From Vryheid take the R69 towards Louwsburg for about 30 km; bear right onto the R618 towards Nongoma and travel for 53 km. The reserve lies to the south of this road.
Accommodation: A camping site with ablution facilities (R7 to R15 per stand per night). No caravans are allowed at the site and no camping is permitted in the wilderness area.
Other facilities: A 25-km network of hiking paths; an information centre.
Open: Throughout the year.
Opening time: Wilderness area – 24 hours; camping site – sunrise to sunset.
For further information: Ngome State Forest, Private Bag X9306, Vryheid 3100. Tel: (0386) 7-1883. Fax: (0386) 7-1883.

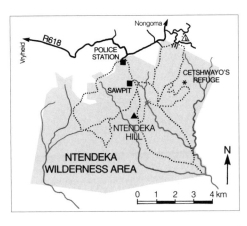

The Ntendeka Wilderness Area is 5 230 ha in extent, of which approximately half is covered by coastal and inland tropical forest, and the remainder by grassland. The area is steeped in Zulu history and was at one time the refuge of the Zulu king Cetshwayo. The area is incised by high dolerite and sandstone cliffs with dense forest covering the steep valley slopes, while above the cliffs is a gently undulating plateau. The main appeal of Ntendeka is the extensive indigenous forest, in which more than 180 tree and shrub species have been recorded. Many of the waterwood trees in the forest exceed 30 m in height, and this is the only area in Natal where the bastard stinkwood and Natal myrtle are known to occur. More than 60 fern species have been recorded. Epiphytic orchids are also well represented. To observe some of the shy forest creatures it is best to sit quietly at the edge of a clearing. Blue and red duiker, bushbuck and samango monkey may be seen, although the monkeys' loud 'jack' calls are more likely to be heard, and the rare Ngoye red squirrel lives in this extensive patch of forest. The birdlife includes such rarities as cuckoo hawk, wattled crane and blue swallow. In all 194 bird species have been recorded, some of which you are not likely to see clearly, although the calls of trumpeter hornbill, purple-crested lourie and narina trogon will indicate their presence.

141 NYALA GAME RANCH

Location: Zululand; north-west of Empangeni.
Access: From Empangeni take the R34 in the direction of Nkwalini; watch out for the sign-

posted turn-off to Nyala Game Ranch. The last stretch of road is gravel.
Accommodation: *Mbondwe camp* has ronda-

64. Cliffs in the Mhlopeni Nature Reserve provide nesting sites for black eagles.

65. Although primarily a recreational area, the Midmar Public Resort does have an adjoining nature reserve.

66. Loteni Nature Reserve is a convenient starting point for many mountaineering expeditions.

67. Female nyala with a lamb in the Mkuzi Game Reserve.

68. A waterfall descends the Drakensberg Escarpment at Vulture's Retreat in the Mdedelelo Wilderness Area.

69. Cathedral Peak can be seen from the camping site in the Mlambonja Wilderness Area.

70. Waterholes at Ndumu Nature Reserve attract a variety of birds.

71. A view across the Nsumu Pan to the hunting camp at Mkuzi Game Reserve.

72. A charming cottage at Tendele Camp in the Royal Natal National Park.

73. There are spectacular views from the rest camp at Oribi Gorge Nature Reserve.

74. The Royal Natal National Park offers many pretty walks.

75. In the Royal Natal National Park some of its most majestic scenery can be viewed from horseback.

vels, tents, electricity, a lounge, full ablution facilities and a swimming pool; a trained cook prepares visitors' food. *Hlati camp* provides similar facilities, but without a lounge or electricity. *Umvumvu camp* has rustic huts, tents, ablution facilities and pit toilets; a trained cook prepares visitors' food. The camps accommodate between 15 and 60 children on an environmental education programme.

Other facilities: Game-viewing on foot, from hides or in open vehicles (including night walks and drives); horse trails. The ranch is open to day visitors.

Open: Throughout the year.

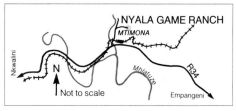

Opening time: Sunrise to sunset.
Beware: Malaria.
For further information: Nyala Game Ranch, P.O. Box 647, Empangeni 3880. Tel: (0351) 2-4543/7.

The main function of the 500-ha Nyala Game Ranch is to provide a venue for environmental education. A wide variety of game species can be seen and birdlife is varied. Winters are cool and generally more pleasant than the summers in this area.

142 OCEAN VIEW GAME PARK See map Dlinza Forest Nature Reserve

Location: Zululand; Eshowe.
Access: From Eshowe follow the R68 south towards Gingindlovu; the reserve is on the right.
Accommodation: None.
Other facilities: Accompanied walks.

Open: Throughout the year.
Opening time: 07h00 to 17h00.
For further information: The Town Clerk, Borough of Eshowe, P.O. Box 37, Eshowe 3815. Tel: (0354) 4-1141.

A variety of game species, including impala, kudu, reedbuck and blue wildebeest, have been released in the 45-ha Ocean View Game Park, and a wealth of bird species can be found here.

143 ORIBI GORGE NATURE RESERVE

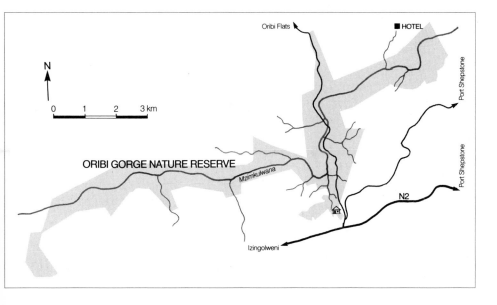

Location: South-eastern Natal; west of Port Shepstone.

Access: From Port Shepstone follow the N2 westwards towards Harding for about 10 km, then take the signposted right turn to Oribi Gorge. A public road traverses the reserve.

Accommodation: 1 7-bed cottage and 6 3-bed rest huts. Oribi Gorge Hotel is nearby.

Other facilities: Trails; picnic sites with fire-places; fishing (permit obtainable at the office).

Open: Throughout the year.

Opening time: 24 hours; visitors to the camp should arrive before 16h30.

Beware: Bilharzia.

For further information: The Natal Parks Board (see page 365).

The Mzimkulwana River has carved its way through layers of sandstone to produce one of Natal's most dramatic landscape features, the Oribi Gorge. The surrounding reserve conserves 1 837 ha of rugged cliffs, boulder-strewn river bed, impressive waterfalls, forested slopes and open grassland. Forty mammal species are known to occur in the Oribi Gorge Nature Reserve, and sightings of the elusive samango monkey are not uncommon. The calls of baboons echo across the gorge and visitors may catch a glimpse of bushbuck, reedbuck, vervet monkeys, blue and common duiker, and rock dassies. Ironically, the oribi, the small antelope from which the reserve takes its name, is not found here. Of the 268 bird species that occur, raptors are particularly well represented and crowned, black and long-crested eagles as well as jackal buzzard may be spotted.

144 PARADISE VALLEY NATURE RESERVE See map Durban

Location: Central Natal; Pinetown.

Access: From Durban follow the N3 to Pinetown and turn right at the St Johns Ave intersection; turn right again into Old Main Rd and follow this road eastwards; turn right into Stapleton Rd and drive under the freeway, turning left into Eden Rd; continue into Oxford Rd to the reserve.

Accommodation: None.

Other facilities: Short walks; picnic sites.

Open: Throughout the year.

For further information: The Officer-in-charge, Paradise Valley Nature Reserve, Municipality of Pinetown 3610.

This 28-ha patch of coastal forest lies on the banks of the Umbilo River. Bushbuck and blue duiker are present, as well as an interesting variety of forest birds.

145 PONGOLAPOORT PUBLIC RESORT NATURE RESERVE

Location: North-eastern Natal; north-east of Mkuze.

Access: From Mkuze travel north on the N2 for about 10 km; turn right at the signpost to Jozini/Sodwana; travel east for approximately 2 km down this road; road then veers sharply left and entrance is on left just before hill going up to Jozini.

Accommodation: None.

Other facilities: Fishing for tiger fish.

Open: Throughout the year.

Opening time: Sunrise to sunset.

Beware: Malaria; bilharzia; crocodiles; hippos.

For further information: The Natal Parks Board (see page 365). (Reserve) Officer-in-charge: Tel: (035662) 1421.

Pongolapoort Public Resort Nature Reserve surrounds the dam of the same name and covers a total area of 11 693 ha. The reserve is totally undeveloped at this stage and proclamation is still pending. The dam attracts many water-related bird species and it can be expected that a number of game species will be brought into the area.

146 QUEEN ELIZABETH PARK
NATURE RESERVE See map Doreen Clark Nature Reserve

Location: Central Natal; north-west of Pieter-maritzburg.
Access: From Pietermaritzburg follow the N3 towards Mooi River. The reserve, east of this road, is reached via the Montrose exit.
Accommodation: None. There is accommodation in Pietermaritzburg.

Other facilities: Self-guided walks; picnic sites with fireplaces; game-viewing on foot; a curio shop, which is closed at weekends.
Open: Throughout the year.
Opening time: Sunrise to sunset.
For further information: The Natal Parks Board (see page 365).

Headquarters of the Natal Parks Board, this 93-ha reserve has a range of attractions for the visitor. Cycads, aloes and proteas grow in abundance and a number of game animals found in Natal, including white rhinoceros, can be viewed.

147 ROYAL NATAL NATIONAL PARK

Location: The Drakensberg; north-west of Bergville.
Access: From Mooi River follow the N3 northwards for 52 km; turn left onto the R615 and drive past Winterton and Bergville. At the bottom of the Oliviershoek Pass turn left and follow the signposts to the park. There are no internal roads, except those to the camps.
Accommodation: *Tendele camp* has 8 3-bed and 5 5-bed bungalows, 2 6-bed cottages and the luxury 6-bed Tendele Lodge. *Mahai camping site* has facilities for 400 persons, with 2 kitchens and 5 ablution blocks. *Rugged Glen* camping site is privately run. There is a hotel in the park; Mont-aux-Sources Hotel is on the eastern boundary. Book in advance for school and public holidays.
Other facilities: An extensive network of footpaths; guided and self-guided walks (a booklet describing the climbs and walks is available from the office); visitor centre; picnic sites with fireplaces; climbing (permits must be obtained at the office; carry a passport if you intend ascending the Namahadi Pass to Lesotho); horse-riding; trout fishing (a permit is available at the office); washing machines; tumble dryers.
Open: Throughout the year.
Opening time: Sunrise to sunset.

Speed limit: 40 km/h.
Beware: Sudden changes in the weather.
For further information: The Natal Parks Board (see page 365). (Camping site) The Officer-in-charge, Mahai Campsite, P.O. Mont-aux-Sources 3353. Tel: (0364) 38-1803. (Royal Natal National Park Hotel) P.O. Mont-aux-Sources 3353. Tel: (0364) 38-1051.

This magnificent 8 094-ha park was proclaimed in 1916 and is, arguably, in the most beautiful part of the Drakensberg. The crescent-shaped rock face of the Amphitheatre, the 850-m Tugela Falls and the 3 282-m peak of Mont-aux-Sources provide spectacular scenery which can be admired even by the most sedentary visitor.

The vegetation is varied, ranging from open grassland and mountain fynbos (heath) to patches of riverine woodland.

Although the park is best known for its scenery, a variety of mammal species may be seen, including grey rhebok, mountain reedbuck, klipspringer, common duiker, bushbuck and baboon, and almost 200 bird species have been recorded.

148 RUGGED GLEN NATURE RESERVE See map Royal Natal National Park

Location: The Drakensberg; north-west of Mooi River.

Access: Adjacent to the Royal Natal National Park; see that entry for directions.

Accommodation: Camping site (accommodating a maximum of 45 people) with communal ablution facilities.

Other facilities: Walking trails; horse-riding; trout fishing.

Open: Throughout the year.

Opening time: Sunrise to sunset.

For further information: The Officer-in-charge, Rugged Glen Nature Reserve, P.O. Mont-aux-Sources 3353. Tel: (0364) 38-1803.

This 762-ha reserve is managed as part of the adjoining Royal Natal National Park. Similar mammals, birds and vegetation can be found in both areas.

149 SODWANA BAY NATIONAL PARK

Location: North-eastern Natal; east of Mkuze.

Access: From the N2 just north of Mkuze turn right towards Ubombo, and continue eastwards beyond this village to Mbazwana; from here drive southwards and follow the signposts to the reserve. Sodwana lies 90 km from Ubombo. Alternatively, from the N2 north of Hluhluwe, follow signposts to Sodwana Bay.

Accommodation: 20 self-contained log cabins. There is a camping and caravan site with 600 open stands (maximum 4 000 people) and ablution blocks. Book well in advance.

Other facilities: Short trails; fishing bait and ice for sale; power supply available; boat storage facilities; picnic sites; supermarket; fuel.

Open: Throughout the year.

Opening time: Sunrise to sunset.

Beware: Malaria.

For further information: The Officer-in-charge, Sodwana Bay National Park, Private Bag 310, Mbazwana 3974. Tel: (035672) 1102.

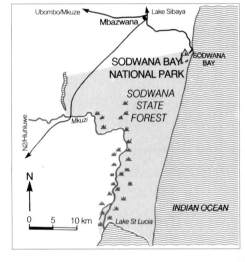

Set among 413 ha of forested sand dunes, the Sodwana Bay resort attracts large numbers of holiday-makers, particularly in school holidays, when the area is alive with the sound of ski-boats and 4x4 vehicles. Out of season the park is somewhat quieter, although beach and ski-boat fishermen visit throughout the year.

Despite its popularity, much of the park remains unspoilt. The sand-dune forest and swamp forest with its majestic fig trees are a short walk from the camping site and here there is a chance of seeing bushbuck, suni, red duiker and the rare Tonga red squirrel. Steenbok, reedbuck and common duiker inhabit the more open country.

Birdwatchers will find this area very rewarding, as it is particularly rich in the smaller birds. Some unusual species that are likely to be seen are the pink-throated longclaw, Rudd's apalis, black coucal and Dickinson's kestrel. An exploration of the shoreline can be productive too, revealing a wealth of marine organisms.

Stretching southwards from Sodwana Bay National Park to the northern shore of Lake St Lucia is the 42 424-ha Sodwana State Forest. This area consists mainly of seasonally flooded grassland, with a coastal belt of sand-dune forest. The forest has recently been taken over by the Natal Parks Board and is not yet open to the public.

This is a subtropical area with hot, humid summers, although temperatures are usually cooled by sea breezes. Winters are mild.

150 SPIOENKOP PUBLIC RESORT NATURE RESERVE

Location: Western Natal; south-west of Ladysmith.
Access: From Ladysmith take the N3 southwards, turning right onto the R616 after 6 km. The reserve is clearly signposted.
Accommodation: *Main camp* has 30 6-bed chalets. *Ntenjwa rustic camp* has 4 2-bed A-frame thatched structures with camp beds and sleeping bags, kitchen equipment and a refrigerator (this camp is 14 km from the main camp and can be reached on foot or by ferry across the dam). There is a camping site (maximum 150 persons) with ablution facilities. A 'Schools' Village' is available for educational groups.
Other facilities: Picnic sites; game-viewing walks; boating and watersports permitted; horse-riding; museum; battlefield tours; tennis, badminton, table tennis; swimming pool; children's playground; tractor rides; boat rides.
Open: Throughout the year.
Opening time: 24 hours.
For further information: The Natal Parks

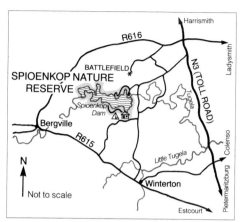

Board (see page 365). (Camping site and rustic camp) The Camp Superintendent, Spioenkop Public Resort, P.O. Box 140, Winterton 3340. Tel: 03682, ask for 78.

Situated around Spioenkop Dam on the Tugela River, this resort is mainly geared towards water-related activities. However, the adjacent 2 000- and 500-ha game parks contain a wide variety of introduced species, such as white rhinoceros, Burchell's zebra, blue and black wildebeest, red hartebeest, blesbok, eland, impala, kudu, mountain reedbuck and giraffe. Guided tours of the Spioenkop battlefield and the Anglo-Boer War historical museum add an interesting dimension to this reserve.

151 SPRINGSIDE NATURE RESERVE

Location: Central Natal; west of Pinetown.
Access: From central Durban take the N3 towards Pietermaritzburg; just to the west of Kloof turn off into Old Main Rd and from here into Stonewall Rd and right into Springside Rd. The entrance to the reserve lies just off Springside Rd.
Accommodation: None.
Other facilities: Self-guided walks.
Open: Throughout the year.
Opening times: Sunrise to sunset.
For further information: The Wildlife Society of Southern Africa (see page 365) or S. Soane, 4 Shortlands Avenue, Hillcrest 3610.

Springside Nature Reserve has been developed jointly by local service organisations, the Wildlife Society and the Hillcrest Town Board.

A narrow stream runs through the 16-ha reserve and there are wetland areas along its course. The vegetation includes tree ferns and patches of bush, grassland and indigenous forest, with such trees as waterberry and wild pomegranate present. The birdlife is varied and more than 60 species have been recorded, including forest weavers.

ST LUCIA GAME RESERVE See map St Lucia Park

Location: Coastal Zululand; east and north-east of Mtubatuba.
Access: From Mtubatuba follow the R620 for about 26 km to St Lucia Estuary. Various parts of the lake can be reached by boat.
Accommodation: None. See St Lucia Park, False Bay Park and Cape Vidal State Forest.
Other facilities: See St Lucia Park, False Bay Park and Cape Vidal State Forest.
Beware: Malaria; crocodiles; sharks.
For further information: The Natal Parks Board (see page 365).

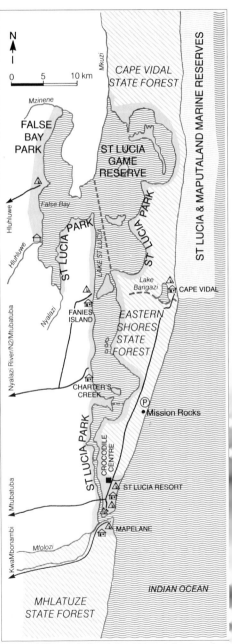

St Lucia Game Reserve consists of the water area and islands of the St Lucia estuary, and covers 36 826 ha. It is at its narrowest in the south and stretches over 20 km at its widest point in the north. The water is shallow, with an average depth of 1 m, although there are many deeper channels and gulleys.

More than 600 hippopotamuses spend the daylight hours in the water, and in the evenings make their way out to the grazing grounds surrounding the estuary along the hippo paths that criss-cross the area. Crocodiles are common in all parts, but the greatest numbers concentrate where rivers enter St Lucia. The Crocodile Centre near the village is well worth a visit as it explains the biology, way of life and importance of this reptile. Sharks sometimes enter the estuary.

The waters of the lake teem with fish, crustaceans, insects and micro-organisms, and it is this abundance that attracts the great variety of waterbirds. A large breeding population of fish eagles is found here, between 1 000 and 2 000 pairs of white pelicans are regularly counted, and 12 heron species breed around the lake shore. Many species of wading birds feed along the mud shallows, particularly in the winter months when the waters reach their lowest level. In total, more than 350 bird species have been recorded at St Lucia Game Reserve.

ST LUCIA PARK

Location: Coastal Zululand; north-east of Mtubatuba, surrounding most of Lake St Lucia.
Access: *Charter's Creek:* From Mtubatuba drive along the N2 towards Mkuze for 25 km and turn right at the Nyalazi River Halt turn-off signposted Charter's Creek and Fanies Island; follow this road for 13 km to the camp, which is clearly signposted. *Fanies Island:* Continue be-

yond Charter's Creek for 11 km, following signposts. *St Lucia Resort:* From Mtubatuba follow the R620 for about 26 km to St Lucia Estuary; signposts in the village indicate Natal Parks Board offices and the camping and caravan sites. *Mapelane:* From Empangeni travel northwards on the N2 for about 30 km, then turn right at KwaMbonambi lighthouse signpost; continue for about 40 km along the well-signposted road to Mapelane. This road is sandy in places and at times ordinary vehicles may have difficulty in reaching the camp.

Accommodation: *Charter's Creek* has 1 7-bed cottage, 1 2-bed, 4 3-bed and 10 4-bed rest huts. There are no camping facilities here. *Fanies Island* has 1 7-bed cottage and 12 2-bed rest huts; there is a camping site here with 20 stands and ablution facilities. *St Lucia Resort* has 3 camping and caravan sites near the village, accommodating up to 1 600 people; all have ablution facilities. *Mapelane* has 10 5-bed log cabins and a camping site with 44 stands and ablution facilities. There are several privately owned hotels and holiday flats in St Lucia village.

Other facilities: Charter's Creek has a swimming pool, self-guided trail, motor launch tours, fuel. *Fanies Island* has a swimming pool, self-guided trail, fishing (bait sold), boat hire, fuel. *St Lucia Resort* offers fishing (bait sold), boat hire, shops, hotels, a crocodile centre, fuel. *Mapelane* offers fishing (bait sold); shops and fuel are 40 km away at KwaMbonambi.

Open: Throughout the year.

Opening time: Sunrise to sunset; resort camps – 24 hours.

Beware: Malaria; crocodiles and occasionally sharks; hippopotamuses roam through some of the camps at night.

For further information: (Accommodation and trails) The Natal Parks Board (see page 365). (Fanies Island camping site booking) The Camp Superintendent, Fanies Island, P.O. Box 201, Mtubatuba 3935. Tel: 03552, ask for 1431. (St Lucia Resort booking) The Officer-in-charge, St Lucia Resort, Private Bag, St Lucia Estuary 3936. Tel: (03592) 20. (Mapelane camping site booking) The Officer-in-charge, Mapelane, Private Bag, St Lucia Estuary 3936. Tel: (03592) 20.

St Lucia Park is an approximately 1-km wide strip around most of Lake St Lucia, reaching from the mouth of the Nyalazi River in the south to the Mkuzi River in the north. It covers a total area of 12 545 ha, including the village at the mouth of the estuary. Most of the vegetation consists of a mixture of woodland types with many interesting trees, reed beds and some grassed areas. This mixture provides habitats for many bird species, as well as mammals which include vervet monkey, red duiker and bushbuck. During the rainy season many frog and toad species emerge to breed, and each species has a different call; it is quite possible to sit in the evening and hear the males of 10 or more species calling to attract mates.

A number of other reserves are linked to St Lucia Park. Mapelane Nature Reserve is situated along the southern bank of the estuary mouth and covers 900 ha of coastal forest. At its southern boundary is Mhlatuze State Forest, a 1 103-ha area which has recently been incorporated into Mapelane and is controlled by the Natal Parks Board. It is not yet open to the public.

With a total surface area of 88 480 ha, St Lucia and Maputaland marine reserves together make up the most extensive marine reserve in Africa, stretching in a continuous strip from 1 km south of Cape Vidal to Ponto de Ouro on the Mozambique border, and extending 5,6 km out to sea. The northern sector protects turtle-nesting areas and is a breeding ground for many popular angling fish species. The St Lucia sector contains the southernmost coral reefs in the world and is an important breeding area for game fish. Except for fish taken by line, no bait or any other marine organisms may be collected. There are two marine sanctuary areas, one in each marine reserve, in which no fishing in any form, snorkelling or diving is permitted.

154 TEMBE ELEPHANT RESERVE See regional map only

Location: Northern Zululand; on the Mozambique border.

Access: Follow the route past Jozini, continuing beyond Ndumo Game Reserve turn-off in the direction of Kosi Bay. The road to Tembe Elephant Reserve is on the left.Check the road conditions with the authorities. Permits must be obtained in advance.

Accommodation: 3 tented camps, each with 4 safari tents and a kitchen tent equipped with a stove, refrigerator and deepfreeze. Each camp has a thatched ablution block and a central braai area.

Other facilities: Cook in each camp; ranger will take visitors on open Landrover drives; network of hides; no fuel or supplies are available in the reserve.

Open: Throughout the year.

Opening time: Check with the authority.
Beware: Malaria.

For further information: The Kwazulu Bureau of Natural Resources (see page 365).

The 29 000-ha Tembe Elephant Reserve consists mainly of dense woodland and sand forest, with areas of shrub veld and swampland. It was set aside to protect a small, remnant population of elephant, now numbering approximately 100. Other game species include square-lipped rhinoceros, giraffe, kudu, waterbuck, nyala, impala, red duiker and suni. The bird population is rich and varied. Summers are hot, with mild winters.

155 THE SWAMP NATURE RESERVE

Location: Drakensberg foothills; west of Pietermaritzburg.
Access: From Pietermaritzburg follow the N2 northwards in the direction of Howick for about 25 km and then take the R617 to Himeville via Bulwer and Underberg; from Himeville follow signposts to Pevensey; the reserve lies along this road.
Accommodation: None. Himeville Nature Reserve (see page 118) has camping facilities and there is a hotel in Himeville itself.
Other facilities: None.
Open: Throughout the year.
Opening time: Sunrise to sunset.
For further information: The Natal Parks Board (see page 365).

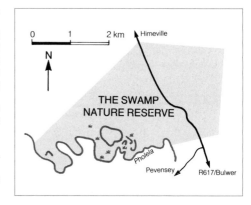

Approximately 60 ha of this 220-ha reserve consists of wetlands which provide suitable habitat for a wide range of waterfowl species, as well as the rare wattled crane. Reedbuck also occur in the wetland areas. The Polela River forms 3 km of the southern boundary of the reserve.

156 UBIZANE GAME RANCH

Location: Northern Zululand; north-east of Mtubatuba.
Access: From Mtubatuba travel along the N2 for 50 km and turn left towards Hluhluwe Game Reserve; follow this road for about 6 km to the game ranch. The route is clearly signposted.
Accommodation: 2-bed huts with bedding, refrigerator, kitchen and ablution facilities (R35 per person per night, excluding meals; meals can be provided by prior arrangement). The Zululand Safari Lodge is situated on the ranch.
Other facilities: Walking trails; game-viewing in open vehicles; trips to neighbouring game reserves; horse-riding; restaurant and bar.
Open: Throughout the year.
Opening time: 24 hours.
For further information: Ubizane Game Ranch, P.O. Box 102, Hluhluwe 3960. Tel: (03562) 3602.

Ubizane Game Ranch covers 1 500 ha of bushveld which supports about 2 300 head of game, including white rhinoceros, giraffe, Burchell's zebra, nyala, blue wildebeest, kudu, waterbuck, impala, blesbok and warthog, as well as a wide range of smaller mammals and birds.

76. At Sodwana Bay National Park sand-dune forest is separated from the sea by a narrow strip of beach.

77. Eastern Shores Nature Reserve, part of the St Lucia complex, has a very large reedbuck population.

78. The rest camp at Charter's Creek, St Lucia, is beautifully situated.

79. St Lucia is well known for its hippopotamus population; more than 600 occur in the game reserve alone.

80. A Sontuli bush camp hut glows in the early-morning sun at Umfolozi Game Reserve.

81. The shores of False Bay are more remote than other parts of the St Lucia complex.

82. The Umfolozi Game Reserve protects more than 1 000 white rhinoceros, a species that almost became extinct.

83. A trail through the mangrove swamp at Umlalazi Nature Reserve allows visitors to see these fascinating trees at close quarters.

84. Comfortable chalet accommodation at Umlalazi.

85. Burchell's zebra in the grassland of the Vernon Crookes Nature Reserve.

86. Cape vultures nest on the cliffs of the Umtamvuna Gorge in the reserve of the same name.

87. Sehlabathebe National Park has no public road system, but hikers can enjoy many scenic walks.

UMDONI BIRD SANCTUARY See map Ilanda Wilds Nature Reserve

Location: South Coast; at Amanzimtoti, south of Durban.
Access: From Durban take the N2 southwards into Amanzimtoti; the reserve lies to the north of Umdoni Rd.
Accommodation: None. There are hotels and a camping site in Amanzimtoti.
Other facilities: Short trail; birdwatching hides; information centre; tea kiosk open at weekends.
Open: Throughout the year.
Opening time: 06h00 to 18h00.
For further information: The Chief Health Inspector, Borough of Amanzimtoti, P.O. Box 26, Amanzimtoti 4125. Tel: (031) 903-2121. Fax: (031) 903-7382.

In this small area of indigenous forest and dams visitors may watch the birdlife from strategically placed hides. Species that may be observed include the green-backed heron, and giant and pygmy kingfishers. In addition, a section of the sanctuary has been set aside in which both exotic and indigenous waterbirds are enclosed.

Many of the trees and other plants in the forest are labelled.

UMFOLOZI GAME RESERVE

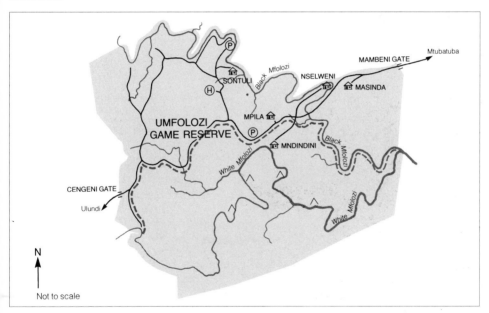

Location: Northern Zululand; north-west of Mtubatuba.
Access: From Mtubatuba take the R618 towards Nongoma; follow this road for 22 km and then turn off onto a clearly signposted gravel road to the reserve. All internal roads are gravel and are generally in good condition, although during the summer rains lower-lying roads may become impassable.
Accommodation: 6 5-bed chalets (self-catering), 2 7-bed cottages, 18 3- to 4-bed rest huts,
1 7-bed lodge, 3 8-bed bush camps. All the camps have separate kitchens where cooks prepare food provided by visitors, and communal ablution blocks. There are no camping facilities.
Other facilities: Wilderness trail; hiking trails (March to November); auto-trail; picnic sites; 86-km network of game-viewing roads; 2 game-viewing hides; fuel and a shop selling curios, books, charcoal and cool drinks. The nearest store is 50 km away at Mtubatuba.

Open: Throughout the year.
Opening time: Sunrise to sunset.
Speed limit: 40 km/h.

Beware: Malaria; bilharzia; pepper ticks.
For further information: The Natal Parks Board (see page 365).

Despite being one of South Africa's oldest nature reserves, having been proclaimed in 1897, the Umfolozi Game Reserve has seen a great deal of slaughter. The area once served as the hunting domain of the Zulu Royal House and was later penetrated by white ivory hunters. In an attempt to prevent the spread of the disease nagana, which affects hoofed animals, many thousand head of game were shot. Only in the 1960s was Umfolozi's future in conservation terms assured.

Much of the reserve's 47 753 ha consists of hilly country with level flood plains along the Black and White Mfolozi rivers. Savannah woodland and thicket, interspersed with open areas of grassland, cover large parts, and reserve staff clear bush and burn regularly to open up more areas for grazing species. The once fine riverine forests and large numbers of fig trees were largely destroyed during the floods caused by Cyclone Demoina.

Umfolozi is best known for the role it has played in saving the white rhinoceros from extinction. Today there are more than 1 000 of these mammals in the reserve, as well as smaller numbers of the black rhinoceros.

Other species that can be seen are buffalo, elephant, giraffe, Burchell's zebra, nyala, impala, kudu, waterbuck, blue wildebeest and warthog. Predators are well represented by lion, leopard, cheetah, wild dog and spotted hyena. More than 400 bird species have been recorded within the Umfolozi/Hluhluwe complex.

The best time of year for game-viewing is during the dry winter months when water sources are most limited. Summer visitors are most likely to see game on early morning and late afternoon drives. Temperatures of over 38 ^{o}C are common during summer, particularly in the lower-lying valleys.

159 UMGENI VALLEY NATURE RESERVE See map Albert Falls Public Resort Nature Reserve

Location: Natal Midlands; north-west of Pietermaritzburg.
Access: From Pietermaritzburg follow the N3, branch off at Howick and drive through the town, turning right onto the Karkloof/Rietvlei road; continue for about 1 km. The reserve is approximately 27 km from Pietermaritzburg.
Accommodation: 1 5-bed cottage. 3 camps accommodating up to 40 children; 1 smaller camp accommodating 30 children. Each camp has dormitary-type huts, a kitchen and ablutions.
Other facilities: Resource centre; 5 walking trails; picnic sites; swimming in river.
Open: Throughout the year.
Opening time: Sunrise to sunset; office – 08h00 to 16h30.
For further information: The Secretary, Umgeni Valley Nature Reserve, P.O. Box 394, Howick 3290. Tel: (0332) 30-3931 or 30-4332.

Umgeni Valley Nature Reserve, which lies just below the impressive Howick Falls, is one of the best-known and more successful conservation education centres – for both children and adults – in South Africa.

Covering 656 ha, it contains a variety of habitats, dominated by mixed open woodland and grassland above the river valley.

Apart from the mammal species that occur here naturally, game species such as eland, nyala, impala and giraffe have been introduced.

More than 200 bird species have been recorded here.

160 UMHLANGA LAGOON NATURE RESERVE

Location: North Coast; north of Durban.
Access: From Durban follow the N2 northwards for about 18 km and turn off to Umhlanga Rocks. The Umhlanga Lagoon Nature Reserve is north of this resort.
Accommodation: None.
Other facilities: Picnic site; nature trail; trails guided by the Wildlife Society.
Open: Throughout the year.
Opening time: Sunrise to sunset.
For further information: Tel: (031) 25-1271 or The Natal Parks Board (see page 365).

(Guided trails) Natal branch of the Wildlife Society (see page 365).

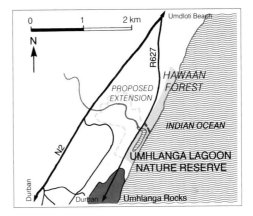

Situated on one of the few unspoilt river mouths in Natal, the Umhlanga Lagoon Nature Reserve conserves a patch of sand-dune forest, as well as the lagoon. A great number of bird species occur here, including fish eagle and crested guineafowl, and red and blue duiker and bushbuck also live in this 26-ha reserve.

A shell midden estimated to be some 1 400 years old is of historical interest.

The adjacent Hawaan Bush is privately owned and can be explored by arrangement with the Natal Wildlife Society; this 65-ha area differs in floral composition to Umhlanga and attracts many different species of birds.

161 UMLALAZI NATURE RESERVE

Location: North Coast; north of Durban.
Access: From Durban follow the N2 northwards in the direction of Empangeni; 18 km north of Gingindlovu turn right to Mtunzini; from Mtunzini take the road eastwards and follow the signposts to the reserve.
Accommodation: 1 5-bed leisure home; 13 5-bed log cabins; a camping site (maximum 70 people) with ablution facilities and plug points.
Other facilities: Fishing (bait sold); boating and water-skiing permitted; rowing boats can be hired; 3 self-guided walking trails which lead through the mangrove swamp and sand-dune forest; picnic sites.
Open: Throughout the year.
Opening time: 24 hours.
Beware: Crocodiles; sharks may enter the estuary.
For further information: The Natal Parks Board (see page 365). (Camping site bookings) The Officer-in-charge, Umlalazi Nature Reserve, P.O. Box 234, Mtunzini 3867. Tel: (0353) 40-1836.

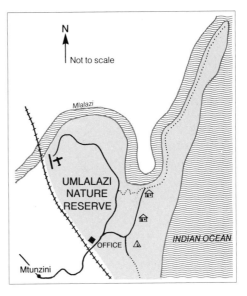

The nearby beach and fishing opportunities attract many people to this reserve, while others come to water-ski. The reserve covers 1 028 ha of sand-dune forest and mangrove swamp. The short trail through the mangroves can be very rewarding, but be prepared to get muddy. Along the way it is possible to see several crab species, including the comical male fiddler crabs, tree-climbing whelks and the amphibious mudskipper fish that spends much of its life on land. The birdlife is varied and interesting spider and butterfly species may be spotted. Red and blue duiker, bushbuck and vervet monkey inhabit the reserve.

162 UMTAMVUNA NATURE RESERVE

Location: Extreme south-eastern Natal; south-east of Port Shepstone.

Access: From Port Shepstone take the R61 southwards to Port Edward; at Port Edward take the road westwards towards Izingolweni and drive for about 8 km. The Umtamvuna Nature Reserve lies to the west of this road and is signposted.

Accommodation: None. There are hotels, self-catering accommodation and camping sites along the South Coast.

Other facilities: Self-guided trails.

Open: Throughout the year.

Opening time: Sunrise to sunset.

Beware: Bilharzia.

For further information: The Officer-in-charge, Umtamvuna Nature Reserve, P.O. Box 25, Port Edward 4295. Tel: (03930) 3-2383.

This 3 257-ha reserve consists mainly of a forested gorge with steep rocky cliffs bordering the Mtamvuna River.

As well as its scenic beauty, Umtamvuna Nature Reserve has a rich plantlife and nearly 1 300 different species have been recorded, including 25 orchid species and a number of other rare plants.

A colony of Cape vultures breeds in the reserve and the presence of other rare bird species, such as peregrine falcon, crowned eagle and Gurney's sugarbird, make a visit here well worthwhile.

Reedbuck, common and blue duiker, and bushbuck may also be seen.

Rain falls in summer and temperatures are high at this time. Winters are generally mild, but nights can be cold.

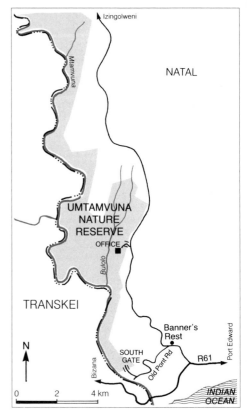

163 UVONGO NATURE RESERVE

Location: South Coast; south of Port Shepstone.

Access: From Port Shepstone drive southwards on the MR359 for 12 km, into Uvongo; in the resort Edward Ave gives access to the south bank of the Uvongo River, and Marine Dr. to the north bank.

Accommodation: None. There are hotels, self-catering accommodation and camping sites along the South Coast.

Other facilities: Picnic sites; short trails (an information booklet can be obtained at the municipal offices).

Open: Throughout the year.

Opening time: Sunrise to sunset.

For further information: The Town Clerk, Borough of Uvongo, P.O. Box 13, Uvongo 4270. Tel: (03931) 5-1222. Fax: (03931) 7-6236.

The main attractions of this 28-ha reserve are the clear waters of the Uvongo River, a waterfall that plunges 23 m into a lagoon, coastal forest and many different tree and bird species.

164 VERGELEGEN NATURE RESERVE

See map Mkhomazi & Mzimkulu Wilderness Areas

Location: The Drakensberg; north-west of Pietermaritzburg.

Access: From Pietermaritzburg travel towards Howick on the N3 for about 25 km; take the R617 exit to Himeville via Bulwer and Underberg; continue past Himeville towards Lower Loteni and after 16 km turn left at the signpost to the reserve. Vergelegen lies 19 km further on. From December to March, and occasionally at other times, the access road may be flooded or parts of it may be washed away. Check on conditions by telephoning the Natal Parks Board.

Accommodation: 2 5-bed cottages.

Other facilities: Trout fishing (permits obtainable at the reserve office); footpaths.

Open: Throughout the year.

Opening time: Sunrise to sunset.

For further information: The Natal Parks Board (see page 365).

Similar to the nearby Loteni Nature Reserve, Vergelegen is composed mainly of steep hill slopes and deep valleys with a vegetation that is predominantly grassland. The 1 159-ha reserve is situated near the headwaters of the Umkomaas River and rises to an altitude of approximately 1 500 m above sea-level. Thaba Ntlenyana, at 3 482 m southern Africa's highest mountain, can be seen from it. There are a number of short walks within Vergelegen, but a permit must be obtained to explore Mkhomazi Wilderness Area.

165 VERNON CROOKES NATURE RESERVE

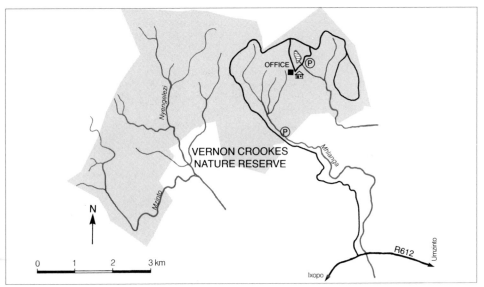

Location: South Coast; north-west of Park Rynie.

Access: From Park Rynie follow the R612 inland to Umzinto and continue past this village for 4 km; turn right and drive for 6 km.

Accommodation: 5 4-bed rustic huts.

Other facilities: A picnic site; a network of game-viewing roads; walking is allowed.

Open: Throughout the year.

Opening time: Sunrise to sunset; office – 08h00 to 19h00.

Speed limit: 40 km/h.

Beware: Ticks.

For further information: The Officer-in-charge. Tel: (03231) 4-2222, office hours.

Vernon Crookes Nature Reserve is an island of natural vegetation surrounded by sugar cane and softwood plantations. Much of this 2 189-ha reserve comprises steep to undulating ridges and hills, dissected by deep drainage lines. The vegetation consists mainly of patches of coastal forest interspersed with grassland, but a number of exotic plant species are a problem in the area. Apart from naturally occurring game species such as blue and common duiker and bushbuck, a number of other species, such as Burchell's zebra and impala, have been introduced.

166 VRYHEID NATURE RESERVE
See map Klipfontein Public Resort Nature Reserve

Location: Northern Natal; north of Vryheid.
Access: From central Vryheid take the R33 towards Paulpietersburg and after a short distance turn right to the reserve, which lies to the north of the town on Lancaster Hill.
Accommodation: None.

Other facilities: A picnic site; birdwatching hide; game-viewing roads; walking is allowed.
Open: Throughout the year.
Opening time: Sunrise to sunset.
For further information: The Natal Parks Board (see page 365).

Leased by the Natal Parks Board from the Borough of Vryheid, this reserve covers 720 ha and consists of forested slopes and open grassland. It has been stocked with Burchell's zebra, eland, impala, mountain reedbuck, springbok, oribi, bushbuck and blesbok.

167 WAGENDRIFT PUBLIC RESORT NATURE RESERVE
See map Moor Park Nature Reserve

Location: Natal Midlands; north-west of Pietermaritzburg.
Access: From Pietermaritzburg take the N3 towards Estcourt; west of Estcourt take the Ntabamhlope road, reaching the reserve after 7 km.
Accommodation: A camping and caravan site; an education centre with 80 beds.
Other facilities: Fishing; sailing; hiking; motor-

boating; picnic sites.
Open: Throughout the year.
Opening time: 24 hours.
For further information: (Education centre) The Natal Parks Board (see page 365). (Camping site) The Officer-in-charge, Wagendrift Public Resort, P.O. Box 316, Estcourt 3310. Tel: (03631) 2-2550.

Adjacent to the Wagendrift Dam Public Resort, this reserve covers 758 ha. An environmental education centre is run by the Natal Parks Board in conjunction with the adjacent Moor Park Nature Reserve.

168 WEENEN NATURE RESERVE

Location: Natal Midlands; north-east of Pietermaritzburg.
Access: From Pietermaritzburg take the N3 northwards to Colenso and turn right onto the R74 towards Weenen; after 21 km turn right to the reserve The route is clearly signposted.
Accommodation: A camping and caravan site with 12 stands and ablution facilities.
Other facilities: Picnic sites with fireplaces; self-guided walking trails; fishing; curio shop.
Open: Throughout the year.
Opening time: Sunrise to sunset.
For further information: The Officer-in-charge, Weenen Nature Reserve, P.O. Box 122, Weenen 3325. Tel: (0363) 4-1809.

Weenen Nature Reserve consists of 4 908 ha of thorn scrub and grassland, and has a wide range of game species, including the most westerly population of black rhinoceros in Natal. White rhinoceros also occur here, as do buffalo, giraffe, kudu, eland, mountain reedbuck and steenbok.

169 WINDY RIDGE GAME PARK

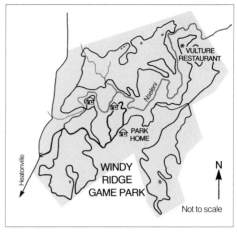

Location: Zululand; west of Empangeni.
Access: From Empangeni follow the R34 towards Melmoth; after 8 km, just after the Cactus drive-in cinema, turn right and drive for 9 km to Heatonville; continue northwards across the railway line, following the game park signposts for a further 11 km. The road is graded gravel for 11 km. An entrance fee is charged.
Accommodation: A camp with 6 rustic huts, each with a gas stove, refrigerator, cooking and eating utensils and bedding; communal ablution facilities (R18 per adult per night). A second camp with 6 8-bed rustic huts caters for school groups and has a separate kitchen unit and ablution facilities (R7 per person per day; R16 with meals). Park Home, isolated from the camps, sleeps 6 people (R80 per day).
Other facilities: A 60-km network of gravel game-viewing roads; guided walking trails; conference facilities; picnic site; guided game-

viewing drives; night drives can be arranged.
Open: Throughout the year.
Opening time: 07h30 to 18h00.
For further information: P.O. Heatonville 3881. Tel: (0351) 2-3465/7. Fax: (0351) 2-7208.

Windy Ridge, in the Nseleni River valley, is in flat to hilly country, dominated by acacia and mixed woodland, with riverine bush along the river. The park covers 1 300 ha and is home to white rhinoceros, giraffe, nyala, kudu, bushbuck, impala, warthog, leopard and crocodile. This is a good location for birdwatching.

170 PHINDA RESOURCE RESERVE

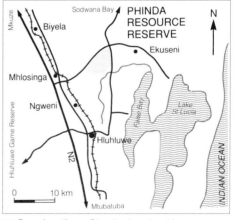

Location: North-eastern Zululand; north of Hluhluwe village.
Access: From the north on the N2 through Pongola and Mkuze, turn left to Mhlosinga Station, cross the railway line and turn right; continue for 13 km to the reserve signpost. From Durban follow the N2 northwards to the Ngweni/Sodwana Bay turn-off (after the Hluhluwe village turn-off), crossing over the N2; turn left at the stop sign; after 4 km turn right towards Sodwana. From here it is 13 km to the reserve entrance. There is a 1 500 m airstrip.
Accommodation: Luxury main lodge, rock chalets and bush suites.
Other facilities: Game-viewing drives and accompanied walks through widely differing ecosystems including wetlands, Fever Tree forests and Ilala Palm veld. Diving and snorkelling tours to the Maputaland coast can be arranged.

Opening time: Check when booking.
Beware: Malaria.
For further information and reservations: P.O. Box 1211, Sunninghill Park, 2157. Tel: (011) 803-8421; Fax: (011) 803-1810.

The recently established Phinda Resource Reserve, an upmarket 'eco-tourism' showpiece 15 000 ha in extent, provides visitors with a memorable wilderness experience and at the same time shares its considerable resources with the local rural community. The reserve encompasses hilly terrain, flat acacia bush, open savannah and riverine woodland. Some 10 000 head of game are present, such as elephant, lion, leopard, cheetah, hippo, white rhinoceros, giraffe, Burchell's zebra, nyala, blue wildebeest, impala, kudu, southern reedbuck, suni and warthog. Birdlife is varied (360 recorded species).

LESOTHO

171 Sehlabathebe National Park

The tiny kingdom of Lesotho, which shares its borders with South Africa and Transkei, is known as the 'mountain kingdom' and justifiably so. To the east lies the Drakensberg escarpment, the Central Range lies in the middle of the country, the Maluti Mountains in the north-west, the Blue Mountain range in the west, and the Southern Border range in the south-east. The only conservation area is the Sehlabathebe National Park, which lies right on the edge of the escarpment.

All visitors to Lesotho must carry a valid passport, and nationals other than South Africans may require visas. It is advisable not to wear camouflage or military-like clothing, and to be aware of the country's strictly enforced regulations on the transportation of alcohol. With a few exceptions, roads are usually in a poor state of repair and a 4x4 vehicle is needed for many routes. There are plans to upgrade a number of roads as part of the Highlands Water Scheme, although this same development, to harness the country's water resources, threatens the continued existence of Sehlabathebe. A large new conservation area has been proclaimed on the Natal border, as part of the Highlands Water Scheme.

In Lesotho rain falls in summer and during this season many routes become impassable. Winters are cold to very cold, and snow is quite common.

171 | SEHLABATHEBE NATIONAL PARK

Location: Far eastern Lesotho, on the Natal border; north-west of Kokstad.
Access: From Kokstad in Natal follow the R56 westwards for 70 km to Matatiele, then continue northward on a secondary road for about 34 km to the border post at Qacha's Nek; once in Lesotho drive for approximately 10 km to the T-junction and turn right to Tsoelike, continuing along this road to the reserve. The reserve can also be reached via Ramatseliso's Gate or Sani Pass. For all these routes a 4x4 vehicle is strongly advised. Access is difficult during summer rains, and winter snows could cut off all roads. It is possible to reach the reserve via a tarred road from Maseru to Mt. Moorosi, but beyond Mt. Moorosi the road becomes very poor. Hikers can reach the park via Bushman's Nek after a 6-hour hike. Air Lesotho will arrange flights from Maseru to the Ha Paulus airstrip and from there visitors can be transported to the lodge.
Accommodation: The park lodge provides fully equipped accommodation for up to 12 people; there is also a 5-bed hostel with basic facilities. Visitors must bring their own bedding and food. Camping is allowed in the park but there are no facilities.
Other facilities: Walking; trout fishing. There

are no shops or fuel supplies.
Open: Throughout the year.
Beware: Flooding rivers; be well equipped to cope with adverse weather conditions.
For further information: Sehlabathebe Lodge Reservations, Lesotho National Parks (see page 365). (Flights) Air Lesotho, P.O. Box 861, Maseru 100, Lesotho.

Sehlabathebe National Park lies within the Drakensberg, the highest mountain range in southern Africa, and covers 6 500 ha. The park's main appeal is its superb scenery and there is little game, although the occasional eland or grey rhebok may be sighted. One of the rivers running through the park, the Tsoelikana, protects a very rare fish, the Maluti, or Drakensberg, minnow which was once thought to be extinct. Several rare birds, such as the bearded vulture, bald ibis and orange-breasted rockjumper, may be seen here. Summers are wet and afternoon thunderstorms are common.

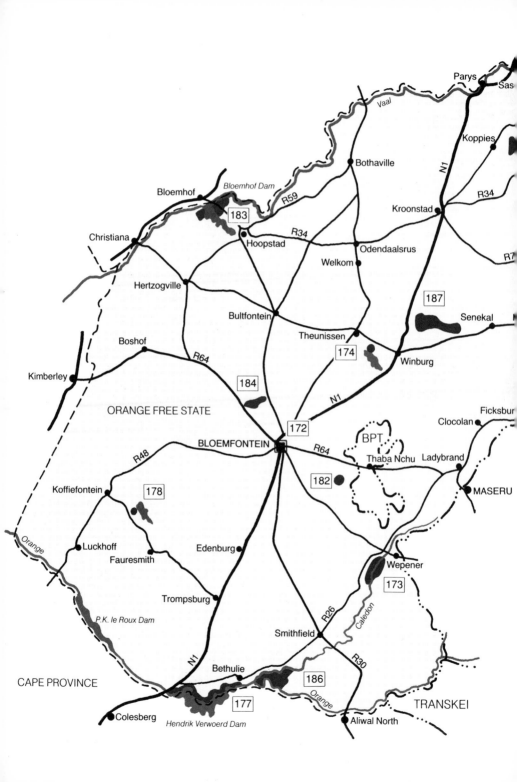

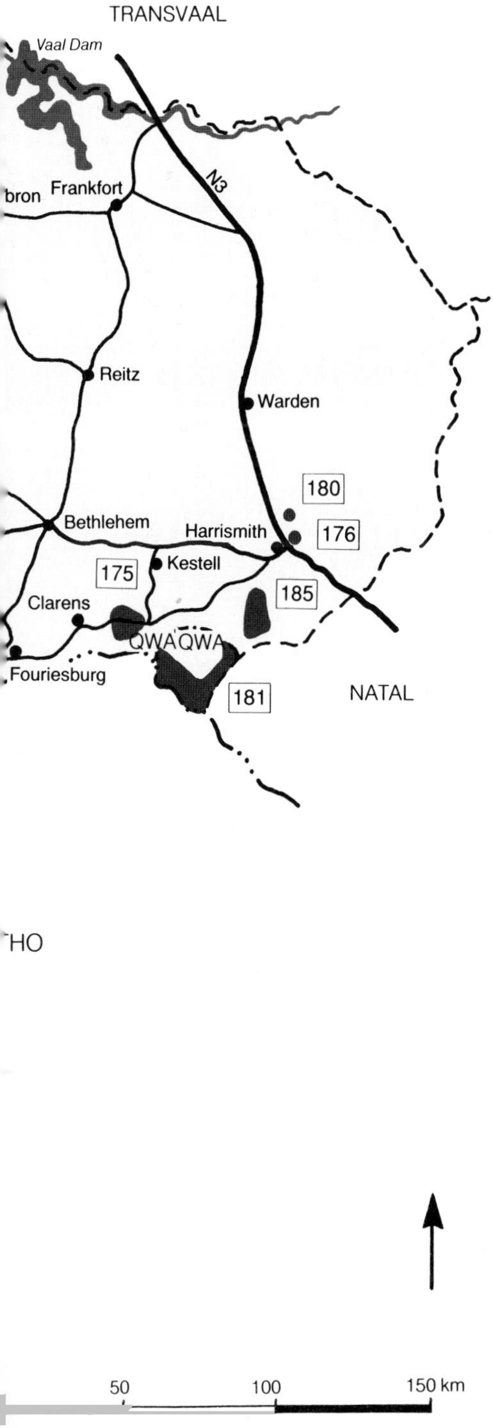

ORANGE FREE STATE AND QWAQWA

TRANSVAAL

Vaal Dam

bron Frankfort

N3

Reitz

Warden

Bethlehem   Harrismith

Kestell

175

Clarens

QWAQWA

Fouriesburg

181   NATAL

180

176

185

HO

50   100   150 km

172 Bloemfontein
173 Caledon Nature Reserve
174 Erfenis Dam Nature Reserve
175 Golden Gate Highlands National Park
176 Harrismith Botanic Garden
177 Hendrik Verwoerd Dam Nature Reserve
178 Kalkfontein Dam Nature Reserve
179 Koppies Dam Nature Reserve
180 Mount Everest Game Reserve
181 Qwaqwa Conservation Area
182 Rustfontein Dam Nature Reserve
183 Sandveld Nature Reserve
184 Soetdoring Nature Reserve
185 Sterkfontein Dam Nature Reserve
186 Tussen-die-Riviere Nature Reserve
187 Willem Pretorius Game Reserve

In the Orange Free State little remains of the once seemingly endless grassland that sustained vast herds of game. Much of the province consists of flat land on the Highveld plateau, although the south-eastern section bordering Lesotho and the Natal Drakensberg is very mountainous. This is a summer-rainfall area, with most rain falling in the form of thunderstorms.

The province has one national park, the Golden Gate Highlands National Park, and 14 nature reserves, which are controlled by the Directorate of Environmental and Nature Conservation. Most of the reserves are located around dams and are intended primarily for recreational use. However two, Seekoeivlei and Wuras Dam, are at present closed to the public. Seekoeivlei Nature Reserve protects an area of marsh wetland habitat on the banks of the Klip River and the birds it supports, while Wuras Dam is used principally by scientists researching aquatic organisms. A third area, the 134-ha Ficksburg Nature Reserve 15 km west of Ficksburg, has recently been opened to the public. For further information contact the Orange Free State Directorate of Environmental and Nature Conservation (see page 365).

In the corner formed by the borders of the eastern Orange Free State, Natal and Lesotho lies the tiny self-governing homeland of Qwaqwa. It has no conventional nature reserves, but a mountainous region known as the Qwaqwa Conservation Area has been set aside for the protection of wildlife and the development of tourism.

172 BLOEMFONTEIN

Franklin Nature Reserve

Delville Dr. The Franklin Nature Reserve covers approximately 200 ha of Naval Hill, a prominent feature of Bloemfontein on which are sited a number of historical landmarks. The reserve, which is open daily, harbours game species such as springbok, blesbok, red hartebeest and eland.

Orange Free State National Botanic Garden

Rayton Rd, Bloemfontein North. Lying approximately 10 km from central Bloemfontein, this botanic garden covers just over 45 ha and includes both formally laid-out displays and an area of natural vegetation. The garden is dominated by dolerite outcrops and protects remnants of grassland, low open woodland and elements of Karoo vegetation. There are fine collections of Rhus trees and Mesembryanthemum species, as well as a garden displaying grasses of economic importance. A number of small mammals occur and 83 bird species have been recorded.

173 CALEDON NATURE RESERVE

Location: Southern Orange Free State; southwest of Wepener.

Access: From Wepener follow the R26/R702 towards Bloemfontein for about 7 km, then turn left onto the graded gravel R701 in the direction of Smithfield; the reserve lies on the Welbedacht Dam to the left of the road.

Accommodation: None.

Other facilities: None.

Open: Throughout the year.

Opening time: Sunrise to sunset.

For further information: The First Nature Conservator, P.O. Box 84, Wepener 9944. Tel: (05232) 572.

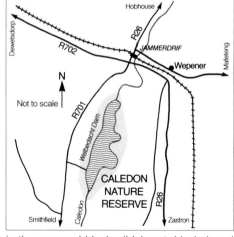

Caledon Nature Reserve covers 1 500 ha and surrounds the Welbedacht Dam on the Caledon River. The vegetation is mostly mixed grassland, with karee thorn, wild olive and white stinkwood growing in ravines and along rocky ridges. Mountain reedbuck and steenbok occur naturally in the area and black wildebeest, blesbok and springbok have been introduced. Many waterbirds are attracted to the dam, and the black stork breeds here.

174 ERFENIS DAM NATURE RESERVE

Location: Central Orange Free State; east of Theunissen.

Access: From Theunissen drive east along the R708 for about 8 km; at the Erfenis

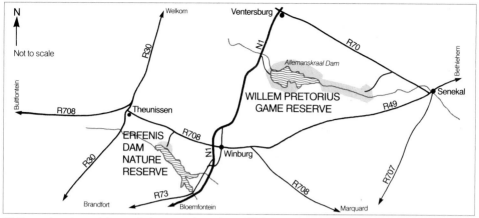

Dam sign turn right and then continue for approximately 9 km; turn at the nature conservation sign and drive 100 m to the reserve entrance.
Accommodation: Caravan and camping site with ablution facilities.
Other facilities: Game-viewing; boating;

fishing; picnic sites with fireplaces.
Open: Throughout the year.
Opening time: 06h00 to 21h00.
For further information: The First Nature Conservator, Erfenis Dam Nature Reserve, P.O. Box 131, Theunissen 9410. Tel: (0175) 4211.

The Erfenis Dam on the Vet River extends over 3 308 ha when full, and is a popular venue for boating and fishing. Black wildebeest, yellow blesbok, springbok, ostrich, red hartebeest and Burchell's zebra have been released in the adjacent reserve, which comprises a little over 400 ha of grassland.

175 GOLDEN GATE HIGHLANDS NATIONAL PARK

Location: Far eastern Orange Free State; south-west of Harrismith.
Access: From Harrismith follow the R49 towards Bethlehem for about 44 km, then turn left to Kestell on the R712; about 2 km beyond Kestell turn right onto a graded gravel road and follow this to the entrance.
Accommodation: *Brandwag camp* has suites with a double bed, lounge, bathroom and TV; single and double rooms, each with a bathroom and TV; 4- and 6-bed chalets, each with a bathroom, kitchen and TV. *Glen Reenen* has huts equipped with crockery, cutlery and cooking utensils, some with shower and toilet, some using an ablution block. The camping site has 60 stands, fireplaces and scullery and ablution facilities. The Rhebok trail hut sleeps 18 and has cooking facilities, firewood and drinking water. The Wilgenhof Youth Hostel for school and youth groups sleeps a maximum of 4 teachers and 60 children.
Other facilities: Network of game-viewing roads; 1- to 3-hour walks; 2-day hiking trail; horses for hire. *Glen Reenen* has a picnic site with fireplaces, a shop selling food and drink,

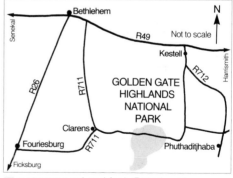

a stream pool and fuel; *Brandwag* has a restaurant and ladies bar, a coffee shop, an information centre and a curio shop, bowls and tennis courts.
Open: Throughout the year.
Opening time: 24 hours.
For further information: (Enquiries and booking) National Parks Board (see page 365). (Park address) P.O. Golden Gate 9708. Tel: (014326) 711.

The Golden Gate Highlands National Park is principally a scenic park of 6 241 ha in the foothills of the Maluti Mountains and extending to the borders of Qwaqwa and Lesotho. The park takes its name from sentinel-like 'gate-posts' of sandstone, one of several impressive formations carved by the Little Caledon River in the foothills of the Malutis, which range in altitude from 1 892 to 2 770 m. The vegetation is predominantly grassland, with pockets of forest in the ravines. Mountain reedbuck, grey rhebok and oribi occur naturally in the area, and a number of species have been re-introduced, including black wildebeest, eland, red hartebeest, blesbok and Burchell's zebra. The birdlife is not prolific (159 species have been recorded), but black eagles and bearded vultures may occasionally be seen.

176 HARRISMITH BOTANIC GARDEN

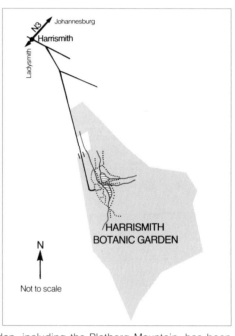

Location: Far eastern Orange Free State; east of Harrismith.
Access: The garden lies 5 km from Harrismith and is well signposted from the town.
Accommodation: None. Harrismith has hotels and a caravan and camping site.
Other facilities: Self-guided walking trails; information centre; picnic sites.
Open: Throughout the year.
Opening time: August to May – 07h00 to 16h45; June and July – 07h30 to 16h45.
For further information: The Town Clerk, Municipality of Harrismith, P.O. Box 43, Harrismith 9880. Tel: (01436) 2-1061.

Harrismith Botanic Garden, previously known as the Drakensberg Botanic Garden, covers 114 ha at the foot of Platberg, the flat-topped mountain which dominates this Free State town. More than 1 000 plant species from the Drakensberg area are displayed in the cultivated section, including some high-altitude ones which are concentrated in a rockery. Several walks wind through the natural areas, where more than 100 bird species have been recorded, as well as a variety of small mammals, including rock dassies, common duiker and yellow mongoose.

The 4 070-ha area adjacent to the botanic garden, including the Platberg Mountain, has been proclaimed the Platberg Nature Reserve. This is being developed at present; day visitors are allowed to enter the reserve on foot; there is one overnight house which may be hired; a number of walking trails are to be opened.

177 HENDRIK VERWOERD DAM NATURE RESERVE

Location: Extreme southern Orange Free State; north-east of Colesberg.
Access: From Colesberg take the R58 to Norvalspont and continue for 4 km; turn left and cross the Orange River; the reserve lies to the right of the road.
Accommodation: An Overvaal resort adjoining the reserve has 44 4- to 6-bed rondavels, each with a bathroom, kitchen and lounge/dining room (R37 or R59 per rondavel per night); a camping site with full ablution facilities; a caravan park.
Other facilities: Game-viewing; boating; fishing (permit required); hunting during winter; swimming pool; sporting facilities.
Open: Throughout the year.
Opening time: (Reserve) Summer – 06h00 to 19h00; and winter – 08h00 to 18h00.

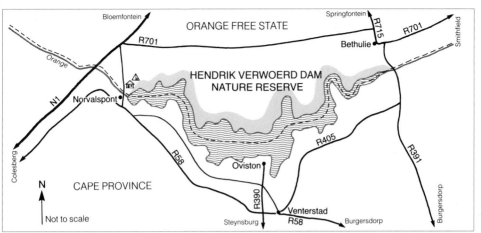

(Resort) 24 hours.
For further information: The First Nature Conservator, Hendrik Verwoerd Dam Nature Reserve, P.O. Hendrik Verwoerd Dam 9922.

Tel: 052172, ask for 26. (Resort) The Manager, Overvaal Hendrik Verwoerd Dam Resort, Private Bag X10, Hendrik Verwoerd Dam 9922. Tel: 052172, ask for 45.

With a surface area of approximately 36 000 ha when full, the Hendrik Verwoerd Dam is the largest expanse of inland water in South Africa. Built across the Orange River, the dam is practically surrounded by nature reserves: the Oviston Nature Reserve lies on its southern shore, in the Cape Province, Tussen-die-Riviere Game Farm is situated to the east, and the reserve bearing the dam's name stretches along its northern shore.

The 11 237-ha Hendrik Verwoerd Dam Nature Reserve is predominantly grassland, with the occasional rocky ridge and outcrop. A number of game species, such as springbok, black wildebeest, blesbok, mountain reedbuck and steenbok, can be seen, as well as a breeding herd of Cape mountain zebra, released here in 1985.

178 KALKFONTEIN DAM NATURE RESERVE

Location: South-western Orange Free State; north of Fauresmith.
Access: From Fauresmith take the R704 in the direction of Koffiefontein; take the Petrusburg turn-off. Turn left at the nature conservation signpost.
Accommodation: None. Camping is permitted.
Other facilities: Boating and fishing are permitted; picnic sites with fireplaces.
Open: Throughout the year.
Opening time: 24 hours.
For further information: The First Nature Conservator, Kalkfontein Dam Nature Reserve, P.O. Box 78, Fauresmith 9978. Tel: 05822, ask for 1422 or 1441.

This tiny reserve, only 162 ha in extent, surrounds the 5 075-ha Kalkfontein Dam. It is principally a recreational area (the dam is a favourite haunt of fishermen), although more than 50 waterbird species have been recorded, and many of them breed here.

179 KOPPIES DAM NATURE RESERVE

Location: North-eastern Orange Free State; north-east of Kroonstad.

Access: From Kroonstad take the N1 towards Parys; after approximately 6 km turn right onto the tarred secondary road to Koppies; turn right again at the town and then left onto a gravel road to the dam. Alternatively, take the toll road to Johannesburg from Kroonstad; take the Koppies turn-off and proceed as above.

Accommodation: None. Camping is permitted and there are basic ablution facilities.

Other facilities: Game-viewing; boating and fishing (licence required) are permitted.

Open: Throughout the year.

Opening time: 07h00 to 21h00.

For further information: The First Nature

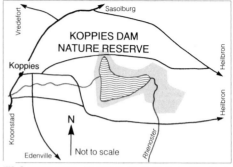

Conservator, Koppies Dam Nature Reserve, P.O. Box 151, Koppies 9540. Tel: 016152, ask for 2521.

Koppies Dam Nature Reserve covers 4 325 ha and surrounds the Koppies Dam on the Rhenoster River. This is grassland country, interspersed with patches of sweet thorn along the river banks. A few game species have been released here and these include black wildebeest, blesbok, springbok, Burchell's zebra, buffalo and impala. The dam attracts a broad spectrum of waterbirds.

180 MOUNT EVEREST GAME RESERVE

Location: Far eastern Orange Free State; south-east of Harrismith.

Access: 3 km north of Harrismith on the N3 (Johannesburg/Durban) turn east onto the Verkykerskop road; follow for 13 km and turn right. The reserve turn-off is a further 5 km and lies on the right.

Accommodation: 2 to 6-bed log chalets, fully equipped; rondavels (4 rondavels make up one living unit), fully equipped; 4 x 'rustic rooms' in a farmhouse. Two caravan parks with full ablution facilities. Rates range from R40-R70 per person per night (additional R15 per person in season). Sleeping in caves permitted (R15 per person) but only sleeping bags/stretchers provided.

Other facilities: Conference centre; curio shop and fast-food outlet; four hiking trails; horse-riding; swimming pool; 'vulture restaurant'; game-viewing (accompanied if required); bass and trout fishing.

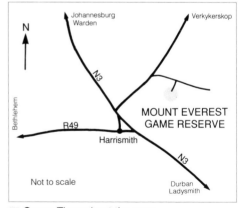

Open: Throughout the year.

Opening times: Check with owner.

For further information: P.O. Box 471, Harrismith 9880. Tel: (01436) 2-3493 or 2-1816.

Mount Everest Game Reserve lies in mountainous terrain and incorporates the mountains Mooihoek, Glen Paul and Everest. The vegetation is dominated by high-altitude Drakensberg species, with pockets of indigenous forest.

There are 21 game species present, including white rhinoceros, blesbok, black wildebeest, eland, gemsbok and a number of exotics such as fallow deer and camels. More than 130 bird species have been recorded. This high-altitude area experiences cold winters.

88. Eland have been re-introduced to Golden Gate Highlands National Park.

89. The most noticeable feature of Golden Gate is the cliffs with their coloured layers of sandstone.

90. Golden Gate Highlands National Park in the foothills of the Maluti mountains.

91. The buffalo in the Willem Pretorius Game Reserve comprise the largest disease-free herd in South Africa.

92. The Platberg forms a backdrop to Harrismith Botanic Garden.

93. Tussen-die-Riviere Game Farm lies at the confluence of the Orange and Caledon rivers.

94. The paradise flycatcher inhabits forest in the coastal reserves of Transkei.

95. Nodules of hard rock embedded in softer sandstone are a feature of the coast at Hluleka Nature Reserve.

96. Several streams flow through the Mkambati Nature Reserve to the sea.

97. Open grassland and coastal forest are components of the Dwesa Nature Reserve.

98. Springbok flourish in the Tsolwana Game Park.

99. The crowned eagle finds sanctuary in the Katberg Forest.

100. Much of the Tsolwana Game Park is covered by grassland.

Location: Qwaqwa; south-west of Harrismith.
Access: From Harrismith travel along the R49 towards Bethlehem for 8 km, then turn left onto the tarred R712 to Phuthaditjhaba. A new route via Reitz has recently been opened and is 30 km shorter than via Bethlehem. There are roads to Metshi-Matsho (Swartwater) Dam and Witsieshoek Mountain Resort, but much of the area is accessible only on foot.
Accommodation: Within the Conservation Area there are basic huts on the various hiking trails. *Witsieshoek Mountain Resort* offers hotel-type accommodation. *Fika Patso Dam Resort* has 20 self-catering chalets and conference facilities. There is a hotel in Phuthaditjhaba (Witsieshoek).
Other facilities: 3 1-day hiking trails (Mont-aux-Sources, Metshi-Matsho and Wetsi Caves) with overnight facilities (more hiking trails are planned); trout fishing (licence required) in the Metshi-Matsho Dam; *Korfshoek Day Resort* has picnic sites – self-catering chalets and camping and caravan sites are planned, as well as horse trails, fishing and a day hiking trail.
Open: Throughout the year.
Opening time: 24 hours; it is wise to travel only by day. Visit the Tourist Information Centre near Phuthaditjhaba (08h00 to 16h30; Sats. 08h00 to 13h00) before venturing into the mountains.

Beware: Weather extremes may be expected at all times; thunderstorms are common in summer, as are snow and bitter cold in winter.
For further information: Qwaqwa Tourism and Nature Conservation Corporation (see page 365).

The Conservation Area covers about 30 000 ha of mountainous terrain high in the Maluti Mountains and Drakensberg. Short grassland dominates the vegetation but there are small patches of indigenous forest and open areas dominated by protea bushes, and tree ferns grow along some of the streams. Although wildlife is scarce, the hiker may see grey rhebok, baboons and rock dassies, and rare birds such as the bearded vulture, Cape vulture, bald ibis and wattled crane. The high altitude ensures that summer temperatures are mild to cold, and in winter snow falls on the mountain peaks.

182 | RUSTFONTEIN DAM NATURE RESERVE

Location: South-eastern Orange Free State; south-east of Bloemfontein.
Access: From Bloemfontein follow the R64 towards Thaba Nchu for approximately 60 km; turn off to the right and watch for signposts.
Accommodation: None. Camping is permitted and there are basic facilities.
Other facilities: Watersports and fishing; picnic sites with fireplaces.
Open: Throughout the year.
Opening time: 24 hours.
For further information: The Director, Directorate of Environmental and Nature Conservation (see page 365).

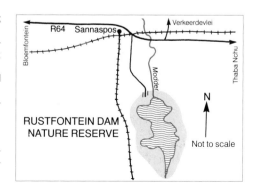

This 393-ha reserve surrounding the Rustfontein Dam on the Modder River is a popular recreational area and is not recommended for those seeking tranquillity.

Large numbers of waterfowl may be seen on the dam and a few head of game are present on the grassland plains.

183 SANDVELD NATURE RESERVE

Location: North-western Orange Free State; north-west of Bloemfontein.
Access: From Bloemfontein take the R700 towards Hoopstad via Bultfontein; continue along the R700 towards Bloemhof and watch out for signposts on the left, just before the bridge.
Accommodation: Caravan park with electricity and ablutions blocks. Camping is permitted and there are basic ablution facilities.
Other facilities: Game-viewing; fishing (licence required); picnic sites with fireplaces; boating is permitted.
Open: Throughout the year.
Opening time: 06h00 to 21h00.
For further information: The First Nature

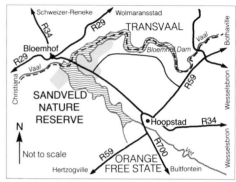

Conservator, Sandveld Nature Reserve, P.O. Box 414, Bloemhof 2660. Tel: (018022) 1103.

The Sandveld Nature Reserve is situated at the confluence of the Vet and Vaal rivers along the southern bank of the Bloemhof Dam. The dam covers approximately 25 000 ha and the reserve a further 14 700 ha.

Kalahari thornveld, comprising camel thorn trees and sweet grassland, dominates and supports a number of introduced game animals, among them giraffe, eland, gemsbok, red hartebeest and blue wildebeest.

The varied birdlife includes flocks of ducks and geese on the dam, as well as a range of typical thornveld species, such as white-backed vulture, yellow-billed and grey hornbills, pygmy falcon, sociable weaver, and crimson-breasted and long-tailed shrikes.

184 SOETDORING NATURE RESERVE

Location: Western-central Orange Free State; north-west of Bloemfontein.
Access: From Bloemfontein follow the R700 in the direction of Bultfontein for approximately 40 km, then watch out for signposts; the Soetdoring Nature Reserve is to the left of the road.
Accommodation: None.
Other facilities: Game-viewing; predator park; picnic sites with fireplaces; fishing; no powered boats permitted.
Open: Throughout the year.
Opening time: 07h00 to 18h00.
For further information: The First Nature

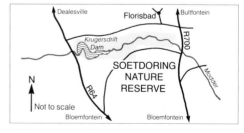

Conservator, Soetdoering Nature Reserve, P.O. Box 517, Bloemfontein 9300. Tel: (051) 33-1011.

The Soetdoring Nature Reserve covers 4 117 ha around the Krugersdrift Dam on the Modder River. The vegetation is a mixture of False Upper Karoo vegetation, dominated by low, scrubby bushes, and sweet grassland. Dense stands of sweet-thorn trees line the river. Many game species associated with grassland plains have been re-introduced, including Burchell's zebra, black wildebeest, blesbok and springbok. The dam attracts large flocks of ducks and geese when it is full, and martial eagles and secretary birds breed in the reserve.

185 STERKFONTEIN DAM NATURE RESERVE

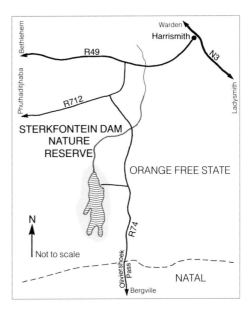

Location: Far eastern Orange Free State; south-west of Harrismith.
Access: From Harrismith take the R49 towards Bethlehem and after about 5 km turn left onto the R712 towards Qwaqwa and the Oliviershoek Pass; continue for about 8 km; turn left onto the R74 towards Bergville/Oliviershoek Pass. After about 8 km follow the signposts, pointing right, to the Sterkfontein Dam.
Accommodation: 10 chalets (self-catering); a farmhouse for groups; caravan park with electricity, a modern ablution block and laundry facilities; camping at the water's edge is permitted. Qwantani time-sharing resort is situated on the western side of the resort.
Other facilities: Limited walking; watersports and fishing are permitted; boat sheds; ramp for boats; clubhouse for watersports may be hired.
Open: Throughout the year.
Opening time: 06h00 to 21h00.
For further information: The First Nature Conservator, Sterkfontein Dam Nature Reserve, P.O. Box 24, Harrismith 9880. Tel: (01436) 2-3520.

This nature reserve is being developed around the Sterkfontein Dam, a 7 000-ha catchment area which is unusual in that it is filled with water pumped over the Drakensberg escarpment from the Tugela River. The reserve is situated in the foothills of the Drakensberg range and its vegetation is predominantly mountain grassland. Yellowwood trees are found in the ravines, however, and proteas and Natal bottle brush grow on the slopes.
Future plans include the development of hiking trails and overnight facilities and the stocking of game.

186 TUSSEN-DIE-RIVIERE NATURE RESERVE

Location: Extreme southern Orange Free State; east of Bethulie.
Access: From Smithfield follow the R701 towards Goedemoed for about 15 km before taking the signposted right turn to Tussen-die-Riviere.
Accommodation: 6 chalets with communal ablution facilities (R30 per chalet per day); a camping site with full ablution facilities; and a few 'shelters' for hikers.
Other facilities: Network of game-viewing roads; walking trails; picnic sites.
Open: October to April (controlled game hunting takes place between May and September).
Opening time: 07h00 to 18h00.
For further information: Principal Nature Conservator, Tussen-die-Riviere, P.O. Box 16, Bethulie 9992. Tel: (05862) 2803.

A roughly triangular wedge of land at the confluence of the Orange and Caledon rivers, Tussen-die-Riviere Nature Reserve covers 22 000 ha. Its terrain comprises rocky ridges and ravines interspersed with areas of open plain, with Aasvoëlkop rising to a peak on the eastern boundary. The plains are covered by grass and low Karoo bushes, with a variety of tree species growing on the ridges and along

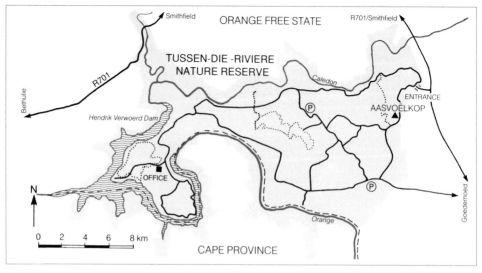

the river banks. Apart from the small mammals that occur naturally in the area, such as the bat-eared fox, aardwolf and steenbok, many game species have been introduced. Visitors may see white rhinoceros, Burchell's zebra, blue and black wildebeest, blesbok, springbok, kudu, eland, gemsbok, mountain reedbuck, red hartebeest, ostrich and klipspringer. The birdlife is abundant, the game birds and waterbirds associated with the riverine habitats being of particular interest.

187 WILLEM PRETORIUS GAME RESERVE See map Erfenis Dam Nature Reserve

Location: Central Orange Free State; north-east of Bloemfontein.

Access: From Bloemfontein take the N1 towards Kroonstad; approximately 30 km north of Winburg take the signposted right turn to the reserve and continue for 8 km to the entrance. Access is also possible from the R70 between Ventersburg and Senekal. An entrance fee is charged.

Accommodation: An Overvaal public holiday resort at the western entrance has 2-bed rondavels, each with a lounge/dining room, kitchen and bathroom; more basic 2-bed rondavels, cabins and family cottages are also available. There is also a caravan and camping site with ablution facilities.

Other facilities: Extensive network of game-viewing roads; fishing (permit available from office); boat tours; boating permitted; swimming pool; sporting facilities; licensed restaurant; picnic sites; shop selling fresh produce and fuel. An environment education centre, controlled by the Directorate of Environmental and Nature Conservation, opened in December 1990: 10 chalets; accommodation for groups of up to 140 children; recreation hall; conference facilities; restaurant; swimming pool; environmental education lectures to organised groups; open to general public on a booking basis.

Open: Throughout the year.

Opening time: (Reserve) Summer – 06h00 to 19h00; winter – 08h00 to 18h00. (Resort) 24 hours.

Speed limit: 50 km/h.

For further information: The First Nature Conservator, P.O. Willem Pretorius Game Reserve, via Ventersburg 9450. Tel: (01734) 4168. (Resort) The Resort Manager, Overvaal Willem Pretorius, address as above. Tel: (01734) 4229. (Environment education centre) The Manager, Tel: (01734) 4003/4.

This 12 005-ha reserve surrounds the Allemanskraal Dam, which has a surface area of 2 771 ha. Stone ruins lying in different parts of the reserve are of archaeological interest, and a number of historical sites are situated nearby. The southern part of the reserve is mainly open grassland, but in the north the land is broken by ridges, ravines and watercourses. A variety of tree species are scattered throughout the area, and dense stands of sweet thorn grow at the foot of the ridges.

Many game species, such as white rhinoceros, buffalo, giraffe, Burchell's zebra, reedbuck, black wildebeest, red hartebeest, kudu, eland, springbok and blesbok, have been released into the Willem Pretorius reserve. Large numbers of waterbirds are attracted to the dam, while game birds are abundant on the plains. Approximately 220 bird species have been recorded, including martial and fish eagles which are known to breed here each year.

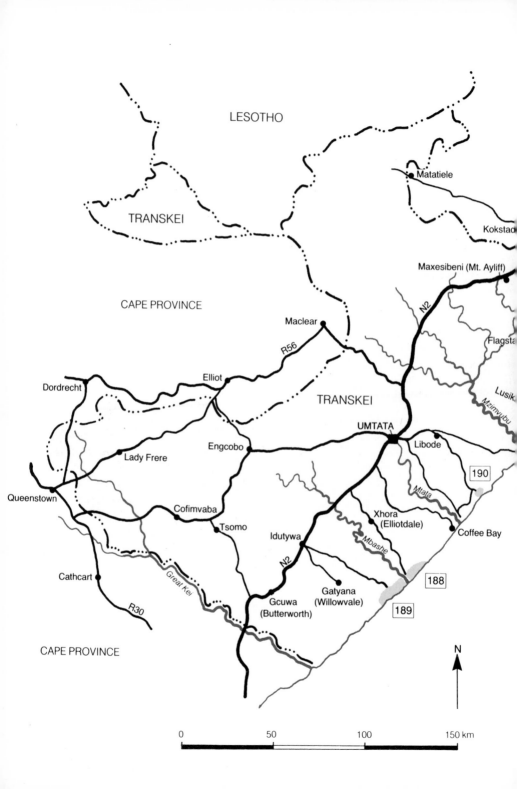

TRANSKEI

188 Cwebe Nature Reserve
189 Dwesa Nature Reserve
190 Hluleka Nature Reserve
191 Mkambati Nature Reserve
192 Silaka Nature Reserve

Declared independent from South Africa in 1976, Transkei covers approximately 45 000 km² between the Great Kei River in the south-west, the Drakensberg in the north-west, and the Mtamvuna River in the north. The country's rugged terrain ranges in altitude from sea-level to 2 400 m in the Drakensberg, and a number of impressive rivers which rise in the highlands deeply incise the landscape as they run their course before flowing into the Indian Ocean to the east.

A high human population has resulted in extensive modifications to the countryside, but the coastline, where all the country's nature reserves are situated, remains relatively unspoilt. Stretching 250 km, the Wild Coast, as it is known, contains a number of distinct habitats, including rugged cliffs, estuaries rich in birdlife, mangrove swamps, dense indigenous forests and grassland. The constantly changing scene makes this a popular venue for hiking. Transkei receives most of its annual rainfall (750 to 1 400 mm) in the summer months, between October and March.

Secondary roads to the coastal reserves vary in condition, but are often in a poor state of repair, particularly during the rainy season. Information on road conditions can be obtained from local police stations or from the Transkei Department of Commerce, Industry and Tourism (see page 365). Some confusion may be caused by changes that are being made to the road numbering system.

South African visitors must carry passports or identity documents and other foreign nationals must be in possession of a valid passport and a visa. Identity documents should be carried in a safe place at all times and a careful watch kept on any items of value. As thefts from camps and cars in reserves are apparently on the increase, all valuables should be locked out of view in the car boot.

A number of new reserves have been proposed, but their future is still uncertain. Information about them can be obtained from the Department of Commerce, Industry and Tourism.

188 CWEBE NATURE RESERVE

Location: Southern Transkei; east of Idutywa.
Access: From Idutywa follow the N2 towards Umtata for 49 km; turn right onto a gravel road and drive southwards for 23 km to Xhora (formerly Elliotdale); continue beyond Xhora, following signposts to 'The Haven'.
Accommodation: Self-catering accommodation and a camping site are being developed. The Haven Hotel lies within the reserve.
Other facilities: Pathways; fishing.
Opening time: Sunrise to sunset.
For further information: Transkei Department of Agriculture and Forestry (see page 365). (Haven Hotel) P.O. Xhora (Elliotdale), Transkei.Tel: (0471) 2-5344/5.

A newly established nature reserve, Cwebe contains a variety of habitats – forest, grassland, mangrove and beach – which support a wide range of birds and small mammals. The Mbanyana River is an added attraction, with its spectacular waterfalls and beautiful lagoon where Cape clawless otters may be observed. The 2 149-ha reserve is bounded to the south by the Mbashe River and from here a sandy beach, popular with anglers and shell-collectors, stretches northward.

189 DWESA NATURE RESERVE See map Cwebe Nature Reserve

Location: Southern Transkei; east of Idutywa.
Access: From Idutywa turn right towards Gatyana (formerly Willowvale); at the next signpost to Gatyana take the left fork and follow the signposts south to the reserve.
Accommodation: 5 5-bed chalets; 3 4-bed chalets (R50 to R60 per chalet per night); all have gas refrigerators and stoves. A camping site has 20 stands and ablution facilities.
Other facilities: Pathways; fishing within a demarcated zone. Visitors are advised to take all their requirements, including fuel.
Open: Throughout the year.
Opening time: 06h00 to 18h00.
For further information: Transkei Department of Agriculture and Forestry (see page 365).

Dwesa Nature Reserve, the first reserve to be proclaimed in Transkei, is separated from Cwebe Nature Reserve by the Mbashe River. Although the two reserves are very similar in habitat and vegetation and support many of the same small mammals and birds, Dwesa also contains a number of introduced species, including red hartebeest, blesbok and blue wildebeest. Crocodiles have been re-introduced to the rivers and buffalo, eland and warthog once again roam the grassland and forest fringes. The birdlife in this 3 900-ha reserve includes such rarities as the narina trogon and mangrove kingfisher.

190 HLULEKA NATURE RESERVE

Location: Central Transkei; east of Umtata and north of Coffee Bay.
Access: From Umtata follow the R61 eastwards for 29 km to Libode; shortly after Libode turn right onto a gravel road and follow it southwards for 90 km to the reserve.
Accommodation: 12 fully equipped 6-bed chalets (R60 per chalet per night). Book in advance.
Other facilities: Self-guided walks; fishing.

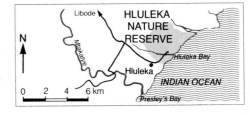

Visitors are advised to take all their require-ments, including fuel.
Open: Throughout the year.

Opening time: 06h00 to 18h00.
For further information: Transkei Department of Agriculture and Forestry (see page 365).

This small, hilly reserve, covering 772 ha, contains patches of indigenous forest and grassland. Although a few game species, such as eland and Burchell's zebra, have been introduced, the main appeal for the naturalist is the abundant birdlife. The rocky coastline provides excellent fishing and attracts large numbers of fishermen during holiday periods. Anglers should be aware that here, as at all Transkeian reserves, collecting bait is not permitted.

191 MKAMBATI NATURE RESERVE

Location: Northern Transkei; south-east of Kokstad.
Access: From Kokstad follow the N2 south-wards for 7 km to the border crossing at Brooks Nek; continue for another 7 km, then turn left towards Bizana; after about 36 km turn right at Magusheni onto the R61 to Flagstaff. About 29 km further on turn left towards Holy Cross and watch out for signposts to the reserve. Alternatively, to reach Umtentu to the north of the reserve, turn left at Magusheni onto the R61 and drive for 28 km; turn right to Impisi and continue past this settlement to Umtentu.
Accommodation: 3-bed rondavels (R30 per rondavel per day); a 20-bed thatched house and 6- or 8-bed cottages (R25 per person per day); a 10-bed serviced lodge (R65 per person per day); communal ablution facilities for all. A cook will prepare visitors' food.
Other facilities: Pathways; fishing; canoeing.

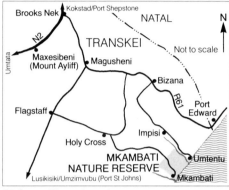

Open: Throughout the year.
Opening time: 06h00 to 18h00.
For further information: Transkei Department of Agriculture and Forestry (see page 365).

Lying between the Msikaba and Mtentu rivers and dissected by perennial streams, the Mkambati Nature Reserve has mainly grassland vegetation, similar to that of other Transkeian reserves. Subtropical influences, however, are stronger in its more northerly position, and a wide variety of plants are found within the reserve, including the Pondoland palm or 'mkambati' coconut. Eland, red hartebeest, blue wildebeest, blesbok and gemsbok have been introduced, and the birdlife is prolific.

192 SILAKA NATURE RESERVE

Location: Central Transkei; east of Umtata.
Access: From Umtata take the R61 eastwards towards Umzimvubu (Port St. Johns); just be-fore this village, the road turns off to the reserve.
Accommodation: 14 self-contained 4-bed chalets (R30 per chalet per night).
Other facilities: Short trails; fishing.
Open: Throughout the year.
Opening time: 06h00 to 18h00.
For further information: Transkei Department of Agriculture and Forestry (see page 365).

This beautiful reserve lies in a forested valley, with grassy hills near the coast which support blesbok, blue wildebeest and Burchell's zebra. The birdlife includes a variety of forest birds.

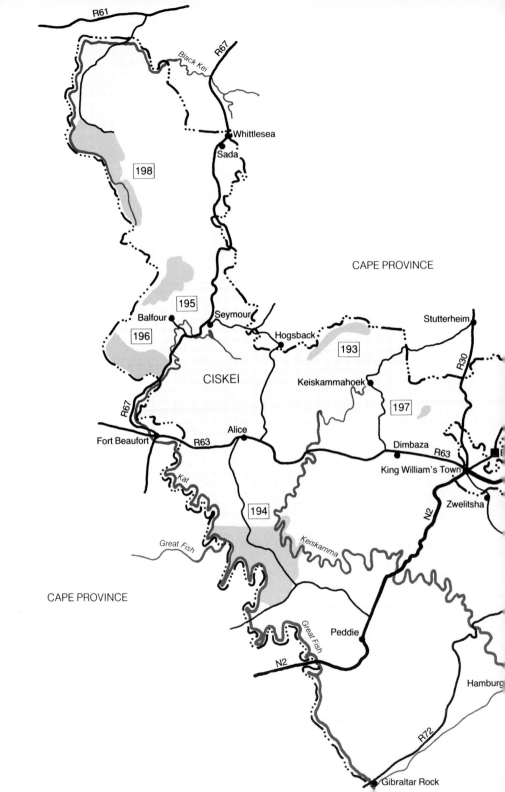

R61

R67

Black Kei

Whittlesea

Sada

198

CAPE PROVINCE

195

Seymour

Stutterheim

Balfour

196

Hogsback

193

R30

CISKEI

Keiskammahoek

197

R67

Alice

Dimbaza

R63

Fort Beaufort

R63

King William's Town

Kat

Zwelitsha

N2

194

Great Fish

Keiskamma

CAPE PROVINCE

Great Fish

Peddie

N2

Hamburg

R72

Gibraltar Rock

N

10   20   30   40   50 km

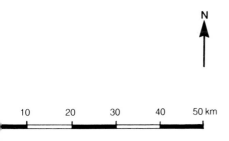

erlin
N2
Mdantsane

EAST LONDON

R72

Kidd's Beach

INDIAN OCEAN

CISKEI

193 **Amatola Forest**
194 **Double Drift Game Reserve**
195 **Katberg and Readsdale Forests**
196 **Mpofu Game Reserve**
197 **Pirie Forest**
198 **Tsolwana Game Reserve**

Ciskei, granted independence in 1981, is a small country of approximately 8 500 km². Despite its size, it is an ecologically diverse region, containing several distinct vegetational zones and ranging in altitude from sea-level to some 2 000 m above it. There are tracts of indigenous forest, semi-arid Fish River Valley Bushveld – dense, thorny, succulent bush with occasional open glades – and grassland, and on the plateau to the north dry, scrubby, Karoo-type vegetation occurs. At the coast there are 11 tidal estuaries, which are of particular interest to the birdwatcher.

Most of the annual rain falls during thunderstorms in the period from October to March. Winter days in the interior are generally clear and cool, although nights can be cold; towards the coast average temperatures become higher. Mist occurs frequently, particularly in the warm, wet summer months, but it usually clears by midmorning.

There are no passport or visa requirements at Ciskei's border crossings, but all visitors should carry a passport or identity document when touring in the country.

AMATOLA FOREST

Location: Eastern-central Ciskei; north-west of Bisho.
Access: From Bisho follow the R63 westwards in the direction of Fort Beaufort for 24 km and then turn right onto the R352 to Keiskammahoek. The reserve is clearly signposted from this settlement and is approached on graded gravel roads.
Accommodation: 5 trail lodges.

Other facilities: Hiking trails varying in length from 1 to 6 days (booking is essential); trout fishing (permit is required).
Open: Throughout the year.
Opening time: 24 hours.
For further information: The Department of Forestry, Private Bag X501, Zwelitsha 5608, Ciskei or The Department of Tourism (see page 365).

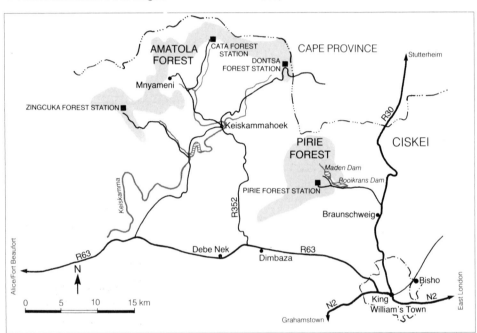

Superb mountain scenery, large blocks of indigenous forest and an extensive grass-covered plateau make Amatola Forest well worth a visit. Hikers have a good chance of seeing common duiker, bushbuck, samango monkey (their loud 'jack' call is frequently heard), baboon and rock dassie. This area is also the home of the nocturnal tree dassie, and although its blood-curdling screams carry through the forest after dark, the animal is not often seen. Two rare amphibians, the Hogsback frog and Amatola toad, find refuge here. The birdlife is particularly rich, and a number of rarities, such as the crowned eagle and narina trogon, may be spotted.

This area receives a high annual rainfall (up to 2 000 mm), most of which falls during the summer months. Mist is common at this time.

DOUBLE DRIFT GAME RESERVE

Location: Western Ciskei; north of Peddie, on the Great Fish and Keiskamma rivers.
Access: From Peddie drive along the N2 for approximately 8 km and turn left onto the R345

to Breakfast Vlei, which lies on the reserve's southern boundary. The road continues through the reserve to Alice, via Lekfontein and Victoria Post. Access is also possible through the Andries Vosloo Kudu Reserve (see page 187) at Double Drift, but this crossing should not be attempted if the Great Fish River is in flood. There is no internal road network open for public use as yet.

Accommodation: *Mbabala Lodge* sleeps 10 and is fully furnished and serviced; *Double Drift Lodge* is on the hiking trail and can accommodate 10 people; *Mvubu Bush Camp* is situated right on the Fish River and offers luxurious accommodation for 8 people in 4 stone and thatch huts.

Other facilities: 1- to 3-day guided hiking trails; game-viewing; trophy hunting in the winter months. Horse trails and white water rafting are planned for the future.

Open: Throughout the year.

Opening time: Sunrise to sunset (public road open 24 hours).

Beware: Water on the hiking trails should be boiled.

For further information: The Manager, Double Drift Game Reserve, P.O. Box 408,

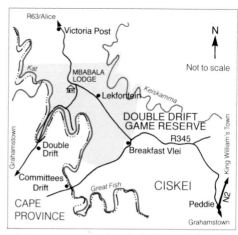

Alice 5700, Ciskei. Tel: 04049, ask for Alice 1403 or 1421. For bookings, or if you experience difficulty, contact Ciskei Safaris (see page 366).

The Double Drift Game Reserve is still being developed, but promises to become one of the finer reserves in the region. Covering approximately 22 000 ha, it adjoins the Andries Vosloo Kudu Reserve/Sam Knott Nature Reserve in the eastern Cape Province. Most of the reserve lies in the rugged Great Fish River valley and the vegetation is predominantly the dense, semi-succulent thorn scrub associated with this location. Away from the river, small patches of forest occur in the gorges and grassland areas.

It is planned to introduce a great variety of game species to the area – even elephant have been discussed. Species that can be seen at present include bushbuck, kudu, blesbok, common duiker, impala, blue wildebeest, Burchell's zebra, warthog, hippopotamus, giraffe and a wide range of smaller species. The birdlife is particularly rich along the Great Fish River and in the wooded gorges.

This area has a low annual rainfall (less than 500 mm), most of which occurs in summer.

195 KATBERG AND READSDALE FORESTS

Location: Ciskei; north of Fort Beaufort.

Access: From Fort Beaufort follow the R67 northwards for approximately 25 km and then turn left onto the R351, following the signposts to Katberg.

Accommodation: The Highlands/Katberg resort and Katberg Hotel lie just outside the Katberg State Forest and provide a variety of accommodation.

Other facilities: Nature trails lasting between 1 and 4 hours; a hiking trail; horse-riding trails. The hotel and resort offer a wide variety of sporting activities, as well as fuel and a shop selling basic foodstuffs.

For further information: The Department of Forestry, Private Bag X501, Zwelitsha 5608, Ciskei. (Highlands/Katberg Resort) P.O. Box 40, Balfour, Ciskei. Tel: 040452, ask for 1002. (Katberg Hotel) P.O. Box Katberg 5742, Ciskei. Tel: 040452, ask for 3.

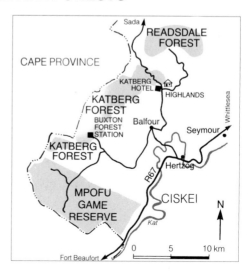

Mountainous terrain and indigenous forest make this an area of outstanding scenic beauty. A number of small mammals occur here and these include baboon, samango monkey, bushbuck and other small antelope. The birdlife is rich, and Cape parrot, Knysna lourie, chorister robin and crowned eagle may be observed.

196 MPOFU GAME RESERVE See map Katberg and Readsdale Forests

Location: Northern Ciskei; north of Fort Beaufort.
Access: From Fort Beaufort drive along the R67 towards Seymour and after approximately 25 km turn left onto the R351 towards Balfour; about 4 km further on, at the entrance to Balfour, turn left, following the road south-westward towards Buxton Forest Station; the road to the reserve branches to the left after approximately 10 km.
Accommodation: *Ntloni Lodge* sleeps 8 people and is luxuriously furnished and fully serviced.
Other facilities: Guided walking trails from August to March (maximum 10 walkers per day); trophy hunting during the winter months.
Open: Throughout the year.
Opening time: Sunrise to sunset.
For further information: The Manager, Mpofu Game Reserve, P.O. Box 647, Fort Beaufort 5720. Tel: 040452, ask for 11. For bookings, or if you experience difficulty, contact Ciskei Safaris (see page 366).

Mpofu Game Reserve extends from the Katberg Mountains in the north to the Kat River in the south and covers approximately 12 000 ha of rolling grassland and Fish River Valley Bushveld, with isolated pockets of indigenous forest. A number of game species have been introduced. The reserve is still under development as a conservation area.

197 PIRIE FOREST See map Amatola Forest

Location: Eastern-central Ciskei; north of King William's Town.
Access: From King William's Town follow the R30 towards Stutterheim for 13 km, then turn left onto the gravel road to Maden Dam, which lies 7 km further on. The entrance to Pirie Forest is a short way beyond the dam; no vehicles are permitted in the forest.
Accommodation: None. King William's Town has hotels and a caravan and camping site.
Other facilities: 2 hiking trails, 8 km and 9 km long; a picnic site at Maden Dam; an information centre.
Open: Throughout the year.
For further information: The Ciskei Department of Tourism (see page 365). Kaffrarian Museum, P.O. Box 1434, King William's Town 5600.

This beautiful forested area is steeped in tribal history and was one of several scenes of conflict between the British and Colonial soldiers and the Xhosa people during the Frontier Wars of the nineteenth century. For many years the forest's timber was exploited for commercial and military purposes, and evidence of the early woodcutters' activities can still be seen. The indigenous vegetation harbours a rich and varied birdlife.

198 TSOLWANA GAME RESERVE

Location: Northern Ciskei; south-west of Queenstown.
Access: From Queenstown drive along the R61 towards Tarkastad; turn left to Thornhill and follow the road past the town to the reserve. Tsolwana lies 57 km from Queenstown, to the left of the road. Alternatively, from Queenstown take the R67 towards Whittlesea; shortly after crossing the Black Kei River turn right and follow this road for 36 km to the park office. Both routes are clearly signposted.
Accommodation: Tsolwana has four fully serviced luxury lodges: *Thibet Park* sleeps 10 people; *Lillyfountain* sleeps 14; *Otterford* sleeps 12 and *Indwe* sleeps 8 people. *Fundani* and *Phumlani* are rough trail camps, which each sleep 10 people.
Other facilities: A network of game-viewing

roads (a guide will accompany you on your drive through the reserve); organised night drives, horse-riding and hikes can be pre-arranged; hunting safaris can be arranged for the winter months. There is a well-stocked curio shop and picnic facilities at the entrance to the park.

Open: Throughout the year.

Opening time: 08h00 to 18h00.

For further information: The Manager, Tsolwana Game Reserve, P.O. Box 1424, Queenstown 5320. Tel: (0408) 2-2104 or 040892, ask for Tsolwana 1. Fax: (0408) 2-2105. For bookings, or if you experience difficulty, contact Ciskei Safaris (see page 366).

Tsolwana Game Reserve is unusual in that it is run on a basis of environmental conservation coupled with resource management. The local inhabitants, provided with jobs and cheap meat, benefit directly from activities in Tsolwana and the adjacent Hinana Tribal Resource Area, and because of this involvement poaching and other negative influences, such as fence cutting and uncontrolled burning, have been virtually eliminated.

The most prominent features of this rugged 17 000-ha park are the Black Kei River valley and the Tsolwana Mountains. The area can be divided into three major vegetation types: Karoo scrub, thornveld savannah and a combination of grassland and mountain heath. Tsolwana is stocked with a wide range of indigenous and exotic game species, including white rhinoceros, giraffe, Hartmann's mountain zebra, red hartebeest, black wildebeest, blesbok and springbok. The exotics, which include Barbary and mouflon sheep, Himalayan tahr and fallow deer, are kept mainly for trophy hunters. More than 120 bird species have been recorded.

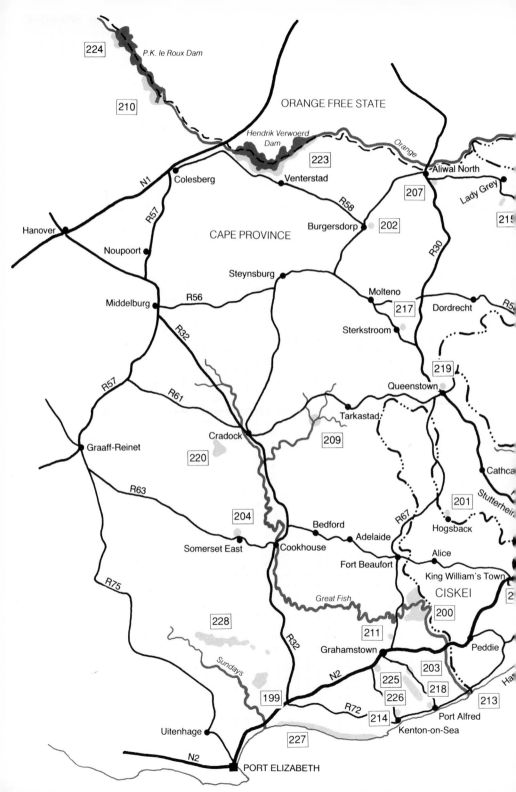

EASTERN CAPE PROVINCE

LESOTHO

Barkly East

Maclear

R58

Elliot

TRANSKEI

N2

Kei

222
205
21
212
208
Kei Mouth
Haga Haga
Gonubie
EAST LONDON

N

INDIAN OCEAN

50   100   150 km

199 **Addo Elephant National Park**
200 **Andries Vosloo Kudu Reserve**
201 **Auckland Nature Reserve**
202 **Berg Nature Reserve**
203 **Blaauwkrantz Nature Reserve**
204 **Bosberg Nature Reserve**
205 **Bosbokstrand Private Nature Reserve**
206 **Bridle Drift Dam Nature Reserve**
207 **Buffelspruit Nature Reserve**
208 **Cape Henderson Nature Reserve**
209 **Commando Drift Nature Reserve**
210 **Doornkloof Nature Reserve**
211 **Ecca Nature Reserve**
212 **Gonubie Nature Reserve**
213 **Great Fish River Wetland Reserve**
214 **Kariega Game Park**
215 **Karringmelkspruit Nature Reserve**
216 **King William's Town Nature Reserve**
217 **Koos Ras Nature Reserve**
218 **Kowie Nature Reserve**
219 **Lawrence de Lange Nature Reserve**
220 **Mountain Zebra National Park**
221 **Mpongo Park**
222 **Ocean View Guest Farm and Reserve**
223 **Oviston Nature Reserve**
224 **Rolfontein Nature Reserve**
225 **Thomas Baines Nature Reserve**
226 **Waters Meeting Nature Reserve**
227 **Woody Cape Nature Reserve**
228 **Zuurberg National Park**

For the purposes of this guide the eastern Cape Province is taken as that area east of an imaginary line from Port Elizabeth northwards to the P.K. le Roux Dam on the Orange River. To the north it is bounded by the Orange Free State, and to the east by Lesotho and the Kei River. The independent homeland of Ciskei forms an intrusive wedge, stretching inland from the coast.

This region offers a great variety of national parks and nature reserves which protect a broad spectrum of habitats and wildlife. The vegetation comprises extensive areas of grassland plus several forest and bushveld types, and strong elements of dry Karoo scrub which are largely the result of bad farming practices. The landscape has many mountain and hill ranges, scenic river valleys and a varied coastline, all of which make this a highly attractive area to explore.

A number of reserves in the eastern Cape Province are at present closed to the public. Two of these – the Cycad and Roundhill Oribi – have been set aside exclusively for conservation purposes, but special permits are sometimes issued. For further information about the Cycad Reserve contact the Directorate of Nature and Environmental Conservation, Port Elizabeth (see page 365); information about the Roundhill Oribi Nature Reserve can be obtained from the Conservation Division, Algoa Regional Services Council (see page 365). The Black Eagle Private Nature Reserve, between Queenstown and Sterkstroom, is used by the Directorate of Nature and Environmental Conservation, Queenstown (see page 365) to present environmental education courses aimed mainly at underprivileged children, although other groups can be accommodated. Ghio Nature Reserve is an important wetland area near Alexandria; contact the Conservation Division, Algoa Regional Services Council. The Amalinda Nature Reserve just outside East London incorporates a fish hatchery; contact the officer-in-charge, tel: (0431) 41-2212. The Fort Pato, Gulu, Kwelera and Umtiza nature reserves protect small areas of vegetation near East London and fall under the control of the East London Coast State Forester (see page 365).

There is also a marine reserve at various points along the East London coast.

199 ADDO ELEPHANT NATIONAL PARK

Location: South-western part of the region; north-east of Port Elizabeth.

Access: From Port Elizabeth travel on the N2 in the direction of Grahamstown for approximately 11 km before turning left onto the R335 to Addo; the turn-off to the park is on the right, approximately 10 km beyond Addo, and is clearly signposted. The park's internal road network is not surfaced but is usually in good condition. An entrance fee is charged.

Accommodation: 6-bed cottages, each with 2 bathrooms, fully equipped kitchen, living room and air conditioning (R200 per 4 persons per night); 2- to 4-bed huts, with bathroom, fully equipped kitchen and air conditioning (R105 per 2 persons per night); 2-bed huts, each with a shower and toilet, refrigerator, cutlery and crockery; communal kitchen (R74 per hut); towels and bedding are supplied for all types of accommodation. There is also a caravan and camping site with ablution blocks (R9 per stand; R4 per person; maximum 6 persons per stand).

Other facilities: Network of game-viewing roads; game-viewing hide at one of the waterholes; picnic sites with fireplaces; birdwatching hide; swimming pool; restaurant; shop selling basic foodstuffs; fuel.

Open: Throughout the year.

Opening time: Park – 07h00 to 19h00; office – 07h00 to 16h30.

For further information: (Enquiries and booking) National Parks Board (see page 365). (Park address) The Park Warden, Addo Elephant National Park, P.O. Box 52, Addo 6105. Tel: (0426) 40-0556 during office hours.

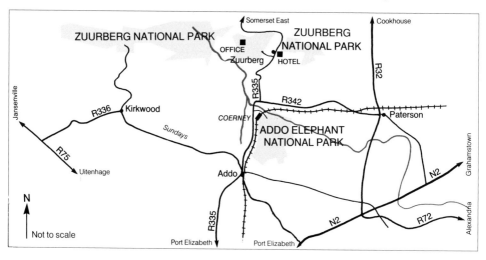

The Addo Elephant National Park was proclaimed in 1931 to protect the remnant population of 11 Eastern Cape elephants and the few free-roaming buffalo in the area. It was only in 1954, however, that the animals were prevented from wandering into surrounding farmland by the erection of an elephant-proof fence. The protection programme proved successful and from 18 elephant in 1954, the number had risen to 100 by 1979.

The park lies in gently undulating country in which 90 per cent of the vegetation consists of spekboom and other woody species (known locally as Addo bush), with Karoo scrub, coastal scrub and grassland making up the remainder. Addo covers more than 9 000 ha of which slightly more than 1 000 ha cannot be reached by the elephants so that examples of the typical vegetation types may be protected from damage. Although Addo is best known for its elephants, there is a naturally occurring population of between 60 and 70 buffalo which are unusual in that they have to rely on browsing rather than grazing to survive. Some 50 mammal species occur in the park, including a small number of black rhinoceros, as well as eland, red hartebeest, kudu and common duiker. More than 160 bird species have been recorded, but because of the dense nature of the vegetation many of them are difficult to observe.

---

200 ANDRIES VOSLOO KUDU RESERVE

Location: Southern part of the region; north-east of Grahamstown.

Access: From Grahamstown follow the N2 towards King William's Town for about 3 km, then turn north onto the R67 and drive for about 22 km; turn right towards Committee's Drift and follow the signposts for 4 km to the Andries Vosloo Kudu Reserve entrance. The approach and internal roads are gravel, but suitable for most vehicles. Permits can be obtained at the office near the entrance gate. A new gate, which will become the main entrance, is soon to be in operation. To reach it, continue on the R67 past Fort Brown for 15 km and turn right at the signpost to the reserve; the entrance is 6 km from the turn-off.

Accommodation: None. There is a variety of accommodation in Grahamstown.

Other facilities: Picnic sites at Double Drift; network of game-viewing roads; game- and birdwatching hide; fishing (licence required).

Open: Throughout the year, although the reserve may be closed during very wet weather.

Opening time: Sunrise to sunset.

Speed limit: 30 km/h.

For further information: The Officer-in-

charge, Andries Vosloo Kudu Reserve, Private Bag 1006, Grahamstown 6140. Tel: (0461) 2-7909.

The Andries Vosloo Kudu Reserve was proclaimed in 1973, but its size has been greatly expanded recently by the addition of several adjoining farms, now known as the Sam Knott Nature Reserve. It is now 23 000 ha in extent, and with the adjoining Double Drift Game Reserve in Ciskei, the total conservation area represented by these three reserves exceeds 45 000 ha. Game-viewing drives to traverse both the Sam Knott/Andries Vosloo complex and the Double Drift Game Reserve are planned for the future.

The vegetation, classified as Fish River Valley Bushveld, consists of very dense, semi-succulent, thorny scrub about 2 m high, although there are patches of forest in gorges and ravines, Karoo scrub elements, open grassland and, of particular interest, euphorbia 'forest'. A number of game species that once roamed the area, including black rhinoceros, buffalo, eland and warthog, have been re-introduced. There is a large, naturally occurring kudu population, as well as bushbuck, common duiker, steenbok and springbok. Other mammals that may be seen are baboon, vervet monkey and caracal. To date 184 bird species have been recorded and a checklist is available at the gate.

201 AUCKLAND NATURE RESERVE

Location: Eastern part of the region; north-west of King William's Town.

Access: From King William's Town travel west on the R63 towards Fort Hare and Alice for about 60 km; turn right onto the R345 to Hogsback and drive for approximately 32 km to the entrance. Alternatively, take the R30 northwards from King William's Town to Cathcart, turn left onto the R351 and then left again onto the R345, following signposts to Hogsback. The reserve is approximately 50 km from Cathcart. Permits are required for both Auckland Nature Reserve and Hogsback State Forest.

Accommodation: The Forestry Department runs a camping site which has basic facilities. Hogsback has hotels and self-catering accommodation.

Other facilities: Network of marked trails within the reserve and Hogsback State Forest.

Open: Throughout the year.

Opening time: Sunrise to sunset.

For further information: The State Forester, Hogsback State Forest, P.O. Box 52, Hogsback 5312. Tel: 0020, ask for Hogsback 55.

Auckland Nature Reserve is part of the Hogsback State Forest and protects a 218-ha patch of indigenous forest. Both Auckland and Hogsback contain many pleasant spots for the hiker and naturalist. The visitor may see samango monkey, bushbuck and bushpig, and the blood-chilling calls of the tree dassie may be heard at night. The birdlife is particularly rich and includes a number of rare species.

202 BERG NATURE RESERVE

Location: Northern part of the region; Burgersdorp.

Access: From Burgersdorp take the gravel road signposted to the waterworks; the reserve lies a short distance to the east of town. Permits can be obtained from the waterworks offices.

Accommodation: None. There is a hotel in Burgersdorp and a camping site with ablution facilities outside the reserve at De Bruin Dam.

Other facilities: Short stretch of gravel road; 7 km of walking trails; game-viewing.

Open: Throughout the year.

Opening time: By prior arrangement.

For further information: The Town Clerk, Burgersdorp Municipality, P.O. Box 13, Burgersdorp 5520. Tel: (0553) 3-1777. Fax: (0553) 3-0056.

Rugged, broken hill terrain covers most of the Berg Nature Reserve, which extends over 425 ha and borders De Bruin Dam. The vegetation is predominantly Karoo scrub and grassland, with scattered trees and bushes. A number of game species, including kudu, black wildebeest, blesbok, red hartebeest and springbok, have been introduced, and mountain reedbuck, common duiker and steenbok occur naturally in the area. The birdlife, typical of semi-arid habitats, includes such species as larks, and waterbirds that are attracted to the dam.

203 BLAAUWKRANTZ NATURE RESERVE

Location: Southern part of the region; south-east of Grahamstown.
Access: From Grahamstown take the R67 towards Port Alfred; this road runs through the reserve as it crosses the Blaauwkrantz River.
Accommodation: None.
Other facilities: Walking is permitted (permit required).
Open: Check with authority.
Opening time: 24 hours.
For further information: The Conservation Division, Algoa Regional Services Council (see page 365).

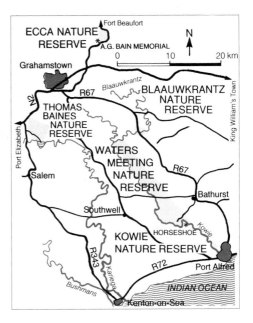

The Blaauwkrantz Nature Reserve lies in the rugged, broken Blaauwkrantz Gorge and protects Eastern Province thornveld vegetation, including aloes and tree euphorbias. To date 215 plant species have been identified. This area is rich in birdlife; 185 species have been observed. Mammal species known to occur include bushbuck, vervet monkey, rock dassie and the Cape clawless otter. Of particular importance, however, is the presence of a rare fish, the Eastern Province rocky, in pools along the Blaauwkrantz River.

204 BOSBERG NATURE RESERVE

Location: Western part of the region; adjacent to Somerset East.
Access: From Somerset East follow the road to the golf course; the reserve lies to the west of the road. There is no internal road network.
Accommodation: Linci Undertakings has a hotel and there are guest farms nearby.
Other facilities: 15-km Bosberg hiking trail; day walks; information centre; game camp.
Open: Throughout the year.
Opening time: Sunrise to sunset.
For further information: Somerset East Municipality, P.O. Box 21, Somerset East 5850. Tel: (0424) 3-1333/4 or 3-2681.

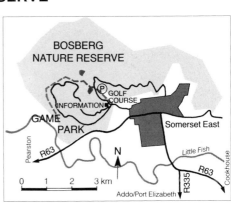

Bosberg Nature Reserve covers 2 050 ha and is situated on the southern slopes of the Bosberg range. The area is well known for its Döhne sourveld, a dense grassland habitat which is to be found in the higher-lying regions. There are thickly wooded parts containing such trees as Outeniqua yellowwood, white stinkwood and wild peach. Mountain fynbos (heath) is dominant on the rocky higher parts of the plateau, while Karoo shrubs and grassland cover the lower-lying areas. Cape mountain zebra and mountain reedbuck have been introduced into the game camp, and steenbok, baboon, vervet monkeys and dassies are commonly seen in the rest of the reserve.

Although only 83 bird species have been recorded, it is certain that many more have still to be added to the list.

205 BOSBOKSTRAND PRIVATE NATURE RESERVE

Location: South-eastern part of the region; north of East London.
Access: From East London follow the N2 northwards for approximately 40 km; turn right onto the gravel road to Haga Haga and continue for about 30 km. The reserve lies along the coast and is clearly signposted.
Accommodation: Fully equipped 6-bed chalets (R35 to R72 per chalet per night); caravan and camping site with ablution facilities (R12 per stand; R3 per person).
Other facilities: Marked walks; the Strandloper Trail passes through the reserve along the coastline; picnic sites with fireplaces; game-viewing; fishing (bait available); shop selling general supplies.
Open: Throughout the year.
Opening time: 24 hours.
For further information: The Manager, Bos-

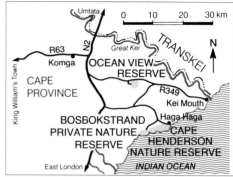

bokstrand Private Nature Reserve, P.O. Haga Haga 5272. Tel: 04372, ask for Mooiplaas 4512. (Bookings) P.O. Box 302, Randfontein 1760. Tel: (011) 696-1442.

Primarily a holiday resort, this 205-ha reserve offers a landscape of indigenous coastal forest, beach and estuary that is particularly rich in birdlife. Several game species may be spotted, including eland, blesbok, impala and bushbuck. The reserve is popular during peak holiday periods.

206 BRIDLE DRIFT DAM NATURE RESERVE

Location: South-eastern part of the region; north-west of East London.
Access: From East London take the R346 towards King William's Town. The reserve turn-off is on the right. There are no internal roads.
Accommodation: None but overnight facilities will shortly be completed.
Other facilities: Walking trails with overnight hut; birdwatching hide; picnic sites with fireplaces; boating and watersports allowed on the dam; fishing (permits are available from East London City Hall during office hours).
Open: Throughout the year.
Opening time: Winter – 0700 to 17h00; summer – 07h00 to 18h00.

For further information: The Director of Cultural and Environmental Services, P.O. Box 984, East London 5200. Tel: (0431) 34-9111 or East London Municipality, Fax: (0431) 43-8568.

The Bridle Drift Dam is a popular boating and fishing venue for inhabitants of East London and the neighbouring area. It also attracts many bird species, as does the natural vegetation in the surrounding 300-ha reserve.

207 BUFFELSPRUIT NATURE RESERVE

Location: North-eastern part of the region; east of Aliwal North.
Access: From central Aliwal North turn into

Barkly Street and follow it for 1 km to the reserve entrance; clearly signposted. Another entrance is due to be opened, and access will then be from the R58 to Lady Grey.

Accommodation: None. Aliwal North has hotels, a caravan and camping site and self-catering accommodation at the Aliwal Spa.

Other facilities: A network of gravel game-viewing roads.

Open: Throughout the year.

Opening time: October to April – 10h00 to 18h00; May to September – 11h00 to 17h30.

Speed limit: 30 km/h.

For further information: Chief of Tourism, Aliwal North Municipality, Private Bag X1011, Aliwal North 5530. Tel: (0551) 2951/3008. Fax: (0551) 4-1307.

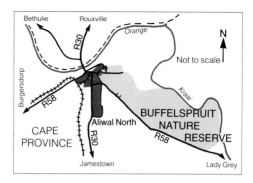

Covering 1 000 ha, the Buffelspruit Nature Reserve lies along the Kraai River. The vegetation supports a number of game animals, including eland, gemsbok, blesbok, springbok, ostriches, black wildebeest, mountain reedbuck, steenbok, Burchell's zebra and red hartebeest.

208 CAPE HENDERSON NATURE RESERVE
See map Bosbokstrand Private Nature Reserve

Location: South-eastern part of the region; east of East London.

Access: From East London follow the N2 northwards for about 35 km before turning right to Haga Haga. The northern tip of the reserve adjoins the village of Haga Haga. Permits are required.

Accommodation: None. Haga Haga has a hotel and a caravan and camping site.

Other facilities: A portion of the Strandloper Trail runs through the reserve.

Open: Throughout the year.

Opening time: Sunrise to sunset.

For further information: The State Forester, East London Coast State Forest (see page 365).

Covering 240 ha, Cape Henderson Nature Reserve lies between Haga Haga and the Bosbokstrand Private Nature Reserve. This is a rugged coastline, with sandy beaches, grassy slopes and coastal forest patches containing such trees as wild banana, milkwood and candlewood, as well as many herbaceous species. The observant walker may spot bushbuck, blue duiker, vervet monkey or Cape clawless otter. The birdlife, influenced by the subtropical climate, is rich and Knysna lourie, collared sunbird and blue-mantled flycatcher are just some of the species that occur in the area.

209 COMMANDO DRIFT NATURE RESERVE

Location: Central part of the region; west of Tarkastad.

Access: 56 km from Cradock (take the sign-posted right-hand fork when the road splits about 10 km outside Cradock) and 34 km from Tarkastad. The access road is R61, which has a good gravel surface. Permits are available at the information centre.

Accommodation: 3 4-bed stone cabins with basic facilities (R26,40 per cabin per night); overnight trail hut; camping and caravan site with ablution facilities (R11 per site per day for 4 persons, R2,60 per person per day).

Other facilities: Self-guided 2-hour hiking trail; 2-day hiking trail; picnic sites with fireplaces; walking; information centre; watersports and

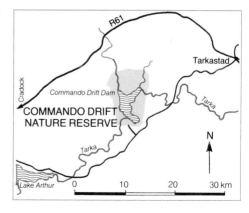

swimming are permitted; fishing (licence required). The nearest shop and fuel supplies are at Tarkastad.
Open: Throughout the year.
Opening time: 24 hours; information centre –

06h00 to 18h00.
For further information: The Officer-in-charge, Commando Drift Nature Reserve, P.O. Box 459, Cradock 5880. Tel: (0481) 3925.

The Commando Drift Nature Reserve covers a total area of 5 983 ha and surrounds the dam of the same name. Before its proclamation as a nature reserve the area was badly overgrazed and the present policy is to allow the vegetation to recover before introducing more game animals. The landscape consists of open plains covered with Karoo scrub, rugged hills, and ravines through which tree-lined watercourses flow. Small populations of Cape mountain zebra, kudu, black wildebeest, blesbok and springbok have aleady been released into the reserve.

A wide variety of waterbirds occur in the reserve and fish, martial and black eagles have been recorded.

210 DOORNKLOOF NATURE RESERVE

Location: North-western part of the region; north-west of Colesberg.
Access: From Colesberg follow the R369 north-westwards in the direction of Petrusville; after approximately 28 km turn right onto a gravel road and drive for 18 km to the reserve. Permits, which are required if you plan to leave the public road, can be obtained at the office during office hours.
Accommodation: None. Camping is permitted, but there are no facilities yet; a trail hut (for 8 people) is planned.
Other facilities: Fishing; picnic sites with fireplaces; 2-, 3- and 4-day trails are planned; canoeing; swimming.
Open: Throughout the year.
Opening time: 24 hours.
Beware: All drinking water should be boiled.
For further information: The Officer-in-charge, Doornkloof Nature Reserve, P.O. Box 94, Colesberg 5980. Tel: (05852) 1304.

Proclaimed in 1981, Doornkloof Nature Reserve covers approximately 10 000 ha. It is dominated by rugged dolerite outcrops, or koppies, and includes 75 km of the P.K. le Roux Dam shoreline at the confluence of the Orange and Seekoei rivers. Dense woodland is found in the sheltered ravines, with grass and more open bush on the ridges and hill slopes, and beds of reeds and sedge along the Seekoei River and Kattegatspruit. In order to allow the vegetation to recover after many years of overgrazing, no attempt has been made to re-introduce large game species, although a small kudu population is present, as well as steenbok, common duiker, baboon, vervet monkey and brown hyena. Mountain reedbuck are particularly abundant and are a feature of Doornkloof. To date 151 bird species have been recorded.

211 ECCA NATURE RESERVE See map Blaauwkrantz Nature Reserve

Location: Southern part of the region; north-east of Grahamstown.
Access: From Grahamstown follow the N2 in the direction of King William's Town for about

3 km; turn left onto the R67 to Fort Beaufort. The reserve lies on the west side of the road at Ecca Pass, about 5 km from the N2.
Accommodation: None.

101. From 18 animals in the mid-1950s, the elephants at Addo now number more than 100.

102. Rondavels at the Addo Elephant National Park overlook a waterhole which is floodlit at night.

103. The Andries Vosloo Reserve was originally proclaimed to protect the kudu that still roamed in this part of the Eastern Cape.

104. The Valley Bushveld vegetation of the Andries Vosloo Kudu Reserve comprises dense thorny scrub, with patches of forest and open grassland.

105. The entrance to the Bosberg Nature Reserve, near Somerset East.

106. Blue cranes find conditions suitable for breeding at the Ocean View Reserve.

107. Canoeists passing stands of euphorbias in the Kowie Nature Reserve.

108. The wetland at the mouth of the Great Fish River is an important gathering ground for waders.

109. Rooiplaat is the best area for watching Cape mountain zebra in the Mountain Zebra National Park.

110. The cycad *Encephalartos longifolius* is protected in the Suurberg National Park.

111. Chalets in the Mountain Zebra National Park are dwarfed by the surrounding landscape.

Other facilities: Marked trail; picnic site.
Open: Throughout the year.
Opening time: Sunrise to sunset.

For further information: The Conservation Division, Algoa Regional Services Council (see page 365).

Ecca Nature Reserve covers 126 ha of rugged country and is famous for its fossils, notably those of the reptile *Mesosaurus* which were discovered by the nineteenth-century geologist A. G. Bain. Information plinths along the trail describe aspects of interest. The vegetation comprises dense, semi-succulent, thorny scrub, and tree euphorbias, aloes and spekboom are abundant. Kudu, bushbuck, steenbok and common duiker occur in the area and rock dassies are often seen.

212 GONUBIE NATURE RESERVE

Location: South-eastern part of the region; north of East London.
Access: From East London follow the N2 northwards towards Umtata, then follow signposts into Gonubie; just before the municipal offices turn right into Seventh Street and follow this road to the reserve parking area.
Accommodation: None. Gonubie has hotels and caravan and camping sites.
Other facilities: Observation platforms outside the boundary fence; pathways; information centre.
Open: Throughout the year.
Opening time: Monday afternoons or by prior arrangement.
For further information: The Town Clerk, Gonubie Municipality, P.O. Box 20, Gonubie 5256. Tel: (0431) 40-4000. Fax: (0431) 40-2358.

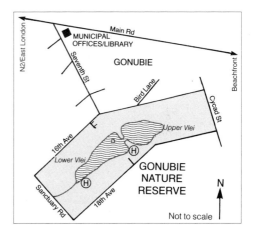

This 8-ha reserve was originally proclaimed for the protection of waterfowl and more than 130 bird species have now been recorded, including crowned cranes that nest here each summer. The reserve has been established around several small vleis which are separated from the sea by coastal bush and a low sand ridge.

213 GREAT FISH RIVER WETLAND RESERVE

Location: Southern part of the region; east of Port Alfred.
Access: From Port Alfred the R72 towards East London crosses the Great Fish River near its mouth; the reserve lies on the west bank; a gravel road runs through it to the beach.
Accommodation: None. Port Alfred has a variety of accommodation.
Other facilities: Fishing is a very popular activity both on the beach and along the river banks.
Open: Throughout the year.
Opening time: Sunrise to sunset.
For further information: The Conservation Division, Algoa Regional Services Council (see page 365).

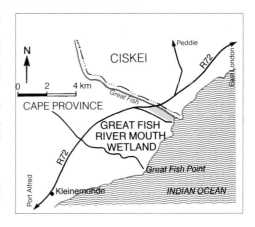

A small reserve has been proclaimed where the Great Fish River flows into the Indian Ocean. At low tide, when extensive areas of mud-flat are exposed, thousands of wading birds – such as green-shanks and little stints – congregate to feed on the numerous invertebrate organisms sheltering in the mud.

214 KARIEGA GAME PARK

Location: Southern part of region; south of Grahamstown.
Access: From the N2 (Port Elizabeth/Grahamstown), take the R343 (Salem/Kenton-on-Sea) which is located 13 km west of Grahamstown. The turn-off to the park is 14 km from Kenton-on-Sea and is clearly signposted. The R343 joins the R72 at Kenton-on-Sea.
Accommodation: Fully-equipped, self-catering, log lodges (from R32 per person per night; minimum two night stay).
Other facilities: Hiking trails; game-viewing; swimming pool.
Open: Throughout the year.
For further information: (Bookings) Kariega Park, P.O. Box 12095, Centrahil 6006. Tel: (041) 52-3533/4. Fax: (041) 55-6931.

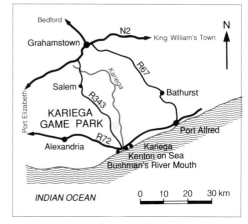

Kariega Park, covering 662 ha, lies above the Kariega River valley, with valley bushveld dominating its vegetation which includes a wide variety of tree species, such as the impressive tree euphorbias.

More than 20 game species may be seen and to date 150 species of bird have been recorded in the reserve. An added bonus when visiting this park is that this area is home to the magnificent crowned eagle.

215 KARRINGMELKSPRUIT NATURE RESERVE

Location: Extreme north-east of region; south of Lady Grey.
Access: Lies adjacent to the R58 (Lady Grey/Barkly East), 12 km from Lady Grey. It is advisable to check with the authorities before visiting this reserve.
Accommodation: None.
Other facilities: None.
Open: Check with authorities.
For further information: The Directorate of Nature and Environmental Conservation (Port Elizabeth) (see page 365).

Karringmelkspruit runs through a steep-sided gorge and the reserve was proclaimed to protect a roosting and breeding colony of the rare Cape vulture. Unfortunately this reserve is far too small to ensure this species' survival, simply because they range over great distances in search of food and are therefore vulnerable to poisoning. It is strongly advised that you consult the authorities before visiting the reserve.

216 KING WILLIAM'S TOWN NATURE RESERVE

Location: South-eastern part of the region; northern suburb of King William's Town.
Access: From the town centre take the R63 towards Komga, following signposts to the reserve.
Accommodation: None.
Other facilities: Walking trails; information boards.
Open: Throughout the year.
Opening time: Sunrise to sunset.
For further information: The Town Clerk, King William's Town Municipality, P.O. Box 33, King William's Town 5600. Tel: (0433) 2-3450. Fax: (0433) 2-2646.

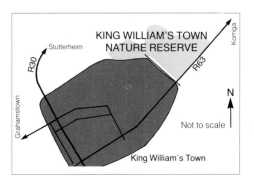

The 59-ha King William's Town Nature Reserve was proclaimed to conserve a patch of Valley Bushveld vegetation comprising thorny scrub.

Despite its proximity to the town, it harbours a few small mammal species, such as common duiker and small grey mongoose, and a varied birdlife.

217 KOOS RAS NATURE RESERVE

Location: Eastern part of the region; north-east of Sterkstroom.
Access: From Sterkstroom take the R344 towards Dordrecht; the entrance to the reserve is on the right, a short distance from the town.
Accommodation: Chalets and rooms with communal kitchen and ablution block; caravan and camping site. R7,50 to R25 per person per night.
Other facilities: Walking trails; game-viewing; information centre.
Open: Throughout the year.
Opening time: 08h00 to 17h30.
Speed limit: 30 km/h.
For further information: The Town Clerk, Sterkstroom Municipality, P.O. Box 25, Sterkstroom 5425. Tel: 04592, ask for 8.

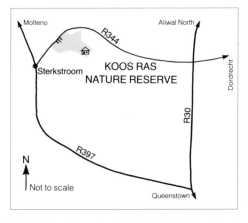

A number of game species, such as kudu, eland, blesbok, impala, springbok, black wildebeest and Burchell's zebra, have been introduced into the 250-ha Koos Ras Nature Reserve.

218 KOWIE NATURE RESERVE See also map Blaauwkrantz Nature Reserve

Location: Southern part of the region; north-western outskirts of Port Alfred.
Access: This is best reached by boat on the Kowie River; the Kowie Nature Reserve lies on the first sharp bend after the sewage works.

Accommodation: None. Port Alfred has hotels and a caravan and camping site.
Other facilities: 2-hour walking trail; picnic areas with fireplaces, accessible by boat only; swimming; boating.
Open: Throughout the year.

Opening time: 07h00 to 17h00.
For further information: The Officer-in-charge, Kowie Nature Reserve, P.O. Box 116, Bathurst 6166. Tel: (0464) 3876 or The Directorate of Nature and Environmental Conservation, Port Elizabeth (see page 365).

Covering 200 ha, the Kowie Nature Reserve on the east bank of the Kowie River offers protection to vegetation and wildlife in an area that is being rapidly changed by large-scale development.
The vegetation of the reserve consists of dense Valley Bushveld, with thorny, semi-succulent scrub and tree euphorbias, as well as areas of open scrub and grass.
Many bird species occur here. This is a popular holiday resort area.

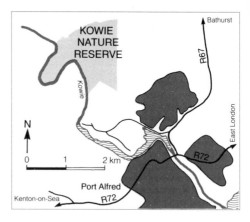

219 LAWRENCE DE LANGE NATURE RESERVE

Location: Eastern part of the region; just outside Queenstown.
Access: At the robot at the Royal Hotel in Queenstown, turn north into Robinson Road and then left into Kingsway; follow this into Hangklip Road. This leads to the gates of the Lawrence de Lange Nature Reserve approximately 3 km from where the gravel road starts.
Accommodation: None. Camping for overnight hikers allowed.
Other facilities: 3 hiking trails (maximum 12 people per trail), including a guided overnight trail (school groups must be accompanied by a teacher); a short network of game-viewing roads; picnic sites. Early booking for the trails is advised. There are 2 hiking trails and picnic sites with fireplaces in the Longhill area.
Open: Throughout the year.
Opening time: 08h00 to 17h00.
For further information: The Town Engineer, Private Bag X7111, Queenstown 5320. Tel: (0451) 3131.

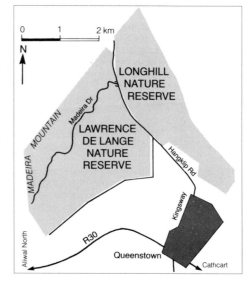

Much of this 818-ha reserve is taken up by Madeira Hill, a steep and stony but well-grassed area; taller vegetation is concentrated in its ravines. Burchell's zebra, black wildebeest, gemsbok, red hartebeest, springbok, eland, kudu, impala and blesbok have been introduced, and to date 35 mammal species have been recorded. A number of bird species may also be seen. A second, 475-ha nature reserve called Longhill has recently been proclaimed and lies across the road from Lawrence de Lange Nature Reserve. Further information can be obtained from the above address.

220 MOUNTAIN ZEBRA NATIONAL PARK

Location: Eastern part of the region; south-west of Cradock.

Access: From Cradock follow the R32 towards Middelburg for 6 km, then turn west onto the R61 in the direction of Graaff-Reinet and continue for 5 km; turn left onto a clearly signposted, graded gravel road to the park. Internal roads are gravel and well maintained. An entrance fee is charged.

Accommodation: 4-bed cottages, each with a fully equipped kitchen, bathroom and living room (R110 for 2 persons per night); the fully equipped, 6-bed Doornkloof Guest Cottage (R240 per night); a caravan and camping site with 20 stands and full ablution facilities (R9 per stand; R4 per person; maximum 6 persons per stand). The 3-day Mountain Zebra Hiking Trail (maximum 12 persons) has 2 overnight huts with basic ablution facilities (R30 per person).

Other facilities: A 40-km network of game-viewing roads; Mountain Zebra Hiking Trail; shorter walking trails; picnic sites; conference facilities; restaurant; swimming pool at main camp; 1-hr fixed horse trail (booking essential); shop selling basic foodstuffs; fuel.

Open: Throughout the year.

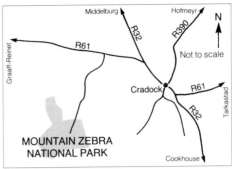

Opening time: 1 October to 30 April – 07h00 to 18h00; 1 May to 30 September – 08h00 to 18h00.

Speed limit: 40 km/h.

For further information: (Enquiries and booking) National Parks Board (see page 365). (Park address) Mountain Zebra National Park, Private Bag X66, Cradock 5880. Tel: (0481) 2427.

The Mountain Zebra National Park, which covers 6 536 ha, was established to protect one of the last remaining populations of the Cape mountain zebra. The park is cradled in a huge amphitheatre on the northern slopes of the Bankberg and mostly consists of grass-covered mountain slopes, flat, open plateaux, deep ravines and the lightly wooded course of the Wilgerboom River. Altitudes range from 1 200 m above sea-level to the 1 957-m peak of Bakenkop. The vegetation lies within a transitional zone between the arid Karoo scrub of the west and the temperate sweet grasslands of the east, and in most areas consists of mixed Karoo scrub and grassland, with trees and taller shrubs growing in the more rugged areas.

The park protects approximately 200 Cape mountain zebra, numbers being maintained at this level in order to prevent overpopulation. Surplus animals are caught and transferred to other parks and reserves. The best area for observing zebra is that known as the Rooiplaat, although in winter many animals spend more time on the hill slopes. Most foals are born during the summer months, between October and March. Of the total of 58 mammal species recorded, others likely to be seen are eland, red hartebeest, black wildebeest, blesbok, springbok and mountain reedbuck. Rock dassies are very common and can be observed close to the camp. More than 200 bird species have been recorded in the park and they include martial, black and booted eagles, Cape eagle-owl, blue crane and pale-winged starling. Forty-five reptile species are known to occur, of which the most easily observed are the large mountain tortoise and the rock monitor, or leguaan.

The park experiences climatic extremes: heavy frost and snowfalls in winter, and very hot days in summer.

221 MPONGO PARK

Location: North-west of East London.

Access: From East London, take the Abbotsford Freeway and continue along the East Coast Resorts/Beacon Bay road to the Macleantown turn-off. Proceed along the Macleantown road for about 23 km. Turn left at the Mpongo Park signpost and continue for a further 6 km. The entrance to the park is on the right. From King William's Town, take the N2 and follow the Mpongo Park signboards from the Fort Jackson turn-off.

Accommodation: Mpongo Park does not have chalets at present, but are planning to build in the near future. There are two caravan/camping sites: one, at the entrance gate, has electricity, but the one inside the park does not. Both have ablution blocks with hot and cold running water.

Other facilities: Guided hiking trails of 1-4 hours duration; guided day and night safaris;

horse-riding trails of three and a half hours' duration leave from the park entrance twice daily. Booking for all trails and safaris is essential. There is a well-stocked curio shop and a museum. Restaurant and take-away facilities are available.

Open: Throughout the year.
Opening time: Sunrise to sunset.
For further information: The Manager, Mpongo Park, P.O. Box 3300, Cambridge, 5206. Tel: (04326) 669. Fax: (04326) 605.

Not to scale

Mpongo Park is a privately owned game reserve. It was established about 20 years ago, but was only opened to the public in December 1987. Today, Mpongo Park, situated in the picturesque Umpongo River Valley, has 4 000 acres of unspoilt wildlife.

It is inhabited by more than 40 game species, including elephant, hippopotamus, rhinoceros, giraffe, zebra, black and blue wildebeest and a wide variety of buck species, from the large eland to the tiny blue duiker. There is an abundance of birdlife, and the great diversity of vegetation allows for a high capacity of a range of species.

222 OCEAN VIEW GUEST FARM AND RESERVE See map Bosbokstrand Private Nature Reserve

Location: South-eastern part of the region; north-east of East London.
Access: From East London follow the N2 northwards for about 50 km; turn right onto the R349 and after 15 km turn right again to Ocean View. The farm is clearly signposted.
Accommodation: 2- and 5-bed rondavels, each with a kitchen, some with a bathroom (R34 to R44 per rondavel per night). Linen provided at a small charge. Caravan and camping site with full ablution facilities (R12 per stand; maximum 4 persons). Meals available at the main house.
Other facilities: Network of walking trails; birdwatching.
Open: Throughout the year.
Opening time: Sunrise to sunset.
For further information: Mrs Monika von Plato, Ocean View Guest Farm, P.O. Komga 4950. Tel: (04372) 2603.

Ocean View is a 260-ha working farm, although the owners have preserved a variety of vegetation types, including high forest and grassland. In this small area more than 180 bird species have been recorded, of which 16 are raptors. Many breed here, including long-crested and crowned eagles, ground hornbill, crowned cranes, Stanley's bustard, Cape parrot, nerina trogon and Knysna lourie. September and November are the best times for birdwatching. Bushbuck, blue and common duiker, samango monkey and tree dassies also occur. Ocean View has been declared a natural heritage site (Nr 75) because of several endangered species of flora and fauna to be found on the farm.

223 OVISTON NATURE RESERVE

Location: Northern part of the region; west of Aliwal North.
Access: From Aliwal North take the R58 to Venterstad; turn right into the town, a short distance further on turn left, then follow signposts. Permits can be obtained at the gate on a self-help basis.
Accommodation: Overnight hut for guided trail. There is a holiday complex at Oviston.
Other facilities: Guided overnight trail in wilderness area (book in advance); trails and walks; 50 km of game-viewing roads; picnic sites with fireplaces; fishing.
Open: Throughout the year.
Opening time: October to March – 06h00 to 20h00 (weekends and public holidays), 07h30 to 16h30 (weekdays); April to September – 07h30 to 16h30.
Speed limit: 30 km/h.
For further information: The Officer-in-charge, Oviston Nature Reserve, P.O. Box 7, Venterstad 5990. Tel: (0553) 5-0000.

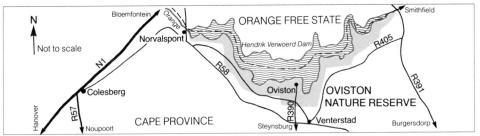

Oviston Nature Reserve is approximately 13 000 ha in extent, of which 3 500 ha is open to the public. Its main purpose is to conserve a part of the False Upper Karoo ecosystem, which comprises grass- and scrub-covered plains, and to maintain breeding populations of indigenous ungulate species for distribution to other reserves. The terrain is generally flat, but there are low hills in the east and west. The reserve has one of the largest game populations in the Cape Province and, of the 48 mammal species which occur here, the most likely to be seen are Burchell's zebra, black wildebeest, mountain reedbuck, red hartebeest, blesbok, springbok, steenbok and ground squirrel. The birdlist for the area is quite extensive, comprising 148 species.

224 ROLFONTEIN NATURE RESERVE See map Doornkloof Nature Reserve

Location: North-western part of the region; north-east of Petrusville.
Access: From Petrusville follow the R48 northwards for 10 km and turn right to Van- derkloof. The entrance to the Rolfontein Nature Reserve is east of Vanderkloof. Permits can be obtained at the gate on a self-help basis.
Accommodation: Overnight shelter on trails. There is accommodation at Vanderkloof, and at Petrusville.
Other facilities: 2 short self-guided trails (more trails are planned); short walks to view-

points; 2-day hiking trails; a well-maintained network of game-viewing roads; picnic sites with fireplaces; fishing (with licence).
Open: Throughout the year.
Opening time: October to March – 06h00 to 18h00 (weekends), 07h30 to 15h30 (weekdays); April to September – 07h00 to 17h00 (weekends), 07h30 to 15h30 (weekdays).
Speed limit: 25 km/h.
For further information: The Principal Na- ture Conservator, P.O. Box 23, Vanderkloof 8771. Tel: 05782, ask for 160.

When the P.K. le Roux Dam is full, Rolfontein Nature Reserve covers approximately 6 200 ha. Much of the reserve – which is separated from the Doornkloof Nature Reserve by a narrow strip of state land – lies on the Renosterberg, which ranges in height from 1 175 to 1 437 m above sea-level, with only a small section of low-lying plains. Although 13 different plant communities have been identified here, the vegetation can be roughly divided into grass-covered plains, shrub-covered hill slopes and riverine woodland. Forty different grass species grow within the area. For a relatively small reserve, there is a remarkable diversity of mammal species. Among the 57 represented are white rhinoceros, Burchell's zebra, 10 antelope species, baboon, vervet monkey and 16 different carnivores. The last-mentioned include the re-introduced cheetah and brown hyena, although they are seldom seen. Rolfontein's birdlife includes waterbirds such as fish eagles, white-breasted and reed cormorants and a number of herons, which are attracted by the large fish populations in the dam.

225 THOMAS BAINES NATURE RESERVE See also map Blaauwkrantz Nature Reserve

Location: Southern part of the region; south of Grahamstown.
Access: From Grahamstown follow the N2 westwards for 15 km and turn left onto the R343 towards Salem; after travelling 2 km turn

left again to the reserve entrance. Internal roads are gravel but they are suitable for all vehicles except buses.
Accommodation: Hostel facilities for organ- ised educational groups only. Grahamstown

has hotels and a camping site.
Other facilities: Network of game-viewing roads; environmental education centre; picnic sites with fireplaces at the Settlers' Dam.
Open: Throughout the year.
Opening time: 07h00 to 17h00.
Speed limit: 30 km/h.
For further information: The Officer-in-charge, Thomas Baines Nature Reserve, Private Bag 1006, Grahamstown 6140. Tel: (0461) 2-8262.

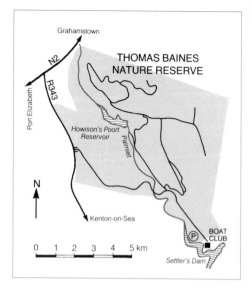

Although this 1 005-ha reserve lies within the Valley Bushveld vegetation zone and is covered with low, thorny bushes, there are also extensive areas of mixed grassland and fynbos (heath). The terrain is mostly hilly, and the Palmiet River flows through the reserve. The 42 mammal species occurring here include white rhinoceros, buffalo, eland, bontebok, black wildebeest, impala and mountain reedbuck. The birdlife is abundant and 171 species have been recorded, as have 24 reptile species.

226 WATERS MEETING NATURE RESERVE See map Blaauwkrantz Nature Reserve

Location: Southern part of the region; southeast of Grahamstown.
Access: From Grahamstown follow the R67 towards Port Alfred; at Bathurst bear right onto a graded gravel road and follow the signposts to the Horseshoe and the Waters Meeting Nature Reserve. Permits are required.
Accommodation: Basic camping site for

canoe hikers. Bathurst has a hotel.
Other facilities: Walking trails; picnic sites with fireplaces.
Open: Throughout the year.
Opening time: 07h00 to 17h00.
For further information: The State Forester, Bathurst State Forest, P.O. Bathurst 6166. Tel: (0464) 25-0876.

Waters Meeting Nature Reserve is one of the most attractive conservation areas in this region. It covers 4 247 ha and, with the Kowie River as its western boundary, extends up the slopes of the river's forested east bank.

The forests – which consist of many thorny tree species and tree euphorbias – and their inhabitants are the main reason for setting aside this conservation area. The dense nature of the vegetation makes mammal-spotting difficult, but there are bushbuck, blue duiker, rock and tree dassies, bushpig, caracal and Cape clawless otter. Although no comprehensive birdlist is available, more than 150 species occur in the area, including crowned eagle, fish eagle, Knysna lourie and several different kingfisher species.

227 WOODY CAPE NATURE RESERVE

Location: South-western part of the region; east of Port Elizabeth.
Access: From Port Elizabeth follow the N2 towards Grahamstown for 56 km; turn right onto the R72 towards Kenton-on-Sea, and at Alexandria take the gravel road to Alexandria State Forest. This follows the northern boundary of the eastern part of the reserve and

should be suitable for most vehicles. Permits are required. There are no internal roads.
Accommodation: An overnight hut on the Alexandria Trail accommodates 12 persons.
Other facilities: The Alexandria Trail runs through the reserve (book well in advance); trees marked with National Tree List numbers.
Open: Throughout the year.

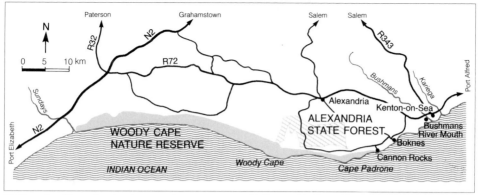

Opening time: Sunrise to sunset.
For further information: The State Forester,

Alexandria State Forest, P.O. Box 50, Alexandria 6185. Tel: 04652, ask for 1103.

The Woody Cape Nature Reserve forms part of the Alexandria State Forest and covers 15 460 ha, most of which is an extensive sand-dune 'sea', with patches of thicket and forest. This is a young and expanding dune system and one of the largest areas of active coastal dunes in the world. No detailed survey of the reserve's wildlife has been undertaken, but mammal species such as steenbok and common duiker may be seen. The rich birdlife of the area includes the most southerly population of the trumpeter hornbill.

228 ZUURBERG NATIONAL PARK See map Addo Elephant National Park

Location: Western part of the region; due north of Port Elizabeth.
Access: From Port Elizabeth travel 11 km northward on the N2 before taking the R335 to Addo; continue north to the Zuurberg Hotel. This road becomes graded gravel shortly before the entrance to the Zuurberg park. To get to the western end of the park, take the tarred R336 from Addo to Kirkwood and continue northward on gravel beyond the town to the entrance. There are no internal roads.
Accommodation: None at present. Zuurberg Hotel to the east of the reserve.
Other facilities: Hiking trails (numbers of hikers are controlled and permits are required).
Open: Throughout the year.
Opening time: Sunrise to sunset.
For further information: The Warden, Zuurberg National Park, P.O. Box 76, Addo 6105. Tel: 04252, ask for 106.

Formerly a state forest, Zuurberg was proclaimed a national park in 1985 and lies within the Winterhoek mountain range. The mountainous terrain, with its deep valleys and rounded peaks, ranges in altitude from 300 to 920 m above sea-level. The park is of particular interest to botanists as it contains three major vegetation types: False Heathland, which has elements of fynbos (heath) combined with other influences, evergreen coastal forest and Valley Bushveld, with low, thorny bushes, including tree euphorbias. Several rare plant species, such as the Zuurberg pincushion and the cycad *Encephalartos longifolius*, grow here.

The park has already been restocked with Cape mountain zebra, and it is planned to re-introduce other species, including elephant and buffalo. Grey rhebok, mountain reedbuck, bushbuck, Cape grysbok, kudu, bushpig, baboon and vervet monkey still survive in the area, and there are also many interesting bird, reptile and fish species.

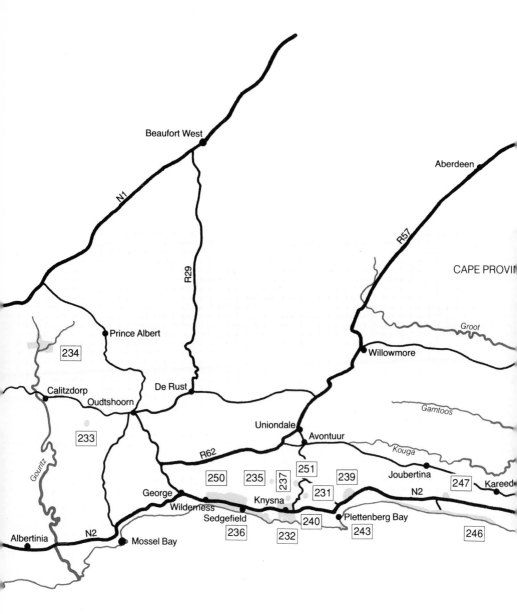

SOUTHERN CAPE PROVINCE

229 Cape Recife Nature Reserve
230 Cape St Francis Nature Reserve
231 Diepwalle State Forest
232 Featherbed Nature Reserve
233 Gamka Mountain Nature Reserve
234 Gamkapoort Nature Reserve
235 Goudveld State Forest
236 Goukamma Nature Reserve
237 Gouna State Forest
238 Groendal Wilderness Area
239 Keurbooms River Nature Reserve
240 Knysna National Lake Area
241 Loerie Dam Nature Reserve
242 Maitland Nature Reserve
243 Robberg Nature Reserve
244 Seekoei River Nature Reserve
245 Settlers Park
246 Tsitsikamma National Park
247 Tsitsikamma State Forest Reserve
248 Uitenhage Nature Reserve
249 Van Stadens Wild Flower Reserve
250 Wilderness National Park
251 Ysternek Nature Reserve

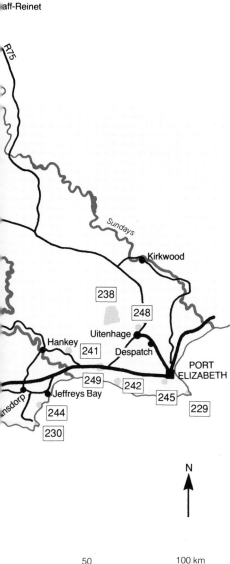

The southern Cape Province is generally considered to be the narrow piece of land sandwiched between the northernmost ranges of the Cape Folded mountains and the Indian Ocean, with the Gouritz and Sundays rivers as its boundaries in the west and east respectively. The region is well watered, receiving some 700 mm rainfall annually at the coast and about 1 300 mm on the mountains. This relatively heavy, year-round precipitation ensures dense, species-rich vegetation, which includes large areas of indigenous forest. Several types have been defined, ranging from dry to wet forest, and there are superb examples of true high forest, in which giant yellowwoods and stinkwood trees grow. Tall mountain fynbos (heath), including many rare plant species, covers the south-facing mountain slopes, whereas on the northern slopes Karoo species, better adapted to arid conditions, predominate.

In this area of great scenic beauty and temperate climate a burgeoning tourist industry has caused the demise, or drastic modification, of many natural areas. However, a good complement of reserves ensures that at least part of the natural environment is conserved.

Many of these protect forest areas on the coastal plain, where tourist pressure is heaviest, but some lie among the mountains and valleys of the eastern Little Karoo. It has been proposed that large tracts of indigenous forest on the coastal plain and adjacent mountains be proclaimed a national park.

Rain falls throughout the year; summers are mild to warm, and winters cool, with snow a possibility on the higher peaks.

229 CAPE RECIFE NATURE RESERVE

Location: Eastern part of the region; Port Elizabeth.
Access: In Port Elizabeth follow Marine Drive through Summerstrand, following signposts to Cape Recife. Obtain permits for vehicles at the Happy Valley beach manager's office.
Accommodation: None.

Other facilities: Paths; birdwatching hides.
Open: Throughout the year.
Opening time: Sunrise to sunset.
For further information: The Department of Parks and Recreation, P.O. Box 12435, Centrahill, Port Elizabeth 6006. Tel: (041) 55-9711. Fax: (041) 55-2907.

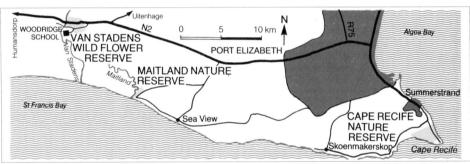

This 336-ha nature reserve protects not only the fragile shoreline and sand dunes of Cape Recife, but also the many organisms that rely on these habitats. The marine, shore, bush and freshwater habitats attract over 100 bird species, including large concentrations of waders in summer.

230 CAPE ST FRANCIS NATURE RESERVE

Location: Eastern part of the region; south of Humansdorp.
Access: From Humansdorp take the R330 to the village of Cape St Francis. From there the reserve is best reached on foot.
Accommodation: None. There are cottages and a camping site at Cape St Francis.
Other facilities: Walking; fishing permitted.
Open: Throughout the year.
Opening time: 24 hours.
For further information: The Officer-in-charge, Cape St Francis Nature Reserve, P.O. Box 38, Humansdorp 6300. Tel: (04231) 92-0339.

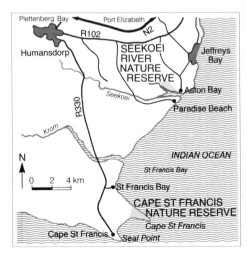

Covering only 36 ha, the Cape St Francis Nature Reserve protects a delicately balanced habitat of sand dunes and coastal fynbos (heath) in an area that has seen much destruction by property developers. The varied birdlife attracted to the reserve includes marine and terrestrial species.

231 DIEPWALLE STATE FOREST

Location: Western part of the region; north-east of Knysna.
Access: From Knysna follow the N2 east-wards towards Plettenberg Bay; after 7 km turn left onto the R339 towards Avontuur and Uniondale, and continue for about 16 km. Diepwalle is clearly signposted. The R339 becomes graded gravel about 6 km from the N2.
Accommodation: An overnight hut which can be used only by hikers on the Outeniqua Trail.
Other facilities: Elephant Walk, an 18-km circular trail with shorter alternatives (permits required); picnic sites.
Open: Throughout the year.
Opening time: 06h00 to 18h00.
For further information: The Regional Direc-

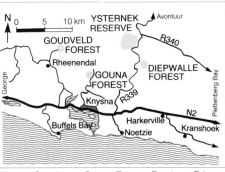

tor, Southern Cape Forest Region, Private Bag X12, Knysna 6570. Tel: (0445) 2-3037.

Much of Diepwalle State Forest consists of flat to gently undulating country covered by indigenous forest and montane fynbos (heath). The main attraction of this forest is the 'Elephant Walk' which traverses some of the best-preserved natural forest in South Africa. The trail passes a number of large Outeniqua yellowwoods and takes one through areas of moist high-forest comprising large stinkwood, real yellowwood, ironwood, hard pear, white pear and numerous other canopy-forming species. The area also forms part of the remaining home range of the so-called 'Knysna elephants'. Only four survive, and the chance of seeing one of these shy animals is remote. Mammals more likely to be spotted are vervet monkey, bushbuck and baboon.

232 FEATHERBED NATURE RESERVE
See map Knysna National Lake Area

Location: Western part of the region; south of Knysna.
Access: From Knysna by means of the 'Featherbed Ferry' only, or by private boat; no public road access. Visitors must be accompanied by an approved trail leader.
Accommodation: None. There is a variety of accommodation in and around Knysna.

Other facilities: Guided 5-km scenic trail; educational tours for schoolchildren; meals can be provided; swimming from beaches.
Open: Throughout the year.
Opening time: Sunrise to sunset.
For further information: The Manager, Featherbed Nature Reserve, P.O. Box 1261, Knysna 6570. Tel: (0445) 2-4489.

The 70-ha Featherbed Nature Reserve, situated on the more westerly of the Knysna Heads at the mouth of the Knysna Lagoon, may be explored under the guidance of a trail leader who explains the ecology and history of the area. The vegetation is predominantly coastal fynbos (heath). Bushbuck, Cape grysbok and blue duiker may be spotted, and more than 100 bird species have been recorded.

233 GAMKA MOUNTAIN NATURE RESERVE

Location: North-western part of the region; west of Oudtshoorn.
Access: From Oudtshoorn take the R62 west-wards towards Calitzdorp; turn left after 12 km onto the concrete-paved old Calitzdorp road; continue for 18 km, turn left at the Uitvlugt signpost onto a gravel road, cross the Olifants

River and travel another 7 km to the reserve, following signposts. There are no internal roads. Vehicles must be left at the entrance gate where permits can be obtained from the information centre.
Accommodation: None. There is accommodation at Calitzdorp Spa, 10 km further west.

Other facilities: A 2-day guided hiking trail for groups of 6 to 12 people (arrangements should be made in advance); 1-day hiking trail; 4 short trails; information centre.
Open: Throughout the year.
Opening time: 07h00 to 19h00.
For further information: The Officer-in-charge, Gamka Mountain Nature Reserve, Private Bag X21, Oudtshoorn 6620. Tel: (04437) 3-3367.

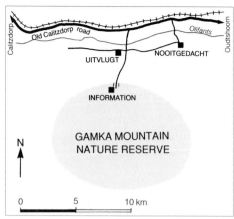

The Gamka Mountain Nature Reserve protects a 9 428-ha area in a rugged, isolated mountain range, where deep ravines dissect the upper plateau. The vegetation is adapted to dry conditions and includes several rare plants, among them a recently discovered species of *Mimetes*. The reserve was established in 1970 with the specific purpose of conserving a small population of Cape mountain zebra. Other mammals that occur here are klipspringer, grey rhebok, common duiker, steenbok and Cape grysbok. Leopard also roam these mountains but they are rarely seen. Over 140 bird species have been recorded.

234 GAMKAPOORT NATURE RESERVE

Location: North-western part of the region; north-west of Oudtshoorn.
Access: From Oudtshoorn take the R328 over the Swartberg Pass to Prince Albert, and then turn west onto the gravel road to Gamkapoort Dam, continuing for 35 km. To reach Prince Albert from the N1, take the R328 south-eastwards at Prince Albert Road station.
Accommodation: None, but camping may be arranged.
Other facilities: A short walking trail; overnight trail; fishing, boating and picnicking permitted.
Open: Throughout the year.
Opening time: Sunrise to sunset.
For further information: The Officer-in-

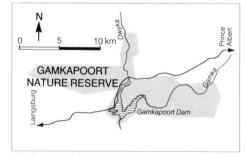

charge, Gamkapoort Nature Reserve, P.O. Box 139, Prince Albert 6930. Tel: (04436) 905.

The Gamkapoort Nature Reserve extends over 8 250 ha, of which about one-sixth is taken up by the Gamkapoort Dam, at the confluence of the Gamka and Dwyka rivers. Situated on the northern slopes of the Great Swartberg range, the reserve boasts some fine rugged scenery, including a deep and impressive gorge below the dam wall. Dwarf succulent shrubs grow in the low-lying areas, taller bushes and shrubs on the hill slopes, and dry montane fynbos (heath) can be seen on the highest ridges. Sweet-thorn trees form dense stands along the watercourses. Kudu, grey rhebok, springbok, klipspringer, common duiker, steenbok and rock dassie occur naturally in the area, as well as leopard and caracal.

235 GOUDVELD STATE FOREST See map Diepwalle State Forest

Location: Western part of the region; north-west of Knysna.
Access: From Knysna take the N2 westwards towards George, turning right onto the road to

Rheenendal; continue along this road for 12,6 km, then follow the signposts to Goudveld.
Accommodation: None. Millwood Hut is available only to hikers on the Outeniqua Trail.

Other facilities: Walking trails; picnic sites; historical sites; natural swimming pools.
Open: Throughout the year.

Opening time: 06h00 to 18h00.
For further information: The Regional Director, Southern Cape Forest Region (see page 365).

Goudveld State Forest lies in the foothills of the Outeniqua Mountains, in an area once the site of goldfields which flourished for a short period in the late 1880s. Today nothing remains of the gold-mining town, Millwood, but many of the tunnels and shafts excavated during the boom are scattered among the hills. A trail from the Jubilee Creek picnic site leads upstream past some of the old alluvial diggings.

236 GOUKAMMA NATURE RESERVE

Location: Western part of the region; west of Knysna.
Access: From Knysna travel 16 km westward on the N2; turn left to Buffels Bay and continue for 6 km to the entrance to the reserve. Permits can be obtained at the gate or office. There are no internal public roads. A small entrance fee is charged during December, January and April.
Accommodation: None.
Other facilities: 35 km of trails; picnic sites with fireplaces at the estuary; canoes and rowing boats permitted; swimming in the river; board-sailing; fishing (permit necessary).
Open: Throughout the year.
Opening time: 08h00 to 18h00.
Beware: Swimming in the sea is dangerous; snakes, particularly puff adders.

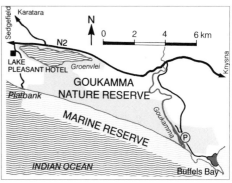

For further information: The Officer-in-charge, Goukamma Nature Reserve, P.O. Box 331, Knysna 6570. Tel: (0445) 83-0042.

The Goukamma Nature Reserve, established in 1961, covers 2 230 ha and includes the freshwater lake Groenvlei, the lower sections of the Goukamma River and its estuary, extensive sand dunes and 14 km of rocky coastline and beaches. The adjacent Goukamma marine reserve, which includes Buffels Bay and Walker Point and also extends one nautical mile seawards from the high-water mark, protects all organisms, although angling with rod and line from the shore is permitted. No marine organism may be removed or disturbed, bait collecting is forbidden and no angling from ski boats, spearfishing or use of cast nets is allowed within the marine reserve. Coastal fynbos (heath) covers much of the reserve, but there are also impressive stands of milkwood. Bontebok have been released here and bushbuck, common and blue duiker, Cape grysbok, small grey mongoose, otter, honey badger, bushpig, caracal and vervet monkey also occur. To date 211 bird species have been listed, including the most westerly record of the African finfoot.

237 GOUNA STATE FOREST See map Diepwalle State Forest

Location: Western part of the region; north of Knysna.
Access: From Knysna drive 2 km westward on the N2, then turn right onto the road to Gouna.
Accommodation: None. Rondebossie hut is available only to hikers on the Outeniqua Trail.

Other facilities: Terblans Nature Trail; picnic site; natural swimming holes.
Open: Throughout the year.
Opening time: 06h00 to 18h00.
For further information: The Regional Director, Southern Cape Forest Region (see page 365).

Gouna lies slightly to the west of Diepwalle State Forest and its forests are similar in structure. The Outeniqua Trail passes through a portion of Lilyvlei reserve which encloses the only remnant of unworked natural forest in the southern Cape. Due to its relative inaccessibility, this 100-ha section of forest escaped the axe during the last century.

238 GROENDAL WILDERNESS AREA

Location: Eastern part of the region; west of Uitenhage.
Access: In Uitenhage drive northwards up Caledon St, turn left into Gibbon St and then right into Groendal Rd, following it to the entrance. Permits are required.
Accommodation: None. Camping or sheltering in caves is allowed with a permit, but there are no facilities.
Other facilities: 3 hiking trails – 14, 36 and 38 km; groups not to have less than 3 persons.
Open: Throughout the year.
Opening time: Sunrise to sunset.
Beware: It is easy to become lost if paths are not followed; sudden changes in the weather.
For further information: The Officer-in-charge, Groendal Wilderness Area, P.O. Box 445, Uitenhage 6230. Tel: (0422) 2-5418.

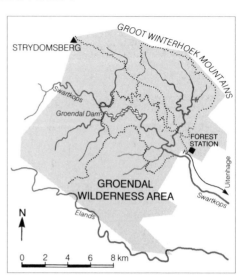

The 21 793-ha Groendal Wilderness Area protects the water catchment area of the Swartkops River, with the Groendal Dam in its centre. Lying within the Groot Winterhoek Mountain range, this wilderness area has rugged terrain, incised by numerous streams and ravines. The vegetation is predominantly fynbos (heath), with a great diversity of individual species. Isolated pockets of indigenous forest occur in the ravines, and there are also elements of thorny, semi-succulent Valley Bushveld scrub. There is not a wide range of mammal species, but hikers may see baboon (more often heard than seen), common duiker, Cape grysbok, bushbuck, grey rhebok and mountain reedbuck.

239 KEURBOOMS RIVER NATURE RESERVE

Location: Central part of the region; east of Plettenberg Bay.
Access: From Plettenberg Bay follow the N2 eastwards for 6 km and turn left immediately before reaching the Keurbooms River. A short tar road leads to the Keurbooms River resort. A permit is required.
Accommodation: *Overvaal Keurboom* has 15 6-bed family cottages, each with a fully equipped kitchen, bathroom and bedding; 6 fully equipped 4-bed rooms. A camping site with ablution facilities. A canoe trail hut accommodating 12.
Other facilities: A 2-day canoe trail; 1-hr hiking trail; boating allowed within zoned areas (permits can be obtained from the Nature Conservation Office at 7 Zenon St, Plettenberg Bay); boat trips upriver during summer holidays; Plettenberg Bay Angling Club hires out boats; picnic sites with fireplaces.
Open: Throughout the year.
Opening time: 08h00 to 18h00.

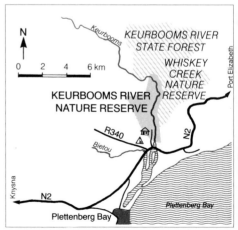

For further information: The Officer-in-charge, Keurbooms River Nature Reserve, Private Bag X1003, Plettenberg Bay 6600. Tel:

112. Wood sandpipers find rich pickings in the Cape Recife Nature Reserve.

113. The estuary of the Goukamma River forms part of the Goukamma Nature Reserve.

114. The Cape St Francis Nature Reserve protects a delicate coastal environment.

115. In the Goudveld State Forest, north-east of Knysna.

116. The Robberg Nature Reserve is a favourite site for anglers.

117. The rugged Gamka Mountain Reserve is intersected by many ravines, including Tierkloof.

118. The Otter Trail in the Tsitsikamma Coastal National Park takes its name from the Cape clawless otter, which is occasionally seen by hikers.

119. Comfortable 'oceanettes' at Storms River Mouth in the Tsitsikamma Coastal National Park.

120. The Storms River as it enters the sea in the Tsitsikamma Coastal National Park.

121. Its call and a flash of red in flight are usually the only signs of the Knysna lourie in the Tsitsikamma and other forest areas.

122. A boardwalk forms part of the Kingfisher Trail in the Wilderness National Park.

123. The Ebb and Flow rest camp in the Wilderness National Park.

The main feature of this 760-ha reserve is the Keurbooms River with its steep, forested banks, and the best way to explore it is to paddle quietly upstream in a canoe or rowing boat. Apart from the indigenous forest, there are large areas of fynbos (heath) on the plateau above the river, where Cape grysbok may be seen. In this and the neighbouring Keurbooms River Forest Reserve to the north the visitor has a good chance of seeing bushbuck, rock dassie, baboon and vervet monkey. To date 124 bird species have been recorded, including Caspian terns (which breed on a protected sand bar near the river mouth) and such rarities as the African finfoot.

Whiskey Creek, a 3 404-ha nature reserve on the east bank of the Keurbooms River, forms a natural extension to the Keurbooms reserves. For further information contact the Regional Director, Tsitsikamma Forest Region, Private Bag X537, Humansdorp 6300. Tel: (0423) 5-1180. Fax: (0423) 5-2745.

240 KNYSNA NATIONAL LAKE AREA

Location: Western part of the region; Knysna.
Access: The park surrounds Knysna, including the lagoon; several public roads, including the N2, traverse the area.
Accommodation: None. There is a variety of accommodation in Knysna.

Other facilities: Most watersport activities are permitted in zoned areas of the lagoon.
Open: Throughout the year.
Opening time: 24 hours.
For further information: The Warden, Knysna National Lake Area, National Parks Board, Knysna (see page 365).

The Knysna National Lake Area, like the Wilderness and West Coast national parks, is in an area where the demands of leisure activities are heavy, and the National Parks Board aims to maintain a healthy balance between conservation of the environment and the utilisation and development of recreational facilities. The lake area covers approximately 15 000 ha, of which 1 800 ha is taken up by Knysna Lagoon, one of South Africa's largest estuaries. The lagoon is rich in invertebrate organisms and fish (including the rare Knysna seahorse), which in turn support a wide variety of waterbirds. The Knysna Marine Reserve, which falls within the lake area, has been established as a closed breeding area for invertebrates (bait organisms) to be used for restocking areas open to exploitation. Fishing is thus allowed but no bait may be collected in this area. Few mammals remain in the area, but bushbuck, Cape grysbok and common duiker are occasionally sighted, and bushpig, leopard, baboon and vervet monkey also occur.

241 LOERIE DAM NATURE RESERVE

Location: Eastern part of the region; west of Port Elizabeth.
Access: From Port Elizabeth follow the N2 westwards; after 40 km take the R331 to Hankey; Loerie is 11 km from the N2, and the reserve turn-off just beyond the town.
Accommodation: A dormitory accommodates 48 persons and a timber hut 18 persons; used by hikers and educational groups.
Other facilities: A 3- and a 7-km walking trail.
Open: Throughout the year.
Opening time: Sunrise to sunset.
For further information: The Nature Conservation Division, Algoa Regional Services Council (see page 365).

This 1 000-ha reserve around the Loerie Dam is open to all, but is intended primarily for use by school and other groups to promote an awareness of the environment and conservation. Situated in scenic, mountainous terrain, it protects both the dense, thorny, Valley Bushveld scrub and the Eastern Cape fynbos (heath) vegetation, and is particularly colourful in winter.

242 MAITLAND NATURE RESERVE See map Cape Recife Nature Reserve

Location: Eastern part of the region; west of Port Elizabeth.
Access: From Port Elizabeth take any route to Sea View, then continue westwards for about 7 km along the coastal road to the Maitland Nature Reserve.
Accommodation: There is a camping and caravan site at the river mouth.

Other facilities: Self-guided 3,2-km walking trail with information boxes; picnic site. A further 9-km walking trail encompasses the reserve.
Open: Throughout the year.
Opening time: Sunrise to sunset.
For further information: The Nature Conservation Division, Algoa Regional Services Council (see page 365).

The Maitland Nature Reserve, situated at the mouth of the Maitland River, covers 127 ha and protects a fine stand of coastal forest and bush, including fruiting plants which attract a variety of birds.

243 ROBBERG NATURE RESERVE

Location: Central part of the region; south-east of Plettenberg Bay.
Access: From Plettenberg Bay follow the road towards the airport; the reserve is signposted.

There are no internal roads. Permits required which can be obtained at the gate (entrance fee: R2,20 per person, R4,40 per vehicle).
Accommodation: There is a variety of accom-

modation in and around Plettenberg Bay.
Other facilities: An 11-km walking trail and alternative shorter routes; an interpretation centre; rod and line fishing from seashore; picnic sites with fireplaces at the car park.
Open: Throughout the year.
Opening time: 07h00 to 17h00 (1 December to 15 January – 07h00 to 20h00).
Beware: Freak waves and dangerous currents; hikers should carry water.
For further information: The Officer-in-charge, Robberg Nature Reserve, Private Bag X1003, Plettenberg Bay 6600. Tel: (04457) 3-2125 or 3-2185.

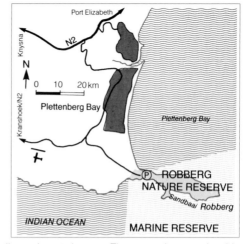

The Robberg, a promontory of about 175 ha, juts some 4 km into the Indian Ocean at the southern end of Plettenberg Bay. To the north its cliffs drop almost sheer to the sea, but the southern slope is more gentle and there are overhangs which show evidence of occupation by primitive Khoikhoi 'strandlopers' centuries ago. The vegetation covering this rocky extremity consists mainly of low, wind-blown scrub. The Robberg's name – 'mountain of seals' – is derived from the fur seals that once beached here in large numbers; today only a few are occasionally seen. The area is a breeding ground for the southern black-backed gull, white-breasted cormorant and black oystercatcher.

Extending 1 nautical mile beyond the coastline, the entire area is a reserve and no bait collecting, no spearfishing, no angling from boat or craft and no disturbance of any marine organism is allowed.

244 SEEKOEI RIVER NATURE RESERVE
See map Cape St Francis Nature Reserve

Location: Eastern part of the region; west of Port Elizabeth.
Access: From Port Elizabeth follow the N2 in the direction of Humansdorp, take the turn-off to Jeffreys Bay and continue to Aston Bay; the Seekoei River Nature Reserve lies just north-west of this town.
Accommodation: None.

Other facilities: Walking is allowed; there is a birdwatching hide.
Open: Throughout the year.
Opening time: 07h00 to 17h00.
For further information: The Officer-in-charge, Seekoei River Nature Reserve, P.O. Box 38, Humansdorp 6300. Tel: (04231) 92-0339.

Situated at the common estuary of the Seekoei and Swart rivers, this 66-ha reserve is an important bird sanctuary. The vegetation, defined as false coastal fynbos (heath), consists of low scrub, with patches of bush and reedbeds along the river. Many waterbirds, such as yellow-billed duck, red-knobbed coot, little egret and various tern species, are attracted to the estuary.

245 SETTLERS PARK

Location: Eastern part of the region; Port Elizabeth.
Access: From the Old Cape Road turn southward into Rink Street, following it into Park Drive; turn off into How Avenue and continue to the main entrance, where there is a parking area. There are other entrances to Settlers Park from Cudmore Street, Fordyce Road, and Hunter and Newton avenues.

Accommodation: None. There is a variety in Port Elizabeth.
Other facilities: Network of footpaths.
Open: Throughout the year.
Opening time: Sunrise to sunset.
For further information: The Nature Conservation Division, Port Elizabeth Municipality (see page 365); or The Curator. Tel: (041) 33-6794.

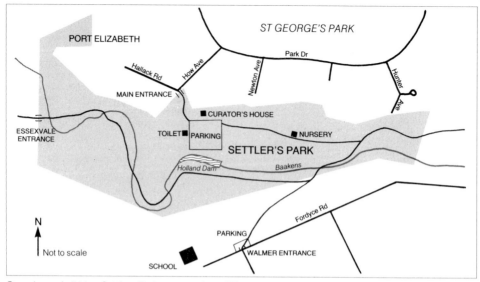

Covering only 54 ha, Settlers Park protects four different vegetation types: fynbos (heath), coastal forest remnants, grassland and Karoo. The Baakens River meanders through the reserve and is flanked by cliffs and ravines which provide a natural setting for bushbuck, common duiker and water mongoose, despite the proximity of the city centre.

246 TSITSIKAMMA NATIONAL PARK

Location: Central part of the region; east of Plettenberg Bay.

Access: From Plettenberg Bay follow the N2 eastwards for 50 km, then take the signposted right turn to the Tsitsikamma National Park and continue 6 km to the entrance of the park; the camp at Storms River Mouth is 4 km further on. To reach De Vasselot Nature Reserve, from the N2 take the turn-off in the direction of Nature's Valley; once in the village turn northwards and drive for a short distance to the camping site.

Accommodation: *Storms River Mouth camp* has 4-, 7- and 8-bed cottages, each with a fully equipped kitchen, bathroom and living room (R200 per 4 persons per night); 4-bed 'oceanettes', each with a fully equipped kitchen, bathroom and living room (R200 per 4 persons per night); 3-bed 'oceanettes', each with a fully equipped kitchen and bathroom (R105 per 2 persons per night); 4-bed huts, each with a fully equipped kitchen and bathroom (R105 per 2 persons per night); bedding supplied. There is

a camping site with ablution facilities (R22 plus R8 per person per night; maximum 6 persons per stand). *De Vasselot camping site,* near Nature's Valley, has 45 stands and ablution facilities. There are 4 hiking trail huts with basic facilities.

Other facilities: Hiking trails, including the 46 km Otter Trail; shorter walks; water sports and a 30-km network of pathways in the De Vasselot reserve; an underwater trail at Storms River Mouth; scuba-diving permitted (certified divers only); rock-fishing within a demarcated area; a restaurant, swimming pool and a shop at Storms River Mouth.

Open: Throughout the year.

Opening time: Tsitsikamma National Park – 05h30 to 21h30; the De Vasselot reserve – 24 hours.

For further information: (Enquiries and booking) National Parks Board (see page 365). (Park address) The Park Warden, Tsitsikamma National Park, P.O. Box Storms River 6308. Tel: (04237) 607 or 651.

The Tsitsikamma National Park is a narrow strip of land along the southern Cape coast which stretches from the mouth of the Groot River at Nature's Valley in the west about 80 km to another Groot River in the east. Along the entire length a marine reserve extends an average 5 km out to sea. The park was

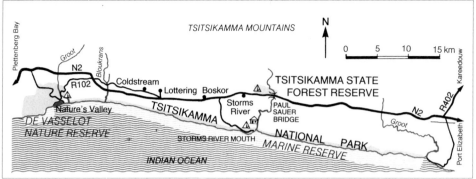

proclaimed in 1964 and at the end of 1987 the De Vasselot Nature Reserve was transferred to the stewardship of the National Parks Board from the Forestry Department.

The coastal plain, with cliffs falling sheer to the sea, and the deep, narrow valleys cut by rivers flowing down from the Tsitsikamma Mountains are the dominant topographical features of the park. The interior of the De Vasselot reserve is hilly and rugged, and also deeply incised by narrow valleys.

There are two major types of vegetation: areas of indigenous forest with many large trees, such as Outeniqua yellowwood, white stinkwood, Cape chestnut and white milkwood; and fynbos (heath) which includes several protea species, as well as the endangered *Leucospermum glabrum* in De Vasselot. Bushbuck, blue and common duiker, baboon, vervet monkey, rock dassie, small grey mongoose and Cape clawless otter occur in the park, and whales and dolphins are sometimes seen from the rocky shore. To date 280 bird species have been recorded, 25 of which are seabirds and the rest inhabit the forest and fynbos areas. The shore life is particularly rich, with a variety of marine organisms including 65 fish species and many molluscs and other invertebrates.

247 TSITSIKAMMA STATE FOREST RESERVE See map Tsitsikamma National Park

Location: Central part of the region; east of Plettenberg Bay.
Access: From Plettenberg Bay follow the N2 eastwards towards Port Elizabeth for about 60 km to the signpost 'Big Tree'; this is one entry to the forest reserve, the other being at the Paul Sauer Bridge 3 km further on.
Accommodation: A camping site with ablution facilities at the Paul Sauer Bridge.

Other facilities: Short walking trails; part of the 63 km Tsitsikamma Hiking Trail; restaurant and petrol station at the bridge.
Open: Throughout the year.
Opening time: Sunrise to sunset.
For further information: The Regional Director, Tsitsikamma Forest Region, Private Bag X537, Humansdorp 6300. Tel: (0423) 5-1180. Fax: (0423) 5-2745.

Covering about 500 ha, the Tsitsikamma State Forest Reserve protects a large block of indigenous coastal forest which contains some giant trees, the best-known being the 'Big Tree', an Outeniqua yellowwood taller than 36 m. There are fine examples of many other trees, such as stinkwood, candlewood and assegai, and a prolific undergrowth which includes many ferns and shrubs, as well as creepers. An area of fynbos (heath) surrounding the forest adds to the diversity of the vegetation. A wide variety of creatures inhabit the forest, but most are secretive. The most likely to be heard, if not seen, are birds such as the Knysna lourie and narina trogon, and the best way to observe these and other animals is to sit quietly in one of the forest clearings.

248 UITENHAGE NATURE RESERVE

Location: Eastern part of the region; Uitenhage.
Access: From Uitenhage take the R75 north-

wards towards Graaff-Reinet and after 8 km turn off to the clearly signposted Springs Holiday Resort; the resort is within the reserve.

Accommodation: The holiday resort has self-catering accommodation and a camping site.
Other facilities: A network of footpaths; guided tours at 15h00 every weekday except Thursday, and at 14h00 and 16h00 at weekends and on public holidays; picnic sites with fireplaces; swimming pool at resort; look-out tower.
Open: Throughout the year.
Opening time: 08h00 to sunset.
For further information: The Town Clerk, Uitenhage Municipality, P.O. Box 45, Uitenhage 6230. Tel: (0422) 992-6011, ext 291/299. Fax: (0422) 2-7562.

The 824-ha Uitenhage Nature Reserve is located around 'The Eyes', freshwater springs that contribute to the town's water supply. The reserve protects a variety of plantlife associated with Valley Bushveld, grassland and dry Karoo vegetation. Aloes offer a particularly fine spectacle when they flower between June and August. Birdwatchers will find the most productive area near the springs.

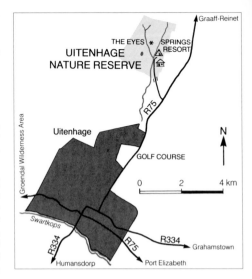

249 VAN STADENS WILD FLOWER RESERVE See map Cape Recife Nature Reserve

Location: Eastern part of the region; west of Port Elizabeth.
Access: From Port Elizabeth follow the N2 westwards for 29 km before taking the exit to Van Stadens Pass; the reserve is clearly signposted.
Accommodation: None.

Other facilities: Walking trails; information centre; picnic sites.
Open: Throughout the year.
Opening time: Sunrise to sunset.
For further information: The Nature Conservation Division, Algoa Regional Services Council (see page 365).

The Van Stadens Wild Flower Reserve was established to protect a largely unspoilt area which contains a combination of fynbos (heath) and Alexandria forest, the latter with elements of the Knysna as well as more tropical eastern forest. Of the reserve's total area of 500 ha, some 60 ha are cultivated. April to September, when many of the plants are in flower, is considered the best time to visit.

250 WILDERNESS NATIONAL PARK

Location: Western part of the region; east of George.
Access: From George take the N2 eastwards to Wilderness; the reserve lies on either side of the highway, from Wilderness in the west to the borders of the Goukamma Nature Reserve in the east. To reach the Ebb and Flow camp, from the N2 turn left into Wilderness, passing the Karos Hotel, and continue through the residential area; 3 km further on cross a road/rail bridge, then turn left to the camp. To reach the Wilderness camp, continue past Wilderness on the N2 and turn left shortly after the Lakes Holiday Resort, following signposts.
Accommodation: *Ebb and Flow camp* has

2-bed huts, each with a shower and toilet but no kitchen (R45 per night); 2-bed huts (R35 per night); bedding included; a camping site with 70 stands and ablution facilities (R12 per stand per night, plus R6,50 per person per night; maximum 6 persons per stand). *Wilderness camp* has 4-bed log cabins, each with a fully equipped kitchen, bathroom and living room (R165 per night); 6-bed cottages, each with a fully equipped kitchen, bathroom and living room (R155 per 4 persons per night); 6-berth caravans with stove, refrigerator and adjoining room on site (R55 plus R8 per adult and R7 per child per night); bedding supplied; a camping site with ablution facilities (R12 per stand per

night, plus R6,50 per person per night; maximum 6 persons per stand). Booking is essential.
Other facilities: Walking trails, including the 12-km Kingfisher Trail; watersports within zoned areas; boats can be hired; swimming; fishing.

Open: Throughout the year.
Opening time: 24 hours.
For further information: (Enquiries and booking) National Parks Board, George (see page 365). (Park address) Wilderness National Park, P.O. Box 35, Wilderness 6560. Tel: (0441) 9-1197.

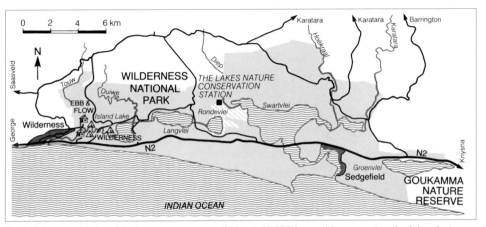

The Wilderness National Park covers an area of about 10 000 ha and incorporates the lakes between Wilderness and the Goukamma Nature Reserve and their interlinking waterways. These are: the Touw River estuary, Wilderness Lagoon, the Serpentine, Island Lake, Langvlei, Rondevlei, Swartvlei and the western fringe of Groenvlei. The National Parks Board has taken over management of the area so that pollution and unsightly development around the lakes can be controlled.

The Lakes Nature Reserve and Conservation Station, which does not fall under the control of the National Parks Board, lies between Rondevlei and Swartvlei and is clearly signposted from the N2. Apart from a section in which bontebok are protected, this reserve is open to the public and has a birdwatching hide which is popular. Sedge and reedbeds provide breeding habitats for 80 waterbird species, and more than 120 other bird species have been recorded. Bushbuck, common duiker and Cape grysbok are occasionally seen. For further information contact: The Officer-in-charge, The Lakes Nature Reserve and Conservation Station, Private Bag X6579, George 6530. Tel: (04455) 3-1302 or 3-1366.

251 YSTERNEK NATURE RESERVE See map Diepwalle State Forest

Location: Western part of the region; north of Knysna.
Access: From Knysna follow the N2 eastwards for 7 km; turn left onto the R339 towards Avontuur and Uniondale; continue for 24 km to the reserve, which is on the left. The R339 becomes graded gravel about 6 km from the N2.
Accommodation: None.

Other facilities: Short walk through wet high-forest at the Dalvan-varings picnic site and a drive up to a view-point.
Open: Throughout the year.
Opening time: Sunrise to sunset.
For further information: The Regional Director, Southern Cape Forest Region, Private Bag X12, Knysna 6570. Tel: (0445) 2-3037.

Covering 1 212 ha, the Ysternek Nature Reserve was set aside to protect montane fynbos (heath) and indigenous forest. Although the larger mammals which occur here, such as leopard, bushpig and bushbuck, are seldom seen, the birdlife is varied and much more visible. The viewpoint offers spectacular views of the Outeniqua and Tsitsikamma mountains to the north and the forested coastal plateaus to the south.

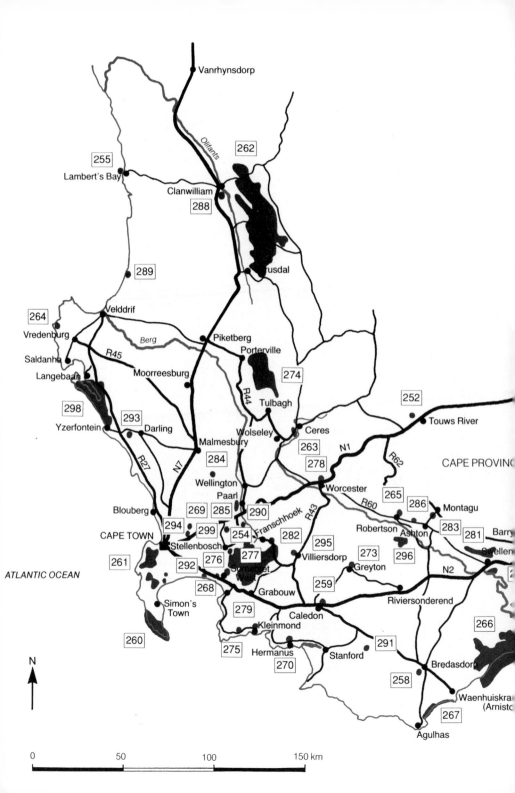

SOUTH-WESTERN CAPE PROVINCE

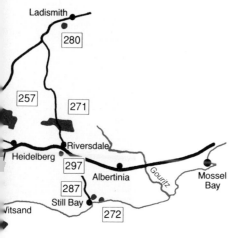

INDIAN OCEAN

296 Vrolijkheid Nature Reserve
297 Werner Frehse Nature Reserve

298 West Coast National Park
299 Wiesenhof Game Park

The south-western Cape Province can be defined as stretching northwards up the West Coast past Lambert's Bay and eastwards along the southern coast to Mossel Bay. The cold Atlantic Ocean washes the West Coast, while the warmer Indian Ocean makes the southern coast a popular holiday area. The coastal plains are separated from the arid interior by the Cape Folded Belt, a chain of parallel mountain ranges. These form important water catchment areas that are the source of rivers such as the Berg, Breede, Olifants and Gouritz.

What makes this region unique is that it is home to the Cape Floral Kingdom, the smallest, yet hectare for hectare the richest, floral kingdom in the world. The vegetation peculiar to this kingdom, known as fynbos, has three main components: broad-leaved, woody protea species, tiny-leaved ericas or heath-like plants, and reedy grasses. Unfortunately, most of the coastal fynbos has disappeared under the plough or beneath urban sprawl. The montane fynbos has fared somewhat better and several large areas have been set aside to conserve this wealth of plant species.

Located in one of the most densely populated areas in South Africa, many of the south-western Cape's conservation areas are heavily utilised. More than two million people ascend Table Mountain, and almost 500 000 tour the Cape of Good Hope Nature Reserve each year. Cape Town is the major city and probably one of the best-known ports in the world, dominated as it is by the sandstone massif of Table Mountain. Despite the limitation of being situated on a narrow peninsula, the city is well endowed with nature reserves.

The Directorate of Nature and Environmental Conservation (see page 365) is the provincial authority in charge of many of the conservation areas

in this region. Some – such as the 850-ha Maanschynskop Nature Reserve near Caledon, which was proclaimed to protect the endangered marsh rose – are closed to the public. Another six were proclaimed specifically to protect the endangered geometric tortoise. It is believed that no more than 3 000 of these distinctly marked reptiles survive and their decline is directly related to the destruction of 96 per cent of their habitat, the coastal renosterveld. For further information contact the Herpetology Section, Jonkershoek Nature Conservation Station, Private Bag X5014, Stellenbosch 7600.

Within this region there are also several marine reserves, as well as sanctuaries set aside to protect the rock lobster (crayfish). The three rock lobster sanctuaries are at St Helena Bay, at Saldanha and Langebaan, and from Melkbos Point, north of Cape Town, to Chapman's Peak, just to the south of the city. The western shore of the Cape of Good Hope Nature Reserve is a general marine reserve but angling and spearfishing are permitted, and a limited number of rock lobsters may be taken. Five marine reserves within False Bay extend from 500 m to one nautical mile seawards from the low-water mark. Although angling is permitted in most areas, there are regulations governing such aspects as catch size and bait collection, and it is wise to obtain clarification from the Directorate of Nature and Environmental Conservation.

The south-western Cape Province has a typical Mediterranean climate, with cool, wet winters and warm, dry summers. The region is well known for its strong south-easterly winds in summer and for the north-westers which often blow at gale force in winter.

---

252 A.S. LE ROUX NATURE RESERVE

Location: The Little Karoo; north-west of Touws River.
Access: From Touws River take the N1 southwards and after 2 km turn right into the A.S. le Roux Nature Reserve.
Accommodation: None. Touws River has a hotel and a camping and caravan site.
Other facilities: 15-km hiking trail; picnic area; pathways.
Open: Throughout the year.
Opening time: On request.
For further information: The Town Clerk, Touws River Municipality, Private Bag X1124, Touws River 6880. Tel: 02382, ask for 191.

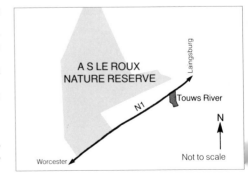

Previously known as the Landdrosdrift Nature Reserve, A.S. le Roux covers 2 700 ha and contains five different vegetation types, namely western mountain Karoo (which occurs in very stony country and includes low shrubs and some bush), succulent Karoo, mountain renosterveld (which comprises straggly woody shrubs), montane fynbos (heath) and false heathland (characterised by daisy-like plants). This amazing diversity offers visitors the opportunity to examine hundreds of different plant species. There is a flourishing herd of springbok and many species of birds are to be seen.

253 ANYSBERG NATURE RESERVE

Location: The Little Karoo; south-east of Laingsburg.
Access: From Laingsburg take the R323 south-eastwards towards Riversdale for approximately 60 km. The turn-off to the reserve is on the right and is clearly signposted.
Accommodation: A basic camping site with 6 stands and limited ablutions.
Other facilities: An overnight trail is being developed; at present hikers may make arrangements with the Officer-in-charge to hike in the reserve.
Open: Throughout the year.
Opening time: 24 hours.
For further information: The Directorate of Nature and Environmental Conservation, Private Bag X6546, George 6530. Tel: (0441) 74-1567. (Reserve) The Officer-in-charge, Private Bag X216, Ladismith 6885. Tel: 02372, ask for 1913 or 1921.

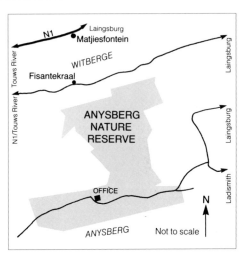

Anysberg Nature Reserve lies in part of the Anysberg Mountain Catchment Area, whose waters drain eventually into the Gouritz River system. Recently enlarged to more than 34 000 ha, the reserve consists mainly of mountains interspersed with wide, open valleys. Two major plant communities are present, Karoo scrub and bush on the lower northern and southern slopes, and montane fynbos (heath) higher up. Several plant species, including two rare ericas, are only known to grow in this mountain range. Mammals that occur here include baboon, leopard, caracal, klipspringer, grey rhebok, common duiker, Cape grysbok, spectacled dormouse and the Cape spiny mouse. A number of rare birds may be seen, including martial and booted eagles, Cape eagle owl and the protea canary, as well as the Cape sugarbird.

254 ASSEGAAIBOSCH NATURE RESERVE See map Hottentots Holland Nature Reserve

Location: South-western part of the region; south-east of Stellenbosch.
Access: From Stellenbosch take the Jonkershoek road, and watch out for a signpost to the reserve on the right. Permits should be arranged telephonically and then collected from the Jonkershoek Fish Hatchery.
Accommodation: None.
Other facilities: Short walks; wild flower garden with labelled plants; picnic sites with fire-places near the entrance gate.
Open: Throughout the year.
Opening time: May to September – weekdays 09h30 to 17h00, weekends – 08h00 to 17h00; October to April – weekdays 09h00 to 18h00, weekends 08h00 to 18h00.
For further information: The Officer-in-charge, Assegaaibosch Nature Reserve, Private Bag 5014, Stellenbosch 7600. Tel: (02231) 7-0111. Fax: (02231) 7-1606.

Assegaaibosch Nature Reserve, adjoining the Jonkershoek State Forest and Hottentots Holland Nature Reserve in the beautiful Jonkershoek Valley, conserves a 204-ha area of montane fynbos (heath) which contains a number of rare proteas. Common duiker, Cape grysbok and small grey mongoose are quite frequently seen. The birdlife is varied and includes grey-winged francolin, black eagle and Cape sugarbird.

The neighbouring Jonkershoek State Forest is open during the day between May and September and has a variety of paths and trails. Permits are required. For further information contact The Regional Director, Western Cape Forest Region, Private Bag 9005, Cape Town 8000.

255 BIRD ISLAND

Location: West Coast; west of Clanwilliam.
Access: From Clanwilliam take the R364 westwards for 62 km to Lambert's Bay. Bird Island lies next to the fishing harbour, and is clearly signposted.
Accommodation: None. Lambert's Bay has a large camping site with ablution facilities, and a hotel.
Other facilities: Birdwatching hide.
Open: Throughout the year.
Opening time: Sunrise to sunset.
For further information: The Town Clerk, Lambert's Bay Municipality, P.O. Box 4, Lambert's Bay 8130. Tel: (026732) 9. Fax: (026732) 217.

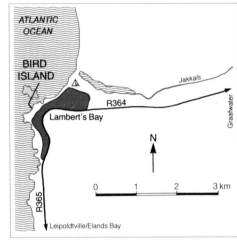

Bird Island was joined to the mainland by a breakwater in 1959 and is now the most accessible of the marine bird breeding islands off the West Coast.

Although the main breeding areas are fenced off from the public to prevent undue disturbance, it is still possible to get close to the birds. Approximately 5 000 pairs of Cape gannets breed here in the spring and summer months, and many thousands of Cape cormorants can be seen throughout the year. There is also a small jackass penguin colony.

The area receives low rainfall. Fog is a common occurrence in the area, but it usually clears by mid-morning.

256 BONTEBOK NATIONAL PARK

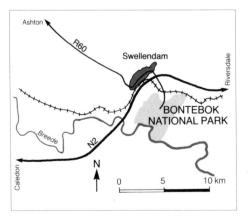

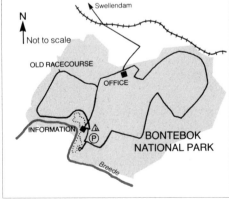

Location: Eastern part of the region; south-east of Swellendam.

Access: Leave Swellendam at the town's eastern end, cross the N2 and follow the gravel road south-eastwards for 6 km to the reserve's entrance gate. The route is well signposted. Internal roads are all-weather gravel. An entrance fee is charged.

Accommodation: A camping and caravan site with 25 stands and ablution facilities is situated on the banks of the Breede River. Fully equipped caravans are available for hire. There are plans to provide self-catering accommodation.

Other facilities: A 25-km network of game-viewing roads; 2 short walking trails; swimming in the Breede River; fishing; shop selling cool drinks, nonperishable groceries and curios; fuel; information centre; picnic sites with fireplaces.

Open: Throughout the year.

Opening time: From 1 October to 30 April – 08h00 to 19h00; from 1 May to 30 September – 09h00 to 18h00.

Speed limit: 25 km/h.

For further information: (Enquiries and booking) National Parks Board (see page 365). (Park address) The Warden, Bontebok National Park, P.O. Box 149, Swellendam 6740. Tel: (0291) 4-2735.

The original Bontebok National Park was proclaimed in 1931 in the Bredasdorp district to protect the last 22 animals left alive. All bontebok in existence today are descendants of these 22 animals. In 1960 84 bontebok were moved to the present and much larger Bontebok National Park, which was proclaimed the following year. The improved vegetation in the area resulted in a rapid population increase, to the point where excess animals are now regularly captured alive for relocation. The 2 786-ha park is surrounded by wheatlands and pasture, with the Breede River forming about 6 km of its southern boundary. Its altitude ranges from 60 to 200 m above sea-level and the terrain is mainly flat and open, but interspersed with rocky ridges.

Because the fynbos in the park is virtually the last in the area, great emphasis is placed on the conservation of flora. More than 470 plant species, including a number of rare ones, have been identified in the park. Sweet-thorn trees dominate, while Breede River yellowwood, wild olive and white milkwood are restricted to the river banks.

The low nature of the fynbos vegetation makes game-viewing relatively easy, and in addition to the larger antelope, Cape grysbok, steenbok and common duiker are frequently observed. Although in conservation terms emphasis is placed on the bontebok, a small number of Cape mountain zebra and red hartebeest have been introduced, and this is one of the few reserves where grey rhebok can be easily seen. Of the smaller mammals, both the yellow and small grey mongooses occur. September to November is the period when the bontebok ewes drop their young and, with the vegetation usually at its best at this time, this is a good season to visit.

Approximately 200 bird species have been recorded and birdwatching is particularly rewarding near the camping and picnic sites. In addition, 28 reptile and 10 amphibian species are known to inhabit the park.

Although rain can be expected at any time of year, there is a distinct winter peak.

257 BOOSMANSBOS WILDERNESS AREA

Location: Eastern part of the region; east of Swellendam.

Access: From Swellendam take the N2 eastwards to Heidelberg; from here take the R322 westwards for approximately 12 km and turn off onto a gravel road to Grootvadersbos State Forest; follow this road to the forest station. Alternatively, from Swellendam follow the N2 eastwards for 11 km and turn off onto the R322 to Suurbraak; continue past this village to the Grootvadersbos State Forest turn-off. Permits are required and a maximum of 12 persons is allowed each day.

Accommodation: 2 sets of hiking trail hut shelters without beds. Bookings, which open 3

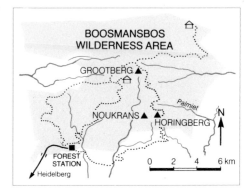

months in advance, should only be made telephonically.
Other facilities: A network of paths and trails.
Open: Throughout the year.
Opening time: Sunrise to sunset; office: 08h00

to 16h00 Monday to Friday.
For further information: The State Forester, Grootvadersbos State Forest, P.O. Box 109, Heidelberg 6760. Tel: (02962) 1812, office hours.

This little-known wilderness area, covering 14 200 ha, lies on the slopes of the Langeberg range and protects large expanses of montane fynbos (heath) and one of the largest pockets of indigenous forest in the Cape Province. There are a number of high peaks, including Grootberg (1 637 m) and Horingberg (1 496 m), as well as impressive gorges containing perennial streams. The patches of forest include such trees as stinkwood and yellowwood, and an isolated stand of the rare mountain cypress.

Bushbuck inhabit the forested areas, while the fynbos provides cover for Cape grysbok and common duiker. On the more open slopes one may catch a glimpse of small groups of grey rhebok, or the agile klipspringer on rocky outcrops.

Birdlife is rich and includes black and martial eagles and jackal buzzard. Several rare butterfly species are protected here.

Lying within the transitional zone between winter and all-season rainfall, the area experiences showers at any time of the year. The summer months are the best time for visiting it.

258 BREDASDORP MOUNTAIN RESERVE

Location: South-eastern coastal part of the region; south-east of Caledon.
Access: From Caledon take the R316 south-eastwards for 74 km to Bredasdorp. From the main road turn right into Independent Rd and then right again into Van Riebeeck Rd, following signposts to the entrance gate.
Accommodation: None. There is a hotel and a caravan and camping site in Bredasdorp.
Other facilities: Nature trails.
Open: Throughout the year.
Opening time: Sunrise to sunset.
For further information: The Town Clerk, Bredasdorp Municipality, P.O. Box 51, Bredasdorp 7280. Tel: (02841) 4-1135.

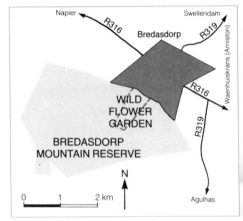

Covering 800 ha in total, this reserve spreads from the southern edge of Bredasdorp up the slope of a 386-m hill, from which there are good views of the town. An 86-ha cultivated area is set aside to protect unspoilt examples of coastal bush and montane fynbos (heath), including a variety of protea and erica species.

A number of small mammals occur here, as do several bird species that are associated with fynbos, such as Cape sugarbird, and lesser double-collared, malachite and orange-breasted sunbirds.

259 CALEDON NATURE RESERVE AND WILD FLOWER GARDEN

Location: Southern part of the region; north-east of Caledon.
Access: From Caledon take the clearly sign-posted road northwards through the town and under the N2 to the entrance gate of the nature reserve.
Accommodation: None. There are 3 hotels in

Caledon.
Other facilities: A 10-km hiking trail; short walks; a picnic area; a tea-room which is open during the spring flower season; an annual flower show.
Open: Throughout the year.
Opening time: 07h00 to 19h00.

For further information: The Town Clerk, Caledon Municipality, P.O. Box 24, Caledon 7230. Tel: (0281) 2-1090/1/2. Fax: (0281) 4-1289.

Famous for its displays of spring flowers, the 214 ha Caledon Nature Reserve and Wild Flower Garden was proclaimed in 1964 on land granted for use as a park by Queen Victoria. It attracts thousands of visitors each year, many of whom attend the annual spring flower show held in September.

The wild flower garden comprises a 56-ha section under cultivation, in which many indigenous tree and fynbos species are nurtured. The reserve lies on the slopes of the Swartberg mountain, from which there are good views of the surrounding region.

The vegetation consists of montane fynbos (heath), among which many different species can be identified.

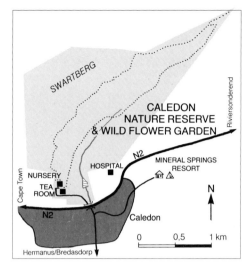

260 CAPE OF GOOD HOPE NATURE RESERVE

Location: Southern part of the region; south of Cape Town.

Access: From Cape Town take the M4 through the Southern Suburbs to Fish Hoek and along the eastern side of the Cape Peninsula to the entrance gate of the reserve. The turn-off is clearly signposted on the left. Alternatively, from Cape Town the M6 runs down the western, Atlantic coastline of the peninsula; after driving through Noordhoek turn right onto the M65 to Kommetjie and follow this road to the entrance gate. An entrance fee is charged. Permits are required and these are available at the main gate.

Accommodation: None.

Other facilities: An extensive network of game-viewing roads; nature trails; a bus up the steep hill to Cape Point; picnic sites; restaurant; kiosk; fishing (permits required) allowed along a section of the coast; slipway for launching boats at Buffels Bay.

Open: Throughout the year.

Opening time: (Entrance time) January to December – 08h00 to 17h00; (exit time) September to April – 20h00, May to August – 18h00.

Speed limit: 60 km/h on main roads; 40 km/h on all other roads.

For further information: The Western Cape Regional Services Council, (see page 365). (Cape of Good Hope) (021) 780-1100.

Situated at the southern tip of the Cape Peninsula, this reserve has a coastline of some 40 km, which is washed by the Atlantic Ocean in the west and the waters of False Bay in the east. Early man inhabited the area more than 200 000 years ago and numerous prehistoric sites have been identified by archaeologists. It is believed that the first European to see the Cape of Good Hope was the Portuguese explorer Bartolomeu Dias, in 1488.

The reserve covers 7 750 ha and its landscape is dominated by two main features: the ridge of hills that runs along the False Bay coast from Smitswinkel Bay to Cape Point, and the gently undulating flatland sloping to the west. The vegetation can be divided into three broad categories: dry, low fynbos (heath) grows on the hills, sedges and ericas dominate the flatland areas, while stands of milkwood trees and a great variety of heaths and succulents cover the sandy coastal zone. Approximately 1 200 different plant species have been identified in the reserve (more than half the total number of plants occurring on the European subcontinent) and these include 52 different ground orchids and 25 protea species.

Although this is primarily a scenic and botanical reserve, it does support small numbers of larger species, such as bontebok, Cape mountain zebra, grey rhebok, Cape grysbok, eland, red hartebeest and common duiker. There are four baboon troops within the conservation area, as well as Cape fox, caracal and rock dassie.

More than 150 bird species have been observed. In addition, the endangered sago-belly frog survives in a few shallow, freshwater pools in a specially protected area. The marine life is of particular interest, as the animals found on the western shore differ considerably from those on the eastern. A marine reserve extends out to sea on the western coast.

Most of the average annual 600 mm of rain falls in winter, between May and August. The area experiences strong winds, particularly from November to March, with wind speeds often reaching up to 40 km per hour.

261 CAPE TOWN

Kirstenbosch National Botanic Garden
Rhodes Ave, Kirstenbosch. Situated on the eastern face of Table Mountain, this 528-ha botanic garden is a major tourist feature of the south-western Cape. Some 60 ha are under cultivation and there are many species from the Cape Floral Kingdom, as well as succulents and cycads. The garden contains many scenic walks, including special trails for the elderly, blind and handicapped, through both the cultivated and the natural areas. The opening times are from 08h00 to 18h00 between April and August, and for an hour later for the rest of the year. For further information contact the Garden Director, Kirstenbosch National Botanic Garden, Private Bag X7, Claremont 7735. Tel: (021) 762-1166.

Raapenberg Bird Sanctuary
Black River Parkway, Observatory. Unless special permits are issued, this 10-ha reserve is open only to members of the Cape Bird Club. Opening times are between sunrise and sunset throughout the year. The sanctuary consists of wetland areas of seasonal open water and extensive reed beds bordering the Black River. To date 55 bird species have been recorded. For further information contact the Parks and Forest Branch, City Engineers Department (see page 365).

Rondevlei Bird Sanctuary
Off Prince George Dr., Grassy Park. Rondevlei, one of the most important waterfowl wetlands in the Cape Peninsula, protects 222 bird species, of which 70 are known to breed here. A small number of hippopotamuses have been introduced in an effort to control certain grass species. The reserve covers a total of 137 ha, surrounding a shallow vlei. Opening times are between 08h00 and 17h00, and there are a number of short trails, birdwatching hides, a picnic area and a natural history museum. For further information contact the Western Cape Regional Services Council (see page 365), or contact Rondevlei Bird Sanctuary direct (Tel: 021 – 706-2404).

Sandvlei Bird Sanctuary
Off the M5, north of Muizenberg. Access is currently restricted to members of the Cape Bird Club and members of the public accompanied by a ranger. Sandvlei was proclaimed a bird sanctuary in 1987 and it is planned to expand this 22-ha area in the near future. To date 132 bird species have been recorded, and the vlei is considered to be a valuable breeding ground for many of them. For further information contact the Parks and Forests Branch, City Engineers Department (see page 365). (Permits) Tel: (021) 75-3040.

Silvermine Nature Reserve
Ou Kaapseweg; extends from Muizenberg and Kalk Bay in the east to Noordhoek Peak in the west. This reserve covers 2 140 ha of some of the finest scenery in the Cape Peninsula and contains many caves, mountain peaks, extensive plateaux and valleys. The area is covered by montane fynbos (heath), although there are also small patches of evergreen forest. Several small mammals and reptiles are present, but the larger species are re-

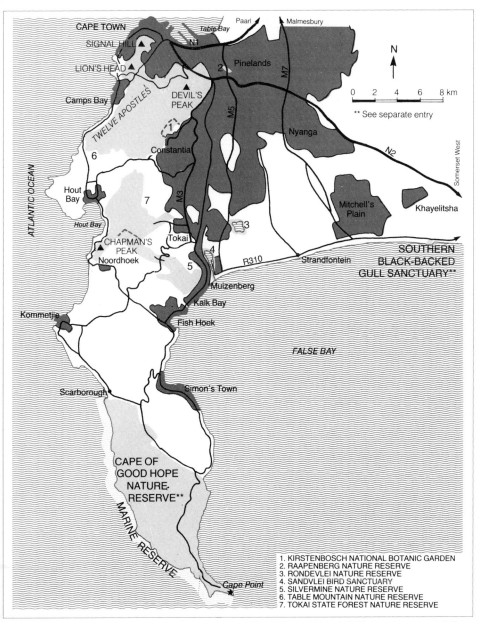

1. KIRSTENBOSCH NATIONAL BOTANIC GARDEN
2. RAAPENBERG NATURE RESERVE
3. RONDEVLEI NATURE RESERVE
4. SANDVLEI BIRD SANCTUARY
5. SILVERMINE NATURE RESERVE
6. TABLE MOUNTAIN NATURE RESERVE
7. TOKAI STATE FOREST NATURE RESERVE

stricted to grey rhebok, steenbok and Cape grysbok. The reserve is open from sunrise to sunset, and offers a network of paths and picnic sites with fireplaces. For further information contact the Parks and Forests Branch, City Engineers Department (see page 365).

Table Mountain Nature Reserve

Tafelberg Rd, Cape Town. This reserve ranges in altitude from 100 to 1 087 m and covers 2 748 ha of mountainous terrain, including Table Mountain, Devil's Peak, Lion's Head and Signal Hill. It is open between sunrise and sunset and offers hiking trails, mountain climbing, picnic sites and a restaurant at the upper cableway station. Montane fynbos (heath) is dominant and no less than 1 470 plant species have been identified, including more than 50 rare and threatened plants. Baboon, Cape grysbok, rock dassie and small grey mongoose are commonly seen. For further information contact the Parks and Forests Branch, City Engineers Department (see page 365).

Tokai State Forest Reserve
Tokai Rd, Tokai. This forest area lies between Table Mountain Nature Reserve in the north and Silvermine Nature Reserve in the south and east, and covers 2 572 ha of terrain similar to that found in the other two reserves. There are many tracks and paths, and a large picnic area with fireplaces. Permits are available at the gate. For further information contact the Department of Environment Affairs, Private Bag 9005, Cape Town 8000. Tel: (021) 72-7471.

262 CEDERBERG WILDERNESS

Location: Western part of the region; north-east of Cape Town.
Access: From Cape Town follow the N7 northwards for about 180 km and, beyond Citrusdal, turn right at the signpost to Algeria; follow this road to the office. 2 public roads traverse the area: in the north, the Pakhuis Pass road (R364) from Clanwilliam, and from Algeria a fairly rough gravel road which links up with the R303 between Citrusdal and Ceres. Permits are required and numbers of visitors are strictly controlled.
Accommodation: *Uitkyk* has 4 rooms for 15 persons (minimum 5) with a kitchen, ablution facilities, beds/mattresses and firewood; *Waenhuis* sleeps 7 persons (minimum 3) and has ablution facilities, beds/mattresses and firewood; book in advance. There are camping and caravan sites at Algeria and Kliphuis with ablution facilities and firewood. Patrol shelters in the mountains may be used by hikers.
Other facilities: An extensive network of hiking trails with overnight huts (maps available at the office); swimming in the river at Algeria; picnic sites with fireplaces at Algeria and on Pakhuis Pass.
Open: Throughout the year.
Opening time: No restrictions on public roads; office – 08h00 to 16h30.
Beware: Sudden weather changes; remember to be well equipped and keep to the designated trails.

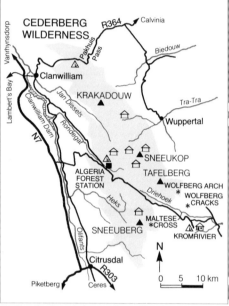

For further information: The State Forester, Cederberg Wilderness, Private Bag X1, Citrusdal 7340. Tel: 02682, ask for 3440. (Private accommodation) The Publicity/Tourist Division, Clanwilliam Municipality, P.O. Box 5, Clanwilliam 8135.

An area of outstanding scenery, the Cederberg range is well known for its rugged broken terrain. The highest peak is the Sneeuberg at 2 027 m above sea-level and there are several other peaks exceeding 1 600 m.

The wilderness area covers 71 000 ha of montane fynbos (heath) and also protects a vast array of plant species, including the Clanwilliam cedar which is now rare as a result of uncontrolled exploitation in the past.

Although no large game species occur, visitors may see Cape grysbok, common duiker, grey rhebok, klipspringer, baboon, rock dassie and small grey mongoose. The area is being used as a pilot sanctuary for leopards, with the intention of reducing the conflict between leopard conservation and stock-farming.

The birdlife is surprisingly rich for a mountainous region and 150 species have been recorded (a checklist is available).

Most of the area's rain falls during winter (May to September), when nights are often cold.

263 CERES MOUNTAIN FYNBOS RESERVE

Location: Central part of the region; Ceres.
Access: From Ceres take the R303 south-westwards towards Wellington. The reserve lies on both sides of the road at the top of Michell's Pass, with the entrance on the right.
Accommodation: None. Ceres has hotels and camping and caravan sites with chalets.
Other facilities: Walking and fishing are permitted; marked hiking trails are planned.
Open: Throughout the year.
Opening time: 24 hours.
For further information: The Town Clerk, Ceres Municipality, P.O. Box 44, Ceres 6835. Tel: (0233) 2-1177. Fax: (0233) 2-1965.

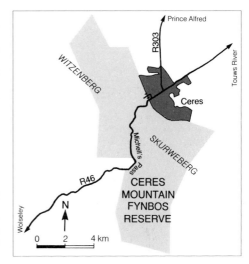

This reserve protects 6 800 ha of mountain fynbos (heath) which includes several rare plant species. From it there are outstanding views of the Witzenberg and Skurweberg mountains, and Bushman paintings are an added attraction. Snow is quite common on the higher slopes in winter.

264 COLUMBINE NATURE RESERVE

Location: West Coast; north-west of Vredenburg.
Access: From Vredenburg take the road westwards to Paternoster; continue on this road for a further 3 km to the reserve.
Accommodation: There is a camping and caravan site with 65 stands and basic ablution facilities.
Other facilities: Fishing and diving for crayfish and abalone (perlemoen) are permitted; walking; picnic sites for day visitors.
Open: Throughout the year.
Opening time: Sunrise to sunset.
For further information: The Town Clerk, Municipality of Vredenburg-Saldanha, Private Bag X12, Vredenburg 7380. Tel: (02281) 3-2231 or (02285) 718. Fax: (02281) 5-1518.

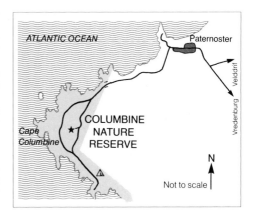

This 263-ha reserve has been set aside to conserve sandveld fynbos indigenous to the area. The terrain is mostly sand-covered with rock outcrops, and to the west includes a number of dunes and bays. The best time to visit is in the spring when the flowers are in bloom.

Rain falls mainly during the winter months, but strong winds can be expected at any time.

265 DASSIESHOEK NATURE RESERVE

Location: Central part of the region; north of Robertson.

Access: From Robertson follow Voortrekker Rd northwards for about 8 km to the reserve. The route is clearly signposted. Permits are required and are available at the entrance gate or at the municipal offices in town.

Accommodation: 35-bed house for hikers only. Robertson has hotels as well as self-catering accommodation and a camping and caravan site at Silverstrand Holiday Resort.

Other facilities: Part of a 37-km hiking trail (which starts at Silverstrand) passes through the reserve; shorter walks; picnic sites with fireplaces. The nearest shops and fuel supplies are at Robertson.

Open: Throughout the year.

Opening time: 08h00 to 18h00.

For further information: The Town Clerk, Robertson Municipality, P.O. Box 52, Robertson 6705. Tel: (02351) 3112. Fax: (02351) 2426.

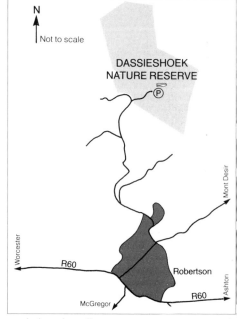

Dassieshoek Nature Reserve lies within the Langeberg West Mountain Catchment Area and extends over 865 ha on the southern slopes of the Langeberg range. Altitudes above sea-level range from 350 to 2 070 m and the steep cliffs and deep gorges provide a magnificent backdrop. Montane fynbos (heath) is dominant and there are many rare and interesting plant species. As is typical of the south-western Cape Province, mammals are not abundant, although baboon, klipspringer, Cape grysbok and small grey mongoose are commonly seen. Leopard and caracal also occur in the range.

The lower-lying areas receive an average annual rainfall of 600 mm, and snow falls on the higher peaks during the winter months. Summers are mild to hot.

266 DE HOOP NATURE RESERVE

Location: South-eastern part of the region; east of Bredasdorp.

Access: From Bredasdorp follow the R319 north-eastwards in the direction of Swellendam for 9 km, then turn right onto a gravel road at the De Hoop signpost; continue for 34 km before turning right again; the entrance lies 7 km further on. Internal roads are well-maintained gravel. Permits are required and are available at the gate.

Accommodation: Cottages and a camping site. Book in advance.

Other facilities: Game-viewing roads; walking trails; cycling is permitted; guided trails and environmental education centres (Potberg and Koppie Alleen) for organised groups; picnic sites with fireplaces. The nearest shops and fuel supplies are at Wydgeleë, which is 15 km away.

Open: Throughout the year.

Opening time: 07h00 to 18h00.

For further information: The Officer-in-charge, De Hoop Nature Reserve, Private Bag X16, Bredasdorp 7280. Tel: (02922) 782.

The De Hoop Nature Reserve is one of the most important in the Cape Province, and together with the marine reserve covers more than 60 000 ha. It is made up of many different types of terrain, including extensive sand and calcrete flats, more than 40 km of beaches and rocky coastline, sand dunes, calcareous ridges, the Potberg hills and De Hoop vlei.

The reserve protects one of the largest remaining areas of coastal fynbos (heath) in the south-western Cape. About 85 per cent of this habitat has already disappeared under the plough and De Hoop thus plays an important part in the protection of what remains. It is estimated, for example, that more than 1 500 plant species occur in the area, 71 of which are rare or endangered and 50 of which are known to grow only within the reserve.

The marine reserve protects a rich diversity of organisms, ranging from the southern right whales,

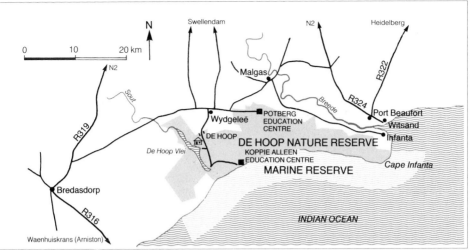

which visit between June and December, to molluscs, seaweeds and even the lowly sandhopper. In all, 70 mammal species have been recorded here, including 13 marine mammals, eland, Cape mountain zebra, grey rhebok, Cape grysbok, common duiker, Cape clawless otter and rock dassie, as well as the largest known single population of bontebok.

However, De Hoop is probably best known for its bird population and to date the checklist records 228 species, many of which – such as the endangered Cape vulture – breed within the reserve. Waterbirds are particularly well represented.

The average annual rainfall is 380 mm and this occurs throughout the year, although there is a distinct peak in August. Strong winds blow all year round.

267 DE MOND NATURE RESERVE

Location: South-eastern part of the region; south of Bredasdorp.
Access: From Bredasdorp follow the R316 towards Waenhuiskrans (Arniston); after 11 km turn right onto a gravel road and continue for 14 km, through Prinskraal, to the entrance gate. Permits are available at the office.
Accommodation: None.
Other facilities: Walking is permitted; fishing (permits are required); seabird watching.
Open: Throughout the year.
Opening time: 08h00 to 16h30.
For further information: The Officer-in-charge, De Mond Nature Reserve, P.O. Box 277, Bredasdorp 7280. Tel: (02841) 4-2170.

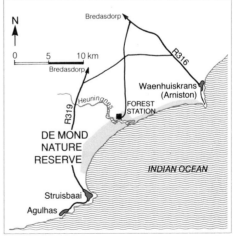

Unlike many stretches of our coastline, De Mond Nature Reserve is peaceful and unspoilt. It covers 954 ha of varied habitat, including sand dunes, coastal fynbos (heath) and the Heuningnes River estuary. There is a rich birdlife and the blackbacked seagull, whitebreasted cormorant and Caspian and Damara terns breed in the reserve. Such mammals as the Cape grysbok, steenbok, common duiker, Cape clawless otter and small grey mongoose may be seen.

268 DICK DENT BIRD SANCTUARY

Location: South-western part of the region; adjacent to Strand.
Access: From the N2 (Cape Town/Somerset West), take the R44 turn-off which leads directly into Broadway; the sanctuary is on the right just before the Lourens River bridge.
Accommodation: None. There are hotels and caravan and camping sites in the area.
Other facilities: Short pathways; 2 birdwatching hides.
Open: Throughout the year.
Opening time: 24 hours.
For further information: AECI (E&C) Ltd, Private Bag 101, Dynamite Factory 7120. Tel: (024) 2-1111. Fax: (024) 2-1901; or Somerset West Bird Club, Tel: (024) 55-1012.

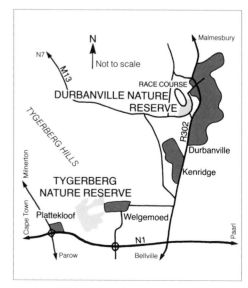

Covering only 7 ha and situated on AECI property, this small bird sanctuary has 6 ponds, previously part of a sewerage treatment plant. The levels of the ponds are manipulated to ensure that there are suitable habitats for a variety of waterbirds. Indigenous trees have been planted to attract birds and tilapia have been established in all the dams. The public are welcome to use the river walk which has an entrance on the Cape Town side of Broadway bridge.

When the sanctuary opened in 1981, 100 bird species were to be seen. There are now 140 different species including white pelican, heron, glossy ibis, 7 raptors and 15 waders. The Cape clawless otter is occasionally seen.

269 DURBANVILLE NATURE RESERVE

Location: South-western part of the region; north-east of Cape Town.
Access: From Cape Town take the N1 in the direction of Paarl and turn off at the Durbanville exit; follow Durbanville Ave, turn left into Tindale Rd and continue to Race Course Rd. The nature reserve is clearly signposted from here.
Accommodation: None.
Other facilities: Pathways; information centre.
Open: Throughout the year.
Opening time: 08h00 to 16h30.
For further information: The Town Clerk, Durbanville Municipality, P.O. Box 100, Durbanville 7550. Tel: (021) 96-3020.

More than 200 plant species, including many protea, erica and aristea species, occur in the Durbanville Nature Reserve, which protects 6 ha of montane fynbos (heath).

The best time to visit the reserve is between September and February.

270 FERNKLOOF NATURE RESERVE

Location: South-western part of the region; south-east of Cape Town.
Access: From Cape Town follow the N2 for approximately 100 km to Bot River; turn right onto the R43 and follow it to Hermanus. The reserve lies on the northern side of the town.
Accommodation: None. Hermanus has hotels, self-catering accommodation and a camping and caravan site.
Other facilities: A 35-km network of trails; an information centre.
Open: Throughout the year.
Opening time: Sunrise to sunset.
For further information: The Town Clerk, Hermanus Municipality, P.O. Box 20, Hermanus 7200. Tel: (0283) 2-1122. Fax: (0283) 2-1894.

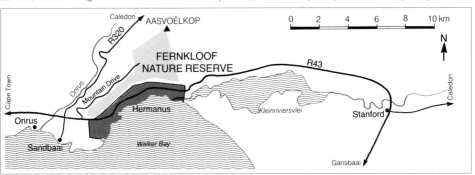

Fernkloof Nature Reserve covers 1 446 ha in the Kleinrivier Mountains above Hermanus and ranges in altitude from 63 to 842 m. It protects coastal and montane fynbos (heath) and a small patch of evergreen forest. Grey rhebok, Cape grysbok and klipspringer are present in small numbers, although they are seldom seen, and 75 bird species have been recorded.

271 GARCIA STATE FOREST

Location: South-eastern part of the region; north of Riversdale.
Access: From Riversdale take the R323 towards Ladismith as far as Garcia Pass and the old Toll House. Footpaths into the reserve leave from this historical monument. Permits are required and are controlled by Grootvadersbos State Forest.
Accommodation: None.
Other facilities: An extensive network of trails and footpaths.
Open: May close during the summer months due to fire risk; contact the State Forester.
Opening time: Sunrise to sunset.
For further information: (Permits) The State Forester, Grootvadersbos State Forest, P.O. Box 109, Heidelberg 6760. Tel: 02962, ask for 1812. (Garcia State Forest) Tel: (02933) 3-2558.

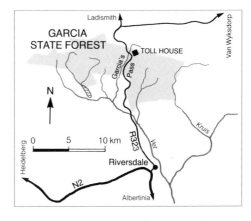

Garcia State Forest lies within the Langeberg Mountains and is managed principally to protect the water catchment area and the great diversity of montane fynbos (heath) species that occur here. The animal life in this 12 000-ha reserve is scarce, but includes the seldom-seen leopard, caracal and honey badger, as well as grey rhebok and Cape grysbok. Bird species such as black eagle, rock kestrel, and malachite and orange-breasted sunbirds are often seen.

272 GEELKRANS NATURE RESERVE

Location: South-eastern part of the region; south-east of Riversdale.
Access: From Riversdale follow the N2 eastwards for 11 km and turn right onto the R323 to Still Bay East. The reserve is on the coast, 5 km east of the town. Permits are required.
Accommodation: None. Still Bay has a hotel and a camping and caravan site.
Other facilities: Walking trail; in December and January the Still Bay Trust conducts guided tours.
Open: Throughout the year.
Opening time: Sunrise to sunset.
For further information: The State Forester,

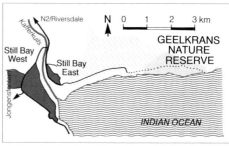

Grootvadersbos State Forest, P.O. Box 109, Heidelberg 6760. Tel: 02962, ask for 1812.

The vegetation of this 165-ha reserve is coastal fynbos (heath), containing a variety of plant species, and the best time to visit is between October and March when the plants are in flower. Bushbuck, Cape grysbok, common duiker and small grey mongoose are common, and rock dassies are particularly abundant.

The birdlife is typical of coastal fynbos regions and includes Cape and red-necked francolin, Cape bulbul, grassbird and southern tchagra.

273 GREYTON NATURE RESERVE

Location: Eastern part of the region; north-east of Caledon.
Access: From Caledon take the N2 westwards for 3 km and turn right onto the R406 to Greyton; at Greyton continue to the end of the main street and turn left and then right to the reserve.
Accommodation: None. Greyton has 3 hotels and a camping site.
Other facilities: Part of the Boesmanskloof Hiking Trail passes through the reserve (permits are required for the trail); short walks.
Open: Throughout the year.
Opening time: Sunrise to sunset.
For further information: The Town Clerk, Greyton Municipality, P.O. Box 4, Greyton 7233. Tel: (02822) 9620. (Hiking trail permits) The State Forester, Sonderend State Forest, P.O. Box 128, Robertson 6705.

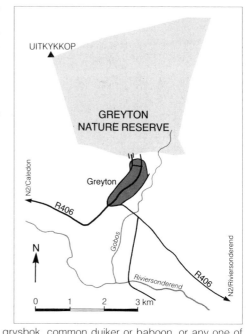

The Greyton Nature Reserve covers 2 220 ha on the southern slopes of the Riviersonderend Mountains, at altitudes which range from 240 to 1 465 m above sea-level. The rugged terrain includes several peaks and deeply incised gorges. Montane fynbos (heath) covers most of the area and the flowers are at their best in spring. The observant visitor may spot grey rhebok, klipspringer, Cape grysbok, common duiker or baboon, or any one of about 25 reptile species.

124. Gannets and several cormorant species have formed colonies on Bird Island.

125. The Bontebok National Park was proclaimed to protect these endangered antelope; bontebok lambs are usually born in spring, in September and October.

126. The Caledon Wild Flower Garden is well known for its springtime display.

127. The drip disa flowers on Table Mountain in December and January.

128. Early spring flowers in Kirstenbosch National Botanic Garden, Cape Town.

129. The Cape of Good Hope Nature Reserve is the haunt of a wide variety of seabirds, including terns.

130. The Middelberg hut provides overnight shelter for hikers exploring the Cedarberg Wilderness Area.

131. The Harold Porter National Botanic Garden combines scenic beauty and colourful displays of indigenous flowers.

132. Sneeukop in the Cedarberg Wilderness Area.

134. In the Marloth Nature Reserve fynbos (heath) covers the slopes of the Langeberg.

133. A combination of low Karoo bushes and succulent shrubs grows in the Ladismith-Klein Karoo Nature Reserve.

135. Hikers in the Hottentots Holland Nature Reserve can overnight in the Landdroskop hut.

GROOT WINTERHOEK WILDERNESS AREA

Location: Western part of the region; north-east of Cape Town.

Access: From Cape Town follow the N7 northwards to Piketberg and turn right onto the R44 to Porterville; from Porterville take the gravel road northwards to Dasklip Pass and follow this road to the forest station. Permits are required and must be obtained 3 months in advance; numbers of visitors are strictly controlled.

Accommodation: 3 huts at De Tronk may be used by hikers for shelter, but there are no facilities; camping is permitted.

Other facilities: Hiking trails.

Open: Throughout the year.

Opening time: 07h30 to 16h30.

For further information: The Forester, Groot Winterhoek Wilderness Area, P.O. Box 26, Porterville 6810. Tel: (02623) 2900.

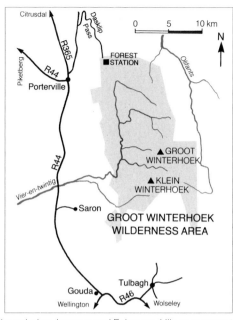

Groot Winterhoek Wilderness Area extends over 30 608 ha and lies within the mountain range of the same name. The highest of several peaks is Groot Winterhoek (2 077 m), and there are also numerous deep gorges and many clear streams and pools. The vegetation is predominantly montane fynbos (heath), with isolated pockets of forest. The area is well known for the abundance of ericas and disas during January and February. Hikers may spot baboon, rock dassie, klipspringer, grey rhebok and common duiker, but the more elusive leopard is seldom seen. Although not abundant, bird species such as black and booted eagles, jackal buzzard, grey-winged francolin and bar-throated apalis may be observed.

Eighty per cent of the average annual rainfall of 1 200 mm occurs between April and September, and snow is also common during winter.

HAROLD PORTER NATIONAL BOTANIC GARDEN

Location: Southern part of the region; south-east of Cape Town.

Access: From Cape Town follow the N2 eastwards for about 60 km, then turn off onto the R44 to Gordon's Bay; continue on the R44 through Gordon's Bay, reaching Betty's Bay 36 km further on. The garden lies to the north of the road and is clearly signposted.

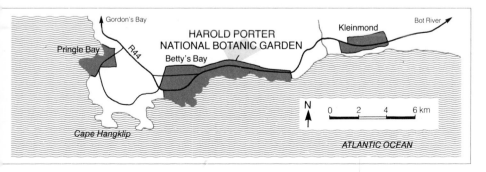

Accommodation: None. Kleinmond has a hotel and a camping and caravan site.
Other facilities: Short walking trails; picnic sites; plants identified by tags; brochure available; dogs are allowed on a leash.

Open: Throughout the year.
Opening time: Sunrise to sunset.
For further information: The Harold Porter National Botanic Garden, P.O. Box 35, Betty's Bay 7141. Tel: (02823) 9711.

This reserve encompasses both coastal and montane fynbos (heath), and covers 188 ha, of which five are under cultivation. More than 50 erica species are displayed in one area and many rare types can be seen. The rare red disa flowers here during December and January. Mammals typical of fynbos, such as baboon, rock dassie, and large- and small-spotted genets, occur here, and 60 bird species have been recorded.

276 HELDERBERG NATURE RESERVE

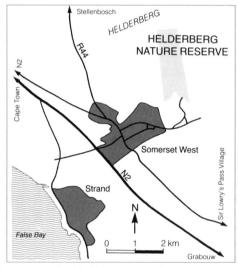

Location: South-western part of the region; adjacent to Somerset West.
Access: In Somerset West drive north-west-wards (in the direction of Cape Town) along Main St and turn right into Lourensford Rd; turn left into Hillcrest Rd, right into Reservoir Rd and then left into Verster Ave. The route is well signposted.
Accommodation: None. There are 2 hotels, 2 guest houses and a caravan park in Somerset West.
Other facilities: Several walking trails ranging from 3 to 8 km in length; picnic sites; kiosk open at weekends.
Open: Throughout the year.
Opening time: Autumn and winter – 07h00 to 18h00; spring and summer – 07h00 to 20h00.
For further information: The Information Bureau, P.O. Box 19, Somerset West 7130. Tel: (024) 51-4022.

Situated against the backdrop of the Hottentots Holland Mountains and beneath the peak of Helderberg mountain, this 385-ha reserve has spectacular scenery as its prime attraction.

It is essentially a botanical reserve, and a small part of it has been cultivated to familiarise visitors with the species they can expect to see in the natural area. Although fynbos covers most of the reserve, there is also a small pocket of indigenous forest. Cape grysbok and common duiker may be seen and there is a rich birdlife.

This is a winter-rainfall area and the Helderberg peak is often shrouded in cloud.

277 HOTTENTOTS HOLLAND NATURE RESERVE

Location: Southern part of the region; south-east of Stellenbosch.
Access: On foot only, along the Boland Hiking Trail. The nearest approach points for vehicles are at Jonkershoek Nature Conservation (off the Jonkershoek road, from Stellenbosch), Grabouw Nature Conservation (off the R321) and at Nuweberg Nature Conservation (off the R321). Permits are required.

Accommodation: 5 30-bed huts with bunks/mattresses for hikers only; ablution facilities at Nuweberg Nature Conservation.
Other facilities: The Boland Hiking Trail (55 km long, but with shorter options) runs through the reserve.
Open: Throughout the year.
Opening time: Sunrise to sunset; some sections may be closed temporarily because of

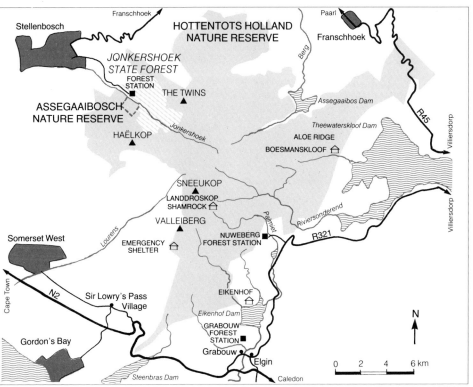

weather conditions: check with Nuweberg Nature Conservation.

Beware: Sudden weather changes.

For further information: The National Hiking Way Board. Tel: (021) 419-4299. (Nuweberg Nature Conservation) Tel: (0225) 4301.

The 26 000-ha Hottentots Holland Nature Reserve lies within part of the very much larger Hottentots Holland Mountain Catchment Area. Situated at the western end of the Cape Folded ranges, and with more folded ranges extending northwards, the reserve lies in a jumble of rugged and broken terrain, with narrow, forested gorges and steep cliffs. Many rivers have their sources in this area and drain in all directions, but mostly to the south-east. Victoria Peak, at 1 589 m above sea-level, is the reserve's highest point.

More than 99 per cent of the area is covered by montane fynbos (heath) and many different endemic species grow here. Several antelope species occur and at least 110 bird species have been recorded in the area.

This is a winter-rainfall area, receiving up to 3 500 mm on the higher peaks, but only 600 mm in the low-lying areas. Winds are strong and frequent.

278 KAROO NATIONAL BOTANIC GARDEN

Location: Western edge of the Little Karoo; north of Worcester.

Access: From Worcester cross the N1 and continue northwards for 3 km. The Karoo National Botanic Garden lies on the right and is clearly signposted.

Accommodation: None. There are hotels and a caravan park in Worcester.

Other facilities: Several short walking trails; picnic area close to the garden; an information brochure; labelled plants; braille trail.

Open: Throughout the year.

Opening time: 08h00 to 17h00.

For further information: The Karoo National

Botanic Garden, P.O. Box 152, Worcester 6850. Tel: (0231) 7-0785.

The Karoo National Botanic Garden was established in 1946 and covers 154 ha, of which 10 ha are under cultivation. The plants in the cultivated section have been grouped climatically, taxonomically and geographically, and there are special displays of succulents, bulbous plants and carrion flowers.

The natural vegetation, classified as Karoo broken veld, comprises mainly succulents, with a few scattered trees.

The best time to visit the garden is during the winter and spring months when the flowers provide a blaze of colour.

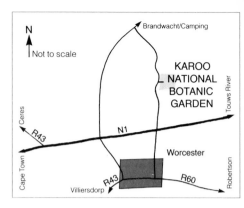

279 KLEINMOND COASTAL AND MOUNTAIN NATURE RESERVE

Location: Southern part of the region; southeast of Gordon's Bay.
Access: From Gordon's Bay take the R44 to Betty's Bay and continue to Kleinmond. The reserve lies to the west and north of this town.
Accommodation: None. There are a number of hotels and camping sites nearby.

Other facilities: Short walking trails; picnic sites with fireplaces at Fairy Glen.
Open: Throughout the year.
Opening time: 24 hours.
For further information: The Town Clerk, Kleinmond Municipality, Private Bag X3, Kleinmond 7195. Tel: (02823) 4010 or 3030.

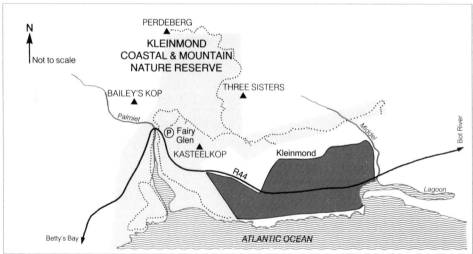

Kleinmond Coastal and Mountain Nature Reserve is about 1 000 ha in extent and incorporates mountain gorges, the Palmiet River estuary and a stretch of sandy and rocky shoreline.

Both coastal and montane fynbos (heath) are represented and, due to the diversity of plant species, this is an incredibly rich floral reserve. A heath species, *Erica pillansii*, is to be found here and nowhere else in the world.

Cape grysbok and common duiker may be spotted in the reserve, and southern right whales occur offshore between June and December. Although strictly speaking not in the reserve, Kleinmond's coastal marshland is the habitat of the rarest amphibian on earth, namely the micro frog (*Microbatrochella capensis*).

LADISMITH-KLEIN KAROO NATURE RESERVE

Location: The Little Karoo; south-west of Ladismith.
Access: From Ladismith take the R62 southwards for 3 km. This road passes through the reserve.
Accommodation: None. Ladismith has a hotel and a camping and caravan site.
Other facilities: Picnic sites with fireplaces; footpaths.
Open: Throughout the year.
Opening time: 08h00 to 17h00.
For further information: The Town Clerk, Ladismith Municipality, P.O. Box 30, Ladismith 6885. Tel: 02942, ask for 20. Fax: (02942) 566.

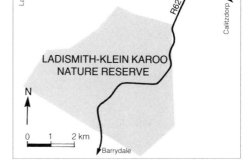

Previously known as Noukloof, this nature reserve covers 2 766 ha of succulent mountain scrub, with a scattering of low bushes. The terrain is mainly hilly and its most prominent feature is the 760-m Ladismith Hill. Eland and springbok have been released here and common duiker and steenbok occur naturally in the area.

The area has a low annual rainfall (approximately 250 mm) which falls mainly in spring and autumn. Summer days are usually hot.

MARLOTH NATURE RESERVE

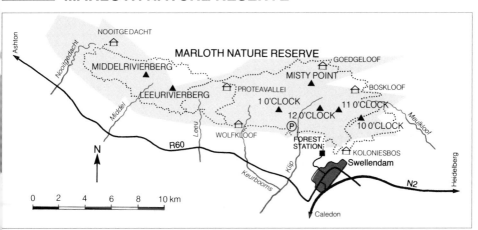

Location: South-eastern part of the region; north of Swellendam.
Access: From Swellendam drive along Andrew Whyte St and follow the signposts to the reserve.
Accommodation: 6 overnight huts with bunks/mattresses for hikers only. Swellendam has hotels, self-catering accommodation and a camping and caravan site.
Other facilities: The Swellendam Trail runs through the reserve; shorter trails; picnic sites at Hermitage Kloof and Duiwebos.
Open: Throughout the year.
Opening time: Sunrise to sunset.
Beware: Sudden weather changes.
For further information: The State Forester, Swellendam State Forest, P.O. Box 28, Swellendam 6740. Tel: (0291) 4-1410. (Hiking trail bookings) Tel: (021) 402-3043 or 402-3093.

The 11 269-ha Marloth Nature Reserve lies in a rugged, mountainous area with many high peaks, gorges and perennial streams.

The 74-km Swellendam Trail is strenuous and should only be tackled by the fit, although there are also several shorter routes allowing access to areas of montane fynbos (heath) and indigenous forest.

Mammal and bird species are typical of the fynbos zone and include Cape grysbok, small grey mongoose, baboon, and black eagle, Cape sugarbird and red-winged starling.

Rain can be expected at any time of year and snow may fall between June and December on the higher peaks. The north-facing slopes of the mountain are warmer and drier than those facing south.

282 MONT ROCHELLE NATURE RESERVE

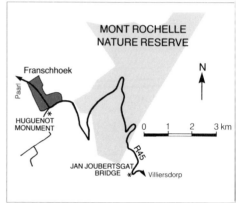

Location: Southern part of the region; north-east of Cape Town.
Access: From Cape Town take the N1 towards Paarl and turn right onto the R303; travel for 16 km and turn left onto the R44 to Franschhoek; continue through the town and over the Franschhoek Pass. This road runs through the reserve. Visitors wishing to walk in the reserve should obtain a permit from the municipality.
Accommodation: None. Franschhoek has 3 hotels and a camping and caravan site.
Other facilities: None.
Open: Throughout the year. May close for a short time because of weather conditions; check with the municipality.
Opening time: 24 hours.
For further information: The Town Clerk, Franschhoek Municipality, P.O. Box 18, Franschhoek 7690. Tel: (02212) 2055. Fax: (02212) 3297.

Mont Rochelle Nature Reserve covers 1 759 ha of rugged, scenic mountain terrain within the montane fynbos (heath) vegetation zone, and adjoins the two large Hawequas and Nuweberg state forests.

Centuries ago generations of migrating elephants and other game wore a track through terrain now covered by the reserve, and this track was used by the first settlers to cross the mountains into the interior.

Today visitors may see grey rhebok, Cape grysbok, klipspringer, baboon and rock dassie, and at least 28 reptile species occur here.

283 MONTAGU MOUNTAIN NATURE RESERVE

Location: Central part of the region; south-east of Worcester.
Access: From Worcester take the R60 through Robertson and Ashton, and on through Cogmanskloof to Montagu. This road runs through the nature reserve. Day hikers pay R1 admission at Old Mill, at the top of Tanner St in Montagu.
Accommodation: 2 6-bed cabins with cooking and ablution facilities for hikers only (R6 per person per night); limited camping is allowed.

There is a variety of accommodation in and around Montagu.
Other facilities: 12- and 15-km hiking trails; shorter walks; picnic sites with fireplaces nearby at Keurkloof.
Open: Throughout the year.
Opening time: 24 hours.
For further information: The Town Clerk, Montagu Municipality, P.O. Box 24, Montagu 6720. (Hiking trail huts) Tel: (0234) 4-2471. Fax: (0234) 4-1841.

Montagu Mountain Nature Reserve extends over 1 200 ha and lies on the northern edge of the Langeberg Mountains. These form part of the Cape Folded Belt and outstanding geological formations which have resulted from the folding and faulting of the rock can be seen in the reserve.

Dry montane fynbos (heath) grows on the mountain's lower slopes, with more moist heathland in the higher regions. Aloes and other succulents dominate the north-facing cliffs.

Leopards do still occur in the mountain range, but klipspringer, grey rhebok, rock dassie and baboon are the species more likely to be seen by the visitor.

The Keisie River, which flows southwards through the nature reserve to join up with the Breede River, is home to a rare fish species, Burchell's red-fin minnow.

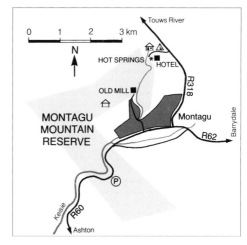

---

284   PAARDENBERG NATURE RESERVE   See regional map

Location: Western part of the region; north of Cape Town.
Access: Contact the authority.
Accommodation: None.

Other facilities: None.
For further information: The Town Clerk, Malmesbury Municipality, P.O. Box 52, Malmesbury 7300. Tel: (0224) 2-2996/7/8.

Proclaimed in 1985, Paardenberg Nature Reserve covers 383 ha and comprises an inselberg of Cape granite formed some 10 million years ago. It protects one of the last remnants of a particular form of montane fynbos (heath), including several extremely rare plant species; one of these, *Erica hippu*, is only known to grow here. This is also where the Cape mountain zebra was first described, but it has long since disappeared from the district.

---

285   PAARL MOUNTAIN NATURE RESERVE

Location: South-western part of the region; north-east of Cape Town.
Access: From Cape Town take the N1 in the direction of Worcester; take the R45 exit to Paarl and follow the road into town for a short distance; turn left at the signpost to the Paarl Mountain Nature Reserve. There is also an entry point to the reserve at the northern end of the town.
Accommodation: None.
Other facilities: There is a limited network of roads and many pathways and also picnic sites with fireplaces.
Open: Throughout the year.
Opening time: 1 April to 30 September – 07h00 to 18h30; 1 October to 31 March – 07h00 to 19h00.
For further information: The Paarl Valley Publicity Association, 216 Main Street, Paarl 7646. Tel: (02211) 2-3829.

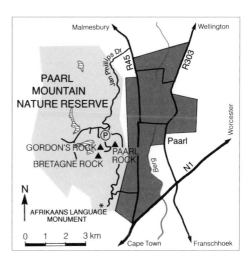

The 1 910-ha Paarl Mountain Nature Reserve is dominated by three giant granite outcrops, known as Paarl, Bretagne and Gordon rocks, whose summits offer magnificent views of the surrounding countryside. Proteas are particularly abundant in the montane fynbos (heath) around the outcrops, and a variety of species are represented. Small patches of indigenous forest grow in sheltered places, and there is also an open forest of the endemic silver tree. A cultivated wild flower garden lies next to the reserve.

There is a pair of black eagles which breeds regularly in the area, and visitors may also see Cape grysbok and rock dassie.

286 PAT BUSCH PRIVATE NATURE RESERVE

Location: Central part of the region; east of Robertson.
Access: From the R60 (Robertson/Ashton) take the signposted left turn-off to Klaasvoogds/Kaktustuin; the road is 9 km from Robertson and 9 km from Ashton. Follow it for 6 km to Bergplaas. All booking must be done in advance.
Accommodation: 1 3- and 1 4-bedroomed farmhouse, each fully equipped, including all bedding, hot and cold water (R25 per person per night for a minimum of two nights); self-catering.
Other facilities: Approximately 40 km of hiking trails; bass fishing.
Open: Throughout the year.

PAT BUSCH PRIVATE NATURE RESERVE
N
Bergendal
Bergplaas
Montagu
Kaktustuin
Klaasvoogds Wes
Robertson
Ashton
R60
Swellendam
R317
Bonnievale
Not to scale

For further information: W.D. Busch, Pat Busch Private Nature Reserve, P.O. Box 579, Robertson 6705. Tel: (02351) 2033.

Located in the foothills of the Langeberg Mountains, this 2 000-ha private nature reserve is also a working fruit and stock farm.

The vegetation consists mainly of montane fynbos (heath) and birds such as the black eagle, orange-breasted sunbird and Cape sugarbird may be seen. Several small antelope species occur naturally in the area and it is planned to bring in other game species.

287 PAULINE BOHNEN NATURE RESERVE

Location: South-eastern part of the region; south-east of Riversdale.
Access: From Riversdale take the R323 southwards for 27 km to Still Bay East; from the main street turn left towards the airfield. This road runs through the Pauline Bohnen Nature Reserve.
Accommodation: None. Still Bay has a hotel and a camping and caravan site.
Other facilities: Pathways.
Open: Throughout the year.
Opening time: Sunrise to sunset.
For further information: The Town Clerk, Still Bay Municipality, P.O. Box 2, Still Bay 6785. Tel: (02934) 4-1577. Fax: (02934) 4-1140.

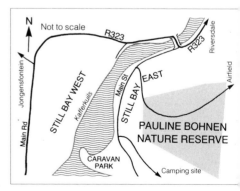

N
Not to scale
R323
Riversdale
R323
Jongensfontein
Main Rd
STILL BAY WEST
Kafferkuils
Main St
EAST
STILL BAY
Airfield
PAULINE BOHNEN
NATURE RESERVE
CARAVAN PARK
Camping site

This reserve covers 140 ha of land which has been donated by Mrs Pauline Bohnen and is being developed for public use. The vegetation is mostly coastal fynbos (heath), although there are some exotic trees, and bushbuck, common duiker, Cape grysbok and small grey mongoose may be seen.

288 RAMSKOP NATURE RESERVE

Location: North-western part of the region; north-east of Cape Town.
Access: From Cape Town follow the N7 northwards; turn right onto the R364 and continue into Clanwilliam. The reserve lies south-east of the town and is well signposted.
Accommodation: None. Clanwilliam has a hotel and a camping and caravan site.
Other facilities: Footpaths; a wild flower garden; tea-room open during the flower season.
Open: Throughout the year.
Opening time: 08h00 to 17h00.
For further information: The Town Clerk, Clanwilliam Municipality, P.O. Box 5, Clanwilliam 8135. Tel: 02682, ask for 215.

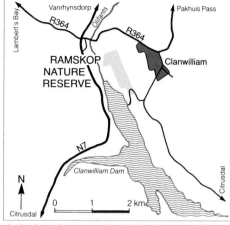

Set aside to protect a small section of the area's rich flora, the 54-ha Ramskop Nature Reserve lies at the meeting place of fynbos and sandveld vegetation. June to September, the peak flowering season, is the best time to explore it, and an annual flower show which is held here each spring attracts large numbers of visitors. A 7,5-ha cultivated area is fenced off and contains more than 200 indigenous species. The reserve is situated on the Clanwilliam Dam and offers magnificent views of the Cederberg range to the east.

289 ROCHER PAN NATURE RESERVE

Location: West Coast; north-west of Cape Town.
Access: From Cape Town take the N7 northwards to Piketberg and turn left onto the R399; travel for 67 km to Velddrif and turn right onto the R27; continue for 15 km. The reserve lies to the west of the road and is clearly signposted. Permits are required and are available at the office.
Accommodation: None. Velddrif offers a variety of accommodation.
Other facilities: Short pathways; observation platforms; birdwatching hides; picnic area with fireplaces.
Open: Throughout the year.
Opening time: 07h00 to 18h00.
For further information: The Officer-in-charge, Rocher Pan Nature Reserve, Private Bag, Velddrif 7365. Tel: (02625) 727.

The Rocher Pan Nature Reserve comprises 914 ha of strandveld and scrub vegetation alongside a shallow seasonal pan fed by the Papkuils River. The pan attracts large concentrations of waders and waterfowl species, many of which breed here, making this one of the most important breeding areas on the West Coast. Between January and mid-May, however, the pan is dry and the birds leave the area; the best time to see them in large flocks is during spring. In addition to the 165 bird species recorded, there are springbok, Cape grysbok, common duiker, steenbok, and yellow and small grey mongooses. The area receives much of its sparse rainfall in winter, and is often swept by strong winds.

290 SAFARILAND GAME PARK

Location: South-western part of the region; north-east of Cape Town.
Access: From Cape Town take the N1 northwards in the direction of Worcester; take the R303 exit towards Wemmershoek and travel for 8 km; turn right again and drive for 1 km to the reserve.
Accommodation: The self-catering accommodation available comprises 12 fully equipped bungalows, each with a kitchen and bathroom.
Other facilities: A 10-km network of game-viewing roads; picnic sites with fireplaces; swimming pools; curio shop.
Open: Throughout the year.
Opening time: 08h00 to 17h30.
For further information: Safariland Game Park, P.O. Box 595, Suider-Paarl 7624. Tel: (02211) 64-0064.

For those wishing to observe a variety of game species, indigenous and exotic, within easy reach of Cape Town, Safariland is ideal.

Giraffe, eland, wildebeest, springbok, Burchell's zebra, llamas, ostrich, camel and water buffalo are allowed to roam freely in the 200-ha park. Elephant are also present, but these animals are kept in an enclosure.

291 SALMONSDAM NATURE RESERVE

Location: Southern part of the region; south-east of Caledon.
Access: From Caledon follow the R316 towards Bredasdorp for 26 km and turn right onto the R326 towards Stanford; follow this road for 19 km and turn left onto a gravel road; drive for 7 km before turning left at the signpost to the reserve. Alternatively, from Hermanus follow the R43 eastwards to Stanford and turn left onto the R326; continue to the gravel road leading to the reserve.
Accommodation: 1 8-bed cottage, with a refrigerator, stove and ablution facilities (R26,40 per night for first 4 persons, then R6,60 per person per night i.e. maximum R52,80 per night for 8 persons); 2 4-bed cottages with refrigerator and stove, but with separate ablution facilities (R26,40 per cottage per night). There are 4 camping and caravan sites with basic ablution facilities (R11 per stand per night for 4 persons plus R2,60 per person extra to a maximum 6 persons per stand).

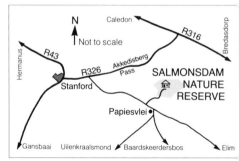

Other facilities: 5 trails varying from 3 to 9 km; picnic sites with fireplaces; information office. The nearest shops and fuel supplies are 16 km away at Stanford.
Open: Throughout the year.
Opening time: 07h00 to 19h00.
For further information: The Officer-in-charge, Salmonsdam Nature Reserve, P.O. Box 5, Stanford 7210. Tel: (02833) 30-0789.

Salmonsdam Nature Reserve has a rugged and attractive landscape containing gorges, streams and waterfalls. It covers 846 ha and its vegetation is primarily fynbos (heath), with pockets of indigenous forest along some streams. Game species that may be spotted include steenbok, bontebok, grey rhebok, Cape grysbok, klipspringer and common duiker. To date 124 bird species have been recorded, and a birdlist is available.

292 SOUTHERN BLACK-BACKED GULL SANCTUARY See map Cape Town

Location: South-western part of the region; east of Muizenberg.
Access: From Muizenberg follow the R310 along the False Bay coastline past Mitchell's Plain. The sanctuary is on the right. There is no direct access and the area is fenced.

Accommodation: None.
Other facilities: None.
Open: Throughout the year.
For further information: The Directorate of Nature and Environmental Conservation (see page 365).

This very narrow strip of land on top of the Swartklip cliffs protects one of the few mainland breeding colonies of the southern black-backed gull, or kelp gull.
The breeding season occurs during the summer months. The birds can be easily observed from the road.

293 TIENIE VERSFELD WILD FLOWER RESERVE

Location: Western part of the region; north-west of Cape Town.
Access: From Cape Town take the N7 in the direction of Malmesbury; from there follow the R315 westwards and drive for 34 km to Darling; at Darling continue on the R315 towards Yzerfontein. The Tienie Versveld Wild Flower Reserve lies a short way out of Darling.
Accommodation: None.
Other facilities: A network of short pathways.
Open: Throughout the year.
Opening time: 24 hours.
For further information: Kirstenbosch

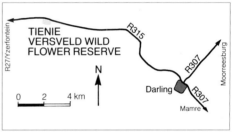

National Botanic Garden, Private Bag X7, Claremont 7735. Tel: (021) 762-1166.

This 22-ha botanical reserve protects a fragment of the sandveld environment and the flora typical of it. The reserve is well known for its spectacular show of flowers each spring.

294 TYGERBERG NATURE RESERVE See map Durbanville Nature Reserve

Location: South-western part of the region; north-east of Cape Town.
Access: From Cape Town follow the N1 in the direction of Paarl, taking the R302 exit to Durbanville; watch out for the signpost to the reserve. Permits are required and are available at the gate.
Accommodation: None.

Other facilities: A network of footpaths; picnic sites with fireplaces.
Open: Throughout the year.
Opening time: Monday to Friday – 08h00 to 16h30; weekends – 09h00 to 18h00.
For further information: The Town Clerk, Bellville Municipality, P.O. Box 2, Bellville 7535. Tel: (021) 918-2911.

A 68-ha island of natural vegetation surrounded by urban development, Tygerberg Nature Reserve protects one of the few remaining pieces of coastal fynbos (heath) left in this area. More than 500 different plant species have been identified.

295 VILLIERSDORP NATURE RESERVE

Location: North-east of Cape Town.
Access: From Cape Town take the N2 over the Sir Lowry's and Houw Hoek passes; about 8 km beyond Bot River, turn left onto the R43 and travel for about 30 km to Villiersdorp; turn left off the town's main street at the signpost to the reserve and continue to the entrance.
Accommodation: There is a camping and caravan site next to the reserve.
Other facilities: Paths in the wild flower garden; 5 thatched summerhouses for picnics.
For further information: The Town Clerk, Villiersdorp Municipality, P.O. Box 23, Villiersdorp 7170. Tel: (0225) 3-1130.

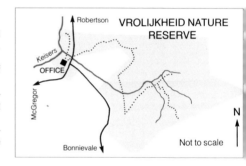

This reserve covers 500 ha of montane fynbos on the slopes of Blokkop Mountain. A small area of 36 ha has been cultivated as a wild flower garden and contains a variety of endemic fynbos.

296 VROLIJKHEID NATURE RESERVE

Location: Little Karoo; south of Robertson.
Access: From Robertson take the tarred road in the direction of McGregor for about 15 km. Telephonic permit bookings are preferred.
Accommodation: None. There is a variety of accomodation in Robertson and McGregor.
Other facilities: Walking is permitted; picnicking on lawns; bird hide on dam; Rooikat Trail (16,5 km) traverses the reserve.
For further information: The Officer-in-charge, Vrolijkheid Nature Reserve, Private Bag 614, Robertson 6705. Tel: (02353) 621.

Most of this 2 004-ha nature reserve lies in an area of low, broken hills and flat gravel plains. On the margin between two vegetation types, it has low Karoo bushes and succulents, with taller bushes in the gorges, as well as fynbos elements in the higher regions.

Springbok have been introduced and klipspringer, grey rhebok, Cape grysbok, steenbok and common duiker occur naturally. More than 180 bird species have been recorded.

297 WERNER FREHSE NATURE RESERVE

Location: South-east of Riversdale.
Access: From Riversdale take the N2 towards Albertinia; the reserve is 2 km out of town.
Accommodation: None.
Other facilities: Game-viewing roads.
Open: By arrangement with the municipality.
For further information: The Town Clerk, Riversdale Municipality, P.O. Box 29, Riversdale 6770. Tel: (02933) 3-2418.

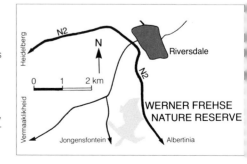

298 WEST COAST NATIONAL PARK

Location: West Coast; Langebaan Lagoon.
Access: From Cape Town take the R27 northwards for about 110 km, turn left and drive another 10 km to Langebaan. The reserve incorporates the lagoon and both shores.
Accommodation: Langebaan Lodge provides accommodation (from R75 to R165 per person per night, room only). Beach bungalows and a camping and caravan site are provided by the Municipality of Langebaan, P.O. Box 11, Langebaan 7357; tel: (02287) 2115.
Other facilities: A 25-km network of game- and flower-viewing roads at Postberg Nature Reserve; watersports permitted; information centre; picnic sites at Postberg; tours to bird islands.
Open: Throughout the year; Postberg is only open from August to October (flower season).
Opening time: 24 hours.
For further information: (Enquiries and booking) National Parks Board (see page 365). (Park address) West Coast National Park, P.O. Box 25, Langebaan 7357. Tel: (02287) 2144.

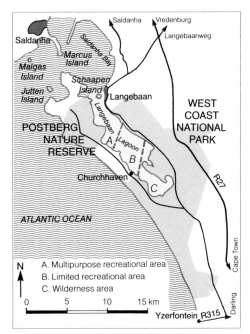

At present the West Coast National Park covers an area of more than 20 000 ha and includes Postberg Nature Reserve. The lagoon and the coastal zone, together with the islands Malgas, Jutten, Marcus and Schaapen, were proclaimed in 1985 and several areas have been added since that date. It is also planned to include privately owned land on a contractual basis. The park's vegetation is predominantly West Coast Sandveld (comprising low bushes, sedges and succulents, with many flowering annuals in spring), but there are also elements of coastal fynbos (heath), particularly in the east. Salt marsh and mud flats covering extensive areas of the lagoon at low tide attract huge flocks of migrant waders in summer. Large numbers of gannets, Cape cormorants, and jackass penguins inhabit the islands, with the largest known colony of southern black-backed gulls on Schaapen Island. Several game species roam freely through the Postberg Nature Reserve, including black wildebeest, bontebok and eland.

299 WIESENHOF GAME PARK

Location: North-east of Cape Town.
Access: From Cape Town follow the N1 for 46 km in the direction of Paarl, then turn right onto the R44 and continue for 4 km. The reserve is clearly signposted.
Accommodation: None.
Other facilities: Game-viewing roads; viewing platform; picnic sites with fireplaces; boating on the lake; swimming pools; roller skating rink.
Open: Throughout the year, except August.
Opening time: Tues – Sun 09h30 – 18h00.
For further information: P.O. Box 50, Klapmuts 7625. Tel: (02211) 5181.

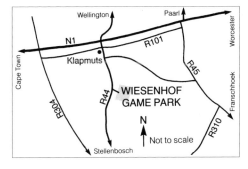

The 300-ha Wiesenhof Game Park has many introduced game species, including blue wildebeest, blesbok, eland, Hartmann's mountain zebra and cheetah.

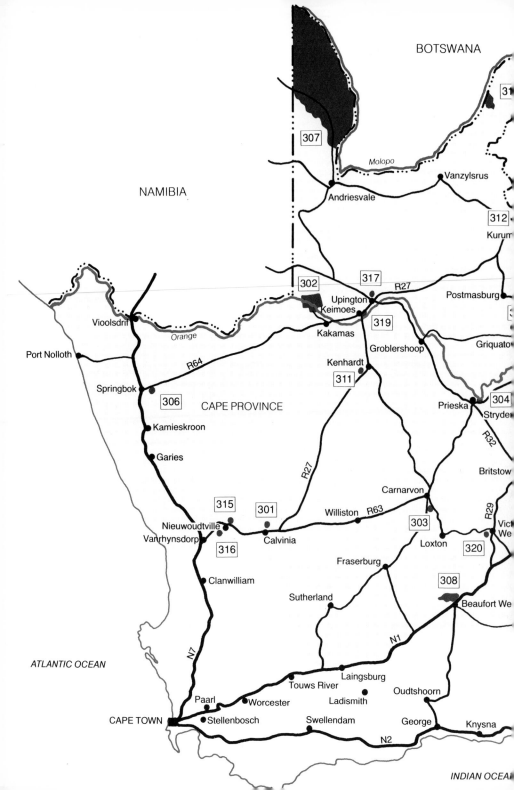

NORTHERN CAPE PROVINCE AND KAROO

300 Aberdeen Nature Reserve
301 Akkerendam Nature Reserve
302 Augrabies Falls National Park
303 Carnarvon Nature Reserve
304 Die Bos Nature Reserve
305 Ganspan Waterfowl Nature Reserve
306 Goegap Nature Reserve
307 Kalahari Gemsbok National Park
308 Karoo National Park
309 Karoo Nature Reserve
310 Klaarwater Nature Reserve
311 Kokerboom Forest
312 Kuruman Nature Reserve
313 Leon Taljaardt Nature Reserve
314 Molopo Nature Reserve
315 Nieuwoudtville Wild Flower Reserve
316 Oorlogskloof Nature Reserve
317 Spitskop Nature Reserve
318 Strydenburg Aalwynprag Nature Reserve
319 Tierberg Nature Reserve
320 Victoria West Nature Reserve

From the southern Cape Province northwards to the Orange River stretches the arid, sparsely populated Karoo. Beyond the river, and with the Botswanan border as its northern boundary, lies the northern Cape, an equally dry and dusty region where only plants and animals adapted to such conditions survive. Between them the Orange River cuts its course from east to west, separating the Karoo plains in the south from the Kalahari sandveld of the north.

Short scrub now covers much of this semi-desert, but once the interior plains of the Cape Province were ranged by vast herds of springbok, black wildebeest, eland, red hartebeest and quagga. Hunting and the introduction of domestic stock sealed their fate; the quagga did not survive, and much smaller herds of other grazing species are now protected in reserves. The conservation authorities are re-introducing species to their former haunts, and black rhinoceros, for example, have recently been released in the Vaalbos and Augrabies national parks, while Cape mountain zebra once again roam the Nuweveld Mountains.

Considering the vast area covered by this region, there are relatively few nature reserves and parks, and only the Kalahari Gemsbok National Park is capable of accommodating viable populations of large predators such as lion and cheetah. Two other national parks, Tankwa Karoo and Vaalbos, have been proclaimed but are not yet open to the public.

The Tankwa Karoo National Park, 90 km south of Calvinia, protects 27 000 ha of succulent Karoo vegetation, with few game animals at present, and in the Vaalbos National Park, near Barkly West, a transitional zone between Karoo, Kalahari and grassland vegetation is being allowed to recover before a major restocking programme begins.

Included within this large region are two distinctive areas of the north-western Cape. The Richtersveld, in the extreme north-western corner, is a mountainous, rugged area with a sparse but unique plant life. Most larger mammals have long since disappeared, but there are still a number of smaller carnivores, rodents and elephant shrews. Plans to set aside part of the Richtersveld as a national park are under discussion.

Further south lies Namaqualand, which is renowned for its colourful springtime displays of wild flowers.

Despite their apparent barrenness, the Karoo and northern Cape regions boast a rich variety of plant and animal species, and it is hoped that greater efforts will be made to increase the amount of land set aside for the conservation of this natural treasure chest.

These arid areas experience extreme climatic conditions, from blistering heat in summer to below freezing temperatures on winter nights. Much of the area receives its meagre rainfall during the summer months.

300 ABERDEEN NATURE RESERVE

Location: South-eastern Karoo; west of Aberdeen.
Access: From Aberdeen follow signposts.
Accommodation: None. There is a hotel and a camping site in Aberdeen.
Other facilities: Walking trail; picnic sites with fireplaces.
Open: Throughout the year.
Opening times: Sunrise to sunset.
For further information: The Town Clerk, Aberdeen Municipality, P.O. Box 30, Aberdeen 6270. Tel: 049212, ask for 14.

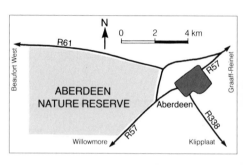

Established in 1982 and covering 573 ha, this reserve is still being developed. Sweet-thorn trees are abundant, and game species that may be seen include springbok and kudu. Gemsbok, eland, red hartebeest and black wildebeest are to be introduced.

301 AKKERENDAM NATURE RESERVE

Location: Western Karoo; Calvinia.
Access: From Calvinia town centre take the road past the hospital and follow it northwards for 2 km to the Akkerendam Nature Reserve's entrance gate.
Accommodation: None. There is a hotel and a camping site in Calvinia.
Other facilities: A short network of gravel game-viewing roads; 2 hiking trails, 1 taking about 1 hour and the other about 7 hours (permission must be obtained in advance; hikers are advised to carry water); picnic sites with fireplaces and water.
Open: Throughout the year.

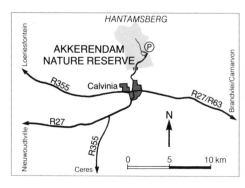

136. Rock dassies are frequently seen in the Paarl Mountain Nature Reserve.

137. The 'folding' of the Cape mountains is clearly shown in the terrain of the Montagu Mountain Nature Reserve.

138. Greater flamingoes frequent Rocher Pan in the winter months.

139. The common duiker is one of five small antelope species which occur naturally in the Vrolijkheid Nature Conservation Station.

140. Sacred ibis at Postberg in the West Coast National Park.

141. The Southern Black-backed Gull Sanctuary, on the False Bay coast.

142. 'Bridal Falls' in the Augrabies Falls National Park.

143. Gemsbok are often seen in the river beds of the Kalahari Gemsbok National Park.

144. Accommodation at Twee Rivieren, in the Kalahari Gemsbok National Park.

145. The Kokerboom Forest, near Kenhardt.

146. Cape cottages in the Karoo National Park are dominated by the Nuweveld Range.

147. The Nieuwoudtville Wild Flower Reserve is a mass of colour in spring.

Opening time: From 1 April to 31 October – 07h00 to 18h15; from 1 November to 31 March – 07h00 to 20h30.

For further information: The Town Clerk, Calvinia Municipality, P.O. Box 28, Calvinia 8190. Tel: 02772, ask for 11 or 241.

The Akkerendam Nature Reserve covers 2 301 ha of Karoo flats and part of the southern slopes of the Hantamsberg, with altitudes ranging from 1 000 to 1 580 m above sea-level. The Akkeren Dam is a prominent feature.

The vegetation is predominantly low Karoo scrub, with occasional small trees such as the karee and the star cliffortia, whose distribution is limited to this part of the Karoo. Ten other plant species are known only from the Hantamsberg. There is a small herd of springbok in the reserve, and at least 25 reptile species are known to occur.

Calvinia lies in a transitional area between winter- and summer-rainfall regions and receives an average of between 200 and 300 mm of rain annually.

302 AUGRABIES FALLS NATIONAL PARK

Location: Northern part of the region; west of Upington.

Access: From Upington take the R27/R64 to Keimoes, then continue on the R64 for about 50 km before bearing right onto the R359; follow this road for 28 km to the entrance to the park, which is clearly signposted. An entrance fee is charged. The internal roads are gravel.

Accommodation: 4-bed cottages, each with a fully equipped kitchen, a bathroom and air conditioning; 2- to 4-bed huts, each with a fully equipped kitchen, a bathroom and air conditioning; 4-bed huts, each with a fully equipped kitchen, a shower, toilet and air conditioning; bedding is supplied. There is a camping site with full ablution facilities (maximum 6 persons

per stand). Hiking trail huts with bunks, toilets and fireplaces.

Other facilities: A short network of game-viewing roads; 3-day Klipspringer Hiking Trail (open April to October); shorter walking trails; scenic view-points; an information centre; picnic sites with fireplaces; a restaurant; a shop with a range of goods, and a fuel supply.

Open: Throughout the year.

Opening time: 07h00 to 19h00.

Beware: Malaria; the summer months are extremely hot.

For further information: (Enquiries and booking) National Parks Board (see page 365). (Park address) The Warden, Augrabies Falls National Park, Private Bag X1, Augrabies 8874.

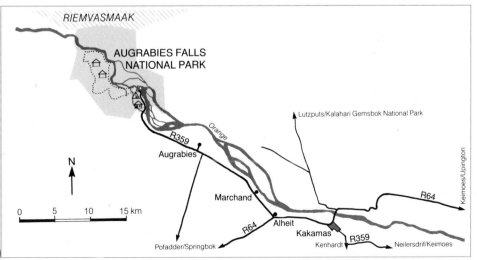

The Augrabies Falls National Park, controlled by the National Parks Board, is primarily a scenic park, with the falls and the gorge as the main attractions. It covers 9 400 ha, and an additional 70 000 ha (known as Riemvasmaak) has been added recently under an agreement with the South African Defence

Force. This makes the park now a truly viable unit and will ensure that its populations of species such as the black rhinoceros can be built up sufficiently to safeguard their survival.

The Orange River is the park's focal point, flowing first over a series of rapids, then through a narrow gorge before dropping 56 m over the main waterfall. This is without doubt one of the most spectacular scenic sights in South Africa and is particularly impressive when the river is high.

The park's vegetation, classified as Orange River Broken Veld, comprises plants that are adapted to extremely dry conditions, and aloes and euphorbias are common. Trees such as camel thorn, karee, wild olive, buffalo thorn and wild raisin bush are concentrated along the dry water courses. When rain does fall grass and small annuals soon appear. The largest mammal in the park, the black rhinoceros, was re-introduced in 1985. Springbok roam the area, and klipspringer and steenbok are frequently seen. The rock dassie is very common, and several regularly feed on the grass at the camping site; ground squirrels, too, are regular visitors to the camp. Baboons and vervet monkeys also occur, as do leopard, caracal, black-backed jackal and bat-eared fox. To date 161 bird species have been recorded, including black and martial eagles. Reptiles flourish in these hot, semi-desert conditions, and one in particular that is frequently seen is the brightly coloured Cape flat lizard; it shows little fear of humans and is common at the viewing area near the main waterfall. Summer temperatures are usually very high and debilitating, but winters are mild, with nights that can be very cold.

303 CARNARVON NATURE RESERVE

Location: Central Karoo; Carnarvon.
Access: From Carnarvon take the R63 southwards towards Loxton; the reserve is on the right, 1 km out of the town.
Accommodation: None. Carnarvon has hotels and a camping site.
Other facilities: A network of good game-viewing roads; walking permitted.
Open: Throughout the year.
Opening time: 08h00 to 17h00.
For further information: The Town Clerk, Carnarvon Municipality, P.O. Box 10, Carnarvon 7060. Tel: 02032, ask for 12.

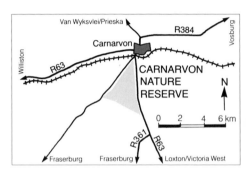

Carnarvon Nature Reserve, also known as the Appie van Heerden Nature Reserve, consists of flat Karoo scrubland and rocky hill country. Several game species have been introduced, including Hartmann's mountain zebra, eland, blesbok, gemsbok, red hartebeest, springbok and black wildebeest.

304 DIE BOS NATURE RESERVE

Location: Central part of the region; Prieska.
Access: From Prieska follow signposts to the nature reserve, which lies 2 km north-east of the town.
Accommodation: Rondavels and a camping site.
Other facilities: Road network; picnic sites with fireplaces.
Open: Throughout the year.
Opening time: 24 hours.
For further information: The Town Clerk, Prieska Municipality, P.O. Box 16, Prieska 8940. Tel: (0594) 3-1113/4. Fax: (0594) 6-1159.

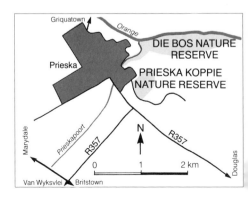

Die Bos Nature Reserve covers approximately 60 ha at the confluence of the Orange and Prieskapoort rivers. It protects no game animals, but vervet monkeys may be seen here and the riverine vegetation attracts an interesting variety of birds.

Prieska Koppie Nature Reserve, on the eastern side of the town, is a small hill that has been developed as a reserve to protect succulents and aloes.

305 GANSPAN WATERFOWL NATURE RESERVE

Location: North-eastern part of the region; Jan Kempdorp.
Access: From Jan Kempdorp drive westwards, cross the R47 and continue on the R370 towards Ganspan; after 2 km turn right onto a gravel road and continue to the Ganspan Waterfowl Nature Reserve.
Accommodation: A camping site with ablution facilities.
Other facilities: Pathways; picnic sites; boating and fishing permitted.
Open: Throughout the year.
Opening time: 06h00 to 18h00.
For further information: The Town Clerk, Jan Kempdorp Municipality, P.O. Box 241, Jan Kempdorp 8550. Tel: (0533) 6-1171.

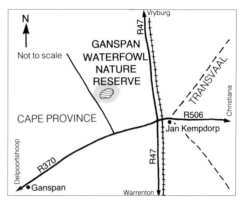

This 100-ha bird sanctuary incorporates the shallow Ganspan and its surroundings, which attract a wide variety of waterbirds. Although this is a popular recreational area, it is also a worthwhile venue for birdwatchers.

306 GOEGAP NATURE RESERVE

Location: North-western part of the region; east of Springbok.
Access: From Springbok drive eastwards towards the airport on the R355; after approximately 4 km turn left to the Goegap Nature Reserve's gate.
Accommodation: None. There are hotels and a camping site in Springbok.
Other facilities: 3 trails, 4 km, 5,5 km and 7 km long; a 7-km network of good gravel roads for game-viewing; picnic sites with fireplaces and water; Hester Malan Wildflower Garden. More trails and facilities are planned.
Open: Throughout the year.
Opening time: 08h00 to 16h00.
Beware: Summer days can be very hot, so carry water on the trails.
For further information: The Officer-in-charge, Goegap Nature Reserve, Private Bag X1, Springbok 8240. Tel: (0251) 2-1880.

The Goegap Nature Reserve covers 15 000 ha, of which approximately one fifth is flat and the rest is made up of large, domed granite outcrops. At present only a small part of this harsh but beautiful reserve is open to the public, but there are plans to make a larger area accessible.

The vegetation, classified as Namaqualand Broken Veld, is dominated by small shrubs and succulents, including the imposing kokerboom. Following the light winter rains a profusion of short-lived plants emerge and flower.

The reserve is inhabited by 46 mammal species, of which the most visible are Hartmann's mountain zebra, eland, gemsbok, springbok, klipspringer, rock dassie, yellow mongoose and the dassie rat. Only 61 bird species have been recorded.

The rainfall is sparse, averaging 162 mm annually, and occurs mainly between May and September. Winters are generally mild, with cold nights, and summer days are often blisteringly hot.

307 KALAHARI GEMSBOK NATIONAL PARK

Location: Far north of the region; north of Upington.
Access: From Upington take the R32 towards Namibia and after 63 km turn right towards Noenieput; continue for about 30 km, then turn left onto the R360; follow this road through Noenieput and Andriesvale, reaching the park's entrance about 280 km from the R32. The clearly signposted, graded gravel roads are usually in good condition, but watch out for rough stretches and soft sand. Fuel is usually available at Noenieput, Koopman Suid and Andriesvale, but these stations have been known to run dry. From Kuruman the R31, via Hotazel and Vanzylsrus, joins the R360 at Andriesvale; this 324-km, graded gravel road varies in condition. From Namibia travel via Keetmanshoop, Aroab, Rietfontein and Andriesvale to Twee Rivieren (360 km); only overnight visitors at Mata Mata may travel in the opposite direction to Namibia. A fee is charged for entry to the park.
Accommodation: *Twee Rivieren camp* has 4-bed huts, each with a fully equipped kitchen, shower and toilet (R100 per 2 persons per night); 2- to 4-bed huts, each with kitchen and bathroom (R100 per 2 persons per night); this is the only camp with air-conditioned accommodation available. *Mata Mata camp* has 6-bed cottages, each with a fully equipped kitchen, shower and toilet (R100 per 4 persons per night); and 3-bed huts (R40 per 2 persons per night). *Nossob camp* has 6-bed cottages, each with a fully equipped kitchen, shower and toilet (R100 per 4 persons per night); 3-bed huts, each with a fully equipped kitchen, shower and toilet (R80 per 2 persons per night); and 3-bed huts (R40 per 2 persons per night). All accommodation is supplied with bedding. There is a camping site with full ablution facilities at each of the 3 camps (R9 per stand plus R4 per person per night; maximum 6 persons per stand).
Other facilities: An extensive network of game-viewing roads; picnic sites; shops selling groceries; fuel supplies. *Twee Rivieren* has supplies of fresh meat, eggs and margarine

(neither bread nor fresh milk is available); an informal lapa; a swimming pool; and a landing strip. *Nossob* has a landing strip and information centre. *Mata Mata* has a landing strip. Cars may be hired but arrangements must be made well in advance.
Open: Throughout the year.
Opening time: Sunrise to sunset.
Beware: Malaria, particularly during the summer rainy season.
For further information: (Enquiries and booking) National Parks Board (see page 365). (Park address) The Park Warden, Kalahari Gemsbok National Park, Private Bag X5890, Gemsbok Park 8815.

The Kalahari Gemsbok National Park is the second largest national park in South Africa, covering an area of approximately 9 590 km². The adjacent Gemsbok National Park in Botswana is considerably larger and their combined area exceeds 36 000 km². No fences have been built between the two and game moves freely from one to the other. The international boundary is marked by unobtrusive beacons along the length of the Nossob River. The two major rivers in the park, the Nossob and the Auob, flow on very rare occasions. Their beds meet near Twee Rivieren camp, and the combined channel continues southward to enter the Molopo River outside the park. Of the three roads open to the public, two follow the courses of the Nossob and Auob.

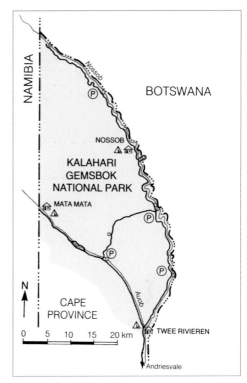

The Kalahari is not a true desert, but semi-desert savannah, and much of the park is covered by low sand ridges, best seen from the road between Rooibrak and Dikbaardskolk. In the central sand-dune area the abundant grassland is dotted with a scattering of low trees and bushes, mainly silver clusterleaf, shepherd's bush and the grey camel thorn. In the river beds the vegetation is more varied and includes camel thorn, black thorn and raisin bush. When the first rains fall a great variety of annuals burst into flower, bringing colour to the arid landscape. Two ground creepers, the 'tsama' melon and the wild cucumber, are important as their fruits are eaten by a wide range of animals, including the larger antelope species, and provide a vital source of moisture.

The park lacks any permanent surface water but the authorities maintain a network of boreholes, most of which lie in the river beds. These artificial waterholes make good sites for game-viewing, and visitors who sit patiently at one of them are usually well rewarded. The sides of the river beds are ridged with limestone, and where networks of small caves have been formed in the limestone a wide range of smaller animals find shelter.

On a larger scale, this is a land of nomadic antelope herds, such as eland, gemsbok, blue wildebeest, red hartebeest and springbok. The movements of the game herds are dictated largely by the rains and by vegetation in this arid area. Usually the best time for spotting game is between February and May, when the herds concentrate in the river beds. During the dry season the animals tend to disperse into the dunes in search of food. Carnivores are well represented and include lion, leopard, cheetah, spotted and brown hyenas, black-backed jackal and a number of smaller species.

The 215 bird species recorded in the park include a rich complement of raptors, ranging in size from the pygmy falcon to the lappet-faced vulture. The vast communal nests of the sociable weaver are prominent features in camel thorn trees along the river beds, and other bird species that may be seen include kori bustard, Namaqua sandgrouse and red-billed quelea.

Summer days are hot, with temperatures often exceeding 40 °C, and the park's meagre rainfall of 200 mm a year occurs at this time. Winter days are mild to cool, but temperatures often fall to well below freezing at night.

---

308 KAROO NATIONAL PARK

Location: Southern Karoo; north of Beaufort West.

Access: From Beaufort West take the N1 southwards; the entrance to the park is a few kilometres out of the town and is clearly sign-posted. An entrance fee is charged. To reach the Mountain View camp (for which permission must be obtained at the office), take the N1 northwards from Beaufort West and turn left onto the R381 to Loxton; continue for about 18 km, over the Roseberg and Molteno passes, and at the foot of the latter turn left onto a gravel road which leads into the northern area of the park; this road gives access only to the Mountain View camp.

Accommodation: *Karoo* camp has 3-bed chalets, each with a fully equipped kitchen and a bathroom (R100 per 2 persons per night); 6-bed cottages, each with a fully equipped kitchen, 2 bathrooms and a living room (R180 per 4 persons per night). There is a camping and caravan site with full ablution facilities (R9 per stand plus R4 per person per night; maximum 6 persons per stand). *Mountain View* camp is a primitive, isolated camp where only beds and mattresses are provided in the huts; there is a communal ablution block; a maximum of 25 persons only is allowed. There are also 2 12-bed hiking trail huts.

Other facilities: A 90-km network of game-viewing roads is being developed; 3-day Springbok Hiking Trail (maximum 12 persons per day); self-guided nature trails; picnic sites with fireplaces; a restaurant and shop, an information centre, conference facilities and swimming pool at the main camp.

Open: Throughout the year; Mountain View camp is closed from March to October; Springbok Hiking Trail is closed from November to end February.

Opening time: October to March – 07h00 to 19h00; April to September – 08h00 to 18h00.

For further information: (Enquiries and booking) National Parks Board (see page 365). (Park address and Mountain View camp booking) The Park Warden, Karoo National Park, P.O. Box 316, Beaufort West 6970. Tel: (0201) 5-2828/9.

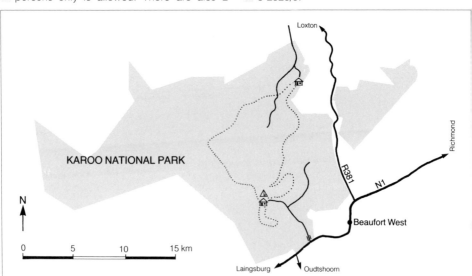

The Karoo National Park, established in 1979, covers 32 792 ha and is dominated by the sheer cliffs and plateaux of the Nuweveld Mountains. River beds descend from the mountains to flat plains in the far western and the eastern parts of the park, but they are dry for most of the year.

Much of the vegetation comprises dwarf shrubs, known as 'Karoo bushes', and sweet-thorn trees are common, particularly along the water courses. A variety of trees and bushes grow in the gorges and along the dry river banks.

A number of game species have been re-introduced, including the second largest population of Cape mountain zebra (approximately 120), as well as red hartebeest, black wildebeest and springbok. Other species that may be sighted include mountain reedbuck, gemsbok, steenbok, grey rhebok, klipspringer kudu, common duiker and the rock dassie. Predators are represented by leopard, caracal, black-backed jackal, Cape fox, bat-eared fox and several mongoose species. More than 180 bird species have been recorded.

The park's average annual rainfall of only 260 mm occurs mainly in the summer months, when days are hot; winter days are usually clear, but nights are cold. The area experiences strong winds, particularly during August.

KAROO NATURE RESERVE

Location: Eastern Karoo; Graaff-Reinet.
Access: From Graaff-Reinet take the R68 northwards, following signposts to the Valley of Desolation; the left turn into the western part of the reserve, in which the Valley of Desolation is situated, is about 5 km from the town. To reach the entrance to the game-viewing area, continue on the R63 for about 3 km to the gate, which is on the right. To reach the eastern part of the reserve, from Church St in Graaff-Reinet turn eastwards along Middel St and continue for about 2 km; shortly after crossing the Sundays River for the second time turn right into Republic St, and after 500 m left into Protea St; the entrance to the reserve is at the end of this road.
Accommodation: Hiking trail huts. There are hotels, self-catering accommodation, and a camping and caravan site in Graaff-Reinet.
Other facilities: Overnight hiking trails (permits are required; they are available from the office and must be booked well in advance); short self-guided trails; picnic sites; a network of game-viewing roads; birdwatching hides at Vanrhyneveld's Pass Dam; boating is allowed on the dam (permission must be obtained from the Graaff-Reinet Boat Club).
Open: Throughout the year.
Opening time: 24-hour access to the Valley of Desolation view-point and the western shore of the dam. Other areas at weekends and public and school holidays in summer – 07h00 to 19h00; in winter – 07h00 to 17h30.
For further information: The Officer-in-charge, Karoo Nature Reserve, P.O. Box 349, Graaff-Reinet 6280. Tel: (0491) 2-3453.

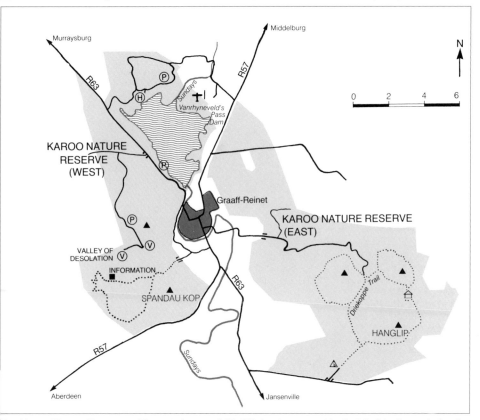

The Karoo Nature Reserve, with a total area of 16 000 ha, is unusual in that it virtually encircles the historic town of Graaff-Reinet. A project of the South African Nature Foundation, it was established in 1975. Much of the reserve is rugged and hilly, with several high peaks, including the impressive Spandau Kop. Probably its best-known feature is the Valley of Desolation, an awe-inspiring cleft at the edge of the mountain. From the view-points there are stunning views southwards towards Spandau Kop and across the Plains of Camdeboo. The Vanrhyneveld's Pass Dam, on the Sundays River, takes up a considerable part of the reserve's area in the north.

The vegetation within the reserve is influenced by the relatively low rainfall and consists of extensive areas of succulent veld dominated by spekboom, high-altitude grassland, savannah dotted with clumps of bush, and the short Karoo scrub of the lowland plains. It is the conservation authority's policy to restock the reserve with game species that once roamed freely in this area, and some of those already re-introduced are the Cape mountain zebra, black wildebeest, eland, red hartebeest, springbok and blesbok. Other game species that occur naturally include kudu, mountain reedbuck, common duiker and steenbok.

310 KLAARWATER NATURE RESERVE

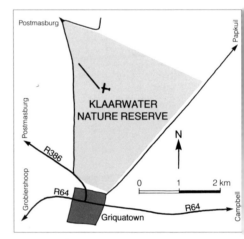

Location: North-eastern part of the region; west of Kimberley.
Access: From Kimberley travel westwards on the R64 to Griquatown; take the R386 towards Postmasburg and after a short distance turn right onto a minor road which flanks the reserve.
Accommodation: None. There is accommodation in Griquatown.
Other facilities: A road network; walking trails; boating permitted; picnic sites with fireplaces.
Open: Throughout the year.
Opening time: Sunrise to sunset.
For further information: The Town Clerk, Griquatown Municipality, P.O. Box 21, Griquatown 8365. Tel: (05962), ask for 19 or 31.

This small municipal reserve covers 765 ha of Kalahari thornveld and protects small herds of springbok and a number of ostrich.

311 KOKERBOOM FOREST

Location: North-western Karoo; south of Kenhardt.
Access: From Kenhardt follow the R27 southwards towards Brandvlei for 7 km; the reserve can be seen clearly from the road.
Accommodation: None. There is accommodation in Kenhardt.
Other facilities: Walking is permitted.
Open: Throughout the year.
Opening time: 24 hours.
For further information: The Town Clerk, Kenhardt Municipality, Private Bag X05, Kenhardt 8900. Tel: 05462, ask for 25.

This kokerboom 'forest', located on a rocky ridge, is one of the largest concentrations of the kokerboom (also known as the quiver tree or tree aloe) in the Cape Province. This area receives little rain and apart from the forest, vegetation is sparse. Summer days can be very hot.

KURUMAN NATURE RESERVE

Location: North-eastern part of the region; Kuruman.
Access: From Kuruman take the R27 westwards towards Sishen; the reserve lies a short distance out of the town, on the right.
Accommodation: None. There is accommodation in Kuruman.
Other facilities: A network of game-viewing roads.
Open: Throughout the year.
Opening time: Weekends between 1 September and 30 April – 15h00 to 19h00; weekends between 1 May and 31 August – 14h00 to 18h00. Otherwise by arrangement.
Speed limit: 20 km/h.

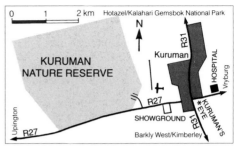

For further information: The Town Clerk, Kuruman Municipality, P.O. Box 4, Kuruman 8460. Tel: (01471) 2-1095.

The Kuruman Nature Reserve covers 850 ha of flat Kalahari thornveld, dominated by large camel thorn trees. The thornveld provides grazing and browsing for white rhinoceros, eland, gemsbok, red hartebeest, kudu, blesbok, impala, springbok, steenbok and Burchell's zebra. Several lark species, Namaqua sandgrouse and white-browed sparrow-weaver, as well as pale chanting goshawk and lanner falcon, are among the bird species which occur.

LEON TALJAARDT NATURE RESERVE

Location: North-eastern part of the region; north-west of Vryburg.
Access: From Vryburg take the R378 towards Ganyesa and Botswana, and after 5 km turn left into the reserve.
Accommodation: Swartfontein Pleasure Resort, on the eastern border of the reserve, has luxury, fully equipped chalets. There is also a camping and caravan site with full ablution facilities.
Other facilities: A network of game-viewing roads, although dense bush obstructs the view in many places; picnic sites with fireplaces; swimming pool at resort.
Open: Throughout the year.

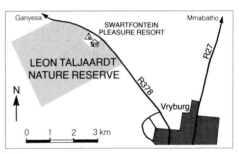

Opening time: Sunrise to sunset.
For further information: The Town Clerk, P.O. Box 35, Vryburg 8600. Tel: (01451) 4461.

This 857-ha reserve is predominantly flat and featureless, and large areas are covered by dense bush, which is classified as Kalahari thornveld. As part of the reserve's restocking programme 21 game species have been released here, although several did not originally occur in this area. White rhinoceros, buffalo, blue and black wildebeest, eland, gemsbok, blesbok, red hartebeest and waterbuck are among the species that have been released. This area can be extremely hot in summer.

MOLOPO NATURE RESERVE

Location: Far northern part of the region; north-west of Vryburg on the Botswana border.
Access: From Vryburg travel north-west for

110 km on the Tosca/Bray tar road, then turn left onto the Vorstershoop gravel road (R379) and travel for 100 km. Drive through Vorsters-

hoop; the reserve is on the left after 14 km. Use the Avondster entrance.
Accommodation: None at present, but a rustic bush camp with ablution facilities is planned. Check with authority.
Other facilities: The bush camp and 10 km of the Phepane River roads are surfaced and suitable for ordinary cars. Otherwise, a 4x4 vehicle is necessary to travel in the reserve. More roads, game-viewing hides and short walking trails are being planned; although no specific trails exist yet, hiking may be permitted by prior arrangement. Some basic supplies can be bought in Vorstershoop, but the nearest shopping centre is Vryburg, more than 220 km away.
Open: The reserve has not yet been officially opened to the public, and intending visitors are asked to make arrangements with the Officer-in-charge.
For further information: Officer-in-charge, Molopo Nature Reserve, P.O. Vorstershoop

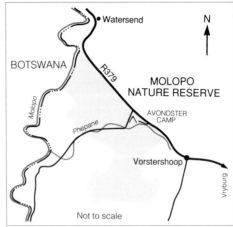

8615. Tel: (0020), ask for Vorstershoop 1322; or Senior Regional Officer, P.O. Box 456, Kimberley 8300. Tel: (0531) 3-4167.

The Molopo Nature Reserve presently covers 23 876 ha. It was created in 1987 to conserve the Molopo thornveld which differs from the more westerly form of Kalahari thornveld in the absence of red dunes and the greater abundance and diversity of acacias. The most abundant trees are camel thorn, black thorn, Kalahari sand acacia, shepherd's bush and silver terminalia. The reserve is still being developed, and presently contains only small numbers of kudu, springbok and red hartebeest. Gemsbok, eland, ostrich and hopefully giraffe will be reintroduced soon. Steenbok and common duiker occur, and smaller carnivores such as the brown hyena, caracal and black-backed jackal are found there naturally. Cheetah and leopard occur in the reserve but are seldom seen.

More than 110 species of Kalahari birds have been observed, and numbers of whitebacked vultures and other large raptors nest on the reserve. The terrain is very flat, the main features being the depressions of the Phepane and Molopo riverbeds. The latter forms the border with Botswana, but neither river has flowed for many years.

315 NIEUWOUDTVILLE WILD FLOWER RESERVE

Location: Far western Karoo; Nieuwoudtville.
Access: From Nieuwoudtville take the R27 eastwards towards Calvinia; the reserve lies about 2 km from Nieuwoudtville, on the left of the road, and is clearly signposted.
Accommodation: None.
Other facilities: Visitors may walk freely in the reserve.
Open: Throughout the year.
Opening time: 08h00 to 18h00.
For further information: The Town Clerk, Nieuwoudtville Municipality, P.O. Box 52, Nieuwoudtville 8180. Tel: (02726) 8-1052.

Covering approximately 66 ha, the Nieuwoudtville Wild Flower Reserve was established in 1974 to protect a portion of the floral diversity found in this area. The reserve consists mainly of flat, open land but a dolerite dyke dominates the northern part. The whole area is a mass of colour when thousands of annuals flower in spring.

316 OORLOGSKLOOF NATURE RESERVE See map Nieuwoudtville Wild Flower Reserve

Location: Far western Karoo; south-west of Nieuwoudtville.
Access: From Vanrhynsdorp take the R27 to Nieuwoudtville; the reserve is 10 km south of Nieuwoudtville.
Accommodation: 4 hiking trail overnight spots with toilets, fireplaces, and tents with stretchers if required (book these spots well in advance).
Other facilities: 46 km of hiking trails which may be hiked as a 3- to 4-day trail or as shorter day hikes (all hiking to be arranged in advance

with the Officer-in-charge); swimming in natural pools in the river; San paintings.
Open: Throughout the year.
Opening time: Weekdays – 08h00 to 17h00. At present there is no public access road and prior arrangements must be made with the Officer-in-charge for transport into the reserve.
For further information: The Officer-in-charge, Oorlogskloof Nature Reserve, Private Bag, Nieuwoudtville 8180. Tel: (02726) 8-1010.

The Oorlogskloof Nature Reserve consists of a large, deeply incised plateau of 5 070 ha, with the gorge of the Oorlogskloof River forming its eastern boundary. This is a scenically dramatic area with magnificent views of the Kners Flats to the west.

Lying at the northern extremity of the Cape Floral Kingdom, the reserve has strong elements of montane fynbos (heath), but these are combined with influences from the Karoo and Namaqualand. Several rare and endangered plant species, e.g. the elephant's foot plant *Dioscorea elephantipes*, grow here. Grey rhebok, klipspringer, common duiker, Cape grysbok, baboon, rock dassie and many smaller mammals occur in the reserve. Leopard occasionally move through the area, and caracal, African wild cat, aardwolf, Cape fox and bat-eared fox are present.

The birdlife in the reserve is rich and includes black and booted eagles, lanner and peregrine falcons, jackal buzzard, gymnogene, Cape eagle owl, white-necked raven, grey-wing and Cape francolin, and a host of smaller species.

The annual rainfall varies between 300 and 450 mm in this part of the country; summers are hot and winters mild to cold.

317 SPITSKOP NATURE RESERVE

Location: Northern part of the region; north of Upington.
Access: From Upington take the R360 towards Noenieput and the Kalahari Gemsbok National Park; the reserve lies to the right, about 7 km out of the town.
Accommodation: None. Upington has a variety of accommodation.
Other facilities: A 30-km network of gravel game-viewing roads; a view-point with telescope on Spitskop; picnic sites with fireplaces.
Open: Throughout the year.
Opening time: April to September – 08h00 to 17h00; October to March – 08h00 to 19h00.
For further information: Spitskop Safaris, Mr W. Strauss, P.O. Box 1788, Upington 8800. Tel: (054) 2-2336.

The Spitskop Nature Reserve covers 2 740 ha of level plain covered with sand and stones, with only two small rocky outcrops breaking the flatness. Its vegetation, classified as Orange River Broken Veld, consists of a sparse covering of shrubs and a scattering of small trees. After the summer rains, which fall mainly in February and March, a carpet of flowering annuals and grasses appears.

A number of game species have been released in the reserve and they include Burchell's zebra, gemsbok, red hartebeest, eland, steenbok, and a large springbok population. Ostrich are also present. No bird list is available, as there are relatively few bird species recorded.

318 STRYDENBURG AALWYNPRAG NATURE RESERVE See regional map

Location: North-eastern Karoo; Strydenburg.
Access: The nature reserve lies within Strydenburg, at the southern end of town and opposite the hotel.
Accommodation: None. There is accommodation in Strydenburg.

Other facilities: A network of footpaths.
Open: Throughout the year.
Opening time: Sunrise to sunset.
For further information: The Town Clerk, Strydenburg Municipality, P.O. Box 60, Strydenburg 8765. Tel: 05762, ask for 16.

One of the smallest nature reserves in southern Africa, the 2-ha Strydenburg Aalwynprag Nature Reserve has been set aside to protect Karoo aloes and other succulents.

319 TIERBERG NATURE RESERVE

Location: Northern Cape; Keimoes, midway between Upington and Augrabies Falls.
Access: From Keimoes town centre, at the traffic lights, follow a tar road eastwards towards Tierberg; after 3 km turn right to the reserve. The internal road is steep and quite rough.
Accommodation: None. There is a hotel and a camping site in Keimoes.
Other facilities: Short footpaths; a picnic site.
Opening time: Sunrise to sunset.
Open: Throughout the year.
For further information: The Town Clerk, Keimoes Municipality, P.O. Box 8, Keimoes 8860. Tel: 05492, ask for 26.

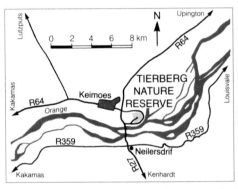

The 77-ha Tierberg Nature Reserve is dominated by the hill of the same name, from which there are fine views of the irrigated farms along the Orange River. This is a botanical reserve which protects many succulent and aloe species, notably the Gariep aloe, which flowers in August and September.

320 VICTORIA WEST NATURE RESERVE

Location: Central Karoo; Victoria West.
Access: From Victoria West drive westwards on the R63 towards Loxton; the reserve is on the left, just out of the town.
Accommodation: None. Victoria West has a hotel and a camping site.
Other facilities: Gravel game-viewing roads; walking trails; picnic sites with fireplaces.
Open: Throughout the year.
Opening time: Contact the authority.
For further information: The Town Clerk, Victoria West Municipality, P.O. Box 13, Victoria West 7070. Tel: 02042, ask for 26/36. Fax: 02042, ask for 368.

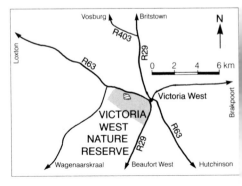

The 428-ha Victoria West Nature Reserve lies deep within the Karoo and short, scrubby vegetation is typical of the area. Game animals that have been introduced include Burchell's zebra, eland, black wildebeest, gemsbok, springbok and blesbok.

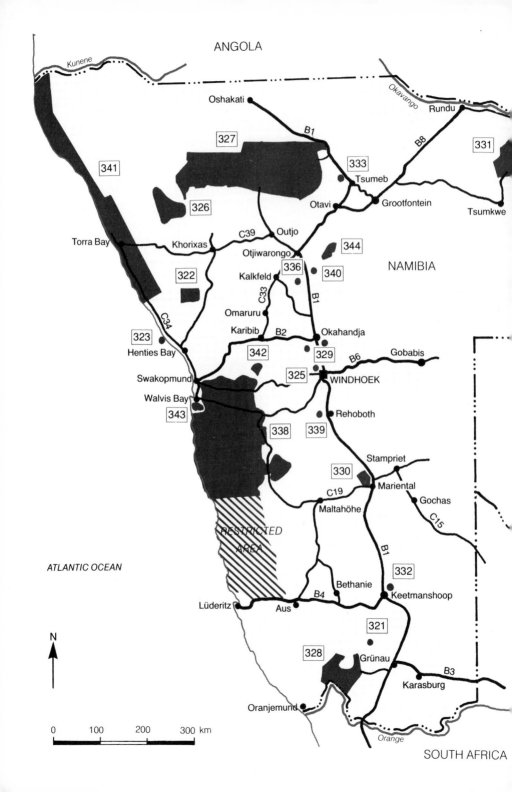

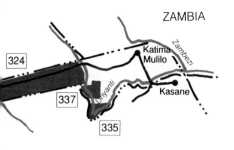

ZAMBIA

BOTSWANA

NAMIBIA

Namibia is a harsh land, with vast areas of desert and arid wilderness, yet it remains one of the most fascinating areas in Africa, drawing large numbers of tourists each year. Covering 823 000 km², the region lies to the north of the Orange River and is bordered by Angola, Botswana, South Africa and, in the extreme north-east, Zambia. The Namib Desert forms a narrow belt of land sandwiched between the Atlantic Ocean to the west and the rugged escarpment of the Khomas Hochland to the east, which separates the desert from the inland plateau. Between the 'true' desert of the Namib and the savannah of the Khomas Hochland lies a transitional zone of flat, open plains known as the Pro-Namib belt. There are only five large, perennial rivers and these border the country: the Orange in the far south and the Kunene River, Okavango, Linyanti/Chobe and Zambezi in the extreme north.

The desert consists of vast areas of sand dunes, flat, gravel-covered plains, great rocky hill ranges and inselbergs, and several large river beds that cut their way from the escarpment to the coast, forming oases of vegetation. The meeting of hot, dry winds blowing across the continent and cold air above the Atlantic Ocean causes fog to roll in across the desert, providing moisture to sustain the vegetation and animal life of the Namib. Most of the central and northern areas consist of different types of woodland savannah, including mopane, tree and shrub savannah, camel thorn and broad-leafed woodland.

This is a land of climatic extremes, with the coastal desert receiving an average annual rainfall of 10 mm and the north-eastern region as much as 600 mm. Summers are hot and the annual rains usually fall between October and April, although this varies from region to region. Winters are dry and generally mild, but temperatures often plummet at night, particularly in the south-eastern part of the country.

Namibia has a small and scattered human population of just over one million, and large areas are unpopulated. The greatest numbers of people inhabit Ovamboland, Kavango and East Caprivi in the far north.

It is strongly recommended that people who intend visiting Namibia's game reserves establish beforehand what changes may have taken place since the publication of this book. South Africans and other nationals require passports to enter the country, and they should check whether visas are also necessary.

The road network is generally good, with a major highway running from south to north and other highways branching off it to the main towns. The numbers of some roads in Namibia are in the process of being changed; the new numbers are used on the map on the previous page, and in the following accounts the old numbers are used, with new numbers in brackets after them. Petrol stations are often few and far between, and travellers are advised to carry spare food and water in the more remote regions.

Namibia's conservation areas range from the world-famous Etosha National Park which protects a vast array of game species, to desert reserves on the west coast best known for plants and animals that have evolved to survive in the harsh environment.

The major parks and reserves are controlled by the Ministry of Wildlife, Conservation and Tourism (see page 365), and the standard of accommodation in them is extremely high, ranking among the best in Africa. As is the case in many countries, pets are not allowed into reserves, and at the entrance to several in Namibia kennels are provided, although the care of the animals remains the responsibility of the owners.

321 AUGARABIES-STEENBOK NATURE RESERVE See map Fish River Canyon Park

Location: South Namibia; north-west of Grünau.
Access: From Grünau take the C28 (C12) north-westwards in the direction of Seeheim; pass the turn-off to Fish River Canyon viewpoint and 11 km further on turn left; follow the signposts to the reserve, which is 10 km ahead.

Accommodation: None. Camping is permitted and there are basic facilities.
Other facilities: Walking is permitted.
Open: Throughout the year.
Opening time: Sunrise to sunset.
For further information: Ministry of Wildlife, Conservation and Tourism (see page 365).

This reserve has only been proclaimed recently and is being developed. It is similar in most respects to the Fish River Canyon area.

322 BRANDBERG

Location: Western Namibia; north of Swakopmund.
Access: From Swakopmund follow the C44 (C34) for 67 km to Henties Bay; continue beyond Henties Bay for 7 km and turn north-eastwards onto the C76 (C35) before travelling 116 km to Uis Mine; continue past this settlement for approximately 14 km and turn left onto the D2359; follow this road for 28 km to Brandberg. From just beyond Henties Bay as far as Brandberg the roads are gravel and, although they vary in condition, most vehicles should be able to negotiate them. Uis Mine can also be reached via Omaruru on the C64 (C36) or from the north via Outjo and Khorixas on the C65 (C39) and the C76 (C35). All these roads are graded gravel.
Accommodation: None. Although there are no facilities, many people camp at the foot of the mountain.
Other facilities: Walking is permitted on the mountain; marked 1-hour trail; Bushman rock paintings. Fuel is available at Henties Bay, Khorixas and Omaruru. Carry all the water and other supplies you require.
Open: Throughout the year.

Opening time: 24 hours.
Beware: Inexperienced hikers should not wander on the mountain; always remember to carry water.
For further information: Ministry of Wildlife, Conservation and Tourism, Windhoek (see page 365).

Although no longer an official nature reserve, Brandberg is an area of great natural beauty and has been declared a national monument. This 500-km^2 massif towers some 2 000 m above the desert plain and contains Namibia's highest peak, Königstein (2 579 m). The Brandberg is perhaps best known, however, for its large number of Bushman paintings, some of which are estimated to be 15 000 to 16 000 years old. There are many great rock overhangs and other magnificent examples of weathering.

The little vegetation that survives here is well adapted to this harsh environment and comprises mainly thick-stemmed succulents and small-leaved bushes. Grasses and annuals spring up within days of a rain shower but are soon scorched by sun and wind.

Some game species, such as springbok and steenbok, still survive in the area, but in such low numbers that it is unlikely that any will be spotted. A number of bird species live in the bushy gorges, and rarities such as Rüppell's korhaan occur on the plains surrounding Brandberg.

This area of Damaraland is extremely hot in summer and rainfall is sparse. Although winters are milder, temperatures during the day may still be high.

323
CAPE CROSS SEAL RESERVE See map Brandberg

Location: Namib Desert; north-west of Swakopmund.
Access: From Swakopmund follow the C44 (C34) northwards past Henties Bay, turn onto the D2301 (C34) and travel for approximately 64 km to Cape Cross. At the signpost turn left onto a good salt road to the reserve.
Accommodation: None. A very large public camping site (Mile 72), 20 km south of the reserve, has basic ablution facilities and fuel supplies.
Other facilities: None.
Open: Every day year round except Fridays. Visitors should check with the authority as this may change.
Opening time: 10h00 to 17h00.
For further information: Ministry of Wildlife, Conservation and Tourism (see page 365).

Cape Cross takes its name from a cross erected here by the Portuguese navigator Diego Cão in 1486, although the original cross was taken to Germany at the end of the last century and a replica now stands in its place.

Today the area protects one of the largest colonies of Cape fur seals in southern Africa; between 80 000 and 100 000 seals live on the rocks here. The most interesting times to visit are during mid-October when the large bulls begin to establish territories, and from the end of November to early December when the black-coated pups are born. Visitors should take care, however, not to cross the barrier and disturb the seals, and not to feed the black-backed jackals which are a common sight.

Huge flocks of Cape cormorants fly past each day on their way from their roosts to feeding grounds.

CAPRIVI GAME PARK

Location: North-eastern Namibia; east of Rundu.
Access: From Rundu follow the B8 eastwards in the direction of Katima Mulilo; this road passes through the game park.
Accommodation: A camp, which can accommodate 40 people, has been developed on the east bank of the Okavango River and there is also a camping site available.
Other facilities: None.
Open: Throughout the year.
Opening time: Sunrise to sunset.
Beware: Do not stray from the main road; malaria.
For further information: Ministry of Wildlife, Conservation and Tourism (see page 365).

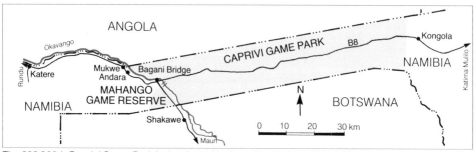

The 600 000-h Caprivi Game Park is dominated by broad-leafed woodland. The dense vegetation makes game-viewing difficult, but elephant, buffalo, kudu and roan antelope do occur. Summers are hot in this area, and rain falls during this season; winter days are warm to cool, with cold nights.

DAAN VILJOEN GAME PARK

Location: Central Namibia; north-west of Windhoek.
Access: From Windhoek follow the C52 (C28) for 20 km towards Swakopmund; take the signposted right turn to the Daan Viljoen Game Park, following this road for a short distance to the entrance gate. The internal roads are gravel.
Accommodation: 2-bed bungalows, each with fridge, hotplate and handbasin, and communal ablution facilities; a large camping and caravan site with communal ablution facilities and kitchens.
Other facilities: Game-viewing drives; walking allowed in the game area on marked trails; fishing allowed in the dam (permits are required and are available from the office); picnic site; a swimming pool; a restaurant. Dogs must be left in the kennels at the entrance gate to the reserve and must be cared for by their owners.
Open: Throughout the year.
Opening time: Sunrise to sunset.
For further information: Ministry of Wildlife, Conservation and Tourism (see page 365).

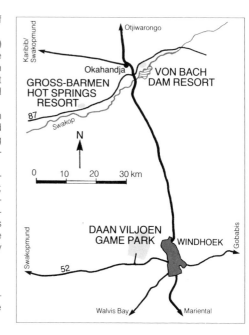

This is a comparatively small game park set around a dam in the hilly country of the Khomas Hochland, within sight of Windhoek. The vegetation of the 4 951-ha reserve is mostly grass, with occasional low trees and bushes. A variety of game species, such as Hartmann's mountain zebra, red hartebeest and blue wildebeest, have been introduced. The best places for birdwatching are around the dam and the rest camp area, and helmeted guineafowl and red-billed francolin are regular visitors to the camping site.

Rain falls in summer, and day temperatures can be high, although nights are pleasantly mild. Winter days are usually mild, but nights can be very cold and frost is not unusual.

326 DAMARALAND WILDERNESS RESERVE See regional map

Location: North-western Namibia; west of Kamanjab.
Access: Private (or charter) aircraft fly to a private strip; alternatively visitors can motor to the Damaraland Wilderness Reserve boundary (which can be reached by most vehicles) where they will be collected. Note: this is a private concession area.
Accommodation: 3 m x 3 m bow tents (maxi-

mum 12 persons), fully equipped, bucket showers, dining tent (R250 per person per night including all meals and activities).
Other facilities: Accompanied game-viewing drives and walks.
Open: 1 March to about 4 January.
Opening times: By prior arrangement.
For further information: Wilderness Safaris (see page 365).

This reserve, covering more than 160 000 ha, lies close to the south-western border of Etosha National Park and is best known for its spectacular desert scenery. This is not an area to visit if you expect teeming game herds but you have a chance of seeing the much publicised desert-dwelling elephants and black rhinoceros, as well as Hartmann's zebra, gemsbok, springbok and ostrich. The winter nights can be very cold in this area.

327 ETOSHA NATIONAL PARK

Location: Northern Namibia; north of Windhoek.
Access: At present there are 2 entrance gates, 1 to Okaukuejo camp in the south and the other to Namutoni camp in the east. To reach Okaukuejo from Windhoek, follow the B1 for 242 km to Otjiwarongo; turn left onto the B2 (C33) and drive for a short distance before turning right, still on the B2 (C33), to Outjo; at Outjo join the C68 (C38) and follow this road for 117 km to the entrance gate; the distance from the gate to Okaukuejo is 18 km. To reach Namutoni from Windhoek, follow the B1 for 242 km to Otjiwarongo and continue north-eastwards for 182 km to Tsumeb; from Tsumeb continue on the B1 for 73 km and turn left onto the C84 (not numbered) to the entrance gate. The camp is 8 km from the gate. *Mokuti Lodge* lies 500 m from the Van Lindequist Gate at Namutoni. Access to Halali camp is by internal roads only.

With the exception of the roads between the gates and Namutoni and Okaukuejo, which are tarred, all internal roads are gravel and well maintained. Etosha Fly-in Safari operates a fly-in service at all 3 camps; there are also charter flights to Tsumeb.

Accommodation: *Okaukuejo camp* has 2-, 3- and 4-bed self-contained bungalows, each with a bathroom, cooking facilities, a refrigerator and bedding; 4-bed tents using communal ablution facilities and kitchen; 2-bed rooms, each with a bathroom and bedding. *Namutoni camp* has 2-, 3- and 4-bed rooms with bedding, some with a bathroom, in the historic Namutoni Fort (the 4-bed rooms also have cooking facilities); 2-bed rooms, each with a bathroom and bedding; 4-bed mobile homes, each with a bathroom, kitchen facilities and bedding; a camping and caravan site with communal ablution and cooking facilities. *Halali camp* has self-contained, 4-bed bungalows, each with a bathroom, cooking facilities, a refrigerator and bedding; 2-bed bungalows with bedding, using communal ablution and kitchen facilities; 2-bed rooms, each with a bathroom and bedding; 4-bed tents with bedding, using communal ablution and cooking facilities; 10-bed dormitory rooms. There is a camping and caravan site with ablution and cooking facilities. Book well in advance during school holidays, as the camps are usually fully booked. *Mokuti Lodge* has double-bedded chalets and 5-bed

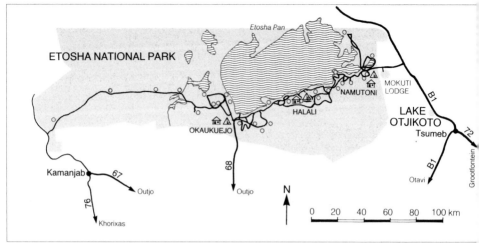

ETOSHA NATIONAL PARK

Etosha Pan

MOKUTI LODGE
NAMUTONI
HALALI
OKAUKUEJO
LAKE OTJIKOTO
Tsumeb

Kamanjab
Outjo
Outjo
Khorixas

N

0 20 40 60 80 100 km

family units, all with *en-suite* bathrooms (total 96 rooms).
Other facilities: An extensive network of game-viewing roads; kennel facilities at the entrance gates. All 3 camps have a licensed restaurant; a shop with a wide selection of goods; petrol and diesel supplies; mail facilities; swimming pools; picnic sites. *Okaukuejo camp* has an information centre and limited car repair facilities. *Namutoni camp* has a museum. *Mokuti Lodge* has 2 restaurants, bar, conference centre, swimming pool and short walking trail in private reserve.
Open: Throughout the year; Halali is closed between 1 November and 15 March.
Opening time: Sunrise to sunset.
Speed limit: 60 km/h.
Beware: Do not get out of your car except at camps and demarcated picnic sites; malaria.
For further information: Ministry of Wildlife Conservation and Tourism (see page 365). (Etosha Fly-in Safari) P.O. Namutoni. Tel (0020) 11. (Mokuti Lodge) Tel: (0671) 3085. Fax: (0671) 3085.

Although it was reduced from 99 526 km^2 to 22 270 km^2 in 1967 for political reasons, Etosha National Park is still one of Africa's greatest game sanctuaries. The pan from which the park takes its name covers 6 133 km^2, and although its origin is not known for certain, it is believed to have once been a great inland lake fed by a large river (probably the Kunene), which over time changed its route and caused the lake to dry out and form a mineral-rich, saline desert plain where no vegetation will grow. During periods of high rainfall and when the rivers in the north-west flow, parts of this 'salt desert' are transformed into shallow lakes. At such times flocks of pelicans, flamingoes and other waterbirds arrive to feed and breed, but these sites are unfortunately situated away from areas open to tourists.

The first Europeans to see the pan were the explorers Francis Galton and Charles Andersson in 1851 In 1901 the German authorities (which then controlled German South West Africa) established a police-post and fort at Namutoni. The first fort was destroyed by Ovambo warriors and was replaced by the more solid structure which today forms part of the Namutoni camp.

The area around the pan consists of short, open grassland with belts of deciduous trees and bushes Mopane woodland covers large areas but in the east, towards Namutoni, this gives way to mixed woodland, with a high percentage of acacias. The game populations of Etosha are large, and many species, including some rarities, are easily seen. The best places for game-viewing are at the waterholes at any one, over a period of a few hours, many different mammals and birds will come to drink. A waterhole in the Okaukuejo camp attracts many different species, including elephant, black rhinoceros and lion, and is floodlit at night. Some waterholes are more suited to photography than others, and some of the better locations are at Klein Okevi, Chudob and Kalkheuwel near Namutoni, and Gemsbokvlakte, about 20 km from Okaukuejo. Conditions vary, however, according to the season and time of day, and it pays to ask the tourist officers about conditions.

During the rainy season many game species move to the western side of the park and it is at this time that the young are dropped. As the dry season sets in, the game herds start to move back to the central and eastern areas where there are permanent waterholes, but towards the end of the dry season large herds of game usually concentrate around the waterholes on the Andoni Flats, to the north of Namutoni

Species that may be seen include giraffe, black rhinoceros, gemsbok, springbok, eland, blue wilde-beest, kudu (particularly abundant around Namutoni), steenbok and Burchell's zebra. One of southern Africa's smallest antelope, the Damara dik-dik, can be seen on the Bloubokdraai road near Namutoni. The rare black-faced impala, too, is most abundant in the Namutoni area, particularly around Klein Namutoni waterhole. Lion are fairly common and regularly seen, and leopard, cheetah, and spotted and brown hyenas also occur. Smaller predators, such as black-backed jackal, bat-eared fox and yellow mongoose, are commonly seen, and ground squirrels live in small colonies around the edge of the pan. At the last count, 325 bird species had been recorded within the park and they range in size from the ostrich to the tiny prinias and sunbirds. Like the game species, birds can best be watched at the waterholes, particularly in the late afternoons. Game-viewing is most difficult in the Halali area because of the dense woodland, but this is a rewarding region for birdwatchers.

Summers are hot and it is at this time that the rains fall (an annual average of 400 mm); March to August is cooler, but some hot days can be expected and night temperatures sometimes drop to below freezing.

328 FISH RIVER CANYON PARK

Location: Extreme southern Namibia; north-west of Vioolsdrif.

Access: From Vioolsdrif follow the B1 north-wards for 37 km, turn left onto the D316 and drive for 82 km to Ai-Ais Hot Springs, in the park. The D316 is good gravel and the park is clearly signposted. Alternatively, from Keet-manshoop to the north follow the B1 south-wards to Grünau and continue for a further 33 km; turn right onto the C97 (C10) and drive along this good gravel road for 76 km to Ai-Ais. A third route turns off the C28 (C12) and runs directly to one of the view-points in the north-eastern part of the park. Internal roads from Ai-Ais to the view-points are gravel.

Accommodation: *Ai-Ais Hot Springs* has 4-bed luxury flats with ablution facilities, a refrigerator, hotplate and bedding; 4-bed, self-contained standard flats; 4-bed huts, each with a refrigerator, hotplate, bedding and communal ablution facilities. There is a camping and caravan site with full ablution facilities and cooking areas. *Hobas Camp* has a camping and caravan site with full ablution and kitchen facilities.

Other facilities: 86-km Fish River Canyon Trail (a recent medical certificate must be sent with the fee when booking; permits are required); short walks; look-out points; kennels at the entrance gate. *Ai-Ais Hot Springs* has a shop selling general supplies, a restaurant, tennis courts and a swimming pool (hot springs); fuel supplies.

Open: Ai-Ais Hot Springs – second Friday in March to 31 October; the hiking trail – 1 May to

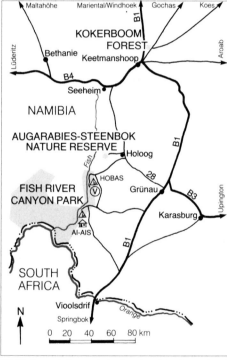

31 August; the main look-out point – throughout the year.

Opening time: Ai-Ais – sunrise to sunset.

For further information: Ministry of Wildlife, Conservation and Tourism (see page 365).

The Fish River Canyon Park is primarily a scenic conservation area, famous for its canyon and the geological wonders contained within it. The park has recently been enlarged to include adjacent mountains to the west and now also extends to the Orange River. The ravine itself is 161 km long, up to 27 km wide and in places almost 550 m deep. Rocks more than 2 600 million years old are revealed at the bottom of the canyon, which has been worn away into its present form by natural forces such as sand-blasting winds, faulting and erosion by the Fish River. The river, one of Namibia's longest, rises south-east of Swakopmund in the Naukluft Mountains and winds its way southwards for 800 km before entering the Orange River. It normally flows only during the rainy season, but pools of varying size remain throughout the year.

Vegetation in the park is sparse, but there are a number of desert-adapted plant species, including a variety of small trees, shrubs and succulents. This is not a reserve to visit if you want to see big game; there are Hartmann's mountain zebra and gemsbok in the greater reserve – although usually the only evidence of them is their tracks around the waterholes at the bottom of the canyon – and klipspringer, baboons and rock dassies may be seen. The birdlife, however, is surprisingly prolific, particularly at the waterholes.

Days are hot, often unpleasantly so in summer, and nights are warm to cool. The little rain that occurs falls in summer, in the form of short showers.

329   GROSS-BARMEN HOT SPRINGS AND VON BACH DAM RECREATION RESORT   <small>See map Daan Viljoen Game Park</small>

Location: Central Namibia; north of Windhoek.
Access: To reach Gross-Barmen from Windhoek, follow the B1 northwards towards Okahandja for 70 km and turn left at the signpost to the resort. To reach Von Bach Dam from Windhoek, turn right at the same junction, following signposts.
Accommodation: *Gross-Barmen resort* has 2-bed bungalows, each with a bathroom but using a communal kitchen; 5-bed bungalows, each with a bathroom and kitchen; 2-bed rooms, each with a refrigerator, hotplate and bathroom. There is a camping and caravan site with ablution and kitchen facilities. *Von Bach*

Dam resort has 2-bed huts without bedding or facilities and with a communal ablution block. There is a camping and caravan site, but only toilets and drinking water are provided.
Other facilities: *Gross-Barmen resort* has a shop, a restaurant, a swimming pool and mineral baths, tennis courts; nature walks; picnic site; fuel supplies. *Von Bach Dam resort* has fishing; nature walks.
Open: Throughout the year.
Opening time: Gross-Barmen – sunrise to sunset; Von Bach Dam – sunrise to sunset.
For further information: Ministry of Wildlife, Conservation and Tourism (see page 365).

The site of an old Rhenish mission station that closed in 1890 after repeated attacks by Hottentots and Hereros, Gross-Barmen is today one of the most popular resorts in Namibia. The neighbouring Von Bach Dam draws watersports and angling enthusiasts. Although not nature reserves in the true sense, they do have limited wildlife and bird populations and are useful stopping-off spots for those travelling to or from Etosha, or other northern reserves.

Daytime temperatures in this summer-rainfall area are often high, although nights are mild. Winter days are usually mild, but nights are often cold.

330   HARDAP RECREATION RESORT

Location: Southern Namibia; north of Mariental.
Access: From Mariental follow the B1 northwards in the direction of Windhoek for approximately 20 km; turn left at the signpost to the Hardap Recreation Resort and continue to the office. Internal roads are graded gravel and are in good condition.
Accommodation: 2-bed bungalows, each with a bathroom, but using communal cooking facilities; 5-bed bungalows, each with a bathroom and kitchen; 10-bed dormitory for youth groups. There is also a camping and caravan site.
Other facilities: A network of game-viewing roads; free-walking trails; a restaurant; shop;

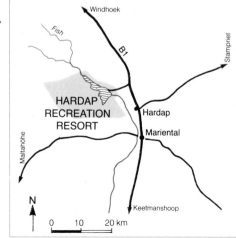

swimming pool; fuel; picnic sites; fishing (permits are available at the office).
Open: Throughout the year.
Opening time: Reserve – sunrise to sunset; rest camp – 24 hours.
For further information: Ministry of Wildlife, Conservation and Tourism (see page 365).

The Hardap Dam covers approximately 10 per cent of the total area of this 25 000-ha reserve and attracts a rich birdlife with more than 100 species, including a large population of white-breasted cormorants. The terrain consists mainly of plains covered with grass and thorny scrub, and rock outcrops.

A wide range of game species may be seen, including kudu, gemsbok, red hartebeest, black rhinoceros, springbok and Hartmann's mountain zebra.

331 KHAUDOM GAME RESERVE

Location: Extreme north-eastern Namibia; east of Grootfontein.
Access: From Grootfontein follow the B8 north-eastwards for 57 km; turn right onto the gravel C74 (C44) and travel eastwards for 222 km to Tsumkwe; at Tsumkwe head north and follow the signposts to the reserve. Beyond Tsumkwe the road becomes sandy and can only be negotiated by 4x4 vehicles. Tracks enter the reserve from the north and west, but it is advisable to consult the authorities before using these routes. The authorities currently insist on a minimum of 2 4x4 vehicles per group as the area is so isolated. No caravans or trailers are allowed.
Accommodation: There are 2 camps, Sikereti in the south and Khaudom in the north. Both have 4-bed huts, with communal facilities, and a camping site. Bookings must be made in advance and only 1 group is allowed per camp (maximum 12 persons per group).
Other facilities: Network of very sandy game-viewing tracks (remember that in heavy sand fuel use increases considerably). The nearest food and fuel supplies are available at Tsumkwe, Bagani, Mukwe and Rundu. Visitors must bring along enough food and water for all passengers for a minimum of 3 days, plus extra in case of a breakdown.
Open: Throughout the year.
Opening time: Sunrise to sunset.
Beware: Malaria; always remember to carry

sufficient water for your needs.
For further information: Ministry of Wildlife, Conservation and Tourism (see page 365).

Khaudom Game Reserve is one of the most recently proclaimed reserves in Namibia. A flat sandveld region with few prominent features, it covers 3 840 km^2 of wilderness within the dry savannah woodland of the northern Kalahari.

This is without doubt one of Namibia's finest game areas, particularly during the rainy season when animals are attracted into it by the presence of water, and the extensive areas of open grassland provide plentiful grazing.

The variety of wildlife to be found here is impressive: 64 mammal species, including herds of elephant, buffalo, giraffe, blue wildebeest, red hartebeest, tsessebe, roan, gemsbok, kudu and eland, as well as all the large predators.

The birdlife in the reserve is varied, and is probably at its best during the rainy season. No comprehensive list is, as yet, available. To date 26 reptile and 12 amphibian species have been recorded.

Summers are hot and rain can be expected during this time; winter days are warm to cool, but nights can be very cold.

332 KOKERBOOM FOREST See map Fish River Canyon Park

Location: Southern Namibia; north-east of Keetmanshoop.
Access: From Keetmanshoop travel in a north-eastward direction towards Koës for 14 km and then turn left to the Kokerboom Forest reserve.
Accommodation: None. There are 2 hotels and a municipal camping and caravan site in Keetmanshoop.
Other facilities: None.
Open: Throughout the year.
Opening time: Sunrise to sunset.
For further information: Ministry of Wildlife Conservation and Tourism (see page 365).

Situated on a private farm, the Kokerboom Forest was declared a national monument in the 1960s and is open to the public.
The 'forest' consists of an unusually dense stand of the giant aloe, *Aloe dichotoma*, known as the kokerboom or quiver tree.

333 LAKE OTJIKOTO See map Etosha National Park

Location: Northern Namibia; north of Tsumeb.
Access: From Tsumeb follow the B1 north-eastwards for 28 km. The lake lies just to the west of this road.
Accommodation: None. There are hotels and a camping and caravan site in Tsumeb.
Other facilities: None.
Open: Throughout the year.
Opening time: Sunrise to sunset.
For further information: Ministry of Wildlife, Conservation and Tourism (see page 365).

A sunken lake of great depth which was formed when the roof of a large dolomite cave collapsed, Lake Otjikoto is home to the very rare, blind cave catfish. This fish only comes to the surface at night, so fish seen during the day are likely to be bream, which have apparently been introduced to the lake.
Although it is not a reserve as such, the lake makes an interesting stop on the main route to Etosha National Park.

334 MAHANGO GAME RESERVE See map Caprivi Game Park

Location: Extreme north-eastern Namibia; north-east of Grootfontein.
Access: From Grootfontein take the B8 in a north-eastward direction and travel for 255 km to Rundu; at Rundu turn right and follow the gravel road eastwards in the direction of Katima Mulilo; after 227 km (just before Bagani) follow signposts to Popa Falls and Botswana; continue for 25 km to the Mahango Game Reserve's entrance gate. The road to and through the reserve is usually in a reasonable condition, but other internal roads are suitable only for 4x4 vehicles, and are almost impassable during the rains. The reserve can also be reached from Shakawe in Botswana. Permits are required and are available at the gate.
Accommodation: None. Popa Falls Rest Camp, situated 19 km from the entrance to the reserve, has self-catering accommodation and is run by the Ministry of Wildlife, Conservation and Tourism. Suclabo, a privately owned rustic camp situated 17 km from the entrance to the reserve, offers a limited number of basic huts and a camping site with ablution facilities.
Other facilities: A limited network of sandy tracks. Fuel is usually available at the turn-off to Mahango just before Bagani; other supplies can be obtained at Rundu or Katima Mulilo.
Open: Throughout the year.
Opening time: 07h30 to 17h00.
Beware: Malaria; bilharzia; crocodiles in Okavango River.
For further information: Ministry of Wildlife, Conservation and Tourism (see page 365). (Suclabo Camp) Suzy Gollwitzer, Suclabo Camp, Rundu 6222.

148. A large colony of Cape fur seals is protected at Cape Cross.

149. The strange welwitschia grows on the gravel plains near the Brandberg.

150. Huts at the popular Daan Viljoen Game Park.

151. Elephant ponder the waterhole adjacent to Okaukuejo camp in the Etosha Pan National Park. The hole is floodlit at night.

152. Lion are often seen or heard at Etosha, particularly in the more open grassland that fringes the pan.

153. Accommodation is provided at Fort Namutoni, Etosha.

154. Klipspringer are often seen bounding up steep rocky slopes in the Fish River Canyon.

155. Ai-Ais Hot Springs provide comfortable and varied accommodation for visitors to the Fish River Canyon Park.

156. Gemsbok flee a storm in the Khomas Hochland, at the edge of the Namib-Naukluft Park.

157. A rock fig on the Waterberg Plateau, its white stem and roots clinging fast to the rock.

158. Thousands of waterbirds are attracted to the rich environment of Sandwich Harbour, in the Namib-Naukluft Park.

159. A ranger accompanies hikers through the Waterberg Plateau Park.

Only recently proclaimed, the Mahango Game Reserve covers an area of approximately 30 000 ha on Namibia's border with northern Botswana. Despite its relatively small size, it protects an amazingly diverse animal and plant life. Its eastern boundary is formed by the Okavango River, and extensive reed and papyrus beds, as well as areas of grassland cover its flood plain. A narrow belt of riverine woodland lines the river bank, while broad-leafed woodland and large, open areas of grassland cover the rest.

More than 60 mammal species have been recorded here, including hippopotamus, elephant, tsessebe, oribi, common duiker, steenbok, roan, sable, buffalo, kudu, bushbuck, sitatunga, lechwe, reedbuck, blue wildebeest and warthog. Lion, leopard, cheetah, wild dog and both brown and spotted hyenas represent the predators. Among the smaller species, Cape clawless otter may be seen at the river, and troops of banded mongoose are active throughout the reserve. A large number of bird species occur, but no formal list has yet been compiled. Fifteen lizard and eight snake species have also been recorded.

Summer days are hot in this region, and rain falls at this time of year; winter days are warm to cool, but nights are cold.

335 MAMILI GAME RESERVE See regional map

Location: Extreme north-eastern Namibia; eastern Caprivi.
Access: The internal road network is poor; prospective visitors should contact the Ministry of Wildlife, Conservation and Tourism in Windhoek, or the local office in Katima Mulilo before contemplating a visit. Three safari companies currently operate in the area: Kalizo Safaris, Afro Ventures Safaris and Wilderness Safaris.
Accommodation: Tented camps run by Kalizo Safaris.

Other facilities: None, except with safari companies.
Open: Throughout the year but movement is severely restricted during summer rains.
Beware: Malaria; potentially dangerous game including lion and buffalo.
For further information: Ministry of Wildlife, Conservation and Tourism (see page 365). Kalizo Safaris, Tel: (011) 886-4067. Wilderness Safaris (see page 366). Afro Ventures Safaris (see page 366).

The Mamili Game Reserve covers 35 500 ha, which encompasses most of the magnificent Linyanti Swamp. In our opinion, this is one of the most fascinating areas in southern Africa and it is hoped that the authorities do not allow it to be spoilt by over-development. During the dry season islands of trees such as apple-leaf and wild date palms are ringed by open, grassy flats but during the rains these islands are surrounded by water. The Linyanti River and a network of hippo channels hold water throughout the year. Elephant, hippopotamus, red lechwe, sitatunga, lion, spotted hyena, leopard and hunting dog occur. The birdlife is a major attraction, with such species as wattled crane, fish eagle, swamp boubou, collared palm thrush, Bradfield's hornbill, Pel's fishing eagle, white-crowned plover and slaty egret. This area can be uncomfortably hot and humid in the summer.

336 MOUNT ETJO SAFARI LODGE

Location: Central Namibia; north of Windhoek.
Access: From Windhoek follow the B1 northwards for approximately 210 km and turn left onto the D2483 to Kalkfeld. The Mount Etjo Safari Lodge lies to the north of the road and is clearly signposted. An airstrip is situated near the reserve.
Accommodation: The lodge has rooms, each with a private bathroom. Advance bookings are essential.
Other facilities: A swimming pool; conducted game-viewing walks; game-viewing drives in open vehicles; hides at waterholes (including a tree-top hide).

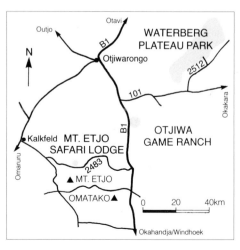

Open: Throughout the year.
For further information: Mount Etjo Safari

Lodge, P.O. Box 81, Kalkfeld 9000, Namibia.
Tel: (06532) 1602.

This game farm, set in an area of mixed woodland and grassland, has a number of dams and waterholes. A wide range of game species has been introduced, including elephant, white rhinoceros, roan antelope, kudu, gemsbok, impala, blesbok, red hartebeest, eland, and Hartmann's mountain and Burchell's zebras. Cheetah and leopard occur naturally in the area. Summers are hot; winter nights can be cold.

337 MUDUMU GAME RESERVE See regional map

Location: Extreme north-eastern Namibia; eastern Caprivi.
Access: Prospective private visitors should contact the Ministry of Wildlife, Conservation and Tourism in Windhoek, or the local office in Katima Mulilo before planning a visit. Kalizo Safaris, Afro Ventures Safaris and Wilderness Safaris operate in Mudumu. Charter flights to Lianshulu can be arranged.
Accommodation: Wildlife Safaris and Afro Ventures Safaris operate *Lianshulu Lodge*: twin-bedded thatched A-frame chalets with *en-suite* facilities (maximum 16 people) and communal bar and dining area (R250 per person per day all inclusive, except alcohol). Kalizo

Safaris operate *Mvubu Camp* which has 6 fully equipped, 2-man cottage-style tents.
Other facilities: Accompanied game-viewing drives, walks and boat trips. As this is a developing reserve, you are advised to contact the conservation authorities or one of the safari operators.
Open: Check with authorities.
Beware: Malaria; potentially dangerous game such as buffalo, crocodiles and elephant.
For further information: Ministry of Wildlife, Conservation and Tourism (see page 365). Wilderness Safaris (see page 366). Kalizo Safaris Tel: (011) 886-4067. Afro Ventures Safaris (see page 366).

Mudumu, which covers 85 000 ha, has its western boundary on the Kwando River, feeding into the Linyanti swamp. Apart from riverine woodland and reedbeds, there are extensive areas dominated by mopane and other tree species. Elephant, buffalo, kudu, sable, hippopotamus, warthog, bushpig, lion, leopard, spotted hyena and wild dog occur. Bird life is richest in the riverine belt. Although summers are hot and humid, winters are generally mild but nights can be cold.

338 NAMIB-NAUKLUFT PARK

Location: Namib Desert; west of Windhoek.
Access: From Windhoek take the C52 (C28) westwards towards Swakopmund; this road passes through the northern sector of the reserve. Alternatively, the C36 (C14) from Walvis Bay also passes through the reserve to the south of the C52 (C28). From Mariental in the south, take the C34 (C19) westwards to Maltahöhe and join the graded gravel C36 (C19); after 160 km there is a left turn to Sesriem camping site, and 20 km beyond it a right to the Naukluft sector of the park. Permits are not required for any of the above public roads, but are necessary for the internal road network in the north. They can be obtained at Hardap or Sesriem, tourist offices in Swakopmund, Lüderitz or Windhoek, or at weekends from Charly's Desert Tours or Hans Kriess Service Station in Swakopmund, and from Troost Transport, Namib Ford or CWB service stations in Walvis Bay. Internal roads, while they can be badly

corrugated, are suitable for most vehicles, with the exception of the road from Walvis Bay to Sandwich Harbour, which requires a 4x4 vehicle as do the last 4 km to Sossusvlei.
Accommodation: *Naukluft camping site* has 4 stands with ablution facilities, water and firewood; groups are only allowed to stay overnight. *Sesriem camping site* has 18 camping and caravan stands with ablution facilities. There are basic camping sites at Kuiseb Bridge, Homeb, Kriess-se-rus, Vogelfederberg, Bloedkoppie, Groot Tinkas, Ganab and Mirabib in the northern sector, with minimal facilities; take all water and supplies. Swakopmund and Walvis Bay have a number of hotels, holiday chalets and camping sites.
Other facilities: Walking is permitted in the northern part of the park as well as Sesriem and Sossusvlei; a 120-km walking trail in the Naukluft sector must be booked in advance from Windhoek only. Fuel is available at Ses-

riem but otherwise this and food must be purchased at Walvis Bay, Swakopmund and Maltahöhe.
Open: Throughout the year.
Opening time: Public roads – 24 hours; internal roads – sunrise to sunset.
Beware: Carry adequate water and food supplies in case of a breakdown; always carry a compass and a sketch map (which can be obtained from the permit offices in Windhoek and Swakopmund) when walking, as it is very easy to lose one's bearings.
For further information: Ministry of Wildlife, Conservation and Tourism (see page 365).

The 23 400-km² Namib-Naukluft Park, together with the adjoining 'Diamond Area', forms one of southern Africa's largest blocks of conservation and, although only a small part of this vast desert reserve is accessible to the general public. Most of the area south of the Kuiseb River consists of a vast 'sea' of sand dunes, separated by flat inter-dune valleys. Between the Swakop and Kuiseb rivers lies a great gravel-covered plain, with a scattering of rocky outcrops and hill ranges. A number of dry, but wooded, river beds run through the western area, and only contain water on a few occasions each century. A portion of the Naukluft Mountains falls within the park, on the eastern side of the southern sector. At Sesriem there is an impressive water-worn gorge with interesting rock formations, and at Sossusvlei there are high sand dunes (reputedly the highest in the world) and between them, large shallow hollows which fill with water during the rains.

As might be expected, vegetation is sparse, particularly in the sand dunes and on the gravel plains. However, ancient welwitschias grow on the Welwitschia Flats north of the Swakop River and near the camping site at Homeb on the Kuiseb River; these unique and fascinating plants are among the oldest in the world. Euphorbias and a variety of low trees survive on the rocky hills. Large camel thorn trees grow along many dry river beds, and on the banks of the Kuiseb and Swakop rivers, where fine examples of ana trees and wild fig trees can also be seen.

Gemsbok, springbok and Hartmann's zebra occur widely in the park, but most concentrate in the better-vegetated eastern plains, and gemsbok are frequently seen in the Kuiseb Canyon where there are pools of water throughout the year. Klipspringer, steenbok and baboon are a common sight along the courses of the Kuiseb and Swakop rivers. Black-backed jackal are common, and leopard and both brown and spotted hyenas also occur. There are many smaller animals, including many lizard and snake species and a great variety of insects, all highly adapted to this desert land. The best areas for birdwatching are the beds of the two main rivers and the Ganab waterhole, but watch out in other areas for such species as Herero chat, Gray's lark, dune lark, Monteiro's hornbill and Rüppell's korhaan. Sandwich Harbour is a veritable bird paradise and well worth a visit for those with a 4x4 vehicle.

Away from the coast, summer days can be very hot and nights mild. Winter days can be pleasant, but temperatures may drop drastically after sunset. Rainfall in this area is very low, but the chances of showers and thunderstorms increases towards the escarpment in the north-east.

339 OANOB DAM NATURE RESERVE

Location: Central Namibia; north-west of Mariental.
Access: From Mariental follow the B1 north-

wards to Rehoboth; from there take the D1237 north-westwards and drive 1,5 km to the entrance gate.

Accommodation: None at present; a camping and caravan site is planned. The nearby Reho Spa has self-catering accommodation and a camping and caravan site.
Other facilities: A picnic area is being developed; existing tracks will be upgraded.
Open: Throughout the year.
Opening time: Contact the authority.
For further information: The College Head, Tsumis Agricultural College, P.O. Box 145, Kalkrand 9000.

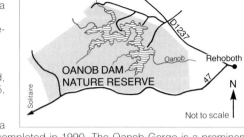

This recently proclaimed reserve covers 7 080 ha and incorporates the Oanob Dam, which was completed in 1990. The Oanob Gorge is a prominent feature and much of the eastern area of the reserve consists of rugged, broken country. The vegetation contains elements of highland savannah and dwarf shrub savannah, and game species include kudu, eland, gemsbok, springbok and Hartmann's mountain zebra.

---

340 OTJIWA GAME RANCH See map Mount Etjo Safari Lodge

Location: Northern Namibia; between Okahandja and Otjiwarongo.
Access: Lies adjacent to the B1, between Okahandja and Otjiwarongo. Book in advance.
Accommodation: *Main camp* has 4-person park homes; two exclusive camps, *Hilltop* and *The Nest*, are self-contained and each can accommodate up to 8 people.

Other facilities: Walking trails (accompanied) game-viewing drives; horse-riding; restaurant swimming pool.
Open: Throughout the year.
Opening time: Check when booking.
For further information: Namib-Sun Hotels P.O. Box 2862, Windhoek, Namibia. Tel: (061) 3-3145. Fax: (061) 3-4512.

Otjiwa Game Ranch is located in typical northern Namibian thornveld and 28 game species are present including white rhinoceros, kudu, eland, gemsbok, Burchell's zebra and waterbuck.

---

341 SKELETON COAST PARK

Location: Coastal Namibia; north of Swakopmund.
Access: From Swakopmund follow the C44 (C34) northwards to Henties Bay; continue past Henties Bay on the D2301 (C34) and then on the D2302 (C34) to the entrance gate at the Ugab River. From Henties Bay the road is salt and is usually in good repair. Alternatively, from Khorixas follow the D2620 (C39) westwards and turn left onto the D3245 (C39) to Torra Bay. This road is graded gravel but is often corrugated in sections. Permits or accommodation receipts are required.
Accommodation: *Terrace Bay* has rooms, each with a bathroom; the all-inclusive tariffs include 3 meals a day and freezer space. Book well in advance. *Torra Bay* has a camping and caravan site. Skeleton Coast Fly-In Safaris runs 5-day fly-in safaris from a tented camp in the

Khumib River valley; this is the only means of visiting the northern section of the park.
Other facilities: Accompanied 3-day hiking trail starting at Ugab River crossing (book well in advance; 6 to 8 persons only; recent medical certificate required); fishing from the beach shops selling basic supplies and a restaurant at Terrace Bay; fuel at Terrace Bay and Torra Bay.
Open: Throughout the year; Torra Bay – 1 December to 31 January only.
Opening time: Southern entrance (Ugab River) – sunrise to 15h00; northern entrance (Springbokwasser) – sunrise to 17h00.
For further information: Ministry of Wildlife Conservation and Tourism (see page 365) (Skeleton Coast Fly-In Safaris) P.O. Box 2195, Windhoek 9000. Tel: (061) 22-4248 or 5-1269. Fax: (061) 22-5713 or 5-2125.

The Skeleton Coast Park is situated in the Namib Desert and covers approximately 16 900 km². Stretching from the Ugab River in the south to the Kunene River on the Angolan border in the north, this narrow strip is nowhere more than 40 km wide. To the uninitiated it is a barren, lifeless moonscape, with its sand dunes, gravel plains and beaches, but for the more interested visitor there is highly adapted plant and animal life to be observed.

The land to the north of the Hoanib River is a wilderness area and is closed to the public. This is a cool desert, although it can be very hot in summer. The 'life-blood' of the Namib Desert is the fog that rolls in from the Atlantic Ocean and provides moisture for the plants, desert-adapted insects and other organisms, such as spiders and scorpions. The northern part of the park is home, at times, to elephants which have adapted to the desert, and also to black rhinoceros which live around the river beds at the fringe of this wilderness. Other species that occur in the park are giraffe, Hartmann's mountain zebra, kudu, springbok, gemsbok, lion and cheetah. Brown hyena and black-backed jackal scavenge on the beaches and there are several lizard species which are only found in this desert environment. Birdlife is abundant, particularly along the river courses.

To the south, and in complete contrast to other parts of the park, is the mouth of the Uniab River, with its freshwater environment and reed beds, and the large numbers of waterbirds associated with them. One of the most interesting plant features of this part of the park are the large 'gardens' of lichens that occur on the gravel plains.

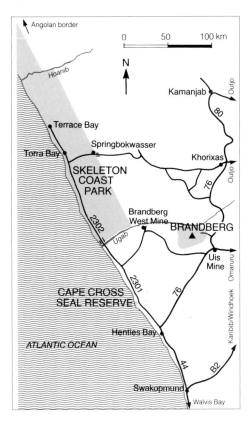

| 342 | **TSAOBIS LEOPARD NATURE PARK** |

Location: Khomas Hochland; west of Windhoek.

Access: From Windhoek follow the B2 towards Swakopmund; at Karibib take the C32 (G77) towards Anschluss and Otjimbingwe. Once on the gravel road outside Karibib, ignore the left turn to Otjimbingwe and follow the C32 (G77) south to the Swakop river for about 52 km. The Tsaobis Leopard Nature Park is 10 km from the main road on the south bank of the river and is signposted. No private vehicles are allowed on internal roads.

Accommodation: 10 fully equipped bungalows with bedding. Booking and deposit are essential. No pets allowed.

Other facilities: A swimming pool; unaccompanied walks; tours of the park are available by prior arrangement only. The nearest food and fuel supplies are at Karibib which is 60 km away.

Open: Throughout the year.

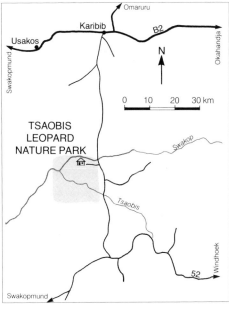

Opening time: 24 hours.
For further information: Tsaobis Leopard

Nature Park, P.O. Box 143, Karibib 9000.
Tel: (062252) 1304. Fax: (061) 3-3690.

Covering 35 000 ha of rugged mountainous country, this park was established in 1969 as a sanctuary for leopard. Because of their mainly nocturnal habits, these predators are seldom seen, but other game species such as springbok, kudu, gemsbok and Hartmann's mountain zebra will be more readily observed. The birdlife is interesting and includes a number of different species which are endemic to arid areas.

Summer days are hot and nights are mild. Winter days are mild, but nights may be cold. This is a low-rainfall area and the little rain that occurs usually falls between October and April.

343 WALVIS BAY NATURE RESERVE See map Namib-Naukluft Park

Location: Namib Desert; south of Walvis Bay.
Access: From Walvis Bay the road south towards Sandwich Harbour passes through the reserve; a 4x4 vehicle is necessary.
Accommodation: None. There are hotels and a camping and caravan site in Walvis Bay.

Other facilities: Fishing from the beach; hiking trails are planned.
Open: Throughout the year.
For further information: The Directorate of Nature and Environmental Conservation, Cape Town (see page 365). (Reserve) P.O. Box 94, Walvis Bay 9190. Tel: (0642) 5971/2.

Situated within the Walvis Bay enclave, this 45 000-ha reserve is politically a part of the Cape Province of South Africa and it falls under the jurisdiction of the Directorate of Nature and Environmental Conservation, Cape Province. It encompasses the Walvis Bay lagoon and the delta of the Kuiseb River, and certain commercial practices, such as the evaporation of sea water to collect salt, are allowed to be carried out within its boundaries.

One of southern Africa's most important wetland habitats, Walvis Bay Nature Reserve forms a link on the route of many migratory birds. During the summer months more than 100 000 birds of 40 species inhabit the area, and many other species live here permanently.

344 WATERBERG PLATEAU PARK

Location: Northern Namibia; north-east of Windhoek.
Access: From Windhoek follow the B1 northwards for approximately 200 km before turning right onto the C101 (C22); continue along this road for about 42 km, then turn left onto a gravel road and travel for another 26 km to the entrance to the park.
Accommodation: Overnight huts for trailists only; camp with hutted accommodation (5-bed chalets with stove and refrigerator, 3-bed bungalows with stove and refrigerator, 2-bed tourisettes, all with bathrooms); camping site; check with the authorities for the latest information.
Other facilities: Accompanied 4-day trail between April and November (minimum 6 persons, maximum 8; book well in advance); daily guided tours to the plateau in special vehicles; restaurant; kiosk; swimming pool. The nearest food and fuel supplies are at Otjiwarongo.
Open: Throughout the year.
Opening time: Sunrise to sunset.

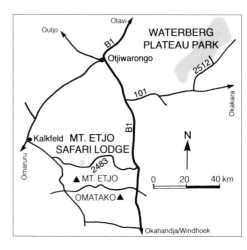

Beware: Malaria.
For further information: Ministry of Wildlife, Conservation and Tourism (see page 365).

A large, flat-topped plateau which has defied forces that eroded surrounding rock over millions of years, takes up most of the 40 000-ha Waterberg Plateau Park. It takes its name from the many springs of fresh water that are located around its base. The park's vegetation is predominantly woodland and grass savannah, with more open areas on the plateau and large trees growing around the springs. Many game species have been introduced or re-introduced to this scenic reserve, mainly on the plateau itself. These include white rhinoceros, buffalo, roan and sable antelope, eland, red hartebeest, blue wildebeest and impala. A wide range of smaller species were present in the area when the reserve was proclaimed and the patient observer may still see klipspringer, rock dassie and elephant shrew. A variety of birds inhabit the wood- and grassland, and a good place for birdwatching is at the springs. Cape vultures may be seen riding the early morning air thermals.

Rain falls in the summer months, between October and April, and temperatures often become uncomfortably high at this time. Winters are mild, but nights can be cold.

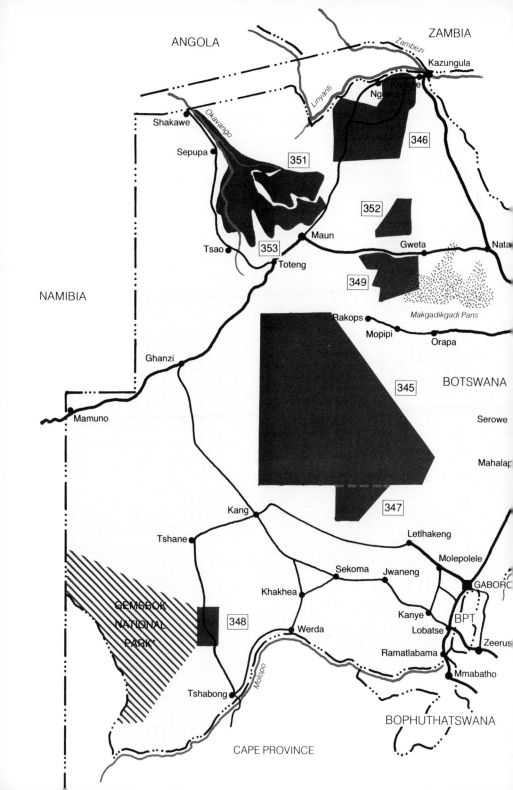

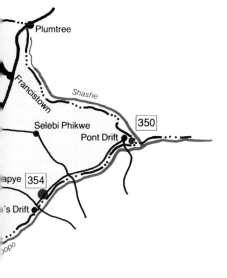

Plumtree

Shashe

Francistown

Selebi Phikwe 350
Pont Drift

apye 354

's Drift

opo

TRANSVAAL

N

100   200   300 km

BOTSWANA

345 Central Kalahari Game Reserve
346 Chobe National Park
347 Khutse Game Reserve
348 Mabuasehube Game Reserve
349 Makgadikgadi Pans Game Reserve
350 Mashatu Game Reserve
351 Moremi Wildlife Reserve
352 Nxai Pan National Park
353 Okavango Delta
354 Stevensford Private Game Reserve

A landlocked republic covering approximately 580 000 km^2, Botswana is bordered by Namibia to the north and west, by the Republic of South Africa to the south, and by Zimbabwe to the east. For a few hundred metres in the north-east, the country also shares a border with Zambia along the Caprivi Strip.

This is a land of great contrasts. Seventy per cent of the total surface area is covered by the vast, waterless Kalahari Desert, while to the north-west the Okavango River drains into the 15 000-km^2 Okavango Delta, the largest inland river delta in the world. The Delta is threatened by a new veterinary cordon fence and dredging to allow easier exploitation of water for mining and agriculture. Between these two extremes lie bare sand dunes, arid savannah, mopane wood-land, dry forest, riverine lushness and flood plains, all of which provide a wide range of habitats for a great variety of mammals, birds, reptiles and invertebrates.

Summers are hot to very hot, with temperatures reaching 38 °C. Most of the annual rainfall occurs

d to public

between November and April and is much higher in the north, often rendering many roads impassable. Winter daytime temperatures are usually warm, but nights can be bitterly cold and it is not unusual to wake up to frozen water bags and ice on the windscreen.

Botswana has several of the largest and most isolated game sanctuaries in southern Africa, most of which are situated in the north and west of the country, away from the more densely populated areas to the south. Until fairly recently vast herds of antelope (red hartebeest, blue wildebeest, springbok and eland) and Burchell's zebra moved freely and widely over much of the country, but the erection of veterinary cordon fences to control the spread of foot-and-mouth disease has resulted in the disruption of many of these seasonal migrations. However, none of the parks controlled by the Department of Wildlife and National Parks (see page 365) are fenced, and game can move freely between the conservation areas and adjacent land. The Gemsbok National Park, in the south-western corner of the country, adjoins South Africa's Kalahari Gemsbok National Park, and is in part administered by the National Parks Board. Only the bed of the Nossob River separates the two parks, and animals can roam unhindered from one to the other. The Botswanan park is, however, closed to the public.

Facilities in the parks are minimal or even nonexistent, and prospective visitors who prefer to be independent must be prepared to 'rough it'. The alternative, particularly in the Okavango Delta and in the western part of the Chobe National Park, is to put yourself in the hands of one of the many safari operators that maintain permanent camps here. (A list of these companies can be found under the appendix 'Safari Operators'.) However, rates at many of these camps are high and booking is essential.

For those visitors who intend to go it alone – be prepared! Most roads are only suitable for 4x4 vehicles and in some areas it is wise to travel in a convoy of at least two vehicles in case of a breakdown or accident. Even the main road between Nata and Maun, which can be used by most vehicles, is very rough and sandy in parts. Fuel, water and general supply points are few and far between and it is not unusual to find garages without fuel stocks. It is advisable to carry a full set of tools and spares and to have a level of mechanical knowledge, as the nearest garage may be several hundred kilometres away and on some tracks you may sit for weeks before another vehicle comes your way. Always carry a good supply of water (for drinking as well as for the vehicle) as surface water is rare, except in the north. If you do use surface water for drinking, it must be boiled or chemically treated. Winter temperatures can drop to well below freezing at night, so remember to take anti-freeze for the vehicle's cooling system.

Lion are still common in some areas, and it is wise to take precautions against large predators in the major game areas. Camping areas are rarely fenced, and visitors are cautioned not to sleep under the stars, despite the romantic appeal. Even when sleeping inside a tent, remember to close firmly all flaps.

Strict regulations have recently been instituted in all national parks and game reserves run by the Department of Wildlife and National Parks, and there are heavy penalties for disregarding these rules. Within most of the parks only 4x4 vehicles are allowed on the roads, except when special permission has been obtained from the warden. Driving at night is forbidden and you must not get out of your vehicle, except at designated sites; nor should you leave the demarcated tracks. The official speed limit within all parks and reserves is 40 km/h. In most reserves camping is allowed only at designated sites and a permit must be obtained to occupy a site.

If travelling with a privately organised tour, an adult will be charged a fee of P50 per day on entering the park, and a further P20 per day for a camping site. Travellers on a tour organised by operators registered, based and licensed in Botswana will pay much lower fees. Rates are reduced for children between eight and 16; there is no charge for children under seven. An additional fee of P10 per day is payable for each vehicle registered outside Botswana (P2 for a vehicle registered in Botswana) and P5 per day for boats (other than canoes or dugouts which are free) being brought into the park or reserve. The unit of currency in Botswana is the pula.

Visitors to Botswana need a valid passport. South African and Commonwealth nationals do not require a visa, but other nationalities may have to obtain one before entering the country.

345 | CENTRAL KALAHARI GAME RESERVE

Location: Central Botswana; north-west of Gaborone.
Accommodation: None.

Other facilities: None.
Open: Limited access is now allowed under permit. Wilderness Safaris offer occasional

birdwatching safaris to Deception Pan in the north-eastern sector of this reserve, and other safari companies sometimes arrange visits. **For further information**: Wilderness Safaris, South Africa (see page 366).

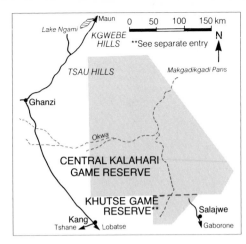

This 51 800-km^2 game reserve is still inhabited by groups of Bushmen and for this reason only limited public access is allowed. Apart from this and occasional tours (see above), only bona fide scientists are allowed access, and then only under exceptional circumstances. Severe penalties are imposed on anyone found in the area without permission.

The game reserve contains large herds of blue wildebeest, red hartebeest, eland, gemsbok and springbok, as well as lion, cheetah, leopard, wild dog, and both spotted and brown hyenas.

---

346 CHOBE NATIONAL PARK

Location: Northern Botswana; north-west of Francistown.

Access: From Francistown follow the main road north-westwards for about 495 km towards Kazungula; just before Kazungula take the signposted turn-off to Kasane village and follow this road to the reserve. If approaching from Victoria Falls in Zimbabwe, follow the main road westwards to the border control at Kazungula and continue westwards to Kasane village. Alternatively, from north-eastern Namibia travel through the Caprivi Strip to Katima Mulilo and turn right to Ngoma passport control; visitors taking this route must continue eastwards through the park to report to border authorities at Kasane or Kazungula. These routes can be negotiated by ordinary vehicles. An alternative route for 4x4 vehicles is from Maun: drive north-eastwards for 138 km to Mababe Gate. This road is closed during the rainy season. The all-weather road between Sedudu and Ngoma Gate is suitable for most vehicles, but in all other sections of the park the roads are generally very sandy and can only be negotiated by 4x4 vehicles. There are landing strips for light aircraft at Kasane, Savuti and Linyanti. A permit must be obtained from the warden and a fee paid to enter the park.

Accommodation: Several privately owned safari camps operate at Savuti and Linyanti, offering luxury tented accommodation. The Chobe Safari Lodge at Kasane has chalets and a camping and caravan site. The luxury Chobe Game Lodge is situated a short distance from Kasane, just inside the park. There are 4 public camping sites: Savuti, Serondela, Nogatsaa and Tshinga. Savuti and Serondela have basic ablution facilities, but there are no facilities at Nogatsaa and Tshinga. Camping is not allowed elsewhere in the park.

Other facilities: Fishing is permitted at Bushbuck Drive, Puku Flats and Serondela camping site (permits are required for this and can be obtained at Kasane office); a store selling liquor and a bar at Chobe Safari Lodge. Petrol and diesel and most supplies are available at Kasane. Clive Walker Trails conduct the Chobe section of their guided Fish Eagle Trail (Okavango/Chobe) from a mobile camp at Savuti.

Open: The northern area of the park is open throughout the year, but movement can be difficult during the rains.

Opening time: 06h00 to 18h00.

Beware: Malaria; crocodiles and other potentially dangerous animals; do not drive at night.

For further information: The Warden, Department of Wildlife and National Parks, Kasane (see page 365). (Chalets and camping site) Chobe Safari Lodge, P.O. Box 10, Kasane. Chobe Game Lodge, P.O. Box 32, Kasane. (Fish Eagle Trail) Clive Walker Trails, P.O. Box 645, Bedfordview 2008. Tel: (011) 453-7645/6/7. Fax: (011) 453-7649.

Chobe was proclaimed a game reserve in 1961 and raised in status to a national park in 1968. It covers an area of approximately 12 000 km^2 and is bordered in the east by large blocks of forest reserve. This vast park is for the most part flat and featureless, except for the minor Gubatsaa and Gcoha Hills in the south-west and the Mababe Depression and Magwikhwe Sand Ridge south of Savuti. There are a number of natural pans in the park, but these are dry for most of the year and the only surface water during the dry season is supplied by the Chobe and Linyanti rivers in the north and north-west, and by waterholes at Savuti, Nogatsaa, Tshinga and Ngwezumba Dam. Some other pans, particularly in the north-east, hold water for at least part of the dry season. Large areas of the park are covered by mopane and mixed woodland, including kiaat and Zimbabwe teak trees; there are belts of acacia trees, particularly in the south. These woodlands are interspersed with extensive areas of grassland. The Chobe River is fringed by an open, grass-covered flood plain, with a narrow band of riverine forest that has, to a large extent, been destroyed by elephants.

Chobe is, in fact, the domain of the elephant. To watch herds moving out of the woodland in the evenings to slake their thirst in the Chobe River, or a grey giant treading carefully between a tent and vehicle to reach leaves or pods on a shade tree, is an unforgettable experience. Buffalo herds, several hundred strong, are a common sight on the Puku Flats, while white rhinoceros, introduced from the Zululand reserves, may be seen near the Chobe River. Small herds of lechwe can be observed close to the river and this is also the only area south of the Zambezi River where puku (an antelope restricted to flood plains) can be seen. The visitor may see sable, roan, tsessebe, oribi, impala, blue wildebeest, eland, waterbuck, reedbuck, kudu, and the Chobe bushbuck, whose colouring is brighter than that of bushbucks further south. Giraffe is another resident species of the park, and warthog are a common sight on the flood plain. Lion occur throughout Chobe, but are most frequently seen in the Savuti area, and wild dog, spotted hyena, leopard and cheetah may also be observed. Smaller mammal species include troops of banded mongoose and tree squirrels at Serondela, and baboon and vervet monkey

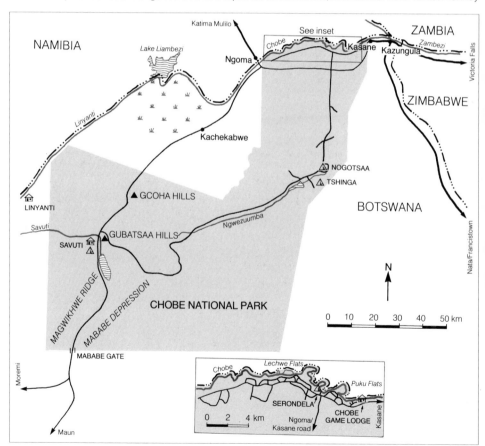

troops near the Chobe River. Hippopotamus and crocodiles are common in the northern rivers and care should be taken close to the river bank.

This park is a birdwatcher's paradise, with more than 350 species having been recorded in the area. Birding is particularly rewarding in the vicinity of the Chobe and Linyanti rivers, and such species as saddle-billed stork, long-toed plover, pink-backed pelican, fish eagle, African skimmer, Bradfield's hornbill, Sousa's shrike, carmine bee-eater and Heuglin's robin can be seen.

347 KHUTSE GAME RESERVE

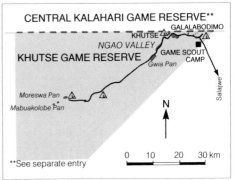

Location: Central Botswana; north-west of Gaborone.

Access: From Gaborone follow the main road north-westwards via Molepolole for approximately 240 km to the entrance. From Letlhakeng the road is sandy and only suitable for 4x4 vehicles. The internal road system is very limited. A permit must be obtained from the warden and a fee paid to enter the park.

Accommodation: 4 public camping sites: Galalabodimo, Khutse, Moreswa Pan and an unnamed one. There are no facilities. Camping elsewhere in the reserve is not permitted.

Other facilities: A borehole at Galalabodimo. It is advisable to carry sufficient fuel, water and all supplies from Gaborone.

Open: Throughout the year.

Opening time: Sunrise to sunset.

Beware: Malaria; watch out for potentially dangerous animals.

For further information: The Department of Wildlife and National Parks, Kasane (see page 365).

Khutse Game Reserve falls within the Central Kalahari bush savannah vegetational zone, and covers 2 590 km^2 of deep sand dotted with acacia and other tree species, with a sparse grass covering.

A feature of the area is the numerous small, open pans, many of which are bare, but others are covered by low shrubs and grass. These pans attract many mammal species, both large and small. All the major migratory antelope occur (eland, gemsbok, red hartebeest, springbok and blue wildebeest), as well as lion, cheetah, brown and spotted hyenas, and many smaller species, such as bat-eared fox, ground squirrel, yellow mongoose and suricate. The lack of surface water limits the number of bird species, but some interesting ones associated with arid areas (such as kori bustard, Burchell's, double-banded and bronze-winged coursers, Namaqua and Burchell's sandgrouse, and several lark species) can be seen.

The climate here is typical of the Kalahari, with very hot summers and occasional showers, and mild to cool winter days, with temperatures often falling to below freezing at night.

348 MABUASEHUBE GAME RESERVE

Location: South-western Botswana; north-west of Tshabong.

Access: From Tshabong follow the main road north-westwards for approximately 80 km to the southern border of the reserve. This road passes through the reserve and continues northwards to Tshane and Ghanzi. Roads are often sandy and corrugated, and can only be negotiated by 4x4 vehicles. If approaching from the northern Cape Province in South Africa on the R380, you must pass through the border post at Tshabong. For your own safety, it is recommended that you report your route to the police station at Tshabong. If exploring any of the western Kalahari areas it is advisable to travel in a convoy of at least 2 4x4 vehicles. A permit must be obtained from the warden and a fee paid to enter the park.

Accommodation: None.

Other facilities: None. Fuel and food supplies are available at Tshabong in the south and Ghanzi in the north.

Open: Throughout the year.

Opening time: Sunrise to sunset.

Beware: Malaria; potentially dangerous animals; it is easy to get lost in this type of environment – carry a compass and take plenty of water.

For further information: The Department of Wildlife and National Parks, Gaborone (see page 365).

Mabuasehube Game Reserve covers about 1 800 km^2 of harsh Kalahari Desert and contains five open pans – Mabuasehube, Khiding, Mpahutiwa, Monamodi and Bosobogola. Vegetation is sparse and consists mainly of scattered scrub and grass. The dominant game species are the migratory red hartebeest, blue wildebeest, gemsbok, eland and springbok, although numbers vary seasonally. Lion and other predators are well represented. Birdlife is typical of the Kalahari region and includes kori bustard, black korhaan, Namaqua sandgrouse, pale chanting goshawk and tawny eagle. Summers are very hot, with sporadic rainfall (usually less than 200 mm annually) and winter days are warm to cool, although nights can be very cold, with temperatures often falling to below freezing.

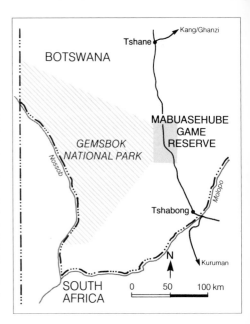

349 MAKGADIKGADI PANS GAME RESERVE

Location: Northern Botswana; west of Nata.

Access: From Nata follow the main road towards Maun for 103 km as far as Gweta; turn left onto a sandy track and travel southwards to the reserve. There are no signposts on this route. Alternatively, from Maun travel eastwards for 106 km and turn right at the signpost to the reserve. Both these routes are only suitable for 4x4 vehicles. The reserve can also be reached from the south. From Francistown drive north for approximately 5 km and turn left onto a rough gravel road to Orapa and Mopipi; continue past Mopipi on a narrow tar road for 29 km, then turn right; follow this track through Toromoja village and continue northwards to the reserve. This last stretch of road has no signposts and is only suitable for 4x4 vehicles. A permit must be obtained from the warden and an entrance fee paid.

Accommodation: None at present. There are plans to develop camping sites in the near future, one of which will be on the Boteti River. Maun and Gweta have hotels.

Other facilities: A network of game-viewing tracks; walking is permitted, but care should be taken as it is easy to become lost and there are lions and other large predators. Fuel is available at Maun, Gweta and Mopipi, although at Gweta and Mopipi the supply is not reliable and

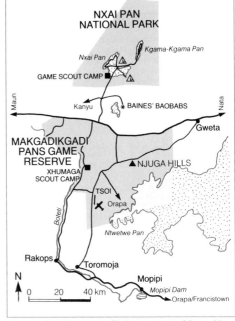

you should carry sufficient to get to Maun, Nata or Francistown.

Open: Throughout the year.
Opening time: Sunrise to sunset.
Beware: Malaria; potentially dangerous animals; keep to the main tracks and carry a compass, as it is easy to become lost.
For further information: The Department of Wildlife and National Parks, Gaborone (see page 365).

The Makgadikgadi Pans are made up of two huge salt pans, Ntwetwe and Soa, and their associated open grasslands. Only a small part of the north-western section of Ntwetwe Pan falls within the boundary of the unfenced 4 144-km² Makgadikgadi Pans Game Reserve, but there are numerous small pans scattered throughout the south and east of the park. The surface of the pans consists of a flat layer of sterile silt that turns into glue-like mud during the intermittent summer rains. One of the great attractions of this reserve is the huge areas of open grassland, although to the north of the park vegetable ivory palms, occurring either as isolated groves or as extensive belts, dominate the landscape. Acacia woodland is found to the west, particularly towards the Boteti River.

Game populations in this area are subject to considerable movement and migration, which is largely dictated by water and food supplies. During the dry season the herds tend to concentrate in the west, in the vicinity of the Boteti River, but with the onset of the rains the animals disperse to the east and north, to Nxai Pan and beyond. Migration routes to the Central Kalahari have been cut off by veterinary cordon fences. Red hartebeest, blue wildebeest, eland, gemsbok, springbok and Burchell's zebra are the most abundant species, and all of the large predatory species – lion, cheetah, leopard, wild dog and brown and spotted hyenas – are present. It is not an uncommon sight to see game far out on the open pans, where they eat the mineral-rich silt. A number of smaller mammals, such as black-backed jackal, bat-eared fox, yellow mongoose and ground squirrel, are common. Although not as abundant as the birdlife in the Okavango, bird species such as white-backed and lappet-faced vultures, bateleur, ostrich, kori bustard, black korhaan and bronze-winged courser can be seen here, as well as for sandgrouse species and many different larks. In years of good rains the pans form shallow lakes and pools, and vast numbers of waterbirds, such as flamingo, avocet and several duck species, move into the area. Soa Pan (access near Nata) is situated well to the east of the reserve, and when there is water it becomes a birdwatcher's paradise. Summers in this central region are very hot, with rain falling between November and April. Winter days are usually mild to warm, but nights are often bitterly cold.

350 MASHATU GAME RESERVE

Location: Far eastern Botswana; east of Pont Drift
Access: The most direct route is from South Africa: from Pietersburg follow the R521 north-westwards for 210 km to Pont Drift border post. Visitors are collected from the South African side of the border. This is a private reserve and casual visitors are not admitted.
Accommodation: Luxury all-inclusive accommodation at Majale Lodge; bush camps providing accommodation in luxury tents. Booking is essential.
Other facilities: Guided walking trails; game-viewing drives in open vehicles; night game-viewing with spotlight; swimming pool at Majale Lodge. Clive Walker Trails offer a relaxed guided 5-day trail (the Mashatu Ivory Trail) from a fully-equipped tented base camp along the Limpopo River (maximum 8 people per group; R940 per person, inclusive of food, transport ex Johannesburg and equipment; guests to supply own liquor requirements).
Open: Throughout the year.
Opening time: Pont Drift border post – 08h00 to 16h00.

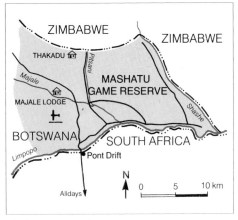

Beware: Malaria.
For further information: Rattray Reserves, P.O. Box 2575, Randburg 2125, South Africa. Tel: (011) 789-2677. Fax: (011) 886-4382. (Mashatu Ivory Trail) Clive Walker Trails, P.O. Box 645, Bedfordview 2008, South Africa. Tel: (011) 453-7645/6/7. Fax: (011) 453-7649.

The Mashatu Game Reserve lies at the eastern end of the Tuli Block in south-eastern Botswana, and is bounded in the east by the Shashe River and in the south by the Limpopo. Inhabited by the Maphungubwe tribe during the Iron Age, the area also had links with ancient Zimbabwean cultures and is of great archaeological interest.

The 30 000-ha reserve consists of narrow flood plains, low, rugged ridges and open plains. Water flows in its two great sand rivers, the Shashe and Limpopo, only when there have been good rains. The vegetation consists mainly of mopane and acacia woodland, grassland and a belt of riverine forest which contains, among other species, large fig trees, nyala berry (*mashatu*) and winterthorn.

Mashatu boasts the largest number of elephant on private land and, depending on the season and conditions, at least 600 may be present. They may be seen anywhere in the area, but during the dry season they come to the Limpopo River to drink at the pools. Other game species include impala, kudu, waterbuck, eland, bushbuck (particularly common along the Limpopo), warthog and a wide variety of small mammals. Large predators, such as lion, leopard, cheetah and spotted hyena, are present but in quite small numbers. Two members of the dassie family – the rock dassie and the yellow-spot dassie – live side by side on the rocky ridges at the confluence of the Shashe and Limpopo rivers. The reserve is also an excellent destination for the birdwatcher, with 375 species having been recorded.

From October to April it is hot in this area and the annual rains occur at this time; winters are cool to cold, although there can be some warm days.

351 MOREMI WILDLIFE RESERVE

Location: North-western Botswana; north of Maun.

Access: From Maun follow the track north-eastwards in the direction of Chobe National Park; after travelling 64 km turn left and then continue for another 34 km to the Moremi South Gate. Alternatively, from Savuti in the north, drive southwards, turn right at the signpost to the reserve and follow this track to Moremi North Gate. Both these routes require a 4x4 vehicle; the latter has long stretches of deep sand and is blocked in places by trees that have been pushed across the road by elephants. The internal roads are sandy. A permit must be obtained from the warden and an entrance fee paid.

Accommodation: A number of safari companies operate lodges and camps on the edge of the reserve, most of which are expensive (see appendix 'Safari Operators'). Booking for these is essential. There are 3 public camping sites, at South Gate, North Gate and Third Bridge. South Gate and North Gate camps have basic, and usually overworked, ablution facilities and tapped water, while Third Bridge has a few pit toilets and the only water source is the river.

Other facilities: Game-viewing drives. Boat trips can be made from Xakanaxa Camp near Third Bridge by arrangement with the safari operators. The nearest fuel and food supplies are at Maun.

Open: Throughout the year, but movement is severely limited in the rainy season and in very

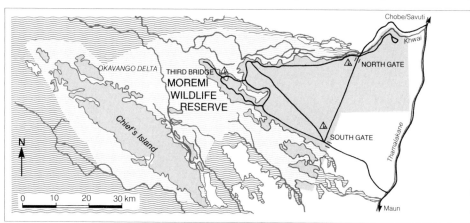

160. The communal nest of the sociable weaver can be seen in many parts of the Central Kalahari Game Reserve.

161. Motorists in the parks and reserves of Botswana can expect to drive along deep sand tracks such as this.

162. The Central Kalahari Game Reserve protects several carnivores, including black-backed jackal.

164. Vegetable ivory palms in the Makgadikgadi Pans Game Reserve.

163. On a flood plain at Moremi Wildlife Reserve saddle-billed storks search for food, unperturbed by a browsing giraffe.

165. Chobe bushbuck at Third Bridge, Moremi Wildlife Reserve.

166. Elephant at the Nogatsaa waterhole in Chobe National Park.

67. Red lechwe seldom stray far from the waters of the Okavango Delta.

68. Accommodation at the Delta Camp, Okavango Delta.

169. A waterhole in Moremi Wildlife Reserve attracts an array of waterfowl.

70. Campers at Third Bridge, Moremi, should be self-sufficient.

171. A 'mokoro' is the traditional vehicle in the Okavango Delta.

172. Even when the Okavango Delta is flooded, wooded islands remain above the water level.

173. A fish eagle in flight is one of the most stirring sights of the Okavango.

wet years is impossible; check road conditions before leaving Maun.
Opening time: Sunrise to sunset.
Beware: Malaria; bilharzia; crocodiles and other potentially dangerous animals.
For further information: The Department of Wildlife and National Parks, Maun (see page 365).

Moremi Wildlife Reserve is situated in the eastern sector of the Okavango Delta and was originally set aside as a sanctuary by the local Tawana tribe. The management of the reserve has since been taken over by the Department of Wildlife and National Parks.

Covering approximately 1 800 km², this unfenced reserve is completely flat, with a network of numerous waterways between reed beds and islands of mixed woodland. Most of the eastern woodland is composed of mopane, but elephants have damaged many of the trees. The South Gate camping site is located in mopane woodland, while the other public camping sites are situated alongside reeded waterways. Only the eastern half of Moremi is accessible to the public.

Although game species move freely between the Okavango Delta and the rest of northern Botswana, their movement to the south is limited by a veterinary cordon fence. It is estimated that as many as 30 000 elephant roam the Okavango Delta and Chobe to the east, and are a common sight in Moremi, particularly during the dry season. Hippopotamus are also common, but dense reed beds make viewing difficult; the best site is at Hippo Pool, 14 km west of North Gate camping site. Large herds of buffalo occur, as do warthog, tsessebe, kudu, impala, roan, reedbuck and waterbuck. Watch out for lechwe on the narrow flood plains, and at Third Bridge camping site there is a good chance of seeing Chobe bushbuck. Large baboon troops occur throughout the park. Predators are represented by lion, leopard and wild dog, as well as a host of largely nocturnal, smaller species such as serval, African wild cat and water mongoose. The routes to and from Moremi also produce sightings of game, particularly in the vicinity of South Gate. Approximately 300 bird species occur here and the area is particularly rich in waterbirds.

Summers are hot and humid, with the rains occurring at this time (October to April). Winters are warm, although nights can be cold.

352 NXAI PAN NATIONAL PARK

Location: Northern Botswana; north-west of Nata.
Access: From Nata follow the main road to Maun for 176 km; turn right at the signpost to Nxai Pan and travel for 18 km; at the 4-way stop continue straight across and drive 19 km to Game Scout Camp. This track is deep sand and only suitable for 4x4 vehicles. A permit must be obtained from the warden and an entrance fee paid.
Accommodation: There are 2 small public camping sites which have basic ablution facilities and water.
Other facilities: Game-viewing drives; walking is permitted, but it is easy to become lost. The nearest fuel and food supplies are at Maun.
Open: Throughout the year, but crossing the pan may prove difficult during the rains.
Opening time: Sunrise to sunset.
Beware: Malaria; potentially dangerous animals (the camps are not fenced).
For further information: The Department of Wildlife and National Parks, Gaborone (see page 365).

The old cattle trek route to Pandamatenga on the border with Zimbabwe used to pass right through

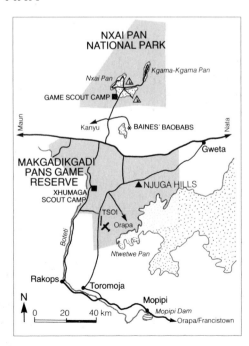

what is now the Nxai Pan National Park, and parts of it can still be seen in places. The 2 590-km^2 par consists mainly of open savannah woodland, acacia thickets and mopane woodland, with large area of open grassland. The scattered stands of acacias on the pan provide browse for giraffe, which ca often be seen feeding on them. Normally the best time for observing large game herds is during th summer at the onset of the rains. Red hartebeest, blue wildebeest, eland, springbok and Burchell' zebra are common at this time. Large numbers of giraffe are present throughout the year and sma numbers of elephant arrive from the north after the first rains have fallen. Lion are commonly heard an a wide variety of other predators, including cheetah, wild dog and brown and spotted hyenas, occu Kudu and impala are present in small numbers. Approximately 250 bird species can be expected in th area, including a variety of birds of prey, and ostrich are common.

353 OKAVANGO DELTA

Location: Northern Botswana; north-west of Maun.

Access: Maun is the main access point to the delta and it is from here that most safari companies collect their clients, some flying them from the airstrip at Maun to their bush camps deep in the delta. Dug-out canoes (*mekoro*) and other watercraft can be hired with guides for excursions.

Accommodation: There is a hotel in Maun. Privately run camps a short distance outside Maun on the road to Moremi offer chalet-type accommodation, camping sites, bars and eating facilities. Boats can be hired from here.

Safari companies offer all-inclusive camps, bu most are expensive.

Other facilities: Fishing; *mekoro* and othe boats for hire; game-viewing and walking ar permitted, but it is strongly recommended tha you make use of the services offered by one c the many companies operating from Maun an do not attempt to enter the delta unaccompar ied. The nearest food and fuel supplies ar available in Maun.

Beware: Malaria; bilharzia along the souther and western fringes of the delta; sleeping sick ness (tsetse fly); crocodiles, hippopotamu and other dangerous animals.

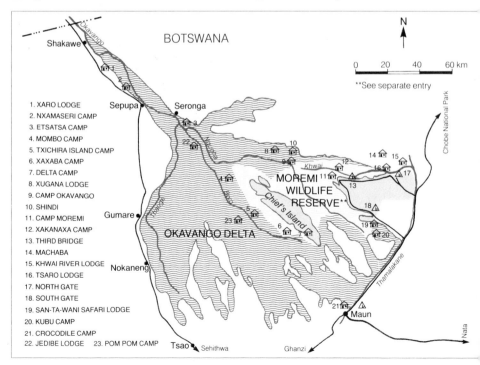

BOTSWANA

Shakawe

0   20   40   60 km

**See separate entry

Chobe National Park

1. XARO LODGE
2. NXAMASERI CAMP
3. ETSATSA CAMP
4. MOMBO CAMP
5. TXICHIRA ISLAND CAMP
6. XAXABA CAMP
7. DELTA CAMP
8. XUGANA LODGE
9. CAMP OKAVANGO
10. SHINDI
11. CAMP MOREMI
12. XAKANAXA CAMP
13. THIRD BRIDGE
14. MACHABA
15. KHWAI RIVER LODGE
16. TSARO LODGE
17. NORTH GATE
18. SOUTH GATE
19. SAN-TA-WANI SAFARI LODGE
20. KUBU CAMP
21. CROCODILE CAMP
22. JEDIBE LODGE 23. POM POM CAMP

Sepupa   Seronga

Gumare

Nokaneng

Tsao Sehithwa

OKAVANGO DELTA

MOREMI
WILDLIFE
RESERVE**

Chief's Island

Khwai

Maun

Ghanzi

Nata

Although only a small section of the Okavango Delta has been proclaimed a reserve (the Moremi Wildlife Reserve), the delta as a whole is nevertheless discussed here briefly because it is a unique and relatively unspoilt wilderness containing large populations of game. Moreover, the operations of a number of safari companies make it reasonably accessible to those interested in wildlife.

The Okavango Delta covers approximately 15 000 km^2 of crystal clear water, wooded islands, grass-covered flood plains and vast reed and papyrus beds. The richness and diversity of this area are probably best appreciated when travelling by boat along the channels. The few vehicle tracks that exist are better left to those familiar with the area, as it is very easy to get lost in this featureless landscape, and the tracks become impassable during the rainy season.

The wildlife in the delta is extremely varied and includes most of the species found in Moremi Wildlife Reserve and Chobe National Park. Hippopotamus are common, and from a boat on the waterways there is a chance of seeing the sitatunga, a rare swamp-dwelling antelope. The lechwe, another antelope adapted to an existence in marshy areas, also occurs here and is active mainly in the early morning and late afternoon.

Many people, however, visit the delta to observe its birdlife, as more than 400 species have been recorded here. The number of different species present is greatest between October and February, and wattled crane, Pel's fishing owl, slaty egret, Hartlaub's babbler, chirping cisticola and coppery-tailed coucal may be seen. Fish eagles are common and there are 16 species of herons, egrets and bitterns which occur. Although rarely seen except by the angler, the fish population is large and varied, and forms an integral part of the ecosystem.

In this northern part of Botswana summer temperatures are high during the day, and winter days are usually warm, although it becomes cold at night. Thunderstorms can occur in March and April and in October and November.

354 STEVENSFORD PRIVATE GAME RESERVE

Location: South-east Botswana; on the Limpopo River.
Access: Take the N1 northwards to Nylstroom; turn westwards on the R517 to Vaalwater; turn right at the NTK silos and continue to Melkrivier and Marken, continuing on to Baltimore, Marmitz, Tom Burke and Groblersbrug. This route is tarred and it is 252 km from Nylstroom to the border. On crossing the border continue for 10 km to Sherwood Ranch, then turn right onto the Bain's Drift road and follow it to the reserve entrance (14 km). Ordinary vehicles are suitable. Note: the border post is open from 08h00 to 18h00.
Accommodation: 6 thatched rondavels (4 with bathroom en suite), with 3 separate kitchen/cooking areas, and ablution facilities (hot and cold water); also tents to house 2 adults and 2 children. Apart from personal requirements and food/drink, everything is supplied. (Rondavels P60 per person per day, children up to the age of 12 - half price.)
Other facilities: Approximately 100 km of game-viewing roads (guided or self-guided); walking is encouraged; fishing (yellowfish, bream, barbel); horses and bicycles are available at a small charge; 3 hides at game drinking

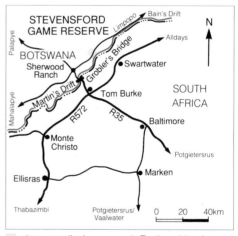

sites; small plunge pool. Fuel and basic supplies are available at Sherwood Ranch.
Open: Throughout the year.
Opening time: Daylight hours.
Beware: Malaria.
For further information: Stevensford Safaris, P.O. Box 26, Sherwood Ranch, Botswana or Phuti Travel, Gaborone. Tel: 31-4166.

Located on the north bank of the Limpopo River, the area consists of mixed woodland, with interesting trees along the river. Game that can be seen includes kudu, blue wildebeest, waterbuck, impala, bushbuck, red hartebeest, warthog and spotted hyena. A bird list is available (272 species).

C. CHIBWIKA-NTAMBU G.M.A.

D. CHISOMO G.M.A.

E. CHIZELA G.M.A.

F. KAFINDA G.M.A.

G. KAFUE FLATS G.M.A.

H. KALUANYEMBE G.M.A.

I. KAPUTA G.M.A.

J. KASONSO-BUSANGA G.M.A.

M. LUMIMBA G.M.A.

N. LUPANDE G.M.A.

O. LUWINGU G.M.A.

P. MACHIYA-FUNGULWE G.M.A.

Q. MANSA G.M.A.

R. MULOBEZI G.M.A.

S. MUMBWA G.M.A.

T. MUNYAMADZI G.M.A.

W. NAMWALA G.M.A.

X. RUFUNSA G.M.A.

Y. SANDWE G.M.A.

Z. SICHIFULO G.M.A.

AA. TONDWA G.M.A.

BB. WEST PETAUKE G.M.A.

CC. WEST ZAMBEZI G.M.A.

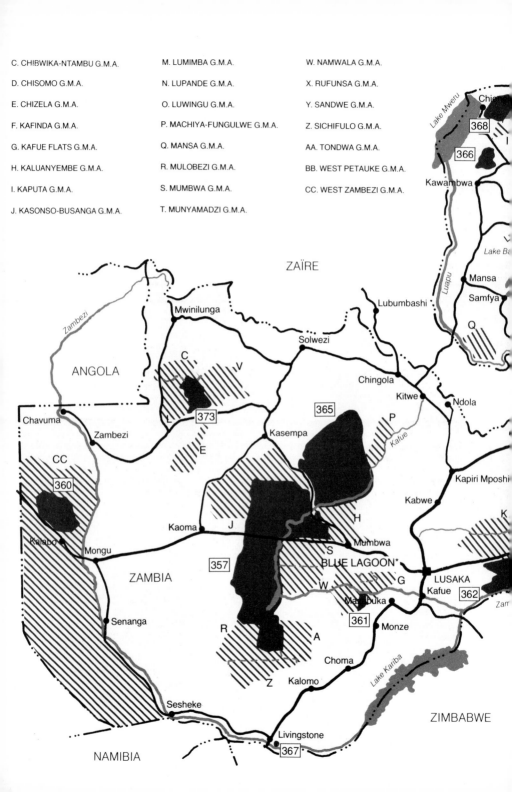

ZAMBIA

Lake Tanganyika

TANZANIA

pulungu

Mbala

72

okoso

Nakonde

Isoka

Kasama

370

O

U

356

B

369

355

359

Mpika

363

M

Lundazi

T

371

enje

364

N

Chipata

MALAWI

Y

Petauke

B

MOZAMBIQUE

Cahora Bassa Dam

N

100   200   300 km

355 Bangweulu Game Management Area
356 Isangano National Park
357 Kafue National Park
358 Kasanka National Park
359 Lavushi Manda National Park
360 Liuwa Plain National Park
361 Lochinvar National Park
362 Lower Zambezi National Park
363 Luambe National Park
364 Lukusuzi National Park
365 Lunga-Luswishi Game Management Area
366 Lusenga Plain National Park
367 Mosi-oa-Tunya National Park
368 Mweru Wantipa National Park
369 North Luangwa National Park
370 Nyika National Park
371 South Luangwa National Park
272 Sumbu National Park
373 West Lunga National Park

A republic 752 972 km^2 in extent, Zambia lies on a high savannah plateau with an altitude ranging from 1 000 to 1 600 m above sea-level. The country's main river is the Zambezi in the south, with its principal tributaries, the Kafue and Luangwa. Lake Tanganyika forms the north-eastern border, and several other large lakes – Kariba Dam to the south, Bangweulu in the interior of the country, and Mweru in the north – and their surroundings are important wildlife refuges.

Miombo woodland, comprising a mixture of grassland and clumps of bushes and trees, makes up 70 per cent of Zambia's vegetation, with mopane trees and bushes dominating the lower-lying regions. This supports an extremely rich and varied wildlife, although heavy poaching has virtually wiped out the country's population of black rhinoceros and has severely reduced the numbers of other large species. Nevertheless, Zambia still has a great deal to offer the wildlife enthusiast. A visit to the country is particularly rewarding for birdwatchers: some 700 bird species have been recorded, many of which are tropical. The miombo woodland harbours barbets, hornbills, sunbirds and bee-eaters (colourful flocks of carmine bee-eaters are a feature of the Luangwa Valley), and many waterbird species are attracted to the extensive wetland areas.

Zambia's rainfall occurs in summer (November to April), with annual average falls of between 700 and 1 600 mm, depending on the region. The middle Zambezi, Luano, Lukusashi and Luangwa valleys become very hot towards the end of the dry season (September to October), but temperatures in the rest of the country are lower because of the

ublic access

altitude of the plateau. The mid-winter months of June and July usually have low temperatures at night, particularly in the higher areas.

In addition to 19 national parks, Zambia has 31 game management areas set aside to conserve a broad spectrum of habitats and their associated wildlife, and at the same time allow the local people to make use of natural resources. Although there are no facilities, the areas are often worth a visit; contact the National Parks and Wildlife Service (see page 365) for further details. Blue Lagoon National Park, west of Lusaka, is well known for its population of Kafue Flats lechwe; however, it is closed to the public. Another national park, Sioma Ngwezi, lies on the Angolan border where poaching is rife. Under current security conditions visits to this area are not recommended.

In view of the difficulty of getting to some of the reserves, visitors are advised to fly into the country and make use of the privately owned reserve camps and lodges. A list of companies operating in Zambia can be found under the appendix 'Safari Operators'. Visitors intending to enter the country by road should check well in advance on the conditions of roads in the parks they wish to visit, and in some cases the access routes as well. During the rainy season some roads become impassable and many parks are closed. A 4x4 vehicle is strongly recommended. Make sure you have sufficient fuel to reach your destination and return, as fuel points are few and their supplies cannot be relied on. It is also a good idea to carry spares and tools, and to have some mechanical knowledge. Driving at night is not recommended, and local security conditions should be established in advance.

All visitors require a valid passport to enter the country. It is a good idea to check the visa requirements well in advance as they tend to change. The unit of currency in Zambia is the kwacha.

Malaria is prevalent and tsetse fly occurs in several areas. Do not swim in rivers and natural pools, as most harbour bilharzia and crocodiles. Check with your doctor for inoculation and vaccination requirements.

A final word of warning: Zambian authorities are sensitive about foreigners photographing police stations, bridges, airports or military installations.

355 BANGWEULU GAME MANAGEMENT AREA

Location: Eastern Zambia; north-east of Lusaka.
Access: From Lusaka follow the road northeastwards towards Mpika; about 60 km beyond the turn-off to Kasanka National Park turn left onto a secondary road to Chiundaponde and continue to Ngungwa; Livingstone camp is a short distance further on. With the exception of the main tar road from Lusaka to Mpika, the roads are negotiable only by 4x4 vehicles and are impassable during the rainy season. Bangweulu can also be reached by driving through Lavushi Manda National Park.
Accommodation: *Nsobe Safari Camp,* near Ngungwa, has chalets for up to 10 persons; each chalet has its own bathroom (K400 per person per night, including all meals). *Livingstone camp* has self-catering accommodation for special-interest safaris, and visitors there should first report to the warden of the neighbouring Kasanka National Park.
Other facilities: Game-viewing drives; accompanied walks; canoeing; portered safaris; game-viewing and birdwatching hides. There are no food or fuel supplies in the area.
Open: *Nsobe Safari Camp* – 5 May to 1 December; *Livingstone camp* – by special arrangement throughout the year, but movement is

limited during the rainy season.
Beware: Malaria.
For further information: Getaway Safaris Ltd, P.O. Box 32212, Lusaka. Telex: ZA 40730. Tel: (1) 21-7230 or 21-3678. (Livingstone camp) Kasanka Wildlife Conservation Ltd, P.O. Box 36657, Lusaka.

One of the last true wilderness areas, the game management area of Bangweulu, meaning 'where the water meets the sky', contains 17 rivers which flow into the Lake Bangweulu Basin, forming magnificent flood plains and marshes. The area is designated a game management area rather than a national park so that the local population can continue to support themselves by fishing. The wildlife of the region is rich and varied, with clawless otter, black lechwe, sitatunga, tsessebe, reedbuck, buffalo, elephant, lion and leopard, as well as more than 400 bird species, including the shoebill.

The area receives an average annual rainfall of 1 300 mm. Summer days are warm, and nights are mild to cold throughout the year.

356 ISANGANO NATIONAL PARK
See map Bangweulu Game Management Area

Location: Eastern Zambia; north-east of Lusaka.
Access: From Lusaka follow the main road north-eastwards for 640 km to Mpika, then take the road to Kasama and Mbala; after approximately 86 km turn left onto a secondary road and drive another 42 km to Mbati village on the park's boundary. The park has no internal road network.
Accommodation: None.
Other facilities: None.
Open: Check with the authority.
Beware: Malaria.
For further information: The National Parks and Wildlife Service (see page 365).

Isangano National Park covers 840 km² of flats and flood plain terrain. The area is well watered, with the Chambeshi River forming the park's eastern boundary and the Lubanseshi River flowing through it. The western area of Isangano is also a flood plain and forms part of the Bangweulu Flats. The vegetation consists of grassland and mixed woodland, with reed beds lining the rivers. Game species include black lechwe, buffalo, bushbuck, eland, Lichtenstein's hartebeest, reedbuck, roan and elephant. Numbers of game are generally low as a result of poaching.

357 KAFUE NATIONAL PARK

Location: Western Zambia; west of Lusaka.
Access: From Lusaka follow the main road westwards for 147 km to Mumbwa; from Mumbwa continue westwards towards Kaoma for 66 km to the turn-off to Lake Itezhi-Tezhi, which lies in the park, 115 km further on. This road is generally in good condition and is suitable for ordinary vehicles. Alternatively, from Livingstone in the south follow the main Lusaka road northwards for 126 km to Kalomo; at Kalomo turn left and drive for approximately 80 km to Ndumdumwense Gate.
Accommodation: A great variety of accommodation is offered at Kafue, ranging from self-catering to single-party luxury camps. The Zambia National Tourist Board operates the 40-bed *Chunga Safari Village* with full-catering and self-catering camps (*Kalala, Kanzhila* and *Chunga*) which provide thatched huts with separate ablution facilities, and a cook to prepare visitors' food. *Ngoma Lodge* and *Musunga Safari Lodge* are privately run. *Lufupa, Ntemwa Safari* and *Moshi* camps are run by Busanga Trails and are fully-catered. There is a camping site at Chunga where camper vans may be parked overnight. Information on official camps should be obtained from the tourist board, as several camps have been closed and others are being renovated. The Wildlife Conservation

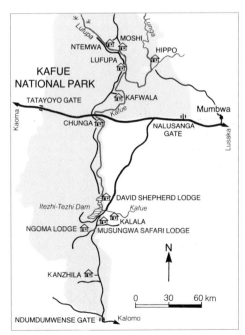

Society of Zambia operates a self-catering camp, *David Shepherd Lodge*, on the shore of

Lake Itezhi-Tezhi. Although the camp is intended only for members, visitors can take out temporary membership in order to stay there. The lodge has 3 4-bed chalets, each with its own bathroom. Busanga Trails Ltd has 4 camps in the northern part of the park, and *Hippo Camp*, in the north-east, is run by Lubungu Wildlife Safaris.
Other facilities: Extensive network of game-viewing roads; several of the private operators conduct fishing or game- and birdwatching trips by boat; fishing at designated sites. Fuel is usually available at several points in the park, but it is advisable to check availability in advance. Unless you are staying at a camp with full-catering, take all food and drink requirements with you.
Open: Although some camps remain open throughout the year, others close from October or November through to May; check with the relevant authority.
Beware: Malaria; visitors may only get out of their vehicles at designated picnic or fishing sites.
For further information: The Zambia National Tourist Board (see page 365). The Wildlife Conservation Society of Zambia, P.O. Box 30255, Lusaka. Tel: (1) 25-4226. Busanga Trails Ltd, P.O. Box 31322 or 30984, Lusaka. Telex: ZA 40081. Tel: (1) 21-1199. Lubungu Wildlife Safaris Ltd, P.O. Box 31701, Lusaka. Telex: Baltic ZA 41530. Tel: (1) 25-1823.

Established in 1924, Kafue National Park is Zambia's oldest and, at 22 400 km^2, its largest national park. It is made up of a vast, gently undulating plateau ranging in altitude from 970 to 1 470 m above sea-level. A few hills are located along the mid-reaches of the Kafue River and much of the area to the west and south is dominated by expanses of Kalahari sand. The region is watered by the Lufupa and Lunga rivers, tributaries of the Kafue, which forms part of the eastern boundary. The vegetation consists of grassland, with the extensive Busanga Plain in the north, and of miombo, mopane and riverine woodland. Stands of teak grow throughout the park, but are most common in the south.

Mammals are well represented in Kafue and include elephant, hippopotamus, buffalo, sable, roan, Lichtenstein's hartebeest, puku, red lechwe on the Busanga Plain, lion, leopard, spotted hyena and wild dog. The Kafue River and its flood plain are particularly well known for their rich birdlife, which is represented by about 450 species.

358 KASANKA
NATIONAL PARK See map Bangweulu Game Management Area

Location: Eastern Zambia; north-east of Lusaka.
Access: From Lusaka take the main road towards Mpika; after 450 km turn towards Samfya and drive 54 km to the park's entrance.
Accommodation: *Lake Wasa Safari Camp* is a private camp for up to 10 persons. *Luwombwa River Fishing Camp* at present has only a 4-bed chalet, but a camp for up to 20 is due for completion shortly.
Other facilities: A 200-km network of game-viewing roads; guided walks; fishing; boats can be hired.
Open: Throughout the year.
Beware: Malaria.
For further information: Kasanka Wildlife Conservation Ltd, P.O. Box 36657, Lusaka.

Run privately by Kasanka Wildlife Conservation Ltd on behalf of the National Parks and Wildlife Service, Kasanka National Park is one of the most attractive parks in Zambia, with its diversity of dry and wetland habitats and their associated wildlife. The 470-km^2 park lies along the south-eastern edge of the Lake Bangweulu Basin in gently undulating country covered by miombo woodland and extensive papyrus and reed beds. Water, in the form of the Luwombwa and Mulembo rivers and the Kasanka stream, as well as lakes, lagoons, marshes and seasonal pans, is abundant.

Many mammals are supported in this rich environment, and sitatunga, puku, elephant, hippopotamus and crocodile are of particular interest. There are plans to establish a core population of the endangered black rhinoceros here. The birdlife is very varied and, among the many waterbirds, includes such species as the shoebill.

359 LAVUSHI MANDA
NATIONAL PARK See map Bangweulu Game Management Area

Location: Eastern Zambia; north-east of Lusaka.
Access: From Lusaka follow the main road towards Mpika; 141 km past the Kasanka National Park turn-off turn left and continue to

174. Kafue National Park is well known for its predators, particularly the leopard.

175. The Mwaleshi River during the dry season, North Luangwa National Park.

176. During the wet season Kafue National Park offers grazers such as the puku an abundance of food.

177. The black lechwe, which occurs only in the vicinity of Zambia's Lake Bangweulu, may be seen in the Bangweulu Game Management Area.

179. Jacana and a battle-scarred hippopotamus in the Luangwa River, South Luangwa.

178. Thornicroft's giraffe — in Luambe National Park — has slightly different markings from other giraffes.

180. The carmine bee-eater is one of many bird species to be seen in South Luangwa.

181. A variety of wildlife is drawn to the river banks in the South Luangwa National Park.

183. Several attractive hotels and campsites located on the shoreline near the reserve provide a base for visitors to the beautiful Lake Malawi National Park.

184. Sapitwa, the highest point of Mulanje.

185. *Protea petiolaris* thrives in the montane environment of Mulanje.

186. A wild fig tree in the evergreen forests of Zomba Plateau.

187. On Mulanje Mountain a hiker looks down into 'The Crater'.

Lavushi Manda, which is not far from the road. It can also be approached from Kasanka National Park; directions can be obtained there.
Accommodation: None.

Other facilities: None.
Open: Check with the authority.
For further information: The National Parks and Wildlife Service (see page 365).

Lavushi Manda National Park lies in the Mpika district and extends over 1 500 km^2. The Lavushi hills, averaging 1 550 m above sea-level, lie in the eastern part of the park, with Lavushi Mountain a prominent landmark. This is an excellent area for hiking. The Lukulu River forms the principal drainage system. Miombo woodland covers most of the park, with riverine woodland lining the major watercourses. Small populations of elephant, sable, roan, eland, waterbuck, buffalo, Lichtenstein's hartebeest and klipspringer roam the area, and lion and leopard are the two major predators.

360 LIUWA PLAIN NATIONAL PARK

Location: Far western Zambia; west of Lusaka.
Access: Difficult! From Lusaka follow the main road westwards for 610 km through Kaoma to Mongu; from Mongu continue westwards to Kalabo, crossing the Zambezi River by ferry; from Kalabo take the secondary road north-westwards to the western edge of the park. There is no internal road network. Check the road conditions and security situation with the authority in advance.
Accommodation: None.
Other facilities: None.
Open: Access is possible only during the dry season.
Beware: Malaria; tsetse fly.

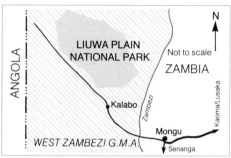

For further information: The National Parks and Wildlife Service (see page 365).

Lying in the northern part of the West Zambezi Game Management Area, Liuwa Plain National Park covers 3 660 km^2. The Luambimba and Luanginga rivers run through the region and are flanked by grass-covered flood plain. Mixed woodland lies on the edges of the plains. As in most conservation areas in Zambia, poaching is a serious problem, and it reaches particularly high levels in the west. However, Liuwa Plain is known for its large herds of blue wildebeest and tsessebe, and buffalo, roan, Burchell's zebra and red lechwe also occur. The area also has a rich birdlife.

361 LOCHINVAR NATIONAL PARK

Location: Western Zambia; south-west of Lusaka.
Access: From Lusaka travel south-westwards on the main road for 186 km to Monze; turn right and follow this all-weather gravel road for 48 km to the entrance gate. There is an airstrip nearby.
Accommodation: A 20-bed lodge; a new lodge is planned.
Other facilities: A limited network of internal roads; walking is permitted. There are no shops or fuel supplies in the park.
Open: Throughout the year.
Beware: Malaria; bilharzia.

For further information: The National Hotels Development Corporation (see page 365).

Lochinvar National Park covers 410 km^2 and consists mainly of flood plains on the southern bank of the Kafue River. This is an outstanding bird sanctuary and the World Wildlife Fund has initiated a wetland project here. More than 400 bird species have been recorded and large flocks of ducks and geese are a notable feature. The park also provides sanctuary for approximately 40 000 Kafue Flats lechwe and small populations of blue wildebeest, Burchell's zebra and hippopotamus.

362 LOWER ZAMBEZI NATIONAL PARK

Location: Southern Zambia; east of Lusaka.
Access: From Lusaka follow the main road eastwards towards Chipata for about 100 km, then take the secondary road towards Chakwenga, which lies about 60 km inside the park. Check with the authority before entering. There is no internal road network.
Accommodation: None.
Other facilities: None. A private company, Circuit Holdings, is planning to develop the park.
Open: Check with the authority.
Beware: Land mines planted during the war in Rhodesia in the 1970s are said to be a hazard.
For further information: The National Parks and Wildlife Service (see page 365).

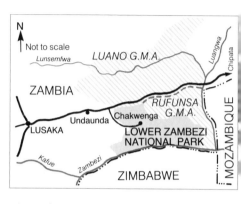

This large, scenically attractive park lies on the northern bank of the Zambezi River, opposite Zimbabwe's Mana Pools National Park (see page 358). Miombo woodland covers the hills, with mopane and acacia dominating the valley floor. A wide variety of game species occur, such as elephant, buffalo, roan, waterbuck, kudu, bushbuck and hippopotamus, but numbers have been greatly reduced by poaching. Lion and leopard are the main predatory species in the park. It becomes very hot in summer.

363 LUAMBE NATIONAL PARK

Location: Eastern Zambia; north-east of Lusaka.
Access: From Lusaka take the main road eastwards to Chipata; from Chipata drive to Mfuwe via Masumba, then take the road to Chama; Luambe is approximately 80 km from Mfuwe, along this road. Apart from the Mfuwe/Chama road, which runs through the park, there is no internal road network.
Accommodation: None.
Other facilities: None.
Open: Check with the authority.
Beware: Malaria; bilharzia; tsetse fly.
For further information: The National Parks and Wildlife Service (see page 365).

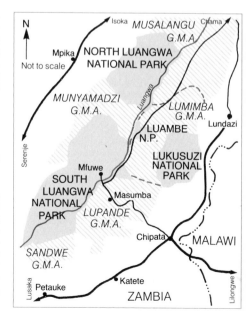

This 247-km² park in the Lundazi district ranges in altitude from 500 to 710 m above sea-level. Much of it is made up of the flood plain of the Luangwa River, which forms the western boundary. Although mopane woodland is the dominant vegetation type, there are also patches of miombo woodland. Mammal species in Luambe National Park include buffalo, elephant, hippopotamus, impala, roan, eland, bushpig and lion. The climate is hot, especially in September and October.

364 LUKUSUZI NATIONAL PARK See map Luambe National Park

Location: Eastern Zambia; north-east of Lusaka.
Access: From Lusaka follow the main road eastwards to Chipata; continue towards Lundazi for approximately 110 km, then turn left onto a secondary road leading to the park. This road is usually in poor condition. There is no internal road network. Permission to be obtained from the authority before entering.
Accommodation: None.
Other facilities: None.
Open: Throughout the year.
Beware: Malaria; bilharzia; tsetse fly.
For further information: The National Parks and Wildlife Service (see page 365).

The 2 720-km^2 Lukusuzi National Park lies in the eastern catchment area of the Luangwa River. Almost half of the park consists of plateau, and the remaining area is dotted with rocky outcrops. Miombo woodland is dominant, with grassland on the plateau and along the rivers. The game species in the park are similar to those found in other areas of the Luangwa Valley and include elephant, buffalo, blue wildebeest, eland, Lichtenstein's hartebeest, roan, sable, klipspringer and warthog. The spotted hyena is the main predatory species.

365 LUNGA-LUSWISHI GAME MANAGEMENT AREA

Location: Central Zambia; north-west of Lusaka.
Access: From Lusaka follow the main road westwards to Mumbwa; from Mumbwa drive north-westwards to Lubungu Pontoon on the banks of the Kafue River. Leopard Lodge lies 3 km further north on this road.
Accommodation: *Leopard Lodge* has 1 4-bed lodge with a bathroom, and 4 2-bed lodges, each with a bathroom; all provide full-catering.
Other facilities: Game-viewing drives; walking safaris; fishing; access to hot springs.
Open: Throughout the year.
Beware: Malaria; bilharzia.
For further information: Bruce and Ina Digby, Summit Safaris Ltd, Leopard Lodge, P.O. Box 33419, Lusaka. Tel: (1) 21-6689 or 21-6318.

The Lunga-Luswishi National Park is similar in most respects to the Kafue National Park, which lies to the south-west. The vegetation is dominated by miombo woodland, with open grassland and flood plain along the Kafue River. Sable, impala, waterbuck, puku, yellow-backed duiker, eland, kudu, bushbuck and hippopotamus are among the game species that visitors are likely to see. The Leopard Lodge camp in the south is privately run, and a number of other safari companies operate in the park.

366 LUSENGA PLAIN NATIONAL PARK

Location: Far northern Zambia; north of Lusaka.
Access: From Lusaka follow the main road towards Mpika for 440 km; turn left and drive for 137 km to Mukuku, then a further 206 km to Mansa; at Mansa turn right and travel northwards for 168 km to Kawambwa; from there take the road towards Mporokoso; the park is on the left. It can also be reached via Mporokoso to the east or Luwingu to the south-east. There are no internal roads.
Accommodation: None.
Other facilities: None.

Open: Check with the authority.
Beware: Malaria; bilharzia; tsetse fly.

For further information: The National Parks and Wildlife Service (see page 365).

Lusenga Plain National Park, 880 km² in extent, consists of a large plain formed by the weathering of a plug dome which has left outcrops of rock exposed. The park is surrounded by hill ridges and bordered in the north-east by the Kalungwishi River, on which there are three attractive waterfalls. Much of the plain is grassland fringed by dry evergreen and swamp forest, while the remainder is covered by dense miombo woodland. Game populations have been greatly reduced by poaching, but buffalo, blue and yellow-backed duiker, bushbuck and reedbuck can still be seen. Summers here are hot and humid.

367 MOSI-OA-TUNYA NATIONAL PARK

Location: Southern Zambia; south of Lusaka.
Access: From Lusaka follow the main road southwards to Livingstone. The park lies 10 km further south. Livingstone has an airport and fly-in package tours can be arranged.
Accommodation: *Rainbow Lodge* provides suites and rondavels; Mosi-oa-Tunya Hotel has Zambian 5-star rating.
Other facilities: Fishing; launch tours on the Zambezi River. *Rainbow Lodge* has a restaurant and swimming pool.
Open: Throughout the year.
Beware: Malaria.

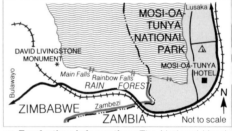

For further information: The National Hotels Development Corporation (see page 365).

Victoria Falls, known locally as Mosi-oa-tunya or 'the smoke that thunders', is one of Zambia's most important tourist attractions. At 66 km², the Mosi-oa-Tunya National Park is one of the smallest in the country, and its main purpose is to protect the riverine area above the falls, the falls themselves and the gorges below. Much of the park is covered by mopane woodland, which provides habitat for buffalo, common duiker and warthog; hippopotamus and crocodile occur in the river. Tall riverine forest grows near the river, and here bushbuck and vervet monkey, as well as bird species such as the coppery sunbird, terrestrial bulbul, wood owl and the rare Taita falcon, may be seen.

368 MWERU WANTIPA NATIONAL PARK See map Lusenga Plain National Park

Location: Far northern Zambia; north of Lusaka.
Access: From Lusaka follow the main road north-eastwards to Mpika, then continue northwards to Kasama; at Kasama turn left and drive

for 173 km to Mporokoso; continue westwards, taking the right turn towards Chiengi, and then another right turn towards Kaputa. This road runs through the Mweru Wantipa National Park

There is no internal road network.
Accommodation: None.
Other facilities: None.
Open: The park is inaccessible during the rainy season.

Beware: Malaria; bilharzia; tsetse fly. The presence of armed poachers could pose a threat; check with the authority.
For further information: The National Parks and Wildlife Service (see page 365).

Lake Mweru Wantipa lies along the eastern border of this 3 134-km^2 national park and from it the land rises gently westwards to a range of deeply incised hills. Dense papyrus beds dominate the vegetation along the lake shore, with a belt of mixed bushwillow and other tree species separating the miombo woodland of the interior from the shoreline. The area was once known for its large elephant and crocodile populations, but poaching has greatly reduced their numbers. There is, however, a large population of bushbuck, and such species as buffalo, blue and yellow-backed duiker, Sharpe's grysbok, puku, reedbuck, roan, sable, sitatunga and hippopotamus also occur. Predators are represented by leopard and lion. The birdlife is particularly rich along the lake shore.

369 NORTH LUANGWA
NATIONAL PARK See map Luambe National Park

Location: Eastern Zambia; north-east of Lusaka.
Access: Difficult! The area is best visited with Shiwa Safaris, the safari company which operates in the park.
Accommodation: None.
Other facilities: None.

Open: No access during rains.
Beware: Malaria; bilharzia; tsetse fly.
For further information: The National Parks and Wildlife Service (see page 365). (Shiwa Safaris) P.O. Box 820024, Chisamba. Telex: ZA 40104. Tel: (05) 22-2730.

North Luangwa National Park covers 4 636 km^2, with the Muchinga Escarpment forming its western border and the Luangwa River along its eastern boundary. Miombo woodland covers most of the area, with some open grassland on the flood plain. The wildlife is similar to that in South Luangwa and includes buffalo, elephant, hippopotamus, impala, kudu, puku, Cookson's wildebeest, lion and leopard.

370 NYIKA NATIONAL PARK

Location: Far north-eastern Zambia; north-east of Lusaka.
Access: From Lusaka follow the main road to Mpika and continue to Isoka; drive eastwards towards Chisenga for 92 km, turn south-eastwards and continue for a further 130 km to Muyombe; drive through this settlement to the park. Alternatively, from Lusaka follow the road to Chipata and continue past Lundazi to Muyombe. The condition of this road varies; check with the authority before trying it.
Accommodation: An 8-bed camp.
Other facilities: None.
Open: Access is difficult in the rainy season.
Beware: Malaria.
For further information: The National Parks and Wildlife Service (see page 365); or The Wildlife Conservation Society of Zambia, P.O. Box 30255, Lusaka.

Only 80 km^2 in extent, Nyika National Park protects the Zambian section of the Nyika Plateau. The vegetation consists of patches of forest at Chowo and Manyanjere, interspersed with areas of open grassland. This is not a good area for big game, but it is rich in small species, such as tree dassie, blue duiker and sun squirrel, and there is a wide variety of birds.

Location: Eastern Zambia; north-east of Lusaka. **Access:** From Lusaka take the main road eastwards to Chipata, then a secondary road northwestwards to the park's main entrance at Mfuwe. Access roads are suitable for all vehicles, although the road between Chipata and Mfuwe is often in poor condition. Within the park there is an all-weather game-viewing circuit in the Mfuwe area, but elsewhere 4x4 vehicles are recommended. Safari operators meet clients at Lusaka, and Zambian Airways run regular flights to Mfuwe Airport, 25 km from Mfuwe Lodge. **Accommodation:** 14 lodges and camps currently operate in South Luangwa, several of which are privately run. *Kapani Safari Camp* has 4 double chalets, each with a bathroom and electricity (US$100 per person per night, all inclusive). Luwi bush camp is available to visitors staying for 5 or more nights at Kapani, for a supplementary charge of US$50. Kapani has a swimming pool, guided game-viewing drives, including night drives, and walking safaris; it is open all year. *Chinzombo Safari Lodge* has fully-catered accommodation in 9 thatched chalets, each with a bathroom. There is a communal dining area and bar, and game-viewing drives, night drives and accompanied walks are offered. Chinzombo is open from late April to mid-January. *Chibembe Lodge* has wooden chalets (maximum 40 persons), some with a bathroom, others using separate ablution facilities; full-catering is provided and meals are served in an open-air dining area. Facilities include accompanied walks, bush camps, game-viewing drives, night drives and a swimming pool. The lodge is open between June and November. *Nsefu Camp* has 6 thatched rondavels, each with a bathroom; full-catering is provided. Nsefu offers game-viewing drives, night drives and a photographic hide, and is open between June and November. *Tena Tena Camp* is a tented camp (maximum 12 persons) with ablution facilities. Full-catering is provided, and there are accompanied game-viewing walks and drives, including night drives. The camp is open between June and October. Book well in advance; cas-

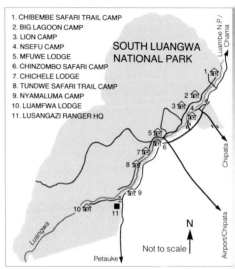

1. CHIBEMBE SAFARI TRAIL CAMP
2. BIG LAGOON CAMP
3. LION CAMP
4. NSEFU CAMP
5. MFUWE LODGE
6. CHINZOMBO SAFARI CAMP
7. CHICHELE LODGE
8. TUNDWE SAFARI TRAIL CAMP
9. NYAMALUMA CAMP
10. LUAMFWA LODGE
11. LUSANGAZI RANGER HQ

SOUTH LUANGWA NATIONAL PARK

ual visitors are not admitted to the private camps. Official lodges offer both full-catering and self-catering accommodation; contact the Zambia National Tourist Board for details (see page 365). **Other facilities:** A petrol pump at Mfuwe. **Open:** Throughout the year, but movement is restricted during the rainy season. **Speed limit:** 40 km/h. **Beware:** Malaria; bilharzia; tsetse fly. **For further information:** The Zambia National Tourist Board (see page 365). (Kapani) Norman Carr Safaris, P.O. Box 100, Mfuwe. Telex ZA 45940. Tel: (1) 21-636. (Chinzombo) Save the Rhino Trust, P.O. Box 320-169, Woodlands, Lusaka. Telex: ZA 42570. Tel: (1) 21-1644 (Chinzombo camping site) The Secretary, The Wildlife Conservation Society of Zambia, Chipata Branch, P.O. Box 510358, Chipata. (Chibembe, Nsefu) Wilderness Trails Ltd, P.O. Box 30970, Lusaka. Telex: ZA 40042. (Tena Tena) Robin Pope Safaris Ltd, P.O. Box 320-154 Lusaka; or Andrew's Travel and Safaris Ltd P.O. Box 31993, Lusaka. Telex: ZA 40104. Tel (1) 21-3147.

South Luangwa National Park lies within the Luangwa Valley, whose floor, for the most part, is gently sloping and well wooded, with isolated, broken ridges and a flat alluvial plain. Two large grassland plains of some 400 km² are located in the park, with smaller grassland areas to the north. The Luangwa River inundates its flood plain periodically, usually in February, and after a flood sometimes changes its course leaving oxbow lakes along the old channel. This instability creates the richness of scenery and the highly productive ecosystem for which the Luangwa Valley is well known. In addition to the open grassland there are areas of miombo and mopane woodland.

Covering 9 050 km^2, South Luangwa was proclaimed a national park in 1938. It has exceptionally rich and varied wildlife, but commercial poaching has brought the once-widespread black rhinoceros population to the brink of extinction and elephant numbers have also declined. Hippopotamus, buffalo, warthog, the endemic Thornicroft's giraffe, bushbuck, kudu, eland, reedbuck, waterbuck, puku, roan and Lichtenstein's hartebeest are just a few of the game species that may be seen. The area is also well known for its predators, which include lion, leopard and spotted hyena. This is an excellent birding area, and amongst others, many raptor and waterfowl species may be seen.

372 | SUMBU NATIONAL PARK
See map Lusenga Plain National Park

Location: Far northern Zambia; north-east of Lusaka.
Access: From Lusaka follow the road to Mpika, then take the road northwards to Mbala; there turn left and continue to the eastern edge of the park. Internal roads are usually in poor condition; check with the authority.
Accommodation: There are chalets, each with a bathroom, at Kasaba Bay, Nkamba Bay and Ndole Bay on the lake shore.
Other facilities: Fishing (best between November and March; boats and tackle can be hired); limited game-viewing and night drives; night boat rides; guided walks.
Open: Throughout the year.
Beware: Malaria; tsetse fly; crocodiles.
For further information: The Zambia National Tourist Board (see page 365).

Sumbu National Park, covering 2 020 km^2, is bordered in part by Lake Tanganyika and the Lufubu River. Away from the lake, much of the park's area is taken up by a plateau which is covered mainly by miombo woodland and small areas of open grassland. Game-viewing in the park is limited because of the lack of a proper road network, but during the dry season a number of species drink from the lake. Visitors may see elephant, buffalo, Lichtenstein's hartebeest, hippopotamus, puku, roan, sable, waterbuck, yellow-backed and blue duiker, lion and leopard. The Tanganyika water cobra, a fish-eating snake, is common in the lake, as are crocodiles. The birdlife is varied, and at the Kalombo Falls near Mbala, many marabou storks breed on the cliffs during the dry season.

373 WEST LUNGA NATIONAL PARK

Location: Western Zambia; north-west of Lusaka.
Access: From Lusaka take the main road to Kapiri Mposhi and then bear left to Solwezi and Mwelemu; from Mwelemu drive southwards, taking the right turn towards Kabompo and Zambezi; after about 240 km turn right and travel 10 km to the park. It is advisable to check road conditions and the security situation in advance. Signposting in rural areas is often poor; it is essential to carry a good map.
Accommodation: None.
Other facilities: None.
Open: Inaccessible during the rainy season.
Beware: Malaria; bilharzia.
For further information: The Zambia National Tourist Board (see page 365).

The 1 684-km^2 West Lunga National Park is situated between the West Lunga and Kabompo rivers; both are perennial and swamps are numerous along the latter. Several forest and woodland types make up the vegetation, including *Cryptosepalum* on the Kalahari sand areas and limited areas of mixed miombo woodland. There are also areas of open grassland and papyrus reed beds. Mammal species are represented by elephant, buffalo, hippopotamus, warthog, sitatunga, puku, blue, common and yellow-backed duiker, oribi, Defassa waterbuck and no less than 22 carnivores.

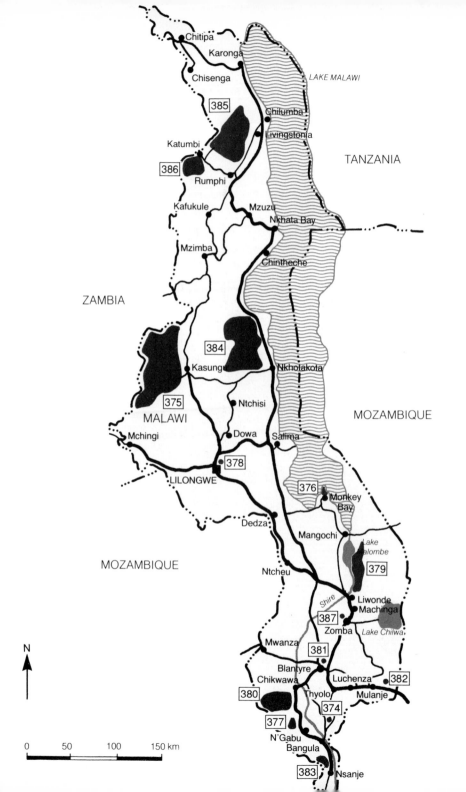

Chitipa

Karonga

Chisenga

LAKE MALAWI

385

Chilumba

Livingstonia

Katumbi

TANZANIA

386

Rumphi

Kafukule

Mzuzu

Mzimba

Nkhata Bay

Chintheche

ZAMBIA

384

Kasungu

Nkhotakota

375

Ntchisi

MOZAMBIQUE

MALAWI

Mchingi

Dowa

Salima

378

LILONGWE

376

Monkey
Bay

Dedza

Mangochi

Lake
Malombe

MOZAMBIQUE

379

Ntcheu

Shire

Liwonde
Machinga

387

Mwanza

Zomba

Lake Chilwa

381

N

Blantyre

Chikwawa

Luchenza

382

380

Thyolo

Mulanje

374

377

N'Gabu

Bangula

0   50   100   150 km

383

Nsanje

MALAWI

A small, landlocked country covering 118 484 km², Malawi is bordered by Tanzania in the north, Mozambique in the east and south, and Zambia in the north-west. The country occupies a narrow strip of land along the East African Rift Valley which runs north to south and contains the Shire River valley and Lake Malawi. Rising steeply from the Rift Valley westwards is a plateau which covers most of Malawi and averages between 1 000 and 1 500 m above sea-level. The country also contains isolated highland areas and two mountain massifs, Zomba and Mulanje. Dry woodlands and woodland savannah cover most of the country, but there are also considerable areas of open grassland and montane forest.

Malawi has a tropical climate, with a rainy season from November to March. Although conditions may become unpleasantly hot and humid in the Shire River valley and around Lake Malawi during the rainy summer months, temperatures are usually cooler in the higher plateau areas at this time. Winters are dry and generally mild to cool, depending on the altitude, and this is the best time for game-viewing.

Despite the country's large and growing population, a considerable amount of land has been set aside for national parks, game reserves and several other conservation areas. These are controlled by the Department of National Parks and Wildlife (see page 365) and the Department of Forestry and Natural Resources (see page 365). Although not reserves in the conventional sense, Chiradzulu Mountain, Chongoni Mountain, Dedza Mountain, Ndirande Mountain and Soche Mountain are worth a visit, as they have interesting scenery and indigenous forest and other vegetation. For further information about these areas contact the Department of Tourism (see page 365). Game is restricted mainly to the reserves, and a broad variety of species can be seen, including buffalo, elephant, rhinoceros, leopard, lion and antelope. More than 600 bird species have been recorded. A particular feature of Lake Malawi is its colourful array of freshwater tropical fish, most of which are cichlids, known locally as 'mbuna'.

All visitors require a valid passport to enter Malawi. South Africans do not need visas, but nationals of some other countries do. Visitors intending to stay more than three months require special permission to do so. The unit of currency is the Malawian kwacha. Visitors should be aware that, in public, women are expected to wear a skirt covering the knees (although this is not enforced in parks and the more remote conservation areas), and it is illegal for men to wear hair that covers the neck or ears. Roads in Malawi are generally in reasonable condition, but may become impassable during the rainy season, and it is always advisable to check conditions before setting out.

374 ELEPHANT MARSH

Location: Southern Malawi; south of Blantyre.
Access: From Blantyre take the main road south-eastwards to Limbe and then to Thyolo; turn right off the main road and drive south-wards for approximately 40 km towards Chiromo. The marsh lies to the west of the road. The only means of getting around the reserve is on foot along the railway causeway.
Accommodation: None.
Other facilities: None.
Open: Throughout the year.
For further information: The Department of National Parks and Wildlife (see page 365).

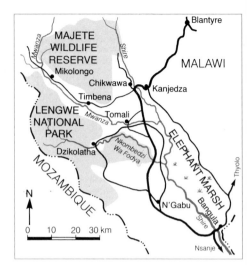

Elephant Marsh, 65 km long and 19 km across at its widest point, is a huge complex of swamps, channels and temporary water bodies east of the Shire River. Although not part of the national park system, it is an important sanctuary for hippopotamus and crocodile, and more than 300 bird species are attracted to this wetland paradise.

375 KASUNGU NATIONAL PARK

Location: Central Malawi; north-west of Lilongwe.
Access: From Lilongwe drive northwards towards Kasungu for about 130 km; turn left and continue for approximately 30 km. This road is suitable for ordinary vehicles, except during severe rains. Many of the park's internal roads are closed between January and June.
Accommodation: *Lifupa Lodge* has 12 2- and 3-bed rondavels, each with a bathroom; meals provided. There is also a tented camp with communal kitchen and ablution facilities.
Other facilities: 280-km network of game-viewing roads; drives accompanied by a game scout, by day or night; a 10-km trail; a restaurant and bar; a swimming pool; an information centre. Fuel is available.
Open: Park – throughout the year; accommodation – April to February.
Beware: Malaria.
For further information: The Department of National Parks and Wildlife (see page 365).

Kasungu National Park covers 2 070 km² and contains several sites of archaeological interest, which the visitor can explore along a 10-km trail. Miombo woodland, which covers much of the park, is interspersed with open, seasonally flooded flats, and there are broken hills to the north.

Game-viewing is good, particularly towards the end of the dry season, and elephant, hippopotamus, buffalo, warthog, eland, Lichtenstein's hartebeest, reedbuck, kudu, roan, sable, puku, oribi and impala may be seen, as well as a small population of black rhinoceros. Lion, cheetah, leopard and wild dog are also present. More than 200 bird species have been recorded.

376 LAKE MALAWI NATIONAL PARK

Location: Southern Malawi; east of Lilongwe.
Access: From Lilongwe take the road to Salima and from there turn south, driving for about 70 km; turn left and follow this road eastward, turning left again to Monkey Bay and Cape Maclear. The authorities advise that the best way to visit the park is by boat.
Accommodation: None. There are hotels nearby at Club Makokola and Nkopola Lodge. Golden Sands Holiday Camp at Cape Maclear has self-catering accommodation and a camping site.
Other facilities: A network of game-viewing roads; walking, diving and snorkelling are permitted; boats may be hired. There is a bar at Golden Sands. Self-catering visitors should take all their requirements with them.
Open: Throughout the year.
Beware: Malaria.
For further information: The Department of National Parks and Wildlife or The Department of Tourism (see page 365).

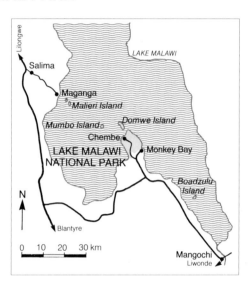

Lake Malawi National Park has a total area of 88 km², covering most of the rugged Nankhumba Peninsula, a section of Lake Malawi, and 12 nearby islands. The clear water of the lake supports a spectacular variety of tropical freshwater fish, with more than 450 species recorded.

Other habitats include sandy beaches, swamps, wooded hillsides, sand dunes and reed marshes. The birdlife is particularly rich; and species include a variety of kingfishers, fish eagle, heron, jacana and egret, as well as large colonies of white-breasted cormorant, which breed on Boadzulu and Mumbo islands.

Vervet monkeys and bushbuck inhabit the woodland, klipspringer may be seen on the rocky outcrops of the mainland, and the reed marshes contain crocodile and hippopotamus.

377 LENGWE NATIONAL PARK See map Elephant Marsh

Location: Southern Malawi; south-west of Blantyre.
Access: From Blantyre take the road towards Nsanje via Chikwawa; after 74 km turn right at the signpost to the park; the entrance is 9 km from the turn-off. All internal roads are gravel and likely to be impassable in the rainy season; although access to the camp is possible all year, 4x4 vehicles are recommended.
Accommodation: 4 4-bed chalets, each with separate kitchen; student hostel.

Other facilities: An 83-km network of gravel game-viewing roads; a self-guided 2,5-km walking trail; walks accompanied by a game scout; game-viewing and birdwatching hides; picnic sites. The nearest fuel and food supplies are 18 km away at Nchalo.
Open: Throughout the year, but movement is limited during the rainy season.
Beware: Malaria; bilharzia.
For further information: The Department of National Parks and Wildlife (see page 365).

Lengwe National Park covers 887 km² of flat to undulating terrain with some lowland flood plains along the Shire River. It contains a mixture of deciduous woodland and thicket, including mopane, miombo and other species associated with savannah environments. The park was originally proclaimed to protect a population of nyala, but other species that may now be seen include buffalo, Burchell's zebra, bushbuck, kudu, impala, sable antelope, suni, and samango and vervet monkeys. Predators are represented by lion, leopard and spotted hyena. The birdlife is prolific, and the gorgeous bush shrike, the barred long-tailed cuckoo and the black-and-white flycatcher may be spotted. Game-viewing is poor between December and June, but the birdlife is at its best in December and January. The area can be uncomfortably hot in October and November.

378 LILONGWE NATURE SANCTUARY

Location: Central Malawi; north-east of Li-longwe.
Access: Lies on the main road between Old and New Lilongwe.
Accommodation: None. There are hotels in Lilongwe.
Other facilities: A network of short walking trails; birdwatching hides; an education centre (brochures are available).
Open: Throughout the year.
For further information: The Department of National Parks and Wildlife (see page 365).

Situated between the old town and the new capital, Lilongwe Nature Sanctuary consists of 120 ha of mixed woodland on the bank of the Lingadzi River. The wildlife of this small sanctuary is surprisingly diverse and includes bushbuck, common duiker, bushpig, Burchell's zebra, serval, leopard and spotted hyena. Crocodile, otter and 14 fish species inhabit the river; more than 200 bird species have been recorded.

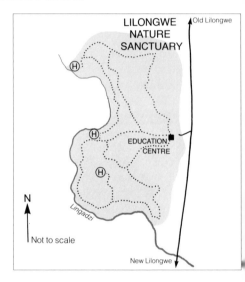

379 LIWONDE NATIONAL PARK

Location: Southern Malawi; north of Blantyre.
Access: From Blantyre take the main road northwards in the direction of Lilongwe; after approximately 120 km turn right and drive a further 6 km to the park's entrance gate. The access road is closed during the rainy season, from late November to early April, but the park and camp can be visited by boat from Liwonde Barrage at this time.
Accommodation: *Mvuu camp* has 8 2-bed and 2 4-bed rondavels with communal kitchen and ablution facilities; visitors should bring their own cooking and eating utensils and bedding. There is also a camping site. Water is fetched from the river nearby.
Other facilities: A 97-km network of gravel game-viewing roads; picnic sites; boating permitted; a 15-seater boat may be hired. The nearest fuel and food supplies are at the village of Liwonde.

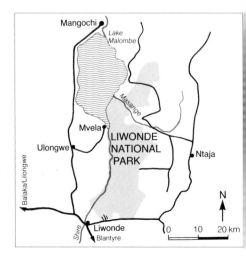

Open: Throughout the year.
Beware: Malaria; bilharzia.

For further information: The Department of National Parks and Wildlife (see page 365).

The 548-km^2 Liwonde National Park is situated on the eastern plain of the Upper Shire Valley, with the river itself as one of its major features. Lake Malombe, which is fed and drained by the Shire, lies at its north-western boundary. The park has a wide variety of habitats, ranging from riverine swamps, through grasslands to extensive areas of mopane woodland on the higher ground. Elephant, sable, kudu, waterbuck, bushbuck, impala and the occasional lion inhabit Liwonde, and hippopotamus and crocodile live in the Shire River. Game-viewing is most productive between August and November. The park supports a variety of birds, including Malawi's only population of Lilian's lovebird.

380 MAJETE WILDLIFE RESERVE See map Elephant Marsh

Location: Southern Malawi; south-west of Blantyre.
Access: From Blantyre follow the main road southwards for about 40 km, then take the right turn to Chikwawa; continue past this settlement to the entrance of the reserve. Only 4x4 vehicles can reach it between December and June. Permission to enter the reserve must be obtained in advance.
Accommodation: *Mkurumadzi camp* has 1

4-bed chalet and a camping site with basic facilities; communal kitchen and ablution facilities. There is no electricity.
Other facilities: Guided walks; picnic site at Kapichira Falls.
Open: Throughout the year, but access is difficult between December and June.
Beware: Malaria.
For further information: The Department of National Parks and Wildlife (see page 365).

Majete Wildlife Reserve covers 691 km^2 of hilly terrain between the Shire and Mwanza rivers. Much of the area's vegetation consists of miombo woodland with some riverine forest, and extensive bamboo thickets in the west. The reserve supports a small elephant population, as well as hippopotamus, kudu, sable, bushbuck, waterbuck, Sharpe's grysbok, Burchell's zebra and warthog. It contains the magnificent Kapichira Falls on the Shire River, and here the birdwatching is excellent.

381 MICHIRU MOUNTAIN CONSERVATION AREA

Location: Southern Malawi; north-west of Blantyre.
Access: Michiru Mountain lies just outside Blantyre; the route is signposted.
Accommodation: Cleared areas are available for camping, but facilities are very basic. There are hotels in Blantyre.
Other facilities: Self-guided walking trails; night hiking is permitted; picnic sites with fireplaces; a curio shop.
Open: Throughout the year.
Beware: Malaria.
For further information: The Co-ordinator, Michiru Mountain Conservation Area, P.O. Box 619, Blantyre.

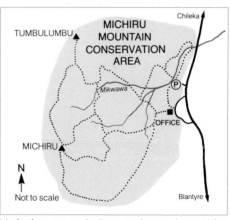

Michiru Mountain Conservation Area covers 5 000 ha of mountain massif and serves as a centre for environmental education, with areas set aside for forestry, agriculture, and natural vegetation with the wildlife it supports. The area contains a large expanse of woodland and includes patches of riverine and montane forest. Mammal species include bushbuck, common duiker, klipspringer, side-striped jackal, spotted hyena, leopard, serval, baboon, vervet monkey and greater bushbaby. More than 200 bird species have been recorded.

382 MULANJE MOUNTAIN

Location: South-eastern Malawi; south-east of Blantyre.
Access: From Blantyre follow the main road south-eastwards to Mulanje. About 20 km beyond this settlement a minor road to the left leads towards the mountain.
Accommodation: There are 6 mountain huts at various points on the mountain, each accommodating between 8 and 20 persons and equipped with very basic facilities; a corrugated iron shelter at the foot of Sapitwa Peak. Huts must be booked well in advance and proof of booking may be requested.
Other facilities: An extensive network of paths.
Open: Throughout the year, although movement may be limited during the rainy season.
Beware: Malaria.
For further information: The Department of Tourism (see page 365). (Booking) The Chief

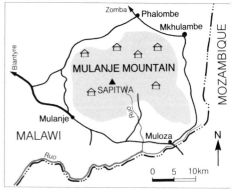

Forester, Ministry of Forestry and Natural Re sources, Mulanje Mountain, P.O. Box 50, Mu lanje. Tel: 46-5218.

Mulanje Mountain is one of the finest scenic areas in Malawi. Its highest point, Sapitwa, rises to 3 002 m above sea-level and the Ruo River flows through the centre of the reserve. Montane grassland and heath cover much of the terrain, although in the gorges there are pockets of forest which contain the massive Mulanje cedars; some of which stand 46 m high. Most game animals have been wiped out by poachers but the area is very rewarding for birdwatchers, and the Knysna lourie and white-tailed flycatcher, as well as several raptor species, may be spotted.

The area is subject to climatic extremes, with high temperatures between August and November, and thunderstorms between November and April, while heavy mist is common during the winter months.

383 MWABVI WILDLIFE RESERVE

Location: Southern Malawi; south of Blantyre.
Access: From Blantyre follow the main road southwards towards Bangula, continuing to the end of the tar; turn right and travel for a short distance to the reserve's gate. Permission to enter the reserve must be obtained in advance.
Accommodation: *Mwabvi camp* has 2 2-bed rondavels and a small camping site, with basic ablution facilities and open wood fires for cooking. *Matope camping site* accommodates 6 people but has no facilities.
Other facilities: A 23-km network of game-viewing roads; walking is allowed; guides can be hired.
Open: April to December.
Beware: Malaria.
For further information: The Department of National Parks and Wildlife (see page 365).

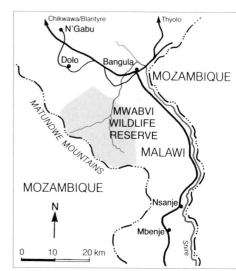

Mwabvi Wildlife Reserve is characterised by spectacular and rugged scenery. It is drained by the upper Thangadzi River and much of its vegetation

comprises mopane woodland. A few black rhinoceros apparently survive here, and there are healthy populations of kudu, sable, suni and warthog, as well as smaller numbers of nyala and buffalo. The birdlife is rich in areas of evergreen thicket along the rivers.
Human settlements in the southern part of the reserve pose a threat to its long-term viability.

384 NKHOTAKOTA WILDLIFE RESERVE

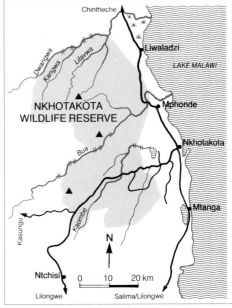

Location: Central Malawi; north of Lilongwe.
Access: From Lilongwe travel north-eastwards towards Salima for about 70 km before turning left and continuing northwards to Nkhotakota village; from Nkhotakota drive westwards towards Kasungu; this road passes through the reserve. During the rainy season access is possible only in 4x4 vehicles. Permission to enter the reserve must be obtained in advance.
Accommodation: *Chipata camp* has a rondavel, a student hostel and a camping site. *Bua camp* has a caravan and a camping site. *Wodzi camp* has a camping site. Facilities are very basic.
Other facilities: Game-viewing roads; guided walks on Chipata mountain and along the Bua River; fishing for lake salmon at Bua (licence required). The nearest supplies are at Nkhotakota village.
Open: Throughout the year.
Beware: Malaria; bilharzia.
For further information: The Department of National Parks and Wildlife (see page 365).

Nkhotakota, which is the oldest wildlife reserve in Malawi, is perhaps best known for its dramatic scenery. Covering 1 802 km², it lies in the hills of the Rift Valley escarpment and is dominated by Chipata Mountain. Several rivers flow through it to Lake Malawi, principal among them being the Bua River, whose course is broken by some impressive waterfalls.
The vegetation, predominantly miombo woodland and rain forest, supports a number of game species, which are generally difficult to spot. These include elephant, Burchell's zebra, sable, bushbuck and buffalo, and some lion occur. Birdwatching can be very rewarding here, with a great variety of species being seen.

385 NYIKA NATIONAL PARK

Location: Northern Malawi; north of Lilongwe
Access: From Lilongwe take the main road northwards in the direction of Kasungu to Mzuzu via Chikangawa (this is a tarred all-weather road, and is in excellent condition); from Mzuzu continue northwards on a tarmac road for about 63 km to Rumphi, then turn westwards towards Katumbi, turning right to the park after about 50 km. Chilinda camp is 60 km from the entrance. A 4x4 vehicle is recommended for travelling in the park during the

rainy season. There is an airstrip 3 km from Chilinda camp.
Accommodation: *Chilinda camp* has 4 4-bed chalets, each with a kitchen, bathroom and lounge, and 6 2-bed rooms (with toilets), with a separate kitchen and dining room and communal ablution facilities. A new 4-bedroomed chalet with bathroom is also available as is a camp with 4 2-bed tents with bathrooms and basic facilities. A 4-bed log cabin 50 km from Chilinda has basic facilities. A youth hostel can take 56 students.

Other facilities: 1- to 5-day walking trails; casual walking is permitted; a 280-km network of game-viewing roads; guided night safaris; an information centre; birdwatching hides; troutfishing; view points; boats for hire; fuel; shop selling basic foodstuffs; bar.
Open: Throughout the year.
Beware: Malaria (but this is minimal).
For further information: The Warden, Nyika National Park, Private Bag 6, Rumphi.

The Nyika Plateau, bounded on all sides by steep escarpments, is one of the most beautiful montane plateaux in Africa. The 3 134-km^2 Nyika National Park encompasses it and is covered by grassland and patches of evergreen forest, with miombo woodland in the lower-lying areas. The best time to see in flower the many plants that grow here is from December to March.

Burchell's zebra, warthog, roan, eland, reedbuck, bushbuck and common duiker are the most common game species in the park, with leopard and side-striped jackal also present, but seldom seen. Small numbers of elephant and hippopotamus occur in the lower-lying areas to the north. The

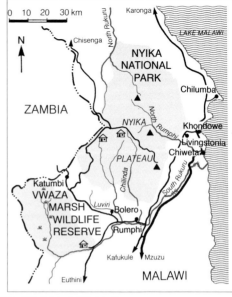

birdlife is very varied, and is particularly good between October and December.

In summer this high-altitude area is much cooler than the adjacent lower-lying regions, and during the winter months, between May and July, frost occurs regularly.

---

386 VWAZA MARSH WILDLIFE RESERVE See map Nyika National Park

Location: Northern Malawi; north of Lilongwe.
Access: From Lilongwe follow the route to Nyika National Park as far as Rumphi; take the gravel road towards Katumbi, turning left to Vwaza Marsh about 10 km from Rumphi. A 4x4 vehicle is recommended to negotiate this road during the rainy season. Permission to enter the reserve must be obtained in advance.
Accommodation: *Lake Kazuni camp* has 5 2-bed tents on concrete bases; pit toilets.

Khaya camping site has basic facilities. Visitors are permitted to camp elsewhere but there are no facilities.
Other facilities: A 124-km network of game-viewing roads, passable only in the dry season; a picnic site at Lake Kazuni.
Open: May to October.
Beware: Malaria.
For further information: The Department of National Parks and Wildlife (see page 365).

This 1 000-km^2 reserve has a wide range of habitats, including miombo and mopane woodland, marshland and rocky hills. A great variety of bird species occur in the marsh, and around Lake Kazuni on the south-eastern boundary, there is a small population of hippopotamus. The woodland on the flood plains of the South Rukuru River supports fairly high densities of elephant, buffalo, roan, impala and warthog, as well as lion and leopard.

---

387 ZOMBA PLATEAU

Location: Southern Malawi; north-east of Blantyre.
Access: From Blantyre follow the main road eastwards to Limbe, then turn northwards and continue to Zomba; from Zomba follow a sign-

posted narrow track north-westwards to the plateau. Internal roads may be difficult to negotiate during the rains.
Accommodation: Kuchawe Inn offers hotel accommodation. There is a camping site with

basic facilities close to the hotel.

Other facilities: A 24-km network of scenic drives; self-guided nature trails; trout-fishing.

Open: Throughout the year.

For further information: The National Faunal Preservation Society of Malawi, P.O. Box 1429, Blantyre. (Kuchawe Inn) P.O. Box 71, Zomba.

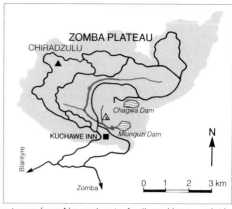

The Zomba Plateau rises 1 000 m above the surrounding plains and protects patches of montane evergreen forest, exotic plantations and open grassland. The plateau offers spectacular views over the Shire River Valley and incorporates several peaks, the highest of which is Chiradzulu at 2 084 m above sea-level. The forest and grassland contain abundant birdlife.

The area is subject to climatic extremes, with high temperatures from August to November, thunderstorms from November to April, and heavy mist in the winter months.

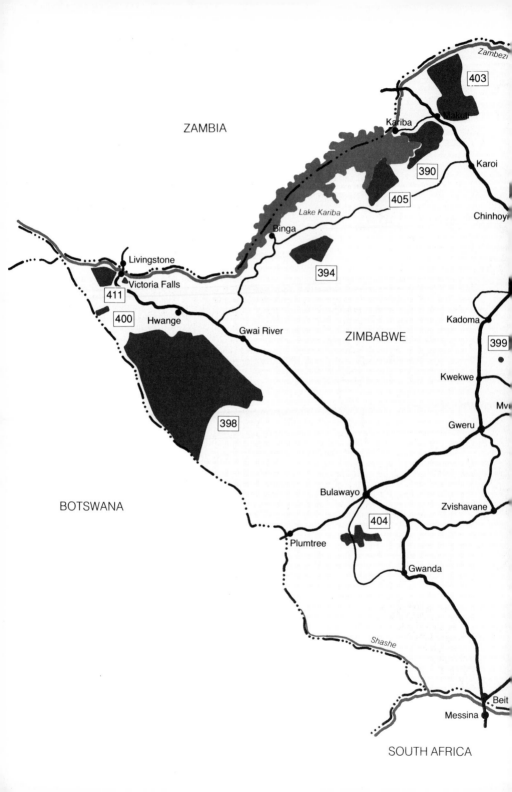

ZIMBABWE

Zimbabwe is a completely landlocked country more than 390 000 km^2 in extent. The mighty Zambezi River and one of Africa's greatest man-made lakes, Kariba, lie on its north-western border, dividing the country from Zambia, while in the south, the Limpopo River forms the border with South Africa. The western border is formed by Botswana, and to the east, beyond the Eastern Highlands, lies Mozambique.

A country of great natural beauty, Zimbabwe has a wide variety of habitats that support its magnificent wildlife. These range from the dry Kalahari sands in the west, through a variety of woodland savannah types (including mopane and miombo, which is known as *Brachystegia* in Zimbabwe) and open grassland, to the lush montane forests and heathland of the Eastern Highlands. The climate is subtropical with a summer rainy season, most of the rainfall occurring between December and the middle of March, with peaks of up to 1 500 mm annually in the Eastern Highlands. Summers are usually warm to hot, October and November being the hottest months, and winters are mild. Malaria is still a danger in many areas and there is tsetse fly in parts of the Zambezi Valley and the south-east. Most rivers, lakes and dams are infected with bilharzia.

Zimbabwe's national parks and safari areas cover more than 12 per cent of the country's total surface area and the vast majority of the conservation areas are controlled by the Department of National Parks and Wildlife Management (see page 365). In addition to the world-famous Hwange National Park, there are parts of the Zambezi Valley which constitute some of southern Africa's last true wilderness areas.

Self-catering accommodation in the parks run by the Department of National Parks and Wildlife consists of one- and two-bedroomed chalets, cottages and lodges. They usually have two or four beds and are equipped with basic furniture, refrigerators, cooking utensils, bedding and towels; lighting is provided by paraffin, electricity or gas. *Chalets* have external cooking facilities and visitors must provide their own crockery and cutlery; ablution facilities are shared. *Cottages* have their own kitchen and bathroom, but no crockery and cutlery. *Lodges* have their own kitchen and bathroom, and are fully serviced and

equipped. All bookings should be made to the National Parks Central Booking Office. They ma be made up to six months in advance and de posits are required in all cases. Enquiries abou exclusive camps (at Hwange, Mana Pools an Matusadona national parks) should also b made to the central booking office.

During the dry, cooler months of the year th Department of National Parks and Wildlife als run three- to four-day wilderness trails for group of up to six in Chizarira, Hwange, Mana Pools an Matusadona national parks. These are not luxur trails and participants must be prepared to carr their own packs, including food, and shoul therefore be in a reasonable state of fitness Details about these trails can be obtaine through the central booking office or the Bula wayo Booking Agency, P.O. Box 2283, Bula wayo. Tel: Bulawayo 63646.

Visitors from outside Zimbabwe require vali passports, and some nationals will need visas The unit of currency is Zimbabwe dollars.

388   BUNGA FOREST AND VUMBA BOTANICAL RESERVES

Location: The Eastern Highlands; south-east of Mutare.
Access: From Mutare drive south-eastwards along Vumba Rd for 27 km and follow the signposts to Bunga Forest. Vumba lies 5 km east of Bunga on the Vumba Rd. The access roads are usually suitable for ordinary vehicles.
Accommodation: None at Bunga. Vumba has a camping and caravan site with ablution facilities. There is accommodation in and around Mutare.
Other facilities: Both reserves have a network of footpaths; picnic site and tearoom at Vumba; swimming pool in the camping site.
Open: Throughout the year.
Opening time: Reserve – sunrise to sunset; office (Mondays to Saturdays) – 07h00 to 17h00, (Sundays) – 08h00 to 17h00.
For further information: The Curator, Vumba Botanical Garden, Private Bag V 7472, Mutare. Tel: Mutare 21-2722 (office) or 21-2713 (home).

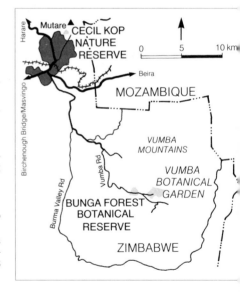

Bunga Forest Botanical Reserve covers 1 558 ha in the magnificent splendour of the Vumba Mountain and preserves a wealth of plant life of the area. The terrain is quite steep and well forested with evergree trees, and although the vegetation is the main attraction of this reserve, the birdlife is rich and sma mammals such as samango monkey and tree civet are present.

The Vumba Botanical Reserve covers 42 ha and contains a 32-ha botanical garden, while th remaining area is covered by indigenous forest.

Temperatures in the area are approximately 5 to 10 °C lower than in other parts of the country and ar subject to rapid changes.

389 CECIL KOP
NATURE RESERVE See map Bunga Forest and Vumba Botanical Reserves

Location: The Eastern Highlands; north of Mutare.
Access: From Mutare drive along Herbert Chitepo St and turn into Arcadia Rd; continue northwards, following the signposts to the reserve.
Accommodation: None. There are hotels and caravan and camping sites in and around Mutare.
Other facilities: A network of roads and paths; pony trails; viewing platforms and hides; educational programme for school-children. A refreshment kiosk is open at weekends.
Open: Throughout the year.
Opening time: 07h00 to sunset.
For further information: The Manicaland branch of the Wildlife Society of Zimbabwe, P.O. Box 920, Mutare. Tel: Mutare 6-1537 or 6-1570.

Cecil Kop Nature Reserve was initiated by the Manicaland branch of the Wildlife Society as an environmental education facility aimed principally at schoolchildren. A full-time education officer runs the programme.

The reserve is 1 740 ha in extent and consists of montane grassland, evergreen forest, *Brachystegia* (miombo) woodland, grassy vleis and man-made dams. As well as the common and blue duiker, bushbuck and kudu which occur naturally in the area, a number of other game species have been introduced and they include elephant, white rhinoceros, giraffe and a wide range of antelope species. Vehicles are allowed into the game area but access to the wilderness block is only on foot or horseback. The latter area has no potentially dangerous game species.

390 CHARARA SAFARI AREA

Location: Northern Zimbabwe; north-west of Harare.
Access: From Harare follow the Great North Road north-westwards through Chinhoyi and Karoi to Makuti, then turn left towards Kariba. The turn-off to Nyanyana camp is about 56 km from Makuti and is clearly signposted. The last 5,5 km is on dirt road. A 4x4 vehicle is recommended for the internal road network.
Accommodation: *Nyanyana camp* has a camping and caravan site with 35 stands, ablution facilities and fireplaces.
Other facilities: Slipway for launching boats; game-viewing on foot is permitted (if accom-panied, a small charge is levied). Part of the Charara Safari Area has been leased to the Wildlife Society of Zimbabwe which has de-veloped a game-viewing platform and some picnic sites; further information and permits can be obtained from Kariba Cruisers. The nearest food and fuel supplies are 28 km away at Kariba.
Open: Throughout the year; movement within the reserve may be restricted during the rains (December to March).
Opening time: Sunrise to sunset.
Beware: Malaria; crocodiles; potentially dan-gerous game frequent the camp.
For further information: Charara Safari Area, Private Bag 2002, Kariba. Tel: Kariba

2257 (main office) or 2-2517 (Nyanyana camp). (Bookings) National Parks Central Booking Office (see page 365). (Kariba Cruisers) Tel: Kariba 2839.

Charara Safari Area covers an area of approximately 1 700 km² along the eastern shore of Lake Kariba. *Brachystegia* (miombo) and mopane woodland dominate the landscape and provide cover for a wide range of game species, such as elephant, black rhinoceros, buffalo, waterbuck, kudu, bushbuck, leopard and lion. Most game species can be seen close to the camp, and elephant frequently pass through on their way to the water's edge 100 m from the camping site. Mining of tin, copper, chrome and other minerals was carried out here in the past and signs of these activities are still visible in some areas. The summer months are hot and the average annual rainfall of 660 mm occurs at this time. Winters are mild, with an average daytime temperature of 25 °C.

391 CHIMANIMANI NATIONAL PARK

Location: The Eastern Highlands; east of Masvingo.

Access: From Masvingo take the main road to Birchenough Bridge; just beyond the town turn right and follow this road towards Chipinge for about 50 km; turn left and travel 56 km further to Chimanimani village. Alternatively, from Mutare follow the main road southwards towards Masvingo for 66 km and turn left towards Mutambara; after 13 km turn right, then drive another 70 km, following the signposts to Chimanimani village. This road ends at the base camp (Mutekeswane). There are no roads in the park. All visitors must report to either the ranger's office at Eland Sanctuary, Chimanimani or the information office at the base camp.

Accommodation: A single communal hut with basic facilities is situated some 3 hours' walk into the park. There is a camping site with a limited number of stands and ablution facilities at the base camp; no caravans are permitted. There is a hotel and a caravan and camping site at Chimanimani village.

Other facilities: A network of footpaths and narrow tracks; an information office at base camp; trout fishing is permitted in the Bundi River from 1 October to 21 April (a licence is required). Food supplies and fuel are available at Chimanimani village.

Open: Throughout the year.

Opening time: Reserve – sunrise to sunset; office – 07h00 to 17h00.

Beware: Inadvertently crossing the border into Mozambique, which is unfenced. It is also advisable to check on the security situation with the warden.

For further information: The Warden, Private Bag 2063, Chimanimani. Tel: Chimanimani 555.

The Chimanimani Mountains are thought to have developed some 1 600 million years ago and now form three distinct ridges within the park. For several centuries the area was used as a route between the coastal ports of Mozambique and the Zimbabwean interior by slave traders and merchants. Although there is some controversy over the origin of the name it is almost certainly derived from the tribal Ndawu word 'tschimanimani', meaning 'to be squeezed together'.

The park covers 17 110 ha of rugged mountain country broken by deep gorges and high peaks, such as Point 71 which rises to 2 436 m above sea-level. There are many perennial mountain streams. The vegetation of the area is principally dry montane forest and grassland, but it has similarities with the montane fynbos (heath) of the western and southern Cape Province of South Africa. A variety of proteas, ericas and everlastings, as well as subtropical ferns, can be seen. Although large game species are not common, eland, sable and bushbuck do occur here. Klipspringer may be observed on the rocky slopes and the secretive blue duiker in the forest thickets. Baboons roam throughout the area. Birdlife is varied and includes fynbos species such as Gurney's sugarbird and the malachite sunbird, forest species such as the trumpeter hornbill and the crowned eagle, and grassland species such as the secretarybird and Shelley's francolin. The winter months are the best for visiting Chimanimani, particularly for a walking holiday. Low cloud, mist and storms can occur at any time of the year.

CHINHOYI CAVES RECREATIONAL PARK

Location: Northern Zimbabwe; north-west of Harare.
Access: From Harare follow the main road north-westwards to Chinhoyi; continue past Chinhoyi for approximately 10 km. The entrance to the park lies to the right of the road.
Accommodation: None. The Caves Motel lies on the boundary of the reserve and a camping and caravan site with ablution facilities is situated nearby (Z$10 per stand per night).
Other facilities: Picnic site; restaurant; cave walks. Fuel is available at the Caves Motel.
Open: Throughout the year.
Opening time: Sunrise to sunset.
For further information: Chinhoyi Caves Recreational Park, P.O. Box 193, Chinhoyi. Tel: Chinhoyi 2550.

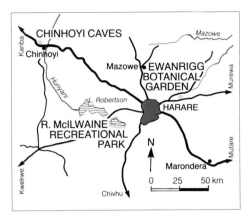

This small park makes an interesting stopping-off spot on the way to Mana Pools National Park or Charara Safari Area on Lake Kariba. It is situated at the foot of the Hunyani Hills and much of the countryside is covered by *Brachystegia* (miombo) woodland.

The Chinhoyi caves were formed by the erosive action of water on soft limestone and are now flooded. Recent exploration has shown that the pool in the main cave, the Sleeping Pool, varies between 88 and 91 m deep and contains several underwater passages. It is believed that the water in the cave may be connected with an even larger body of water, as the temperature of the Sleeping Pool's water remains constant at 22 °C. Pottery and human remains have been excavated in and near the park and have been dated to approximately AD 650. The Shona name for the caves is Chirorodziva, meaning 'pool of the fallen'. This name apparently has its origins in the 1830s, when the people living near the cave were attacked by a marauding tribe and were hurled to their deaths in the deep limestone vaults.

CHIRINDA FOREST BOTANICAL RESERVE

Location: The Eastern Highlands; south-east of Masvingo.
Access: From Masvingo follow the main road eastwards to Birchenough Bridge; just beyond the town turn right towards Chipinge; continue past this village for approximately 86 km towards Mount Selinda Mission; turn right to the reserve just before the mission. There are no internal roads in the reserve.
Accommodation: None.
Other facilities: Picnic sites; pathways.
Open: Throughout the year.
Opening times: Sunrise to sunset.
For further information: National Parks Central Booking office (see page 365).

This reserve was set aside to protect 949 ha of magnificent montane evergreen forest and the rich animal life supported by this habitat. The Chirinda Forest contains more than 100 species of typical evergreen montane trees, such as ironwood, red mahogany and several different figs. The tallest tree in Zimbabwe, a 66-m red mahogany, can be seen here. Spring, when many of the flowering plants are in bloom, is a good time to visit. There is a great variety of undergrowth vegetation, such as creepers, ferns and mosses, and it is this lush vegetation that is home to many vertebrate and invertebrate animal species, several of which are very rare. Species include samango monkey, tree civet, blue duiker, sun squirrel and red squirrel, but many of these animals are elusive and seldom observed. Forest birds abound, although most species are more often heard than seen. Both the Knysna and purple-crested louries occur, as well as the crested guineafowl, trumpeter hornbill, several sunbird species and the black-fronted bushshrike. Most visible of all are the numerous butterfly species, particularly during and shortly after the rains, when food in the form of blossoms and rotting vegetation is most abundant. Well worth a few minutes' observation are the many spider species in the forest.

Interestingly, several plant and invertebrate species that are found here are also known to occur in parts of West Africa, suggesting that a large part of the continent was at one time covered by a continuous belt of rain forest.

The climate is subtropical, but winter nights can be cold. Like the rest of Zimbabwe, this is a summer-rainfall area. Mist can be expected at any time of the year.

394 CHIZARIRA NATIONAL PARK

Location: Western Zimbabwe; west of Harare.

Access: From Harare follow the main road north-westwards towards Chirundu, reaching Karoi after about 200 km; continue past Karoi for 8 km and turn left towards Binga; follow this road south-westwards for about 290 km, then take the signposted left turn to the park, and continue another 20 km to the park's headquarters. This route covers rough dirt roads and 4x4 or high-clearance vehicles are strongly recommended. Alternatively, from Bulawayo follow the main road towards Victoria Falls; about 34 km past Gwai River turn right and travel towards Binga; after about 134 km turn right towards Siabuwa and, near the 47-km peg, take the right turn to the reserve. Most vehicles should be able to negotiate this road without difficulty. It is advisable to check road conditions with the authority in advance. All visitors must report to the warden's office on arrival. The internal roads are in a poor condition, and a 4x4 vehicle is essential.

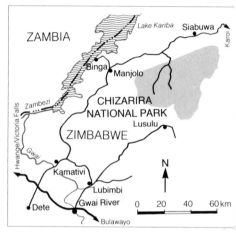

Accommodation: At present there are 3 basic bush camps and several more are in the planning stages. *Kasiswi Bush Camp* is situated on the upper reaches of Lusilukuli River, 6 km from the park's headquarters, and consists of 2 raised sleeping shelters, a dining shelter and ablution facilities. *Mobola Bush Camp* is on the Mucheni River below Manzituba Spring, 6 km from the park's headquarters, and has ablution facilities. *Busi Bush Camp* lies on the banks of the Busi River, 35 km from the park's headquarters, and has 2 sleeping shelters, a dining shelter, a cooking area and basic ablution facilities. The road to this camp is very rough. Chizarira Lodge – 16-bed privately run thatched complex. P.O. Box 18 Victoria Falls. Tel: (0926313) 4337; Fax 4417.

Other facilities: Accompanied wilderness trails of up to 10 days during the dry season the adjoining safari areas, Chirisa and Chewore, also offer wilderness trails; escorted walks with an armed game scout (no unaccompanied walking is allowed). The nearest fuel and food supplies are about 90 km away at Binga.

Open: Throughout the year; movement on some roads is restricted during the rainy season. In future the park may be closed during the rainy season.

Opening time: Sunrise to sunset.

Beware: Malaria; all water should be boiled

188. The magnificent sable antelope is a common sight in Hwange National Park.

189. Kwali Camp, a Cresta Sandstone Lodge, nestles in the Chiredzi region near Zimbabwe's famous Gonarezhou National Park.

190. The Zimbabwe ruins in Great Zimbabwe Park.

191. Mopane woodland of Hwange National Park provides both food and shelter for the shy kudu.

192. Tree-house accommodation at a bush camp in Hwange.

193. Hwange is particularly well known for its large herds of buffalo.

194. Iwaba Wildlife Estate offers comfortable accommodation.

195. The M'Tarazi Falls in the national park of the same name.

196. Msasa trees add colour to the lake shore in the Lake Kyle Recreation Area.

197. Pungwe Falls in Nyanga National Park is one of the scenic highlights of the area.

198. Chalet accommodation at the Robert McIlwaine Recreational Park.

199. At Mana Pools National Park the Zambezi flood plain provides grazing for many animals.

or chemically treated; potentially dangerous game: do not get out of your vehicle except at camps or when accompanied by a ranger. **For further information:** The Warden, Chiza-

rira National Park, P.O. Box 13, Binga. (Bush camps and wilderness trails, including Chirisa and Chewore) National Parks Central Booking Office (see page 365).

Chizarira National Park is a remote and rugged wilderness area set among the Chizarira Hills, where the peak of the highest mountain, Tundazi, rises to 1 433 m above sea-level. The terrain of the 192 000-ha park varies considerably and includes magnificent gorges, plateaux and flood plains. The vegetation, too, is varied, but consists mainly of *Brachystegia* (miombo) and mopane woodland, scrub savannah and grassland.

Game and other mammal species are abundant and include elephant, black rhinoceros, buffalo, eland, bushbuck, kudu, Sharpe's grysbok, klipspringer, tsessebe and warthog. The birdlife is rich, but there is no checklist available.

Summers are hot and the rains occur at this time. The hottest area lies along the Busi River in the south, whereas the upper escarpment area is somewhat cooler. Winters are mild and dry.

395 EWANRIGG BOTANICAL GARDEN See map Chinhoyi Caves Recreational Park

Location: Eastern Zimbabwe; north-east of Harare.
Access: From Harare follow the main road eastwards towards Mutoko; turn left towards Shamva and follow the signposts to the garden. The garden lies 41 km from Harare.
Accommodation: None.

Other facilities: Picnic sites with fireplaces; a network of pathways.
Open: Throughout the year.
Opening time: 08h00 to sunset.
For further information: The Curator, Ewanrigg Botanical Garden, P.O. Box 8119, Causeway, Harare.

The Ewanrigg Botanical Garden is probably best known for its collection of cycads and aloes, many of which do not occur naturally in the area. There is a great variety of other species to be seen, and many of the plants are identified by name plates. The garden contains a 40-ha cultivated area, while natural vegetation flourishes in the remaining 200 ha, where visitors may wander along a network of paths. The best time to see the plants in bloom is during the winter and spring months, although the garden is worth visiting throughout the year. A wide range of bird species occurs.

396 GONAREZHOU NATIONAL PARK

Location: South-eastern Zimbabwe; adjoining Mozambique.
Access: Follow the main road from Ngundu, passing Chiredzi on the Tanganda road; 20 km east of Chiredzi turn right and continue along a graded gravel road past Chipinda Pools. Visitors coming from the south can take the Rutenga/Boli road (check conditions), which is considerably shorter, to Mabalauta/Swimuwini camp. Check details with the authorities.
Accommodation: *Swimuwini camp* (south) has 3 5-bed thatched chalets and 2 3-bed units. Equipment is supplied except cutlery/crockery; ablution facilities in a separate block. Limited camping, with ablution facilities, at Mabalauta. Chipinda Pools and Chinguli (north) have camping areas with ablution facilities. Seven undeveloped camps (Nyahungwe, Madumbini, Bopomela, Lisoda,

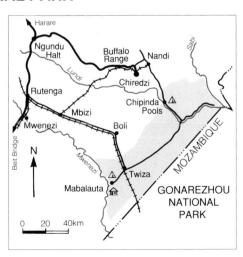

Gata, Chitove and Chamaluvati) with very basic facilities can be hired. Cresta Sandstone Safari Lodges – Induna Lodge and Kwali Camp near park. Tel: (092634) 703253.
Other facilities: A good network of game-viewing roads but conditions on these roads vary and 4x4 or high clearance vehicles are preferable; fishing is permitted in the Lundi River (north) from basic camping sites only. No fuel or food is available in the park; visitors must take along all their requirements.
Open: 1 May to 31 October; closed during the rainy season.

Opening time: Office – 07h00 to 12h00 14h00 to 16h30; gate – 06h00 to 18h00.
Beware: Malaria; bilharzia; exercise caution near elephants.
For further information: (North) The Warden, Gonarezhou National Park, Private Bag 7003, Chiredzi, Zimbabwe. Tel: Chiredzi 397. (South) The Warden, Gonarezhou National Park, Private Bag 7017, Chiredzi, Zimbabwe (Advance booking): National Parks Central Booking Office (see page 365) (Lone Star Lodge) Cresta Hotels and Safaris, P.O. Box 2833, Harare. Tel: 794641, Fax: 794655..

Gonarezhou covers 5 000 km^2 and it is divided into two administrative areas, Chipinda Pools in the north and Mabalauta in the south. The Sabi River forms the northern boundary and the Nwanetsi River laps its southern reaches.

Vegetation consists mainly of open to dense woodland, open grassland and stands of the impressive musimbiti (ironwood) trees.

The red sandstone Tjolotjo (previously called Clarendon) Cliffs lining the Lundi River form a magnificent backdrop. Other features are the Chivilila Falls, also on the Lundi, and the four Gorhwe Pans located in the southern sector. Game species are varied and include elephant, buffalo, hippopotamus, Lichtenstein's hartebeest, Burchell's zebra, giraffe, nyala and roan antelope. Unfortunately, poaching in recent years has depleted numbers of certain game species, most notably elephant and black rhinoceros. Elephant must be treated with great respect and always keep your distance.

Birdlife is very rich, particularly along the wooded river banks, and includes such rarities as the hooded vulture, blue-spotted dove, Pel's fishing owl, Angola pitta, silvery-cheeked hornbill, Mashona hyliota and yellow-bellied sunbird.

Winters are generally mild although nights can be cold, warming up from September, with summer temperatures exceeding 40 °C not unusual. Rain falls at this time.

397 | GREAT ZIMBABWE PARK AND NATIONAL MONUMENT

Location: Eastern Zimbabwe; south of Masvingo.
Access: From Masvingo drive southwards in the direction of Beit Bridge, turning left towards Lake Kyle. The route to the park is well signposted.
Accommodation: None but there are a number of hotels and camping sites situated nearby.
Other facilities: A museum; short trails.
Open: Throughout the year.
Opening time: Park – 08h00 to 17h00; museum – 08h00 to 16h30.
For further information: National Parks Central Booking Office (see page 365).

The Great Zimbabwe Ruins are steeped in legend and tradition and constitute some of Africa's most complex and well-preserved archaeological sites. The ruins, all that remains of a royal stronghold built by the Karanga, ancestors of the Shona, have been dated to between AD 1200 and 1450. It is here that the 'Zimbabwe birds', large soapstone carvings which have become an integral part of the Zimbabwean culture, were discovered.

The adjacent small reserve protects 723 ha of open woodland savannah vegetation and is particularly well known for its aloes.

HWANGE NATIONAL PARK

Location: Western Zimbabwe; north-west of Bulawayo.
Access: From Bulawayo take the main road towards Victoria Falls. To reach *Main Camp,* about 17 km after Gwai River (at the 264,5-km peg) turn left at the signpost to the park and continue for 24 km to the camp. Alternatively, continue along the main road for another 16 km; turn left to Dete village and follow the signposts to Main Camp. To reach *Sinamatella Camp,* about 340 km from Bulawayo turn left and drive 45 km to the camp; this road should be suitable for most vehicles. *Lukosi Exclusive Camp* can be reached from Sinamatella. *Bumbusi Exclusive Camp* lies 24 km north-west of Sinamatella and can be reached by ordinary vehicles during the dry season, but a 4x4 vehicle is required during the rains. To reach *Robins Camp,* approximately 390 km from Bulawayo turn left; follow this road for about 70 km to the camp, along a clearly signposted route. *Nantwich Camp* is close to Robins Camp. *Deka Exclusive Camp* lies 25 km west of Robins Camp and can only be reached by 4x4 vehicles. During the rainy season a number of roads are closed; check with the authority in advance. There is an airstrip at Main Camp and Hwange National Park Aerodrome is nearby. The park can also be reached by train (Dete station is 19 km away). Transport and tours can be arranged through United Touring Company.
Accommodation: *Main Camp* has 1- and 2-bedroomed cottages, lodges and chalets. The cottages and chalets share cooking and dining facilities. There is a camping site with a limited number of stands and ablution facilities.
Sinamatella Camp has similar accommodation to Main Camp. *Bumbusi* and *Lukosi* exclusive camps each have 4 2-bed units and a 4-bed cottage; both have a fully equipped communal kitchen and communal ablution facilities.
Robins Camp has 1- and 2-bedroomed chalets. *Nantwich Camp* has 2-bedroomed lodges. *Deka Exclusive Camp* has 2 3-bedroomed serviced family units, each *en suite.* There is a communal dining room, sitting room and a fully equipped kitchen.
Ivory Lodge, just outside the park in its own wilderness estate, has 10 luxury thatched treehouses, each with a bathroom, and a verandah overlooking a waterhole; shop, dining room and game-viewing platform. *Hwange*

Safari Lodge lies outside the park not far from Main Camp and offers luxury accommodation and tours.
With the permission of the warden, single groups of up to 8 persons may camp for a single night at 6 of the picnic sites (Shumba, Mandavu Pan, Ngweshla, Jambile, Kennedy 1 and Deteema) in the park. These sites are enclosed and have ablution facilities and water.
Other facilities: A 480-km network of game-viewing drives (mostly dirt roads; some sections are closed during the rainy season); picnic sites; large hides at several waterholes. *Main Camp* offers game-viewing by moonlight; escorted walks; a shop selling basic supplies; a restaurant and bar; petrol and diesel. *Sinamatella Camp* offers escorted walks, wilderness trails between April and October; a restaurant; a shop selling basic goods; petrol and diesel. *Robins Camp* offers escorted walks; wilderness trails between April and October; shop selling basic supplies; petrol and diesel. The availability of goods varies from time to time. Ivory Safaris conducts game-viewing drives from *Ivory Lodge.* The nearest point for vehicle repairs is at Hwange town, 101 km from Main Camp and 46 km from Sinamatella.
Open: Main and Sinamatella camps – throughout the year; Robins Camp – 1 May to 31 October.
Opening time: Park – sunrise to sunset; Main Camp office – 07h00 to 18h00.

Speed limit: 40 km/h.
Beware: Malaria.
For further information: (Main Camp) The Warden, Main Camp, Private Bag DT 5776, Dete. Tel: Dete 331/2. (Sinamatella Camp) The Warden, Sinamatella Camp, Private Bag WK 5941, Hwange. Tel: Hwange 4-4255. (Robins Camp) The Warden, Robins Camp, Private Bag WK 5936, Hwange. Tel: Hwange 7-0220. (Ivory Lodge) P.O. Box 55, Dete. Tel: Dete 3402. (United Touring Company) Hwange Safari Lodge, Private Bag 5792, Hwange. (Ivory Safaris) P.O. Box 9127, Hillside, Bulawayo. Tel: 6-1709. (Wilderness trails) National Parks Central Booking Office (see page 365).

Hwange National Park is one of the finest conservation areas in Africa and is said to contain the widest variety and the greatest density of wildlife in the world. The 14 651-km^2 park takes its name from Hwange, a sub-chief of the local Rozvi tribe who, along with his people, was annihilated by the warriors of Mzilikazi, the Matabele chieftain. Until 1928 the game in this region was hunted regularly and on a drastic scale, but in that year the park was set aside to protect the wildlife. Only a relatively small area is accessible to the visitor.

Most of Hwange is covered by Kalahari sand and consists of flat plains and large natural pans, with granite outcrops in the north. There are large, open, grass-covered plains with scattered bush thickets throughout much of the park, and extensive areas of mopane woodland in the north. Although there are no perennial streams or rivers flowing through the area, the numerous natural pans fill up after the rains in summer. At this time game-viewing is more difficult, as the grass is long and the wildlife dispersed, but it can be more rewarding because many species drop their young. During the dry winter months the animals must rely for water on man-made waterholes and boreholes, and vast herds of elephant and buffalo come to drink. More than 26 000 elephant may be present in Hwange in winter, but with the onset of the rains they disperse as far afield as Chobe National Park and the Okavango Delta in northern Botswana.

Black and white rhinoceros have been re-introduced into the park. The former are most abundant in the northern sector, while white rhinoceros favour mixed bush and grassland areas and can usually be seen at the major waterholes around Main Camp. Sixteen antelope species occur in the park, including sable, roan and gemsbok, and giraffe and Burchell's zebra are common and widespread. To date 25 predator species have been recorded here; lion and spotted hyena are found throughout Hwange, and leopard are fairly common in the northern areas, but are rarely seen. Crocodile are present in some of the larger waterholes. Patient waiting at a waterhole for several hours, particularly in the dry season, can be more rewarding than covering long distances on the game-viewing drives, since most species will come to drink during the day. More than 400 bird species have been observed.

399 IWABA WILDLIFE ESTATE

Location: Central Zimbabwe; south-west of Harare.
Access: From Harare take the main road to Bulawayo south-westwards, passing through Kadoma; about 60 km beyond Kadoma turn left onto the Shamwari road; after 36 km take the signposted left turn to the Iwaba Wildlife Estate and continue for another 10 km to the camp.
Accommodation: *Safari Camp* has furnished rondavels *en suite* and caters for single groups of between 4 and 8 persons (US$150 per person per day, all inclusive; it is hoped to be able to cater shortly for groups of between 8 and 12 persons); a tented bush camp is also available (maximum 6 persons). Advance booking is essential for all accommodation.
Other facilities: Accompanied walks and drives; game-viewing; night drives; photo-

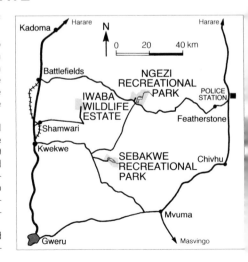

graphy hides; fishing; courses in prehistory and wildlife management (minimum 4 persons).
Open: Throughout the year.
For further information: Iwaba Wildlife Es-

tate, P.O. Box 5, Kwekwe. Tel: Kwekwe 24-7723. Telex: 70006 Travel ZW. Fax: None, but a fax may be sent to the Kwekwe post office (Kwekwe 2169) for placing in the Iwaba post box.

This 10 000-ha, privately owned wildlife estate supports a diversity of mammal and bird species. Mammals that may be seen include black and white rhinoceros, elephant, several antelopes, Burchell's zebra, baboon, vervet monkey, cheetah and leopard, as well as a wide range of smaller species.

400 KAZUMA PAN NATIONAL PARK

Location: Far western Zimbabwe; north-west of Bulawayo.
Access: From Bulawayo take the main road to Victoria Falls; after about 390 km turn left onto the gravel road to Matetsi; drive beyond Matetsi to the park, ignoring the left turn to Robins Camp. The track becomes sandy and only suitable for 4x4 vehicles; check road conditions in advance. Internal roads are usually in poor condition. Visitors should report to the warden at Matetsi Headquarters before proceeding to the park. No day visitors.
Accommodation: None. Camping is allowed in two designated sites with water but no facilities (maximum 10 persons per site).
Other facilities: Walking is permitted.
Open: March to end December.
Opening times: Office (Mondays to Fridays) – 08h00 to 12h00 and 14h00 to 16h30.
Beware: Malaria.
For further information: The Warden, National Parks and Wildlife Management, Matetsi, Private Bag 5926, Victoria Falls. Tel: Victoria Falls 43-3526.

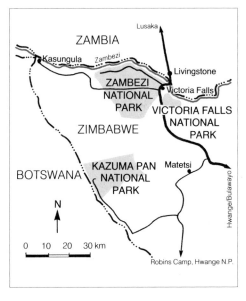

Kazuma Pan National Park covers 31 300 ha of unfenced open grassland savannah, with areas of open woodland. Natural pans fill up during the rainy season and attract large numbers of waterfowl and other birds.
Game species in the park include sable, oribi, kudu, Burchell's zebra and warthog.

401 LAKE KYLE RECREATIONAL PARK
See map Great Zimbabwe Park and National Monument

Location: Eastern Zimbabwe; south of Masvingo.
Access: From Masvingo take the road eastwards towards Birchenough Bridge, turn right at the signpost to Lake Kyle and follow this road to the entrance. Alternatively, from Beit Bridge follow the main road northwards and turn right towards Great Zimbabwe; continue on this road to the park.
Accommodation: Self-catering accommo-

dation comprises 1-, 2- and 3-bedroomed lodges. There are 2 camping and caravan sites, 1 on the southern and 1 on the northern shore of the lake. There are a number of privately owned resorts situated along the southern shore.
Other facilities: Picnic sites with ablution facilities; unaccompanied game-viewing walks in designated areas; accompanied pony trails; fishing is allowed (a licence is required).

The nearest fuel supply is in Masvingo.
Open: Throughout the year.
Opening time: 06h00 to 18h00.
Beware: Bilharzia; crocodiles.

For further information: The Warden, Lake Kyle Recreational Park, Private Bag 9136 Masvingo. (Bookings) National Parks Centra Booking Office (see page 365).

This popular recreational area has been developed around Lake Mutirikwe (Kyle), the second larges dam in Zimbabwe, built at the confluence of the Mshagashje and Mtilikwe rivers. Its total extent is 16 900 ha, just over half of which is taken up by a game park.

The landscape consists of undulating and broken hill country covered mainly by *Brachystegia* (miombo) woodland and grassland. A wide range of game species have been introduced and include white rhinoceros, Burchell's zebra, blue wildebeest, tsessebe, sable, reedbuck, impala, eland warthog, kudu, buffalo and giraffe. Birdwatching is rewarding along the shore of the lake and in particular on Bird Island.

The climate is subtropical, with hot, wet summers. Winters are mild and dry, although nights can be cold.

402 M'TARAZI FALLS NATIONAL PARK See map Nyanga National Park

Location: The Eastern Highlands; south-east of Harare.
Access: From Harare follow the main road south-eastwards in the direction of Mutare as far as Rusape; turn left and follow this road for approximately 100 km to Nyanga National Park. The turn-off to the M'tarazi Falls National Park is indicated in the park via Pungwe. Alternatively turn down the Juliasdale road towards Mutare; after 25 km take the

signposted left turn to the Honde Valley road.
Accommodation: None.
Other facilities: A picnic area with fireplaces short walking trails.
Open: Throughout the year.
Opening time: 07h00 to 18h00.
For further information: The Warden Nyanga National Park, Private Bag T 7901 Mutare. Tel: Nyanga 274.

Although given national park status, M'tarazi Falls National Park is managed as part of the Nyanga National Park. At 762 m the falls are the highest in Zimbabwe and are the main feature of this 2 495-ha park, although it also conserves upland heath and montane mist forest vegetation and the animals that these habitats support. Typical forest dwellers found here are samango monkey, blue duiker, tree cive and crowned eagle.

This is a high-rainfall area, and rain and mist can occur at any time of the year.

403 MANA POOLS NATIONAL PARK See map Charara Safari Area

Location: Northern Zimbabwe; north-west of Harare.
Access: From Harare follow the main road north-westwards in the direction of Chirundu for approximately 310 km to Marongora; continue past Marongora for 6 km, turn right onto a gravel road and drive for 30 km to Nyakasikana Gate. From the gate drive 42 km on a fair to good gravel road past Rukomechi Tsetse Control Camp to Nyamepi Camp. The internal roads are often in poor condition.
Accommodation: *Nyamepi Camp* has a caravan and camping site with 32 stands and ablution facilities. 2 8-bed lodges, serviced and fully equipped, are situated close to Nyamepi Camp. *Vundu Camp*, 13 km from Nyamepi, has 2 sleeping huts accommodat-

ing 12 persons (maximum 2 vehicles), a communal lounge, kitchen and ablution facilities *Nkupe Camp* (1 km from Nyamepi) and *Mucheni Camp* (8 km from Nyamepi) are remote camping sites with basic ablution facilities and braai stands, that can be used by single parties of up to 12 persons with 2 vehicles.
Other facilities: Accompanied wilderness trails; fishing in the Zambezi River; a limited network of game-viewing drives; canoes can be hired. A number of private companies operate walking and canoeing safaris. There are no food or fuel supplies in the park; the nearest fuel is at Makuti.
Open: 1 May to 31 October; check with the authority in advance as these dates may change, depending on weather conditions.

Opening time: Sunrise to sunset.
Beware: Malaria; tsetse flies; crocodiles; potentially dangerous animals; boil or chemi-cally treat all drinking water.
For further information: National Parks Central Booking Office (see page 365).

An unspoilt, remote park situated in the Zambezi Valley, Mana Pools extends over 2 196 km². The name Mana, meaning four, refers to the number of pools on this part of the river's flood plain which form an important feature of the park. From the river the terrain rises southwards to the Zambezi Plateau. The area is bounded in the east by the Sapi and Chewore safari areas, and in the west by Urungwe Safari Area.

The vegetation consists of open areas of grassland and mixed woodland made up mainly of mopane and acacia species, although it also includes giant winter-thorns, great figs and sausage trees, as well as some riverine species.

The park abounds with game such as elephant, buffalo, hippopotamus, black rhinoceros and antelope, and most of the large predator species also occur here. Baboon troops are a common sight near the river. Many people visit the area to enjoy the rich and varied birdlife, particularly near the river and pools. Walking is allowed at visitors' own risk, and can be most rewarding as long as caution is exercised. Avoid walking in dense thickets and high grassland and stay well away from potentially dangerous game species.

The Zambezi Valley has a subtropical climate and temperatures can become extremely high.

404 MATOBO NATIONAL PARK

Location: South-western Zimbabwe; south of Bulawayo.
Access: From central Bulawayo take Grey St and then continue into Matobo Rd; follow this road for 54 km to the rest camp and park's headquarters at Maleme Dam. The route is clearly signposted. The approach to the Maleme Dam is steep and is not recommended for caravans. Internal roads are gravel, but are usually in good to fair condition.
Accommodation: *Maleme Dam* has 1- and 2-bedroomed lodges and chalets. There is also a camping and caravan site with ablution facilities. 4 other camping sites are currently closed, but may be opened again; visitors should contact the warden for further details.
Other facilities: A network of roads; picnic sites; pony trails; walking in designated areas; fishing in the dam (a licence is required); boating (permission must be obtained).
Open: Throughout the year.
Opening time: Park – sunrise to sunset; office – 06h00 to 18h00.
Speed limit: 60 km/h (lower in the game area).
Beware: Bilharzia; malaria; except at Maleme Dam Camp, boil all drinking water.

For further information: The Warden, Matobo National Park, Private Bag K 5142, Bulawayo. Tel: Matopos 0-1913. (Booking) Bulawayo Booking Agency, P.O. Box 2283, Bulawayo.

Matobo National Park covers a total area of 43 200 ha, part of which is set aside for game. The rugged Matobo Hills range consists of broken ridges, valleys and great round capped hills or 'dwalas'. The name Matobo means 'the bald heads', and is said to have been given to these geological formations by the warrior chief, Mzilikazi. Before his time this was the home of the Bushmen, and excellent examples of their paintings can be seen in numerous rock shelters. Cecil John Rhodes is buried in the World's View sector of the park.

Brachystegia (miombo) woodland is the main vegetation type, with msasa and munondo trees predominating and providing a colourful display of fresh foliage in spring. A number of large mammals have been re-introduced to the game area, including white rhinoceros, sable, impala, Burchell's zebra and giraffe. The region is particularly well known for its dense leopard population, but this secretive cat is seldom seen. The careful observer will, however, find tracks and other signs of its presence. This is a true paradise for birds of prey, with a very dense black eagle population and many other raptor species. More than 300 bird species have been recorded at Matobo.

The Matobo range is normally very hot in summer and cold in winter.

405 MATUSADONA NATIONAL PARK See map Charara Safari Area

Location: North-western Zimbabwe; north-west of Harare.
Access: From Harare follow the main road north-westwards to Karoi; continue past Karoi for a further 8 km and turn left; follow this road for 115 km, cross the Sanyati River and drive a further 62 km; turn right to Tashinga and drive 82 km to the Matusadona National Park's headquarters. This is a dirt road and is impassable during the rainy season (November to April). The last stretch should only be attempted by 4x4 vehicles, even in the dry season. The park can also be reached from the west, but check with the authority before using this route. Internal roads are suitable for 4x4 vehicles only. Matusadona can also be reached by boat, and several private operators organise boat safaris along the shoreline throughout the year. There is a small landing strip at Tashinga Camp and safari operators fly in clients to a number of camps nearby.
Accommodation: There are 3 exclusive camps: *Ume*, situated close to Tashinga airstrip on the east bank of the Bumi River, and 55 km from Kariba by boat; *Muuyu Elephant Point*, which is 44 km from Kariba by boat; and *Mbalabala*, which is close to Ume Camp. Each camp has 2 6-bed, fully equipped family units, each with a bathroom, and there is a central unit with communal dining room and a kitchen with a stove and refrigerator. Lighting is by gas. There is a camping site with outdoor cooking facilities at Tashinga on the shore of the lake, a second site with 6 stands and ablution facilities at Sanyati, and a single stand with a shelter and ablution facilities at Changachirere. Camping equipment can be hired, but should be booked well in advance. Luxury accommodation is available at Bumi Hills Safari Lodge on the park's western edge.
Other facilities: Wilderness trails; a limited number of game-viewing roads; game-viewing walks; fishing. The nearest food and fuel supplies are at Kariba village.
Open: The park is open throughout the year to boats, but road access is restricted to between 1 May and 31 October.
Opening time: Sunrise to sunset.
Beware: Malaria; bilharzia; tsetse fly; crocodiles; potentially dangerous animals.
For further information: (Accommodation and wilderness trails) National Parks Central Booking Office (see page 365). (Bumi Hills Safari Lodge) Zimbabwe Sun Hotels, Central Reservations, P.O. Box 8221, Causeway, Harare.

A wild, virtually untouched wilderness, Matusadona National Park covers an area of 1 407 km^2 along the southern shore of Lake Kariba. The Matuzviadonha Hills run through the park, the highest point rising to 1 201 m above sea-level. This part of the Kariba shoreline has several small bays and an estuary-like indentation where the lower part of the Sanyati River valley has been flooded.

Mixed woodland, comprising *Brachystegia*, *Combretum* and *Commiphora* species, covers much of the park and supports such game species as elephant, black rhinoceros, buffalo, waterbuck, eland, bushbuck, kudu and warthog. Hippopotamus are common in Lake Kariba. Large predators such as lion, leopard and spotted hyena are also fairly common. The birdlife is rich and varied particularly along the shoreline.

406 MUSHANDIKE SANCTUARY See map Great Zimbabwe Park and National Monument

Location: Southern Zimbabwe; south-west of Masvingo.
Access: From Masvingo follow the main road westwards towards Bulawayo for 26 km; turn left at the signpost to the Mushandike Sanctuary and follow this graded gravel road to the entrance.
Accommodation: There is a camping and

caravan site with fireplaces and communal ablution facilities.

Other facilities: A picnic area; boating is allowed (boats must be registered at the park's headquarters in Harare); fishing (a licence is required); walking is permitted; a network of game-viewing roads (these are often in a poor condition). The nearest fuel and food supplies are 25 km away at Mashava.

Open: Throughout the year.

Opening time: Sunrise to sunset.

Speed limit: 40 km/h.

For further information: The Warden, Mushandike Sanctuary, Private Bag 9036, Masvingo. Tel: Mashava 2-4412.

Mushandike Sanctuary is a multi-purpose conservation area, combining recreation, game-viewing and a game domestication programme in which attempts are being made to 'farm' certain game species, eland in particular. It is also the home of Zimbabwe's Natural Resources College.

The reserve covers 13 360 ha of *Brachystegia* (miombo) woodland, open grassland and rocky outcrops, and it includes the 417-ha Mushandike Dam.

Sable, kudu, waterbuck, common duiker, klipspringer, steenbok, Sharpe's grysbok, tsessebe, blue wildebeest, impala and warthog are present, as well as a rich variety of birds, including many waterfowl species.

407 NGEZI RECREATIONAL PARK See map Iwaba Wildlife Estate

Location: Central Zimbabwe; south-west of Harare.

Access: From Harare take the main road towards Masvingo; 49 km south of Beatrice, at Featherstone Police Station, turn right; continue for 56 km, following signposts. Or, from Bulawayo drive north-eastwards to Gweru; then follow the main road northwards to Battlefields; turn right and drive 80 km to the park. This route is poorly signposted.

Accommodation: 4 2-bedroomed lodges. There are 25 camping stands scattered throughout the park, some with ablution facilities, others only equipped with toilets.

Other facilities: Fishing in the dam (licences are required and are obtainable at the park office); boating is allowed (boats must be registered with the senior ranger); walking is permitted. Food and fuel supplies are available at Kwekwe, Chegutu and Beatrice, all 80 km from the park.

Open: Throughout the year.

Opening time: Park – sunrise to sunset; office – 07h00 to 13h00 and 14h00 to 17h00.

Beware: Bilharzia.

For further information: The Senior Ranger, Ngezi Recreational Park, Private Bag 8046, Kwekwe, Zimbabwe. Tel: Munyati 2405.

Ngezi Recreational Park covers an area of 6 326 ha, of which 573 ha are taken up by the Ngezi Dam. A variety of game species are present, including sable, kudu, reedbuck and common duiker, and there are hippopotamus and crocodiles in the dam.

408 NYANGA NATIONAL PARK

Location: The Eastern Highlands; south-east of Harare.

Access: From Harare take the main road south-eastwards towards Mutare as far as Rusape; turn left and follow this road for approximately 100 km to the Nyanga National Park. Alternatively, from Mutare take the road northwards to Nyanga, reaching the park after about 100 km.

Accommodation: *Mare Dam, Rhodes Dam* and *Udu Camp* have 2- and 8-bed lodges. *Pungwe Drift* has 2 5-bed luxury lodges; it is recommended that a 4x4 is used to reach the second lodge. There is a camping and caravan site close to the Inyangombe River with ablution facilities, an electricity supply and fireplaces. There is also a caravan park close to the tourist office, with 40 stands and ablution facilities. There are several hotels in the area.

Other facilities: Scenic drives; footpaths; trout fishing (a licence is required); mountain climbing; tennis; swimming; boats can be hired at the 3 main dams; guided pony trails. Supplies and fuel can be purchased 8 km away at Nyanga village.

Open: Throughout the year.

Opening time: Park – sunrise to sunset;

24-hour booking-in service at the Rhodes Dam tourist office.

For further information: The Warden, Nyanga National Park, Private Bag T 7901, Mutare. Tel: Nyanga 274 or 384. (Booking) National Parks Central Booking Office (see page 365).

Most of the Nyanga National Park is situated at an altitude of between 2 000 and 2 300 m, with Zimbabwe's highest peak, Inyangani, rising to 2 593 m above sea-level. A clearly marked path can be followed to its summit. There are several waterfalls within the park, including the 243-m Pungwe Falls and the Inyangombe Falls, which is near the camping sites.

Nyanga National Park covers an extensive area and although it has been developed for agricultural and forestry use, there are still fairly extensive areas that are blanketed by indigenous forest. The acquisition of further lowland forest behind Mount Inyangani offers premier trout fishing in the Gairesi River and this, together with M'tarazi Falls National Park, gives Nyanga a total area of 47 100 ha.

This is primarily a scenic park, but several mammals, such as blue and common duiker, serval, otter, waterbuck, wildebeest, kudu and rock dassie, do occur. Another attraction is the large numbers of forest bird species to be found here.

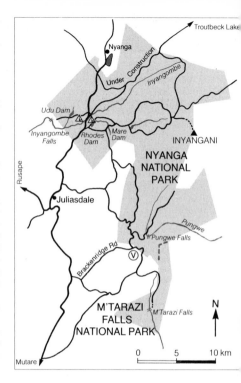

ROBERT McILWAINE RECREATIONAL PARK

Location: Eastern Zimbabwe; south-west of Harare.

Access: From Harare take the main road south-westwards in the direction of Bulawayo; from this road there are 3 clearly signposted turn-offs to the park. To reach the game park and official rest camp, 32 km from Harare take the turn-off to Manyame River Bridge; before reaching the dam wall, fork right and follow this road for 13 km.

Accommodation: 2-bedroomed lodges and 1-, 2- and 3-bedroomed chalets. There are 2 camping sites, both on the northern shore of the lake, with ablution facilities. Several hotels and privately owned camping sites are located in the area.

Other facilities: Game park – bush trails; pony trail; picnic sites; fishing. Recreation area – swimming pools and tennis courts; boats are allowed on the lake. Nearest food supplies are 24 km away at Norton; nearest fuel is 16 km away at Turnpike Garage.

Open: Throughout the year.

Opening time: Recreational park – 06h00 to 18h00; office – 07h00 to 17h00.

Beware: Bilharzia; crocodiles.

For further information: The Warden, Robert McIlwaine Recreational Park, Private Bag 962, Norton. Tel: Norton 2329. (Bookings) National Parks Central Booking Office (see page 365).

he Robert McIlwaine Recreational Park is very popular with people living in and around Harare. The 5 000-ha park is situated around Lake Chivero (McIlwaine) and incorporates a 1 600-ha game park. Most of the animals have been introduced from other areas and they include white rhinoceros, giraffe, Burchell's zebra, eland, tsessebe, kudu, sable and waterbuck. There are crocodiles in the lake. This is a rewarding area for birdwatchers.

410 SEBAKWE RECREATIONAL PARK See map Iwaba Wildlife Estate

Location: Central Zimbabwe; south-west of Harare.
Access: From Harare take the main road south-westwards towards Bulawayo as far as Kwekwe; drive south-eastwards on the road towards Mvuma for 50 km; turn left to the park and drive another 8 km on a dirt road to the entrance.
Accommodation: None.

Other facilities: Short walks; fishing. The nearest fuel and food supplies are at Kwekwe, about 60 km away.
Open: Throughout the year.
Opening time: 06h00 to 18h00.
Beware: Bilharzia.
For further information: The Senior Ranger, Sebakwe Recreational Park, P.O. Box 636, Kwekwe.

The height of the Sebakwe Dam wall has recently been increased and the 278-ha recreational park is gradually diminishing in size as the dam fills. Although there is no official game area, species such as kudu and impala occur here naturally. A variety of birds are attracted to the dam.

411 VICTORIA FALLS AND ZAMBEZI NATIONAL PARKS

Location: Far western Zimbabwe; north-west of Bulawayo.
Access: From Bulawayo follow the main road north-westwards for 440 km to Victoria Falls village. Both parks are adjacent to the village. There are regular air and train services to Victoria Falls. Internal roads may be closed for short periods during the rainy season; check with the authority.
Accommodation: *Zambezi Camp* has 2-bed-roomed lodges. There are 3 fishing camps, at Kandahar, Sansimba and Mpala Jena, each catering for 10 persons, with basic shelters and ablution facilities. Victoria Falls village has a number of hotels and there is a camping site.
Other facilities: Numerous fishing and picnic sites along the Zambezi River; footpaths at the Victoria Falls; guided walks; river cruises; flights over the falls. Zambezi National Park – game-viewing drives. Supplies, fuel and car repairs are available at Victoria Falls village.
Open: Throughout the year.
Opening time: Sunrise to sunset.
Speed limit: 40 km/h.
Beware: Malaria; crocodiles.

For further information: The Secretary, Victoria Falls Publicity Association, P.O. Box 97, Victoria Falls. (Bookings) National Parks Central Booking Office (see page 365).

The 2 340-ha Victoria Falls National Park and the 53 600-ha Zambezi National Park lie next to each other and have the same administrative centre. The former extends in a narrow strip along the southern bank of the Zambezi River and protects the sensitive rain forest around the Victoria Falls which, at 1 700 m wide and 108 m at their greatest height, are among the most spectacular in the world. The flow of water over the falls is lowest between August and December, and this is the best viewing time, as the mist created by the falling water obscures the view when the flow is strong. In addition to the scenic attraction of the falls, this national park boasts a rich and varied animal and plant life in the forest.

The Zambezi National Park has two principal game drives and visitors following them are likely to see elephant, buffalo, giraffe, sable, eland, kudu, waterbuck and white rhinoceros. Smaller species, such as bushbuck, reedbuck and Sharpe's grysbok, may also be sighted. Birdwatching is most productive in the riverine woodland.

The rainy season (November to March) is very hot and uncomfortable. The mid-winter months are cool and dry, and nights can be cold.

USEFUL ADDRESSES

National Parks Board, South Africa
Head office) P.O. Box 787, Pretoria 0001.
Tel: (012) 343-1991.
South-western Cape) P.O. Box 7400, Roggebaai 8012.
Tel: (021) 22-2810.
Southern Cape) P.O. Box 35, Wilderness 6560.
Tel: (0441) 9-1197.
Knysna National Lake Area) P.O. Box 314, Knysna 6570.
Tel: (0445) 2-2095 or 2-2159.

Transvaal
The Directorate of Nature Conservation
Private Bag X209, Pretoria 0001. Tel: (012) 323-3403.
Fax: (012) 21-2530.
The Education Officer of the Wildlife Society
P.O. Box 44344, Linden 2104. Tel: (011) 782-5461.

Bophuthatswana
Central Reservations, Bophuthatswana National Parks Board
Private Bag X2078, Mmabatho 8670. Tel: (0140) 89-5156/9.
Fax: (0140) 2-1468.

KaNgwane, Lebowa and Gazankulu
KaNgwane) KaNgwane Parks Corporation
P.O. Box 1990, Nelspruit 1200. Tel: (01311) 5-3931.
Fax: (01311) 2-3153.
Lebowa) Department of the Chief Minister, Division
and Affairs and Tourism
Private Bag X27, Chuenespoort 0745. Tel: (01529) 3-5529.
Fax: (01529) 3-5244.

Natal and KwaZulu
The Natal Parks Board
P.O. Box 662, Pietermaritzburg 3200. (Reservations) Tel: (0331)
47-1981. Fax: (0331) 47-1980. (General enquiries) Tel: (0331)
47-1961. Fax: (0331) 47-1037.
KwaZulu Bureau of Natural Resources
Private Bag X23, Ulundi 3838. Tel: (0358) 20-2690.
The Regional Director, Water Affairs and Forestry
Private Bag X9029, Pietermaritzburg 3200. Tel: (0331)
42-8101. Fax: (0331) 45-1210.
The Wildlife Society
100 Brand Road, Durban 4001. Tel: (031) 21-3126. Fax: (031)
21-9525.

Lesotho
Lesotho National Parks (Conservation Division Registry),
Ministry of Agriculture
P.O. Box 92, Maseru 100, Lesotho. Tel: (266) 32-2876.

Orange Free State and Qwaqwa
The Directorate of Environmental and Nature Conservation
P.O. Box 517, Bloemfontein 9300. Tel: (051) 405-5245.
Fax: (051) 30-4958.
Qwaqwa Tourism and Nature Conservation Corporation,
Private Bag X826, Witsieshoek 9870. Tel: (01438) 3-0576
or 3-4444. Fax: (01438) 3-4342.

Transkei
The Department of Agriculture and Forestry
Private Bag X5002, Umtata, Transkei. Tel: (0471) 24-9111.
The Department of Commerce, Industry and Tourism
Private Bag X5029, Umtata. Tel: (0471) 3-1190.

Ciskei
The Department of Tourism
Private Bag X0026, Bisho, Ciskei. Tel: (0401) 9-1642 or 9-3214.

Eastern Cape Province
The Directorate of Nature and Environmental Conservation
Private Bag X1126, Port Elizabeth 6000.Tel: (041) 390-2179.
The Directorate of Nature and Environmental Conservation
Queenstown Municipality, P.O. Box 135, Queenstown 5320.
Tel: (0451) 3131.
The Nature Conservation Division, Algoa Regional
Services Council
P.O. Box 318, Port Elizabeth 6000. Tel: (041) 56-1000.
The State Forester, East London Coast State Forest
P.O. Box 5185, Greenfields 5208. Tel: (0431) 46-3532.

Southern Cape Province
The Directorate of Nature and Environmental Conservation
Private Bag X1126, Port Elizabeth 6000. Tel: (041) 390-2179.
The Nature Conservation Division, Algoa Regional Services
Council
P.O. Box 318, Port Elizabeth 6000. Tel: (041) 56-1000.
The Port Elizabeth Municipality
P.O. Box 116, Port Elizabeth 6000. Tel: (041) 56-1056.
The Regional Director, Southern Cape Forest Region
Private Bag X12, Knysna 6570. Tel: (0445) 2-3037.

South-western Cape Province
The Directorate of Nature and Environmental Conservation
Private Bag X9086, Cape Town 8000. Tel: (021) 483-3911.
The Parks and Forests Branch, City Engineers Department
P.O. Box 1694, Cape Town 8000. Tel: (021) 210-2269.
Western Cape Regional Services Council
P.O. Box 1073, Cape Town 8000. Tel: (021) 487-2911.

Namibia
Ministry of Wildlife, Conservation and Tourism, Reservations,
Private Bag X13267, Windhoek 9000, Namibia. Tel: (061)
3-6975 or 3-3875 or 22-0241. Fax: (061) 22-9936.

Botswana
The Department of Wildlife and National Parks
P.O. Box 131, Gaborone, Botswana. Tel: 37-1405.
The Department of Wildlife and National Parks
P.O. Box 17, Kasane, Botswana. Tel: 65-0235.
The Department of Wildlife and National Parks
P.O. Box 11, Maun, Botswana. Tel: 66-0368.

Zambia
The National Parks and Wildlife Service
Post Bag 1, Chilanga, Zambia. Tel: 27-8366.
The National Hotels Development Corporation
P.O. Box 33200, Lusaka, Zambia. Tel: (1) 24-1023.
The Zambia National Tourist Board
P.O. Box 30017, Lusaka, Zambia. Tel: 22-9087.

Malawi
The Bookings Officer, The Department of National Parks
and Wildlife
P.O. Box 30131, Lilongwe 3, Malawi. Tel: 72-3505.
The Chief Forester, Department of Forestry and Natural
Resources
P.O. Box 30048, Lilongwe 3, Malawi. Tel: 73-1322.
The Department of Tourism
P.O. Box 402, Blantyre, Malawi. Tel: 62-0300.

Zimbabwe
National Parks Central Bookings Office, The Department
of National Parks and Wildlife Management
P.O. Box 8151, Causeway, Harare, Zimbabwe.
Tel: 70-6077.

SAFARI OPERATORS

The following are safari companies which, at the time of going to press, are operating in game parks and nature reserves in southern Africa. The list is not exhaustive, nor is the inclusion of any company or organisation in itself a recommendation. It is suggested that anyone intending to visit conservation areas in Namibia, Botswana, Zambia, Malawi or Zimbabwe should also enquire about safari operators from the relevant country's tourist board. Prospective clients are advised to 'shop around' for the company that offers an itinerary and services to match their requirements and to suit their pocket checking for hidden costs and clauses. Safaris offered range from budget to up-market, and several companies offer specialist trips, those for birdwatchers being particularly popular.

Afro Ventures Safaris
P.O. Box 2339, Randburg 2125, South Africa. Tel: (011) 789-1078. Fax: (011) 886-2349.
Operates in: South Africa (Giant's Castle Game Reserve, Hluhluwe Game Reserve, Kalahari Gemsbok National Park, Kruger National Park, Mkuzi Game Reserve, Ndumo Game Reserve, Royal Natal National Park, Umfolozi Game Reserve); Swaziland (Mlilwane Wildlife Sanctuary); Namibia (Daan Viljoen Game Park, Etosha National Park, Mamil Game Reserve, Namib-Naukluft Park); Botswana (Central Kalahari Game Reserve, Chobe National Park, Makgadikgad Pans Game Reserve, Moremi Wildlife Reserve, Nxai Pan National Park); Zimbabwe (Chizarira National Park, Hwange National Park, Mana Pools National Park, Matusadona National Park, Zambezi National Park).

Bonaventure Botswana
P.O. Box 84540, Greenside 2034, South Africa. Tel: (011) 787-0219. Fax: (011) 787-5077.
Operates in: Botswana (Chobe National Park, Moremi Wildlife Reserve, Okavango Delta); Zimbabwe (Zambezi Nationa Park).

Ciskei Safaris
P.O. Box 3300, Cambridge 5206. Tel: (04326) 669. Fax: (04326) 605.

Drifters Adventours
P.O. Box 48434, Roosevelt Park 2194, South Africa. Tel: (011) 888-1160. Fax: (011) 888-1020.
Operates in: South Africa (many, including Cederberg Wilderness Area, Kalahari Gemsbok National Park, Karoo Nationa Park, Kosi Bay Nature Reserve, Mkuzi Game Reserve, Wolkberg Wilderness Area); Bophuthatswana (Pilanesberg Nationa Park); Transkei (Mkambati Nature Reserve); Namibia (Etosha National Park, Fish River Canyon Park, Hardap Recreatior Resort, Khaudom Game Reserve, Mahango Game Reserve, Namib-Naukluft Park); Botswana (Chobe National Park Moremi Wildlife Reserve, Okavango Delta); Malawi (Kasungu National Park, Liwonde National Park, Mulanje Mountain Nyika National Park); Zimbabwe (Kazuma Pan National Park, Mana Pools National Park, and in the Zambezi Valley).

Gametrackers
P.O. Box 4245, Randburg 2125, South Africa. Tel: (011) 886-1810. Fax: (011) 886-1815.
Operates in: South Africa (Timbavati Private Nature Reserve); Bophuthatswana (Pilanesberg National Park); Namibia (Etosha National Park); Botswana (Chobe National Park, Moremi Wildlife Reserve, Okavango Delta); Zimbabwe (Hwange National Park).

Karibu Safaris
P.O. Box 35196, Northway 4065, South Africa. Tel: (031) 83-9774. Fax: (031) 83-1957.
Operates in: South Africa (Augrabies Falls National Park, Addo Elephant National Park, Blyde River Canyon Nature Reserve, Golden Gate Highlands National Park, Kalahari Gemsbok National Park, Kruger National Park, Mkuzi Game Reserve, Tsitsikamma National Park, Willem Pretorius Game Reserve); Namibia (Etosha National Park, Fish River Canyon Park, Namib-Naukluft Park); Botswana (Chobe National Park, Makgadikgadi Pans Game Reserve, Moremi Wildlife Reserve, Nxai Pan National Park, Okavango Delta); Malawi (Kasungu National Park, Lake Malawi National Park Liwonde National Park, Mulanje Mountain, Zomba Plateau).

Okavango Explorations
P.O. Box 69859, Bryanston 2021. Tel: (011) 708-1893. Fax: (011) 708-1569.
Operates in: Botswana (Okavango Delta).

Overland Safaris
P.O. Box 82, Warden 9890, South Africa. Tel: 013342, ask for Roadside 7-7330. Fax: 014372, ask for 670.

Operates in: South Africa (Augrabies Falls National Park, Kalahari Gemsbok National Park); Lesotho (Sehlabathebe National Park); Namibia (Daan Viljoen Game Park, Fish River Canyon Park, Khaudom Game Reserve, Mahango Game Reserve, Namib-Naukluft Park, Waterberg Plateau).

Penduka Safaris
P.O. Box 55413, Northlands 2116, South Africa. Tel: (011) 883-4303. Fax: (011) 883-4303.
Operates in: Botswana (Central Kalahari Game Reserve, Chobe National Park, Mabuasehube Game Reserve, Makgadikgadi Pans Game Reserve, Moremi Wildlife Reserve, Okavango Delta).

Safari Par Excellence
P.O. Box 5920, Harare, Zimbabwe. Tel: 72-0527. Fax: 72-2872.
Operates in: Botswana, Zambia, Malawi and Zimbabwe. This company acts as an agent for several other operators.

Safariplan
P.O. Box 4245, Randburg 2125, South Africa. Tel: (011) 886-1810. Fax: (011) 886-1815.
Operates in: South Africa (Manyeleti Game Reserve, Timbavati Private Nature Reserve). Also agents for Gametrackers.

Shearwater Adventures
P.O. Box 3961, Harare, Zimbabwe. Tel: Harare 73-5712. Fax: Harare 73-5716.
Operates in: Zimbabwe (Chizarira National Park, Hwange National Park, Kazuma Pan National Park, Mana Pools National Park, Matusadona National Park, and in the Zambezi Valley). The company is an agent for a number of other operators.

Skeleton Coast Safaris
P.O. Box 2195, Windhoek, Namibia. Tel: (061) 22-4248. Fax: (061) 22-5713.
Operates in: Namibia (Etosha National Park, Skeleton Coast Park).

Sobek Expeditions
P.O. Box 60957, Livingstone, Zambia. Tel: Livingstone 32-1432.
Operates in: Zambia (Zambezi Valley).@BODY1B = *SWA Safaris*
P.O. Box 20373, Windhoek, Namibia. Tel: (061) 3-7567. Fax: (061) 22-5387.
Operates in: Namibia (Etosha National Park, Khaudom Game Reserve, Skeleton Coast Park); Botswana (Chobe National Park, Moremi Wildlife Reserve, Okavango Delta).

Ubizane Safaris
P.O. Box 102, Hluhluwe 3960, South Africa. Tel: 03562, ask for 3602. Fax: 03562, ask for 193.
Operates in: South Africa (Zululand parks).

Wilderness Safaris
P.O. Box 651171, Benmore 2010, South Africa. Tel: (011) 884-1458. Fax: (011) 883-6255.
Operates in: Namibia (Damaraland Wilderness Reserve, Etosha National Park, Fish River Canyon Park, Hardap Recreation Resort, Khaudom Game Reserve, Mahango Game Reserve, Mamili Game Reserve, Mudumu Game Reserve, Namib-Naukluft Park, Skeleton Coast Park, Waterberg Plateau Park); Botswana (Central Kalahari Game Reserve, Chobe National Park, Moremi Wildlife Reserve, Okavango Delta); Malawi (Kasungu National Park, Lake Malawi National Park, Lengwe National Park, Lilongwe Nature Sanctuary, Liwonde National Park, Mulanje Mountain, Nyika National Park, Vwaza Marsh Wildlife Reserve); Zimbabwe (Chizarira National Park, Hwange National Park, Kazuma Pan National Park, Mana Pools National Park, Matusadona National Park, and in the Zambezi Valley); South Africa (Kruger National Park, Ndumo, Mkuzi, Hluhluwe, Umfolozi, Maputaland Coastal Forest Reserve and Marine Reserve – Rocktail Bay Lodge, Phinda Resource Reserve, Drakensberg).

Wilderness Trails
P.O. Box 30970, Lusaka, Zambia. Telex: ZA 4-0143.
Operates in: Zambia (South Luangwa National Park).

Wilderness Leadership School
P.O. Box 53058, Yellowwood Park 4011, South Africa. Tel: (031) 42-8642. Fax: (031) 42-8675.
Operates in: South Africa (Doorndraai Dam Nature Reserve, Nylsvley Nature Reserve, St Lucia Park, Timbavati Private Nature Reserve, Umfolozi Game Reserve);Bophuthatswana (Pilanesberg National Park).

SUGGESTED FURTHER READING

Visitors to the game and nature reserves of southern Africa may find the following books of interest. In addition to these there are many pamphlets, brochures and booklets which are available at a number of the reserves described in this guide.

General
Braack, L.E.O. 1992. *Kruger National Park: A Visitor's Guide.* Struik Publishers, Cape Town.
Campbell, A. 1980. *The guide to Botswana.* Winchester Press, Johannesburg.
Davison, T. 1967. *Wankie: the story of a great game reserve.* Books of Africa, Cape Town.
Duggan, A. (Ed.) 1983. *Reader's Digest illustrated guide to the game parks & nature reserves of southern Africa.* Reader's Digest Association of Southern Africa, Cape Town.
Gordon, R. 1983. *The national parks of South Africa.* Struik Publishers, Cape Town.
Johnson, P. and Bannister, A. 1986. *Okavango: sea of land, land of water.* Struik Publishers, Cape Town.
Levy, J. 1989. *The complete guide to walks and trails in southern Africa.* Second Edition, Struik Publishers, Cape Town.
Main, M., Fowkes, J. and Fowkes S. 1987. *Visitors' guide to Botswana.* Southern Book Publishers, Johannesburg.
Owens, M. and Owens, D. 1985. *Cry of the Kalahari.* Collins, Johannesburg.

Mammals
Ansell, W.F.H. 1978. *The mammals of Zambia.* National Parks and Wildlife Service, Chilanga.
Ansell, W.F.H. and Dowsett, R.J. 1988. *Mammals of Malawi: an annotated check list and atlas.* Trendrine Press, St Ives, England.
De Graaff, G. 1981. *The rodents of southern Africa.* Butterworths, Durban.
Dorst, J. and Dandelot, P. 1983. *A field guide to the larger mammals of Africa.* Collins, London.
Grobler, H., Hall-Martin, A. and Walker, C. 1984. *Predators of southern Africa.* Macmillan, Johannesburg.
Haltenorth, T. and Diller, H. 1984. *A field guide to the mammals of Africa including Madagascar.* Collins, London.
Skinner, J. and Meakin, P. 1988. *Struik pocket guide series: Mammals.* Struik Publishers, Cape Town.
Smithers, R.H.N. 1971. *The mammals of Botswana. Museum Memoir* 4: 1-340. (Trustees of the National Museums of Rhodesia, Salisbury.)
Smithers, R.H.N. 1983. *The mammals of the southern African subregion.* University of Pretoria, Pretoria.
Smithers, R.H.N. and Wilson, V.J. 1979. Checklist and atlas of the mammals of Zimbabwe Rhodesia. *Museum Memoir* 9:1-193. (Trustees of the National Museums and Monuments of Zimbabwe Rhodesia, Salisbury.)
Stuart, C. and Stuart, T. 1988. *Field guide to the mammals of southern Africa.* Struik Publishers, Cape Town.
Stuart, C. and Stuart, T. 1992. *Southern, Central and East African Mammals: A photographic guide.* Struik Publishers, Cape Town.

Birds
Berruti, A. and Sinclair, J.C. 1983. *Where to watch birds in southern Africa.* Struik Publishers, Cape Town.
Kemp, A. and Finch-Davies, C.G. 1986. *Gamebirds and waterfowl of southern Africa.* Winchester Press, Johannesburg.
Maclean, G.L. 1984. *Roberts birds of South Africa.* 5th edition. The Trustees of the John Voelcker Bird Book Fund, Cape Town.
Maclean, G.L. 1981. *Aids to bird identification in southern Africa.* University of Natal Press, Pietermaritzburg.
Newman, K.B. 1980. *Birds of southern Africa: 1. Kruger National Park.* Macmillan, Johannesburg.
Newman, K.B. 1983. *Newman's birds of southern Africa.* Macmillan, Johannesburg.
Pickford, P., Pickford, B. and Tarboton, W.R. 1989. *Southern African birds of prey.* Struik Publishers, Cape Town.
Sinclair, J.C. 1984. *Field guide to the birds of southern Africa.* Struik Publishers, Cape Town.
Sinclair, I. and Goode, D. 1986 *Struik pocket guide series: Birds of Prey* Struik Publishers, Cape Town.
Sinclair, I. and Whyte, I. 1991. *Field Guide to the Birds of the Kruger National Park* Struik Publishers, Cape Town.
Steyn, P. 1982. *Birds of prey of southern Africa.* David Philip, Cape Town.
Ginn, P., McIlleron, G. and Milstein, P. 1990. *The complete book of southern African birds.* Struik Winchester, Cape Town.

Reptiles and amphibians
Boycott, R.C. and Borquin, O. 1988. *The South African tortoise book: a guide to southern African tortoises.* Southern Book Publishers, Johannesburg.
Branch, W. 1988. *Field guide to the snakes and other reptiles of southern Africa.* Struik Publishers, Cape Town.
Broadley, D.G. 1983. *FitzSimon's snakes of southern Africa.* Delta Books, Johannesburg.
Patterson, R. and Meakin, P. 1986. *Snakes.* Struik Publishers, Cape Town.
Patterson, R. and Bannister, A. 1991. *Snakes and other reptiles of southern Africa.* Struik Publishers, Cape Town.

Marine life

Berjak, P., Campbell, G.K., Huckett, B.I. and Pammenter, N.W. 1977. *In the mangroves of southern Africa.* Natal Branch of the Wildlife Society of Southern Africa, Durban.

Branch, G. and Branch, M. 1981. *The living shores of southern Africa.* Struik Publishers, Cape Town.

Griffiths, C., Griffiths, R. and Thorpe, D. 19 .*Struik pocket guide series: Seashore Life.* Struik Publishers, Cape Town.

Insects

Braack, L.E.O. 1991. *Field guide to the insects of the Kruger National Park.*Struik Publishers, Cape Town.

Holm, E. and De Meillon, E. 1986. *Insects.* Struik, Cape Town.

Migdoll, I. 1987. *Field guide to the butterflies of South Africa.* Struik Publishers, Cape Town.

Skaife, S.H. 1979. *African insect life.* Struik Publishers, Cape Town.

Plant life

Acocks, J.P.H. 1975. Veld types of South Africa. *Memoirs of the Botanical Survey of South Africa.* No. 40. B.R.I. and D.A.T.S., Pretoria.

Adams, J. 1976. *Wild flowers of the northern Cape.* Department of Nature and Environmental Conservation, Cape Town.

Batten, A. 1986. *Flowers of southern Africa.* Frandsen Publishers, Fourways, South Africa.

Burman, L. and Bean, A. 1985. *Hottentots Holland to Hermanus: S.A. wild flower guide no. 5.* Botanical Society of South Africa, Cape Town.

De Winter, B. and Vahrmeijer, J. 1972. *National list of trees.* Van Schaik, Pretoria.

Fox, F.W. and Young, M.E.N. 1982. *Food from the veld.* Delta Books, Johannesburg.

Gledhill, E. *Eastern Cape veld flowers.* Department of Nature Conservation, Cape Town.

Jackson, W.P.U. 1980. *Wild flowers of the fairest Cape.* Howard Timmins, Cape Town.

Kidd, M.M. 1983. *Cape Peninsula: S.A. wild flower guide no. 3.* Botanical Society of South Africa, Cape Town.

Le Roux, A. and Schelpe, T. 1988. *Namaqualand: S.A. wild flower guide no 1.* Botanical Society of South Africa, Cape Town.

Moll, E., Moll, G. and Page, N. 1989. *Struik pocket guide series: Common Trees* Struik Publishers, Cape Town.

Moriarty, A. 1982. *Outeniqua, Tsitsikamma and Eastern Little Karoo: S.A. wild flower guide no. 2.* Botanical Society of South Africa, Cape Town.

Onderstall, J. 1984. *Transvaal Lowveld and escarpment (including the Kruger National Park): S.A. wild flower guide no. 4.* Botanical Society of South Africa, Cape Town.

Palgrave, K.C. 1988. *Trees of southern Africa.* Second edition. Struik Publishers, Cape Town.

Palmer, E. 1986. *A field guide to the trees of southern Africa.* Collins, London.

Van Wyk, B. and Malan, S. 1988. *Field guide to the wild flowers of the Witwatersrand and Pretoria region.* Struik Publishers, Cape Town.

Van Wyk, P. 1984. *Field guide to the trees of the Kruger National Park.* Struik Publishers, Cape Town.

Vogts, M. 1982. *South Africa's Proteaceae.* Struik Publishers, Cape Town.

Magazines

African Wildlife (Wildlife Society of Southern Africa)

Custos (National Parks Board, South Africa)

Madoqua (Nature Conservation Department, Namibia)

Lammergeyer (Natal Parks Board)

Getaway (Ramsay, Son and Parker (Pty) Ltd)

Bushcall (Nkwe Publishing (Pty) Ltd & Bophuthatswana National Parks Board)

INDEX

Page numbers given in **bold** type indicate main entries; those in *italic* type denote photographs.